GRAHAM CHAPMAN
JOHN CLEESE
TERRY GILLIAM
ERIC IDLE
TERRY JONES
MICHAEL PALIN

WITH BOB McCABE

HONS
HONS

AUTOBIOGRAPHY BY

Thomas Dunne Books

St. Martin's Press  **New York**

THOMAS DUNNE BOOKS.
An imprint of St. Martin's Press.

The Pythons: Autobiography by The Pythons.
Copyright © 2003 by John Cleese, Terry Gilliam,
Michael Palin, Eric Idle, Terry Jones,
and the Estate of Graham Chapman

For information, address St. Martin's Press,
175 Fifth Avenue, New York, N.Y. 10010.
www.stmartins.com
ISBN 0-312-31144-3

First U.S. Edition: October 2003

10 9 8 7 6 5 4 3 2 1

Designed by Harry Green

Project manager: Nicky Granville

MONTY PYTHON'S
FLYING CIRCUS

CONTEN

PASSING THE AUDITION:
ACKNOWLEDGEMENTS

The late George Harrison used to say that he felt the spirit of the Beatles had passed on to Monty Python. After all, Python came together in late 1969, just as the Fab Four were becoming four fairly fab individuals. Both were groups of men who in a short period of time produced an amazing body of work that came to dominate their particular field, whether it be music or comedy. And of course both, in their own way, changed the world. Maybe George was onto something …

It is often said that history is written by the winners; I think it is also written by those who dare to pass comment on it, subvert it, make a joke of it. Only then do you get the full picture, only then do you really understand – whether it be a bowler-hatted city gent in the early 1970s or the religious order of the world in Judaea, AD 33. That was the task Monty Python took on; I hope you'll agree they more than passed the audition.

When I set out to do this book, one of the things I wanted to do was take the Pythons seriously. I hope ultimately it takes them as seriously as they take themselves.

As with anything as heavy as the thing you now hold in your hands, there are more people to thank than a drunken winner on Oscar night. First and foremost, the Pythons themselves, all of whom were charming, accessible, warm and, without fail, extremely good company. So I would like to thank:

Michael Palin – for his time, the use of his home, several welcome cups of tea, his warmth and good humour, and for having one of the best kept personal archives in town.

Terry Jones – for welcoming me into his home, giving me the run of the place, giving me his food, and for having an equally substantial though slightly less well organised archive(!).

John Cleese – for some fascinatingly entertaining conversations, a walk around the ranch and a sojourn in the aviary. (Check out www.thejohncleese.com.)

Eric Idle (the man responsible for www.pythonline.com) – for getting me to Dublin and for singing 'The Penis Song' while we were alone together in his hotel room.

Terry Gilliam – for allowing me to constantly annoy him, while still offering tea and off-the-record salacious Hollywood scandal.

Overall, I thank them for their openness, honesty, trust and friendship.

Sadly, Graham Chapman is not here to be thanked in person, but is thanked in spirit. However, speaking on Graham's behalf, I can say that without the help of the charming David Sherlock this book would have been sorely lacking. His memories of Graham ensured that Graham had a presence in this book, both in David's comments and in the exchange they sparked off between the others. Similarly, Graham's brother Dr John Chapman and his wife Pam shared many personal memories of Graham with great candour. It was much appreciated.

The vast majority of the 1,000 photographs in this book come from the private collections of those above, and as such they are often personal photos, many of which have never been seen before. Once again we are indebted.

Now, for the backstage people (it really *is* worse than a drunken speech on Oscar night). At Orion Publishing this book would simply never have happened without the publisher Trevor Dolby, who put the idea in motion, landed the talent and saw it through over what seemed like a very long two-year period. He is a fine man, an honest publisher (oxymoron?) and a good friend. His actions in the early days of this book were above and beyond the call of duty, and I hope he knows how appreciated they were. Also at Orion Pandora White has done a splendid, tireless job of keeping the plates up in the air. Thanks also to Laura Meehan.

Without the work of Alison Seiff this book would be coming out around the year 2009, as she took over the job of transcribing literally hours and hours of tape. Also working for hours and hours (days/weeks/months), Harry Green must be thanked for such an amazing design, pulled off with total perfectionism under the most trying of schedules. (He has a dog called 'Monty', you know – strange coincidence.) Colin Grant did a splendid, much valued job of copy-editing and keeping text in motion, while Nicky Granville was fabulous at kicking me up the arse without hurting too much – cheers.

Roger Saunders of Python (Monty) Pictures has been an immense help to this book from early on (we did eventually get the pictures back to him!) – many thanks. Howard Johnson proved not only to be a charming host but a literal oracle of information. Gratitude is also due to Atlanta's very own Jim Yoakum, the man behind the Graham Chapman Archive, for access to rare photos and, along with John Kaufman of Right Recordings, for use of material from the Graham performance CD, *Spot the Loony* (yes, that was a plug). Also, the delightful Humphrey Barclay opened his personal scrapbooks to us, which were a huge bonus and a great help in tracing the early careers of those who became Pythons. Without Eric Albani's record collection, there would be fewer pictures of records in this book – cheers. A special thank you for the tireless efforts of our West Coast connection, Simon Braund, for the pursuit of excellence (well, more pictures really).

Thanks for all sorts of reasons – friendship, sympathy, small amounts of money in manila envelopes – to Rob Churchill, Paul Gillion, Michael Samuels, Glenn & Vicky Archibald, and Susannah Cartwright (the appearance of whose dad twice in this book prompts the exciting new quiz, 'Spot John Cartwright').

Much love as ever to Mary McCabe, a rather excellent mother.

And finally, all my love as ever to Lucy Merritt, for putting up with the insanity of the last two years, to my daughter Jessie for being so beautiful and to my son Jack for, among other things, the way he dances to Bruce Springsteen.

While I was putting this book together my six-year-old daughter was attending our local school. One of her friends there was a nine-year-old boy named Josh. At pick-up one day he came up to me and asked if I knew Monty Python. Given the fact I was totally immersed in Python at this time, I was deeply suspicious so I asked him 'Why?' (Bear in mind that Python had not been on air in the UK for most of his lifetime and was poorly served on video.) 'I'm sorry, is this a five-minute argument or the full half-hour?' he replied, laughing. It was the 'Argument Clinic' sketch. He had performed it along with a mate in their school assembly that very morning. He had never seen it, but he loved it. He loved the words, he loved what it had to say – and he was nine.

That to me, more than anything, shows the enduring appeal of Python. Those that change the world don't necessarily do it with a bang; sometimes they do it when people are just looking the other way. But it changes nonetheless – and for the good. That's not a bad epitaph. (It may be a bad sentence, but it's not a bad epitaph!)

BOB McCABE
Somewhere in England
March 2003

IN WHICH THE PYTHONS MEET THE PYTHONS

'. . . Indeed he wasn't a Python at the time, he wasn't for something like seven years after I first met him, so there we were working together and knowing each other without knowing we were Pythons HELP! . . .'

MICHAEL PALIN

Michael would have been the first Python I ever met, although I didn't know it at the time. Indeed he wasn't a Python at the time, he wasn't for something like seven years after I first met him, so there we were working together and knowing each other without knowing we were Pythons. The first time I ever saw him was at a Union Smoking concert in Oxford where people did turns and sketches. Mike came on with Robert Hewison doing a thing about a bucket. It was kind of conceptual and really good and I just thought Mike was extremely funny. Robert was oddly alienating on stage, whereas Mike was loveable; maybe it was the contrast that made them work together.

Later we all went off and did a cabaret tour of the West Country organised by Robert. It was me, Mike and Robert, and a friend of mine, Mike Wynn-Jones. Like Robert with Michael, it was Mike Wynn-Jones who got me doing cabaret in the first place. We went around hotels and places doing our little cabaret routines. That was in my summer vacation of my second year at Oxford.

JOHN CLEESE

I first saw Cleesey, as I remember, at the Lyric Theatre when he was in *Cambridge Circus*. I went to see a matinée on a Wednesday. At the same time I was doing '****' (*Four Asterisks*) at the Phoenix Theatre. We'd done it in Edinburgh and came down and did two weeks at the Phoenix. We weren't doing matinées, so one Wednesday we went off to inspect the opposition, *Cambridge Circus,* which was packing them in. We weren't quite doing that. John came on stage, I think with Jo Kendall, doing this thing where he slaps his neck all the time, killing mosquitoes. It was set in the Indian Raj, all that stiff upper lip thing. That's also where I saw Graham for the first time.

I've got a feeling that sometime later on he took me out for steak at an Angus Steak House. I was pretty impressed that he could afford to go to an Angus Steak House, but I don't really remember what we talked about. That was when we were doing *The Frost Reports*.

GRAHAM CHAPMAN

I first saw Graham on stage with John in *Cambridge Circus* and I remember thinking John was wonderful, but being even more intrigued by Graham. You could see exactly where John was coming from as soon as he walked on the stage. You could see he was very, very funny and accomplished. I could also see where Tim Brooke-Taylor was coming from, and where Bill Oddie was coming from, but Graham came on the stage and you had no idea what he was doing there. Graham was like a mystery. A wonderful mystery. Why was he funny? Was he funny? What on earth was he doing on a stage? I think my favourite comedy is like poetry in a way. Browning said a metaphor is if you take two completely disparate ideas and you put them together and instead of getting a third idea you get a star. And that is what humour can be – you get ideas together and you make not a star but a laugh. It's especially good if you also can't really see why the ideas have been brought together. Like 'The Spanish Inquisition', when Mike read that out to me the first time I just thought, 'How did he get to that?' It was like that with Graham. One always thought, 'How on earth …?'

I remember having lunch with Graham once and having nothing to say really. That was always my feeling with Graham. He was on a different planet, a wonderful mystery, Graham in his own world.

ERIC IDLE

I first saw Eric on stage in Edinburgh doing a revue in what must have been my third year. We were doing the Oxford Revue and we went to see the Cambridge Revue. I may have seen him the year before, but I just remember seeing this very beautiful young man on stage, with very blue eyes. Then we did a show together, Cambridge and Oxford, called *Rejects Night*. It was an extra show we put on after our proper revue, which we didn't charge for. We had a big dustbin on the stage and we all sat round and got up and read out sketches that we hadn't finished or had rejected for some reason. We read them as long as they got laughs and when they stopped we just crumpled them up and threw them into the dustbin. I didn't meet Eric again until Humphrey Barclay rang me up and said, 'Would you be interested in doing a children's show with Eric Idle?' and I said, 'Well, if my friend Mike can come along as well,' and so that was *Do Not Adjust Your Set*.

We never really met on *The Frost Report*, but I was aware of Eric producing many more one-liners and funny stuff for the CDM – the 'Continuing Developing Monologue'.

TERRY GILLIAM

Terry G arrived on the scene when we were doing *Do Not Adjust Your Set*. Here was this American guy, and there was this strange coat he wore. I can't even remember what it was like now. He started hanging around at script meetings. I thought Eric had brought him along at first, but it must have been the producer, Humphrey Barclay. I just remember him coming along and being very full of ideas and not quite following what he was saying – and being slightly alarmed by his enthusiasm and thinking, 'We're trying to get everything absolutely right, we're trying to control everything and here's somebody else tearing it off into a different direction.'

Eric was much more open to this than Mike and I were. In those days I was very guarded about everything, because I was so aware of things getting diluted and taken off in the wrong direction; it was such a fight to get anything onto the screen in the way that we'd imagined it, everything was a fight. There were so many things that we'd done which I hated on screen, things that Mike and I had written that got altered. That defensiveness came from finding it hard to get our own stuff together and then feeling somebody else is going to then take off in a chariot in a totally different direction.

Michael Palin
blows the gaff on the pythons

TERRY JONES

The first time I saw Terry Jones was on a poster. There was a play on at Oxford called *Professor Taranne*, and there was Terry in his coat with a fag hanging out of his mouth, crouched in a corner looking generally rather strange and alienated. It was probably the end of my first year, the beginning of my second year, so it would be '62 or '63. And then, as you do, you kind of notice people around in the streets and I probably bumped into Terry or saw him wandering around. He was doing some acting then, quite serious acting, and he was a year ahead of me. I suppose you always feel that people above you are their own sort of stars in the university and there was a star status thing in the theatre at Oxford. I might well have seen him on stage next. It must have been '63 when he and I and one or two others got together to rewrite a sketch for the Oxford University end of summer revue. There was an idea around which had come from a guy called Chris Braden, who was the son of Bernard Braden and Barbara Kelly, and he was producing this revue and it was called *Loitering with Intent* because it was staged in a tent. And there was this idea that Braden had come up with which was the analysis of a slapstick joke done in a very po-faced, professorial, undergraduate seminar-ish sort of way, and Terry, myself and a guy called Robert Hewison, who was a big mate of mine at Oxford, got together to write a script to go with this, something for the lecturer to say. And that actually became the 'Custard Pie' sketch which we used to do on charity shows with Graham Chapman as the lecturer. So that's the first time I met Terry. That would have been the summer of '63.

He was quite a charismatic character really. He was small and dark, and he had quite a striking face, someone you noticed. To start with I thought of him as a slightly intense, thespian sort of character – be wary. But of course as soon as I met him and started talking to him I realised that Terry was very funny and friendly and generally very easy to get on with, so we became friends fairly quickly. When someone is a year ahead of you they have a slightly different set of friends and all that and so I wouldn't say we became close friends straight away. But then a year later we did a revue in which we both acted and performed in Edinburgh. That was the time when we became very strong friends. There was definitely an original talent there – I wasn't sure what it was … Terry seemed to have his own integrity and his own little world which he carried around with him and there was no one really quite like him. He was also designing the covers of *Isis* magazine at the time and he actually introduced me to the wonderful world of Letraset.

JOHN CLEESE

I was aware of John before I met him. He had quite a reputation at Cambridge from revue. Although I never saw him performing in the Cambridge Revue, I had written a sketch about an RAF briefing about a bombing raid, one of those things we inherited from all the war books that we read. We were still writing war sketches amazingly enough, and apparently someone said that a man called John Cleese at Cambridge was doing exactly the same kind of material and exactly the same sketch about an RAF briefing almost with the same jokes in. Of course we hadn't colluded at all, it was just coincidence. So that's when I heard about John. Then I heard Terry Jones had seen John doing some sketch about a man who watched stones, and Terry said it was one of the funniest things he'd ever seen. Just brilliant. So I was building up in my mind quite an image of this ace performer who was very special and I eventually met him in 1966 at one of *The Frost Report* recordings.

I don't think John ever came to the script sessions where I first met a lot of people like Barry Took, Marty Feldman, Dick Vosburgh and David Nobbs. All these people would turn up for the writing sessions, in which I was a very junior partner. But John, because he was also a performer in the series, either didn't have time or didn't really want to turn up to script sessions. He and Graham wrote their things quite separately, although Graham occasionally came along. So I met John not at a script session, but at one of the recordings. I can't remember our first words, probably 'Shut up' on his part or 'What? Don't bother me now.'

GRAHAM CHAPMAN

I met Graham around the same time as I met John. Generally we considered ourselves somewhat inferior because we hadn't been on a tour of New Zealand and they had, and the Footlights were much better organised than the Oxford Revue was anyway. But I must have met Graham round about the same time.

It was after he had had this legendary event where apparently he had told people that he had met David Sherlock, they were going to live together and he was in love with him or whatever. I really didn't know him that well at all and certainly wouldn't have been invited to an event like that. But I remember hearing about that and hearing about Graham announcing his homosexuality to the world. And they were all a bit amazed, not least his fiancée, who happened to be invited to the party as well.

ERIC IDLE

Eric has always been a very gregarious character, as long as I've known him. He was always very popular with loads of friends around him. I first met him at the Edinburgh Festival in 1965. He was doing the Cambridge Revue. I think he may have been directing the Cambridge Revue and I was directing the Oxford Revue. I met up with him there and spent a bit of time with him and had a drink.

There was some rivalry of course, but both Oxford and Cambridge tended to get pretty good audiences. There was quite a tradition of going to university revues and the one in '64 – the first one I went to with Terry Jones and Doug Fisher – that did really well. It was incredibly successful and got wonderful reviews, so then one didn't worry too much about the competition. You would be aware of other people's audience levels and also who had been asked to do a bit on the BBC's Edinburgh Fringe programme, where they came up and filmed some of the acts. And who had been visited by David Frost and who hadn't.

TERRY GILLIAM

I met Terry for the first time at Rediffusion Television when Humphrey Barclay said they had somebody who John Cleese had recommended who was a cartoonist and could we see him. He was a wacky American and the last thing we needed was a wacky American. I think he was just someone to meet, and see how you got on. I don't think he'd done anything at that time. We were all just meeting up and there he was in his great big, long coat. A huge long coat. An amazing coat.

Terry was very lively and vivacious, or at least his girlfriend was anyway, and I was quite impressed by him. I remember thinking this was a little touch of American chutzpah in this grey world of the Rediffusion bar and I remember feeling just ever so slightly threatened. There was enough of us doing the show anyway, we had this nice little thing sorted out between us – Eric, Terry and myself writing it – we didn't really want anybody else with bright ideas. But of course then we saw the first animations he started doing and that was the thing that did it.

ABOVE Bill Oddie, John Cleese, Graham Chapman and the cast of *Cambridge Circus* twist the night away on tour in New Zealand.

JOHN CLEESE

I first saw John at the Pembroke Smoker in January or February '63. I had arrived in late '62, and I had done a play for the Pembroke Players. And then they did Brecht's *Caucasian Chalk Circle*. I did a parody of it and sent them all up and people said, 'Oh you must audition for the Smoker.' And I said, 'What's the Smoker?' It was this Pembroke Smoking Concert. I had no idea what it was and so I went along in early January and auditioned for Tim Brooke-Taylor and Bill Oddie with these two other people that I'd been doing the sketches with. I passed the audition and I was in the Smoker.

And on one of the nights I did one of the sketches John had written before, a thing called 'BBC BC' in which Bill Oddie read the news: 'Good evening, here beginneth the news. It has come to pass that …' And I did the weather forecast: 'Over the whole of Egypt, plague followed by floods, followed by frogs, and then death of all the firstborn – sorry about that Egypt.'

So I did that piece and then I met John, this sort of gangly, lanky person. John had always dined in Pembroke; in fact people thought he was in Pembroke but he wasn't, he was at Downing college, but he always dined in Pembroke because he preferred the company of people there. He was friends with Tim Brooke-Taylor and they were all

Footlights. But there was only one person you looked at on stage and that was John. He never admitted to being funny for a second. You had no sense that he knew he was being funny. It was just so controlled that it was brilliant, and it was just head and shoulders above everybody else, he was remarkable. And he remained like that. When he went into the *Frost* show I think he was like that too. He had an extraordinary maturity of performance, very, very controlled and powerful. But he was older than everybody. John was like two years adrift.

GRAHAM CHAPMAN

Graham had gone down when I was at Cambridge. That year's revue was pretty spectacular, it was very funny, *A Clump of Plinths*. I met him because he took over from either Chris Stuart-Clarke or Anthony Buffery, when it went to London, where it ran for a bit, then Graham came in. He did his wrestling thing. Anthony Buffery was hilarious, probably the funniest man at Cambridge, certainly the most improvisational and spontaneous. He was hilariously loony, but he did research into chimp's brains and was doing psychological research, so he had to go back and do that. Graham replaced him. So I only vaguely met him around that time, this pipe-smoking, very quiet man; I certainly knew him well by the time I went to perform the show in Edinburgh that year. Graham was weird, there was no question he was on his own planet, very, very quiet, wouldn't say very much.

Eric Idle
bares his soul about the rest

GRAHAM CHAPMAN
Lanky, and mobile of face, he is a third year Medic in Emmanuel. World famous for his grotesque mimic ability, and Bristol-acclaimed star of the Footlights visit, he refuses to let it affect his confidence. He smokes a cool pipe, and will not admit that he sleeps in a cupboard; understandably he is non-committal about the Common Market.

TERRY JONES

I first met Terry Jones at the Edinburgh Festival in 1963 when I was doing the Cambridge Revue. *Footlights '63* it was called, interestingly enough, but it was the material from *A Clump of Plinths*. Terry was doing the rival Oxford Revue and they always had a night where you could go to their show. I think we clashed most nights because we were both doing the late night revue slot,

but they had this one night where they did a sort of out-takes night, where you could go along and see the end of their show and then they would do material which they'd discarded and they would then read out. It was hilarious actually and some of it was really good, and then they'd discuss it. It was as close as Oxford and Cambridge ever got to improvisation. But Terry was a stand-out, although Doug Fisher and some other very funny people were in that show. I'm not sure, but I think we might even have said hello that night. We met because we were the Cambridge lot and they were the Oxford lot.

MICHAEL PALIN

Palin I met a year later at *Footlights '64*, aptly named, where Michael was in the Oxford show and we went along to the same out-takes night. But I'd also seen his show that year and there was a wonderful piece that Michael did, I don't know what it was called, but it was about a performer. He's on stage and there's a big box with coloured wrapping paper, a present on the stage. He's doing this dreadful performance about 'I love everybody', and then he says 'I just have to open the box', and he opens this box labelled 'To Mikey, with love from the audience', and it's just about how touched he is, and how wonderful and how loving and how deeply thrilled he is that the audience has given him a present. And of course it explodes and leaves him in tatters. I just remember Michael was hilarious, he was really, really funny, and Terry was also in that show.

I had directed the Edinburgh show that year, and I put it all in a box. So it was the year of the box. When people came into the theatre, there was a crate on stage and it opened and we came out and that became the set.

TERRY GILLIAM

Gilliam came to us when we were doing *Do Not Adjust Your Set*. I think we were down at Teddington, and he just appeared. Humphrey Barclay introduced him and he had some drawings and sketches that he'd done. Humphrey was a cartoonist, too, a very good cartoonist, and Gilliam appeared either under a lunch or a bar circumstance, and he had this fantastic coat, this Afghan coat. It was love at first sight. I fell in love with the coat immediately and I liked him. I took to him instantly, and for some reason I supported his wanting to join us, because we hadn't let anybody else be in our gang. We wouldn't even let the other guys write material in *Do Not Adjust Your Set*. It was just Mike, me and Terry, we wrote it all. So I must have been really taken by him because I remember Mike and Terry didn't want him to have anything to do with it. He'd written some not very good sketches, but for some reason I said he should join us. I was really impressed by him. I don't know how or why, I can't explain, except it must have been right. I overruled their objections and talked them into going with him and so that's how he became involved.

Then both he and I were co-opted onto this Frank Muir show, *We Have Ways of Making You Laugh*, where he had to sit around and do cartoons of people. He did drawings and I wrote some sketches.

ABOVE LEFT Terry Jones takes to the stage in the Oxford Revue
ABOVE Michael Palin waits for him down the pub.

John Cleese talks about
himself in relation to the others

GRAHAM CHAPMAN

Chapman I met at an audition for the Footlights my first year at Cambridge. To my astonishment I had been asked to sing, which I was incapable of doing, and also to do a little dance thing. I was kind of bewildered and I knew that I wasn't any good and met Chapman there. We started talking before we auditioned and we went off afterwards to a café and had something to eat. It's very strange but I remember that my reaction to Chapman then was quite a strong feeling of disliking him. It was an absolute gut feeling that I was not able to identify at all. Just a feeling of really not liking him. Then I don't think I saw Chapman again until the beginning of the next academic year, which was my second year and his third. And for reasons that I cannot remember we immediately fell into writing together, the sense of dislike just evaporated and we spent a lot of time that year sitting together, usually in my room, writing stuff, a fair amount of which made it into the Footlights Revue of that year. He and I were in that show, directed by Trevor Nunn. At the end of that he went on down to London to

move on to the next step of being a doctor and started to do a cabaret act with Tony Hendra. He would earn a little money like that and I didn't see much of him then for a year.

ERIC IDLE

I first met Eric at a Pembroke Smoker and saw him perform in that, because at Cambridge we only overlapped one year. My last year was his first. I vaguely remember there were several good people in the Pembroke Smoker and I went along because I spent a lot of time at Pembroke; there were people like Chris Stuart-Clarke, Tim Brooke-Taylor and Bill Oddie in the show.

Eric Idle (front) joins the Footlights.

I had co-written a piece with Bill Oddie called 'BBC BC' which Eric did that night. I remember seeing this very good guy who came on and did the sketch very well. I thought he was rather promising, and I chatted to him briefly afterwards. When the 1963 Footlights were taken to the West End it meant that we were not able to go up to Edinburgh, which we had already undertaken to do as part of the Cambridge drama and light entertainment foray every year. Eric went up to Edinburgh and performed in the revue and did several of the bits that I was doing in the West End. Then I lived in London for about nine months, went off to New Zealand, New York, rattled about America, and so two years later I saw him round the script table at *The Frost Report*. He was a fairly familiar face, although he and I didn't spend a great deal of time together socially. He would usually write these highly verbal monologues, a little bit like a lot of the stuff he wrote for Python. Back then he usually wrote them for Ronnie Barker.

TERRY GILLIAM

Gilliam hunted me down in New York. He saw me in *Cambridge Circus* when it was on Broadway. We were there for three weeks, and he had this story that his magazine, *Help,* did in the style that the Italians called *fumetti,* and he wanted me to do the story because he liked the faces that I pulled. High compliment for an aspiring actor. So he got in touch with me and I remember having an entertaining two-day shoot with him and meeting this guy, Harvey Kurtzman, at the offices of *Help*

knowing what he was talking about but nevertheless disagreeing with what he was saying! I have no idea what the content was. I had been in the Footlights show and he had been in the Oxford Revue, although I don't recall ever seeing him perform until *Do Not Adjust Your Set*.

And then we met again when he was sitting round the writers' table for *The Frost Report*. Mike and Terry always used to write the little visual piece that we shot on the Tuesday, I think it was. So that's when I next remember seeing him.

MICHAEL PALIN

The odd thing is I don't have a first memory of Michael, by which I mean the first time I was really aware of him was when he was sitting round a table at the script meetings we used to have for *The Frost Report*.

There were two things about Michael: one, he and Terry most weeks used to produce a sketch that would need to be filmed. We would usually have a read-through on the Saturday and we would usually be filming the film sketch on the Tuesday. It would be cut together, and then the show was recorded on a Thursday. So that was what they were contributing. And two, my other main memory of Mike was that he had to leave the script meeting early one Saturday in 1966 because he was going off to marry Helen. Isn't that strange? He came to the meeting first and had to leave early. I can't have really known him at that stage because obviously I would have been invited to the wedding. I didn't know either him or Terry that well; they were part of a group around the table.

magazine. Terry and I maintained very faint contact after that, but my main recollection is that he came to London and contacted me while I was rehearsing with Marty Feldman, Aimi MacDonald, Graham and Tim in *The 1948 Show*. He came to a restaurant at the bottom of Kingsway right opposite the old Rediffusion building and we had lunch together. I thought of him more as a magazine man, but he was very keen to try and break out of the magazine world so I put him in touch with Humphrey Barclay, who was producing a show at that time called *We Have Ways of Making You Laugh*, and he started doing cartoons for that. And then, one day, Dick Vosburgh taped some of Jimmy Young's 'inanities', by which I mean Jimmy had said various inane things, and Dick had cut them all together, and they agreed it was terribly funny but they didn't have anything to illustrate it. So Terry got the Jimmy Young pictures and just did the mouth opening and closing; that was I think his first animation.

TERRY JONES

The first memory I have of Terry is when I was working for BBC Light Entertainment. I remember having lunch with him in the canteen at the Aeolian Hall in New Bond Street. I had taken the job at the BBC after the ending of *Cambridge Circus* and before we went off to New Zealand.

I have no idea why we were having lunch! I just remember sitting in the canteen. I have one of those mental photos and a vague sense of not quite

Smoking Concert to which we invited the Footlights committee, and we also provided a lot of good claret. They came to our Smoker, which was quite a reasonable show, drank our claret, and thus we got our invitation to audition and were duly elected. But by then it was my second year. It was when I met John Cleese – he was auditioning at the same time. Afterwards we compared notes, went off to the Kenya coffee house, and that's how the two of us came to work together. We wrote two or three sketches for Smokers that year.[1]

ERIC IDLE

Then along came Eric Idle about a year after us, so three of us knew each other from Cambridge.[2]

TERRY JONES

I remember thinking, 'Why does Terry Jones laugh so much?' They couldn't read out their material without laughing all the time. We weren't like that. What was interesting was that out of the twenty or so writers on *The Frost Report* the most prolific ones came together – Michael and Terry used to be very good at writing the bits of film that were used, Eric Idle was excellent at one-liners, and John and I used to go for a more verbal style of comedy – we realised that we all had something different to offer, and Barry Took brought us together with the idea of doing a series. Terry Gilliam I

JOHN CLEESE

John Cleese and I met at Cambridge University while we were both auditioning for a club called the Footlights Club, which was a kind of revue society.

I, at the age of seven or eight, used to be an avid listener to a radio programme called *The Goon Show*, and at that age I wanted to be a Goon, but that didn't seem to be a very creditable career, certainly to my parents, I didn't even dare mention it. But then later on, around about the age of fourteen, I saw an excerpt on television of a revue produced by the Cambridge Footlights and that had in it a gentleman called Jonathan Miller and I thought, 'That's very good. That's the university I'll go to to read medicine.' [The Footlights] explained that if one wanted to join, one had to be invited to audition. That seemed rather unattainable, so I joined the Mummers instead. Then I found another guy, called Anthony Branch, at my college who was reading Law and was a bit of a pianist. We teamed up and hit on the idea of holding our own

Graham Chapman
speaks from beyond the void

IT'S not often anyone can pull a stroke on David Frost. But 23 colleagues did it, with style, when the *Frost Report* team returned from their Golden Rosebowl triumph at Montreux.

And what's more, it happened in Frost's own home when, after being decoyed outdoors, he returned to find his fellow-artists and back-room team opening the bottles for a celebration party.

After greetings and congratulations under the chandelier – in the smallest room of the Frost residence – they gathered in the garden, with Rosebowl trophy, for more pictures by BEN JONES. This is the 24-strong Frost line-up:

Back Row (left to right): Ray Millichope (film editor), Barry Cryer (scriptwriter), Terry Jones (scriptwriter), Michael Palin (scriptwriter), Dick Vosburgh (scriptwriter).

Middle Row (l to r): Mrs Fiona Gilbert, Mrs Jay Barker, David MacKellar (scriptwriter), Graham Chapman (scriptwriter), John Cleese (writer-actor), Bernard Thomas (assistant director), Tony Jay (writer and assistant producer), Michael Wale (scriptwriter), Eric Idle (scriptwriter), Sally Adams (production assistant), Neil Shand (scriptwriter), Bill Wilson (production assistant), Yvonne Sinclaire (assistant film editor).

Front Row (l to r): Marty Feldman (script editor and writer), Sheila Steafel (actress), David Frost, James Gilbert (producer-director), Julie Felix (singer), Ronnie Barker (actor).

29

didn't know, but John did, and I think that he was responsible for bringing him into the group.[2]

TERRY GILLIAM

When Barry Took hit on the idea of putting us all together, it was fine by us – although at that stage, I knew nothing about Terry Gilliam at all. I'd seen him a couple of times on *Do Not Adjust Your Set*, and that was about it – a shadowy figure![3]

We always used to rib Terry Gilliam somewhat because of his paucity of English language. John Cleese used to say his language use was limited, so things were either 'Great' or they 'really pissed him off'. Not many shades of meaning in between there. I do remember on one occasion we were touring Canada and we were flying over Lake Superior and Terry looked down at Lake Superior and turned round to the rest of us and said 'Hey you guys – a whole bunch of water' which I didn't feel adequately summed up the lake.

He had noticed John Cleese when both John and I were in a revue in New York called *Cambridge Circus* and he was working for some cartoon magazine at the time and he wanted the archetypal English city gent – pin-striped trousers, bowler hat, rolled umbrella kind of person – to have in a photo-montage cartoon of a city gent who has an affair with a Barbie doll. So there are some rather nice pictures in existence of John Cleese doing naughty things with a Barbie doll.[2]

MICHAEL PALIN

Michael Palin and Terry Jones were at Oxford at roughly the same time and we all met up for the very first time at the Fringe of the Edinburgh Festival. Thereafter we began working on a television programme for a gentleman named David Frost. A very modest gentleman who had a programme called *The Frost Report*, and I remember at the end of the programme the credits read 'Starring David Frost' in big letters, 'written by David Frost' in big letters. And then thirty other names just flew by the cameras – and we were amongst those thirty other names. By the end of that series, the five of us all realised that we were actually consistently responsible for the better material in the programme – modest lot that we were![2]

Terry Gilliam pisses on the pythons

JOHN CLEESE

In 1964 *Help* magazine were looking for actors who would work for $15 a day to appear in these *fumetti* strips, which would help the magazine. My roommates and I had written one based on a man who falls in love with his daughter's Barbie doll and basically has some kind of unnatural relationship with it. *Cambridge Circus* was in New York, following on the footsteps of *Beyond the Fringe*, but they hadn't been a success and they were now down in a place called Village Square, a little theatre in Washington Square in Greenwich Village. I went down and they were all performing: John, Graham Chapman, Bill Oddie, David Hatch, Jean Hart, Tim Brooke-Taylor, Jo Kendall … There they were and John, as usual, stood out from the crowd and so I got him to appear in this magazine story. I stayed after the end of the show and I said: 'Hello, I'm the editor of a magazine. We do these little stories, we'd love to have you in one.' Simple as that, and so next week John's out on commuter train platforms, posing for our camera. I remember riding on

John Cleese debuts in *Help* magazine

The Alpine Distress Signal

Mountaineers finding themselves in difficulty and who wish to call for help, should give a distress signal by giving a sign at regular intervals six times within a minute, then a pause of one minute should follow. Thereupon the six signs should be repeated - followed by a minute's pause, and so on until an answer is received from somewhere.

The rescuer's answer will be a sign repeated three times at regular intervals during a minute.

The sign may be audible (shouting, whistling, firing a gun etc.) or visible (moving an eye-catching object, waving a white cloth against a dark background or a dark cloth against a light background, heliography with mirrors lights etc.).

the subway with him in New York and he used to do these weird things where suddenly his arm would float up above his head, just to see what people would do. He was performing publicly then. He was in many ways, I think, bolder then than when he became well known, because he was behaving strangely on subways just to see people's reactions, which he would never do now.

And so we became friends. Then I went off hitchhiking around Europe, he disappeared to work for *Newsweek* and we lost touch with each other completely until I arrived in England in '67. I was still working in magazines and I contacted him when he was doing *The Frost Report*. There he was doing the 'I'm upper class, I'm middle class, I'm working class' sketch and I was able to contact him, so I must have kept a telephone number or something somewhere along the line. I have no memory of contact during the intervening years. That led to me getting him to give me some names of television producers in the hope that I could get out of magazine work and cartooning and could enter television. One of them was Humphrey Barclay who was producing *Do Not Adjust Your Set*, and after three months of my trying to nail Humphrey down he finally made the mistake of picking up his own phone rather than have his secretary answer it and he allowed me to come and see him. I brought my portfolio of drawings and sketches, and some written things; being an amateur cartoonist, he really liked my cartoons and bought a couple of written sketches to impose upon the others in *Do Not Adjust Your Set*.

GRAHAM CHAPMAN

I first saw Graham back in New York, in *Cambridge Circus*, but I didn't meet him then. I was in my typical monomaniacal approach to things, there was only one person in *Cambridge Circus* that counted, and that was John because he was the one we needed for this thing. And so then there was Graham somewhere, and I really don't remember the moment that Graham and I collided. That was the great thing about Graham, there was a sort of

fluidity, he just floated in, he floated out, and so you could have met him anywhere at any time. Maybe I never met him! Maybe that's what happened. I never really felt I'd met Graham.

ERIC IDLE, MICHAEL PALIN & TERRY JONES

The first time I met them was at Teddington studios. I remember walking into the bar after a recording of *Do Not Adjust Your Set*, and Eric was immediately friendly and nice, the first person I bumped into. There were these other two crouching back in a booth being unfriendly and they were Mike and Terry and that was the beginning of a wonderful relationship.

They were ultimately friendly enough but I really felt it was clear that they were quite territorial and there was this interloper in the big sheepskin coat that everybody talks about. I'd bought this coat in Turkey when I was hitchhiking around and it was fantastic, and I'd painted it. That was probably the thing. I'd done some work on it. This coat attracted Eric immediately because he knew he was seeing some major interesting person and the others were threatened by it, so there you go. But what's so funny is that in the end Mike, Terry and I became the closest of the group.

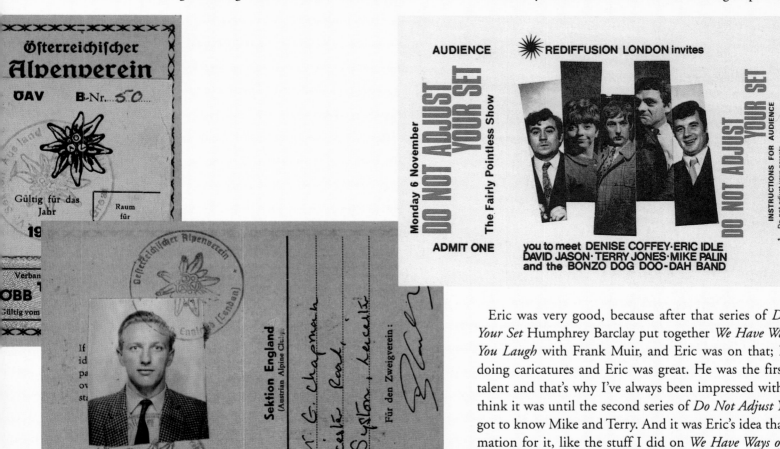

Eric was very good, because after that series of *Do Not Adjust Your Set* Humphrey Barclay put together *We Have Ways of Making You Laugh* with Frank Muir, and Eric was on that; I was on that doing caricatures and Eric was great. He was the first to spot real talent and that's why I've always been impressed with Eric. I don't think it was until the second series of *Do Not Adjust Your Set* that I got to know Mike and Terry. And it was Eric's idea that I do an animation for it, like the stuff I did on *We Have Ways of Making You Laugh*, so that was really good work.

By the second series, I was getting David Jason to do voices on cartoons because he was really good at voice work. I don't even know the moment when I was accepted. Terry talks endlessly of the 'Elephants' cartoon as an early inspiration for Python, so that obviously sparked something. He realised I wasn't just an interloper. And that's what's so funny, years later when Douglas Adams was helping Graham write, my attitude was like them: 'Who is this interloper trying to worm his way into Python?'

IN WHICH
WE ARE BORN

'. . . I got used to dealing with groups of boys and getting on with life in unpleasant circumstances and being smart, funny and subversive at the expense of authority. Perfect training for Python . . .'

Eric Idle

I was born on 29 March 1943 in Harton Hospital, South Shields. My mother was born in the same hospital, but not at the same time, interestingly enough.

I was a war baby. My earliest memories are of a Wellington bomber crashing in flames into the field beside my nursery school. 'The pilot saw the kids and took the plane down,' said the nurses. I remember being forced into a Mickey Mouse gas mask, instilling a lifelong fear of rubber masks and the eponymous rodent.

I remember Christmases with my mother weeping by the tinselled tree for my father. He had joined the RAF in 1941 and was a rear-gunner wireless-operator on Wellingtons and Lancasters with Transport Command. He served in several theatres of operations from India to the Bahamas and came through those dangerous war years unscathed. In December 1945 when the war was over, but before they had been demobbed, he was hitchhiking home to South Shields. It was Christmas time and the trains were jammed, and the troops were told to hitch because everyone stopped for servicemen in uniform. So he got a ride in a truck, sitting in the back with a lorry load of steel. Somewhere near Darlington a car cut in front of them, the lorry swerved and ran off the road, and my dad was crushed by the load. He died on 23 December in hospital with my mother by his bedside. I was two and a half. Christmas was always a bitter-sweet time in my childhood.

I remember the trauma of that moment was very, very strong. My mother disappeared for a while and went into a vast depression, and I was brought up by my gran in Manchester. She wasn't really my grandmother, but my mother's aunt and they lived in Swinton. Her husband, who I called Pop, took me to the circus in Belle Vue, Manchester, and it turned out that we were semi-royalty in circus circles because my great grandfather was Henry Bertrand, a famous ringmaster and circus manager in the 1880s and 1890s. I still have some of his notepaper, with his imposing picture in white tie and tails, announcing he is the manager of 'Robey's Flying Midgets'. It's odd because only afterwards did I realise that I ended up in a circus too, and a flying one at that.

Anyway, we were very well treated and taken backstage to meet the terrifying clowns, who were respectful to him and friendly to me. Pop also took me to various Variety shows at the Manchester Hippodrome where I saw the young Morecambe and Wise, 'Our Gracie' (Gracie Fields), Rob Wilton, Jimmy Edwards, Arthur Askey,

'I was fairly funny at school and I think it's one of the ways for little guys to avoid bullying. The interesting thing about the school was that it was founded, believe it or not, by a man called John Leese. And the school hymn went "Honour to John Leese, our founder, builder he in bygone days". How weird is that? Plus, there was a very tall, bullying figure in our class, **who used to steal my prep and copy it. It all makes sense now!'**

Norman Evans (a drag comic), the Crazy Gang and various other British comedians. The most extraordinary thing, though, for me were the nude tableaux vivants, with a stage full of beautiful girls all stark naked. This was the first time I ever saw a nude woman and suddenly there were twenty-five of them. It was called 'A Scene From Winter', snow fell and they posed with nothing on but discreetly placed drapery. The orchestra played, someone solemnly recited a daft little Hallmark card poem and the girls just sat there because they weren't allowed to move. If they moved they were in big trouble. That was illegal. But if they didn't it was apparently all right and everyone applauded as if it was art. I remember thinking 'This is fucking great!' and ever since then I have always been very fond of bare-assed girls. So that's my background in show business: circuses, comedians and bare-assed women.

At the age of five my gran took me to see three films in one day. I'd never seen a movie before, so I became really hooked on cinema right away. She took me to *Joan of Arc, The Glass Mountain* and a Marx Brothers movie, one after the other. Overkill again! Twenty-five nude ladies all at once and then three movies in a day. We were a pre-television generation of course. The first time I saw television was the Coronation in 1952. My school brought in a tiny 8-inch black and white screen and we were forced to sit around for eight hours watching people walking up and down going 'Vivat Regina!' But they gave us lots of mugs and coronation toys and at least it was a day off school.

My mother was working as a nurse and a health visitor in Cheshire and she sent for me and I went to school for the first time in Wallasey, which is just across the Mersey from Liverpool. I was there for two years, and when I eventually met George Harrison, I had a very strong feeling that we had met before. I often wondered if we'd been lads together playing on the Red Noses at New Brighton, because that was a very popular outing from Liverpool and we were always playing with kids who came from the other side of the Mersey. Anyway, I guess I'll never know.

I suppose it was difficult for my mother to cope with a growing son and a full-time job, and so at the age of seven she put me into a boarding school in Wolverhampton. It used to be called the Royal Orphanage, but it dropped the orphan bit just before I got there. However, we still called it the 'Ophney'. Ironically, the orphanage business had received a shot in the arm from the War and I was at school with a lot of other kids who had also lost their fathers in the War, paid for by the RAF Benevolent Fund. I went there from the age of seven until I finally managed to escape at the age of nineteen to go to Cambridge. There was a junior school from seven till eleven and then came the dreaded senior school, which was bleakly Victorian. It was very grim at the time, and terrifying in retrospect. I still have nightmares that I'm back at the Ophney. It was a physically abusive, bullying, harsh environment for a kid to grow up in, a boarding school where nobody had any fathers. The terms were interminable, fourteen weeks with no emotional support. At the age of seven they seemed to last forever. I look at my daughter now – she's twelve – and I couldn't conceive of sending her away for that long without a cuddle, let alone at seven; how you can do that to seven-year-olds? I have no idea.

At home we had a plaque on the wall thanking my father for making the supreme sacrifice for king and country and it was signed by George VI, so I grew up blaming the king for killing my father. I think my mother got something like £76 for the accident that deprived him of his life and she had a little RAF widow's pension, which of course was taxed, on top of her meagre earnings as a health visitor.

My mother always had problems with communicating and I remember the first day she took me to school she simply disappeared. She didn't say goodbye, she just took off, and later on she said: 'Well, I didn't want to cause a fuss. You were happily playing, so I thought I'd just slip away and avoid a scene.' I had no idea I was going to be left. I was just dumped. One or two abandonment issues there you can see …

I was fairly funny at school and I think it's one of the ways for little guys to avoid bullying. The interesting thing about the school was that it was founded, believe it or not, by a man called John Leese. And the school hymn went 'Honour to John Leese, our founder, builder he in bygone days'. How weird is that? Plus, there was a very tall, bullying figure in our class, who used to steal my prep and copy it. It all makes sense now!

I got used to dealing with groups of boys and getting on with life in unpleasant circumstances and being smart, funny and subversive at the expense of authority. Perfect training for Python. The senior school was very rough when I got there at the age of eleven. Beatings were common. The masters could beat you with canes. The older boys, the prefects, were allowed to whack you with slippers. There was a dormitory 100 yards long which they would patrol at night, and if they heard anybody talking and nobody owned up, everybody had to get out of bed and bend over the end of their beds. They'd go down the line and whack the whole dormitory.

And it was fucking freezing. It was a very grim, Midlands orphanage. I was cold until I was nineteen.

What was good was that we organised our own night life. There was a girls' school under the same roof that they never acknowledged was there. You'd only see the girls in chapel – church was compulsory twice on Sundays – and the girls would be on their side of the chapel and we'd try and slip messages to them. There was a terrible old indoor swimming pool which was full of reeky green water, and we had a system where if you put your name down after prep you'd be woken at two in the morning and could creep silently downstairs to go swimming with the girls. We were very good at misbehaving, sneaking about at night after lights-out and climbing over the wall to buy beer from the off-licence. We called it Colditz, that was our model for the place. It was all about trying to escape. It was like a combination of the army and prison where you learned to adapt and to trust your peer group. Certainly by the last years in the senior school, we were a very highly organised criminal group. We never took a straight exam until O Level because we'd always steal the exam papers. The boys were very adept at picking locks or they'd unscrew the back of cupboards where teachers stored the exams. Then they'd write the answers overnight on stolen exam paper and smuggle these in under their jumpers and substitute them. It was only at O Level that I discovered that I was actually cleverer than most of the others, when a lot of the guys simply didn't come back to school. They'd all failed. That was the first straight exam they'd ever taken.

At school I started performing by doing puppeteering with string marionettes, which involved writing sketches and doing funny voices, hiding in character and poking fun at the masters. We were a big hit and got huge laughs. I also saved up and bought a cheap guitar at the age of about twelve, because it was Elvis time. Elvis saved our lives. Early rock 'n' roll was fabulous and we loved the

Everly Brothers, Chuck Berry and Little Richard. We'd listen to Radio Luxembourg on transistor radios under the sheets at night. I became a bit of a folkie in a trio where I played harmonica with a banjo and a guitar, and we did all black music. We did Sonny Terry and Brownie McGhee, and all those Jim Crow sort of songs. It has always struck me as slightly odd that we identified with the black under-classes in the US, when you think that we were very white boys in an English boarding school, but their songs became our songs of protest too. Our feeling was of being repressed, and I guess the soul of it, the spirit of the music, was very close to what we felt. Then of course along came rock 'n' roll which became the music of our generation. That and the Wolves were the saving grace. They made life worth living. Football and rock. Wolverhampton Wanderers were the first team to play in Europe and I'll never forget the Molyneux football ground packed to the gills, with the huge crowd roaring and the floodlights brighter than day. Our sports master had some connection with the Wolves, so we'd always get their second-hand shirts, and he could get us into the stadium, so I saw some classic games, the very first European matches against Honved and Barcelona, Moscow Dynamo and Red Star of Belgrade. Here suddenly were these strange foreigners coming over

playing our game, wearing tiny, shiny little shorts and super cool shirts, while the Wolves still wore baggy shorts and long sleeves and they looked really untrendy compared to these sleek, skilful foreigners. But Wolves were the top British team. They were the league leaders under Stan Cullis. They even won the Cup in my last year at school and the whole town went delirious.

At boarding school there was nothing else to do but work and after a certain age it became interesting. After sixteen when you're doing A Level (I did history, geography and English literature), reading is your total escape. My gran gave me a typewriter when I was twelve, which was a fantastic gift, so I was always writing little stories. I recently came across a handwritten novel I'd done for my class at about that age called 'The Mystery of the Missing Skull'. The skull was Boadicea's. It's probably an episode of *Xena*. I think I was always interested in words because in such a sterile environment you have to create your own entertainment, and explore your own brain. That becomes your escape, and rock 'n' roll, football, reading and writing were mine. I was more well read than most teenagers because at boarding school there was nothing else to do in the evenings. I didn't have a fucking youth! In the evenings we did prep, then cleaned the school. I did S Level. Nobody's ever done

S Level, because it's above A Level and I once found somebody else who'd done it and we reckoned we were the only two people in England who ever did S Level!

The Goons were a radio show I heard only occasionally. I think we were always in prep when it was on. Mostly radio for me was *The Billy Cotton Band Show*, *The Clitheroe Kid* and awful things like that. My big comedy light bulb was *Beyond the Fringe*. In 1962 I stayed with a friend in London, and we could only get standing tickets for this revue at the Fortune Theatre. Just as well because I would never have stayed in a seat. I rolled around the wall screaming with laughter. I had never laughed so hard in my life. I had no idea you could be that funny, no idea you could laugh at the

'At school we had a very soggy, muddy playing field and I wasn't very good at football, so on a Thursday afternoon, instead of changing for compulsory games, I'd put on my school cap, march out the front door, go down town to Wolverhampton and watch a movie.'

Prime Minister and the War and the Royal Family. Everything I secretly hated was being mocked and they were doing this so wittily. They were just so smart and dangerously funny. I immediately bought the album and I learned everything: Alan Bennett's vicar monologue, Peter Cook's Macmillan speech, Jonathan Miller's whimsical monologue. It was a fucking amazing show and it changed my life. I wanted to be funny from then on.

At school we had a very soggy, muddy playing field and I wasn't very good at football, so on a Thursday afternoon, instead of changing for compulsory games, I'd put on my school cap, march out the front door, go down town to Wolverhampton and watch a movie. I did this regularly every Thursday afternoon, for ages and

ages, marching boldly past the headmaster's study and nobody ever caught me, because if you've got your cap on and you're walking through the front door, you're clearly doing some school business, right? So, I learnt very early on that if you're brazen, nobody questions you. If I'd been sneaking out I would probably have been caught. Well I finally *was* caught in my penultimate year. The headmaster sent for me and he said, 'Did you enjoy the movie this afternoon?' And I annoyed him by saying, 'No, not very much sir, it wasn't very good.' I'd been spotted and reported for watching an X film under-age (actually *Butterfield 8* with Elizabeth Taylor). I'd only been reported because it was an X film. So I was hauled up in front of the whole school next morning and denounced by the headmaster for this dreadful crime – Idle had been caught downtown going to an X movie! Well, I couldn't have given myself a bigger advert, I was a fucking hero. They just loved me! I was publicly sent to the back of the hall, I was no longer a prefect and it was just like 'Yes! Yes!' Kids were slapping me on the back and giving me the thumbs up. I was just the biggest hero! It was brilliant. And then at the end of the year the headmaster left the school with a recommendation that I be made head boy. Odd really.

At the Ophney every Monday afternoon from the age of eleven we had to pretend we were in the army. Joining the CCF (the Combined Cadet Force) was compulsory. So, eleven years old and we're on the fucking playground in army boots, marching up and down the square in itchy baggy uniforms, yelled at by professional drill sergeants. By the age of fourteen not only could I perform arms drill and shoot a .303 Lee Enfield rifle with reasonable accuracy, I could strip a Bren gun, blindfold. Then they'd drop us in the Welsh mountains in full gear and say 'See you', and six hours later if you were lucky you'd stagger into a military camp in North Wales, armed only with a compass and bit of cheese. Very useful little things to know in life. And certainly it prepared me for Python movies …

Since I was head boy (by default) the school insisted I must also be head of the CCF, which I didn't want to be. At the end of military training they had made the mistake of sending us off on a Civil Defence Course which showed just exactly what happened when a nuclear bomb went off, and as a result I had become violently pacifist. During the Easter hols (1962) I went on the Aldermaston March, the annual CND anti-nuclear rally. We marched from Aldermaston in Hampshire to Hyde Park behind banners, singing protest songs, a distance of about 54 miles. We camped overnight in Reading and then marched proudly into town. My friend was at London University and we were very lefty and very committed; it was great. When I got back to school, the padre called me in and said, 'You're a hypocrite, Idle, you're the head of the CCF and you went on the Aldermaston March.' I said, 'Well I resign,' and he said, 'You're not allowed to resign.' So at Parade I would just take the salute, turn the wrong way about to annoy the drill sergeants and slope off and read. I refused to go to Military Camp at the end of term. It was just a sort of 'fuck you' to the school because they couldn't throw me out. I'd been accepted by Cambridge, I was on the Aldermaston March, I didn't take any of their fucking CCF seriously. I was just off in my own world and that was reassuring, that was really good for me because I could finally say 'Screw you'.

Michael Palin

'As I've said, my father was a man

of regular habits, and I think he would

ideally have liked me to replicate

his career, which is what you did then.

He wanted me to go to Clare College,

Cambridge, if the storybook of life

worked out. I took an exam

and they said no, they couldn't take

me, because English was very

over-subscribed that year

and if I had chosen to read forestry

or something like that, I probably would

have got in. Too late by then to go

back and say, **"Oh yes, I want to be a lumberjack."'**

I was born on 5 May 1943, on a quiet Wednesday, quarter to twelve in the morning, at 26 Whitworth Road, Sheffield.

One of my earliest memories is of rationing, which I suppose means I remember shortage. I don't know if I knew why we were short, but I remember ration books with little coupons for butter, sugar and all sorts of things. I remember my mother actually allowing me to tear the coupon off and hand it to the lady in the shop. I wasn't quite sure why one was doing this rather than just paying with money, but I suppose it would have been normal then. So my first memories are of a period of austerity and of going down to a place in Sheffield and having to queue up to get orange juice with my mum.

My parents rented a three-storey house in Sheffield and on the ground floor outside, overlooking the rockery and the little bit of lawn, was a covered, protected entrance to the cellar which was put there because of the war. That was to be our air-raid shelter and we used to play on that a lot. It was rather an odd sort of feature. It was a big concrete platform with a wall on either side, protecting the entrance down to the cellar. I remember not being quite sure why we had it, but there was some story of how it hadn't always been there. And clearly, looking at it now, it would have been added on, I presume, in 1939 or 1940. And I also remember there were bar marks on the windows, like little scabs on the glass window, where it turned out bars had been erected in 1940/41/42 to stop the glass shattering.

So I was dimly aware that there had been some sort of crisis a few years before, but the bombing of Sheffield all took place in 1940 or 1941, so by the time I came into the world there weren't any more bombing raids on Sheffield.

I certainly remember reading a lot of war books and war stories, not particularly encouraged by my parents, interestingly enough; it was just amongst the children at school – stories about war, torture and escape, which were current. That was the bulk of the inspiration for books that were around at that time. I remember reading *The Cruel Sea*, which was quite an event, I think, because it was the first anti-war book, which is why it had a certain celebrity which made it different from the others. I remember reading that in the Cadet edition – no swear words or naughties. I've always liked the Cadet edition idea, I've used it in various sketches – the Cadet edition of the Bible, etc. You could have a Wren's edition, a Cadet edition or a Midshipman's edition …

In the years after the war it was quite hard to find a book. The first hardback book I was ever given, when I was seven, was *The Arabian Nights*. My father gave it to me. Before that books were really quite a luxury.

My mother's family are from Oxfordshire and my father's from Norfolk, and on my mother's side the family were kind of 'gentry', I suppose you'd call them. My father wasn't gentry, but they were both clearly from the professional classes. My father was the son of

Michael's parents at home in Sheffield

Michael with mother and sister Angela

a doctor and he'd been quite well educated at Shrewsbury school and then Cambridge. My mother was the daughter of the High Sheriff of Oxfordshire, and she'd been presented at court. You'd go to Buckingham Palace and be presented to the king or the queen, who'd come along and say hello, and then a big debutante ball would be given. It was a society thing, all about cementing social contacts, and it was expected to happen to you if you were from a certain background. She was part of that because my grandfather on my mother's side was a big landowner in Oxfordshire. In fact he actually lived right on the borders of what became George Harrison's house, Friar Park.

My parents got married and during the Depression, in the mid-1930s, they had to move where the work was. My father was an engineer and so that's how they found themselves up in Yorkshire, because there was just more engineering work up there, first in Hull, where my sister was born, then in Leeds, then in this quite big house in Sheffield. They rented it from a man called Mr Bates who charged them very little. It was never a house that they owned and they always seemed to be very hard up, as I remember it.

I became very close friends with the boy who had come to live in the house next door to us, Graham Stuart-Harris. His family just seemed to have a little bit more than us. It was little, subtle things that showed me how relatively poor we were – next door there'd be a few more things in their fridge. They had a fridge for a start, which we didn't have until 1952. And you were aware that certain people's fathers had cars and we didn't. Little things like that. So I think early on I realised that money was fairly tight, but it didn't seem a lot different from anyone else at the time because there just wasn't much around anyway.

At times during the rest of my early life there were moments when I was slightly embarrassed by the fact that my father would never turn any lights on in the house unless there was someone

Michael with
neighbours
Graham and Susan
Stuart-Harris

actually in that room. We lived in a pool of light round the fire, while the rest of the house remained completely dark. And he used to get very angry if my sister spent more than two and a half minutes on the telephone. I wasn't absolutely certain if it was just my father being naturally like that or whether we really didn't have the money. We did things, we went on holiday for two weeks in the year, which is what people did.

I remember, when I was at boarding school at Shrewsbury, feeling embarrassed that my parents had a rather small car, an A50 Austin Cambridge. Shameful to think of it now. There were a lot of big cars at Shrewsbury, Jaguars and all that. And I can remember then feeling aware that we had less than others, but I don't think it worried me greatly. However, it did slightly affect my father's view of life and he was rather misanthropic anyway, probably partly to do with a stammer he had, which was quite serious.

He couldn't get sentences out, but we never analysed it really. I asked my mother why does he speak like that, and she said a maid jumped out on him, and that was the story – a maid! I don't know what really went on there. Very interesting Freudian thing. It certainly must have affected him in his professional life. If you go into a room full of people to deliver a report and you actually can't get the words out, we can all imagine how awful that must be, especially for him because of his education. Having been to public school and Cambridge, he was expected to go into management. He had worked for Izal, the toilet paper company, but as long as I can remember he worked for Edgar Allen Steelworks. He never got promoted and never got demoted as far as I can see. He was never made a director of the works. I vaguely remember that a younger man called Walter Head was made a director ahead of my father. My father liked Walter Head quite a lot, thought he was good, but there was a sort of a frisson when Walter was made a director, because it was all to do with status and all to do with a bit of money. Every little bit must have mattered. After he died I had to go through some of his papers, and I found out that when I was at Shrewsbury my school fees were half what he earned. That was how important it was for him to send me to a public school.

My mother, I think, had some private money as well. I can remember wishing that we had a bit more money, then my father would be a bit more relaxed and a little slower to get angry.

I wanted to be close to my father, I had the usual feelings towards him. He was my dad and I enjoyed it when we played cricket together or something like that. He took an interest in what I was doing, I suppose. I can't remember year for year, but my general impression was that my mother was much more sympathetic and probably just more relaxed generally. She didn't have to go out to work. She was there more. Most of the time I spent with my mother and in the end my mother was the one who was much more understanding and indulgent. My father was always kind of

preoccupied. But I wanted to please him and I wanted him to be a good dad, like other people have good dads and all that.

I grew up in a fairly protected world, and I remember being very shocked at some age when I heard two people, not my own parents, having a public row. I was just so surprised. I thought that children did that, but we grew out of it. Grown-ups don't do it.

My father was a bit difficult and there would always be quite a number of moments when it was very tense around the table and I could tell he was being a bit sharp with my mother, but I never felt that that was anything that was going to fracture the family. There were moments later on as I grew up when I remember saying to my mother, 'Why don't you divorce him?' I had found this wonderful word 'divorce'. Her response was 'Don't be so silly, dear. You get your nose out of that dictionary and go and plant the marigolds.'

Overall, though, I think I was happy in the sense that I liked my father when he was in a good mood and I wanted our general father–son relationship to work. I think I was aware that, because he had a stammer, people would laugh at it behind his back. I stood up for my father in situations like that. Well, I think I probably tried to.

When I was five years old, I went to Birkdale prep school. There were no kindergartens or nursery schools or anything like that, so Birkdale was my first school and I remained there until I was thirteen. It was a fairly short bus ride away from home, a long walk down the hill and up again at the end of the day, and a bus ride of a few stops. It took us half an hour/forty-five minutes to get there. It was in a big old Edwardian house in a pleasant leafy suburb of Sheffield.

I remember my first teacher was called Miss Forsdyke and I was very fond of her. I remember, as I suppose all of us do, when you're left at the school on your first day, the door closing and it being very dark. Most of my childhood seems to have been in very dark rooms.

I have odd sorts of memories of the first two or three years at school. I even have early sexual memories of teachers that I fancied. I can only have been six or seven and there was one lady, who may still be around, called Miss Cadell, and she was known as 'Bosoms Cadell'. 'Bosom' was a very naughty word for young boys at that time, very, very naughty, and it cropped up a lot in the Bible so there was a lot of giggling at that. There was another teacher called Miss Twyford, who had lovely, long blonde hair, golden hair. I remember her terribly well. She'd have been about twenty and there was something I did respond to – glamour and looks – at that age. It did me no harm.

One of my favourite things as a child was watching Laurel and Hardy and short films like that. We had no television, so that, as they say, was right out. I would go to the News Theatre in the centre of Sheffield and there'd always be a 'B' feature, which I usually hoped would be some slapstick comedy – it might have been Laurel and Hardy, the Three Stooges or Abbott and Costello. I think those were the things that I picked up on first of all. And Norman Wisdom. My father quite liked slapstick humour as well, so that was very much part of it. It's interesting how your humour tastes are shaped a little bit by your parents. And, of course, school was a wonderful gallery of characters, emotions, bizarre situations

1956

and weird behaviour. I think that's why one goes back so often to what people rather disparagingly dismiss as schoolboy humour, but I think if you can use humour and you have a sense of humour, that's where it's first honed and developed, at school. We had some extraordinary teachers. The headmaster himself was an extremely eccentric man, and sometimes the only way to deal with it would be to laugh, usually after he'd flown into one of his strange rages or whatever. Similarly, with a group in the playground, to be able to mimic the voice of one of the teachers, or the way he walked or his expression, was a great cachet. People liked that if you could do it at all well, and I could sort of echo people's voices.

I probably wasn't unique in doing that at my school, but there weren't that many who were seen as the jokers. Others were sporty, or they'd be rather violent in gangs or whatever, whereas I was fairly easygoing and generally I suppose people would be attracted to me because I could make them laugh. I was never a gang member, but sometimes you had to go along with people you really disliked because you realised you might get beaten up if you didn't. But I was happiest in the company of other boys with whom I could laugh and that was my release from this odd, batty world that I was part of.

I was quite keen on acting at that age and I'm not sure why. The chance to show off? Be someone else? I remember a production of *A Christmas Carol* I was in at school, because we had a sort of 'method' producer. He was called Mr Fisher and he would say things like, 'Well Michael, when you go on stage I'm going to throw some water over your bonnet, to show that you've come in from the rain, it'll be rather a nice effect.' I was playing Martha Cratchit, and I had to sit through the meal with my bonnet dripping because my friend Graham, playing my mother, who was supposed to take it off couldn't and practically throttled me.

But I liked that feeling of 'Gosh, things are going out of control here' and as school's all about control, a certain sort of anarchic thrill was going through me that this shouldn't have happened but it was quite enjoyable. And that's when I fell off the stage onto the younger boys in the front row, killing two of them. That story's slightly embellished. At least I think I fell off the stage during that performance, but there's a lurking feeling in my mind that it might have happened to somebody else – a boy called Shaun Snow – but you know I certainly remember it as happening while I was with my back to the audience: either he or I fell off.

I can remember enjoying doing that and also being a little bit nervous. I don't think I was ever really absolutely comfortable with the idea of doing a major acting role and I don't know if I ever would have got the chance.

Later, I remember being cast as Chief Weasel in *Toad of Toad Hall*. It was going to be an outdoor performance but it was cancelled owing to rain and I have a little sneaking feeling that I was rather relieved.

I used to perform at home as well. My parents didn't have many books but they had a beautiful leather-bound edition of Shakespeare. I loved the language and I loved the feel of the book with its delicate thin pages, so just occasionally in the evening I would stride around playing all the roles, reading it aloud to my mother. I didn't always understand it, but it just felt like it demanded to be spoken out loud, which is interesting. My parsimonious father was a bell ringer at the local church and he often went out for bell-ringing practice; I quite liked that because that would be an evening in with just me and my mum and we could have a few more lights on, put a fourth bit of coal on the fire and have a bit of a laugh.

At that age I was very attracted by the prospects of foreign lands and different places. I loved looking at the *National Geographic* magazine and I was fascinated by Biggles stories that were set in the Gobi desert or the North Pole and so on.

My father was the one who introduced me to trains, because I think he was very keen on trains. I don't think he was actually a trainspotter, but he would take me to high places above the Dore and Totley tunnel and watch the trains going in and out. Another Freudian moment – we would watch the trains going in and out of the tunnel!

Then I became a trainspotter because that was the sort of thing that people did at school. It was one of those little competitions. Some people collected cheese labels or cigarette cards; I collected cheese labels, cigarette cards and also went and collected train numbers. But there was something else about standing on a station which wasn't just about collecting the engine numbers. To stand on the station platform and see an express pull in was terribly romantic. The Thames–Clyde Express used to come through and the fact that it had come from London and was going to the Clyde, which was in my imagination absolutely millions and millions of miles away, up in Glasgow, meant a lot to me. So I was very responsive to the romance of that idea of opening up worlds. My sister went to live in London when I was about ten or eleven, and when we would go and see her off at the station, I just wished I was on the train as well.

Another thing I used to do when I was around eleven or twelve years old was to cycle off round the outskirts of Sheffield, up the dry-stone-wall lanes and out onto the moors. It was lovely up there, very wild and very bleak and I used to go on these long bicycle rides without any problem. I would pretend I was a train. I'd be a certain express and I would stop at certain places and wait there for about three or four minutes, or whatever I'd observed trains waiting for. Then I'd get on my bicycle and go on a bit further, then we'd suddenly have to stop because there was some problem with a train ahead. So I'd end up at the imaginary equivalent of Preston or Carlisle or Shap summit, somewhere up in the moors, and I used to think that was great. I always had a keen imagination and I quite liked being on my own. Generally I was gregarious and my friend Graham and I spent an awful lot of time together. But I remember very occasionally I just wanted to go off and have a think myself and do things purely on my own, and they all tended to have a sort of getting-away-from-it, escape theme.

The missionaries who came to speak at our church represented another means of escape. I found a lot of church services fairly boring until the missionaries came along. They were different physical specimens. They were tanned and they didn't look as though they had spent all their lives in the vicarage next door. I was rather impressed by their tales, which always involved suffering of one kind or another. They were either talking about people with appalling deformities and illnesses or they were talking about just how you would have to get from one village to another through a swamp, very often crocodile-infested, and then you'd be aware the man talking had no right hand or something like that. A missionary in church, gripping the side of the pulpit with a hook or whatever, that brightened up my little life.

I didn't really start watching television much until we got our first set, a Kolstar Brandes New Queen, in 1957. Before that I went round to Graham Stuart-Harris's house and watched television, which of course was another uncomfortable reminder that they were a family that had a television and we weren't. I remember coming back from Graham's at night and if I'd seen anything

'My father used to ration television. He hung a little cover over the screen which had to be lifted when we were going to turn the set on and only certain programmes were really allowed to be watched when he was around, whereas the Stuart-Harrises would just leave their set on for most of the evening.'

vaguely unnerving, like this series called *Fabian of the Yard* which had some quite nasty murder moments in it, then I'd have to come down his long drive in total darkness, then along the road and up the drive into our house. I probably could have run it in about thirty seconds, but I remember sometimes being absolutely terrified of what might be lurking in the dark driveways and racing up to my house, throwing open the front door and pushing myself in. When I left his house, I think my imagination took over and sort of created this vision that every shadow might conceal some dismembered limb, or nasty things lurking, and they were quite potent and strong, those fears that I was able to create for myself.

My father used to ration television. He hung a little cover over the screen which had to be lifted when we were going to turn the set on and only certain programmes were really allowed to be watched when he was around, whereas the Stuart-Harrises would just leave their set on for most of the evening. If there hadn't been

the warm haven at No. 28, with relaxed rules, younger parents and more creature comforts, I think my childhood would have lacked something very important.

At the age of thirteen I went to board at Shrewsbury. I was well prepared for it. My father, I knew from very early on, wanted me to go to the school he'd been to and unashamedly fed me all sorts of propaganda with books about the school: the fact that it was founded in 1552, it had a school crest and mottoes in Latin and generally it was one of the top schools in the country. I think that was just partly due to his own disappointment at how life had worked out since he'd been there during the Great War. I knew it was a boarding school. It didn't particularly worry me.

I remember being very pleased that I got in. I got the exams and no one from my prep school had ever been to Shrewsbury before and all around the walls of the school hall they had crests of the various schools to which pupils had gone on to. Because I was the first to go to Shrewsbury, I had to get one of the crests and it was hung up there with great sort of ceremony and it looked rather good because it's got lions round it and God knows what.

Anyway I arrived at school and it was pretty strange suddenly being there, the door closing again, I suppose like it did when I was five years old, but this time my parents were going off for three months, rather than six hours. I had a very, very understanding housemaster, who had a tremendous effect on my life. If you had a bad housemaster, you had a pretty awful time because the school was divided into eight to ten houses, about sixty or seventy boys in each and that's where you lived. That's where you came back to in the evening and that was where you ate and slept. Your whole social life was based on that. We had a real character, a man called R.H.J. Brooke. It's a world of initials, public school, I know lots of boys purely by their initials. I know J.M.M. Sellers, I don't know if you call him John or Jerry or whatever, but I know him as J.M.M. and he probably knows me as M.E. Palin. Anyway R.H.J. Brooke was our housemaster and a man with a very great sense of humour. I'd say he had a softish touch, I wouldn't say he was an easy touch, but you knew you felt you could probably go to him if you got into any real trouble.

So I felt reasonably protected by him and in the first year I shared a study with a man called Geoffrey Fallows, a nice solid guy, and a J.M.M. Sellers, who was about two years ahead of me. I can remember sitting in the toilets once and hearing two of them having a pee, talking about me, 'That new boy, Palin, he's a bit mad, isn't he?' and the other one saying, 'Yes, quite nicely mad though.' It was the 'mad' bit that I quite liked. It was the first time I'd heard anyone discuss me in that way.

There was an air of aggression to some extent, a feeling of having to prove yourself all the time. For instance, you had to decide if you were going to row or play cricket and that was it. You couldn't try both and then decide. One evening somebody came round and said, 'Palin, are you going to be a rower or a cricketer?' 'Oh, um …' 'Are you good at cricket?' 'Not terribly.' 'Rowing then.' So I was down as an oarsman. I spent the rest of the next four years being an oarsman and was never asked to play cricket.

National Service had finished a couple of years before, but we still had the cadet force where we wore uniforms and carried very old rifles around and drilled people. Actually I played one of those characters in *The Meaning of Life*, an RSM with a sash just like the red sash I had in the cadets. I did actually have to shout at people for a bit, I quite enjoyed that really. But it was all a bit of a charade.

One of the good things about school was that we used to have a field day where we would all pile off into the Welsh hills, which were nearby, and these terrible mock battles would be organised. I remember a wonderful one where we were supposed to be defending, and a farmer and his flock got between us and the attackers. We just blasted off, with an apoplectic master shouting, 'Stop! Don't shoot the sheep, don't shoot the sheep.'

There was another time when I went away on a school camp, which was also disastrous, because I and about three or four others were chosen to be the infiltrators looking for an army base. But we were supposed to stay in certain map squares and not move out of those squares and the rest of the force would try and find us over a period of about a day. We found our place in the map reference, sat down in amongst some very thick bracken and were never found. We just sat there. One of the boys was called Rooker and had some cigarettes, which was great, so we spent the whole day smoking in this thick bracken. Very dimly in the distance you could hear some people searching for us. Then the weather got quite bad and so finally, feeling terribly pleased with ourselves, we made our way back to the camp, when it was getting dark around 8 or 9 o'clock. We expected to be greeted as heroes, having done a really good job of avoiding capture, but we got a terrible bollocking because the whole thing had been called off late in the afternoon because of the weather.

One of the most important things in my childhood was the advent of *The Goon Show* on the radio: Spike Milligan, Peter Sellers, Harry Secombe and Michael Bentine originally. They started in 1951 as *The Crazy People*. I picked up on the Goons in about 1954. It was very different from the comedy shows that I'd listened to with my parents. My father liked *Take it from Here* and *Much Binding in the Marsh* and we religiously had to listen to those over tea on Saturday or Sunday afternoon. That was very much part of family life. My father definitely had a sense of humour but *The Goon Show* was beyond him. It was something that I discovered and I used to just hope and pray that he wouldn't come in when it was on. He came in once when Bluebottle was in full swing and was convinced there was something wrong with the radio.

I liked to listen to it on my own. People at school had told me about it originally. Then we'd go through it the next morning and re-live it, as one would. There was nothing before that I felt I'd really discovered for myself. This was it and I used to think, 'How do they do it?' and 'Just how do they create this wonderful world?' I used to find it so funny because it broke the rules. A lot of it was just verbal and I did enjoy the funny voices, there's always been something about funny voices which I've quite liked. Probably goes back to schoolmasters.

I've always felt that civilised behaviour was generally on a knife-edge. I can remember feeling that at school assemblies when someone would get up there and start talking. I can just remember thinking, 'Gosh, if a man on a length of wire, stark naked suddenly swung across the stage, what would happen?' 'What would happen if I ran up there and stuffed a banana in his face?' – something like that. I could almost do it. I don't know if there's a sort of syndrome for that. But I just felt these people are all playing a certain game, terribly sort of straight and focused, but only inches away from insanity. But the great thing about *The Goon Show* was that it was a glimpse of madness, which it probably literally was, because Spike made himself mentally ill just writing them. But there was that feeling, which was wonderful, that they saw behind this thin veneer of civilisation and pushed these characters to limits, which I just thought was exciting and revealing, not just funny but also imaginative and brilliant.

What's special about them was that they broke rules. And most of the other shows, however funny they were, behaved in a certain way, conformed to certain prejudices, reflected the social order and conventions of my parents' generation. Sketch shows were sketch shows and they just reflected the way the world was. During those years after the war everybody was just so relieved it was all over. And it was five or six years after that when the Goons came in and said, 'Right, now let's take it a little bit further.' And then came *Beyond the Fringe*, for instance, the first programme to start putting in jokes about the Prime Minister. I wish in a way that I was able to go back in time and remind myself of what the taboos were, because they were terribly strong and affected our freedom of speech very powerfully. We live in a time now where there seem to be few taboos on anything.

Generally speaking, authority has to win respect now, when in those days it was automatically granted it. I think there was a terrific need after the war to get back to the old hierarchies and make sure church, army, politicians and all that were in place again. I always thought it was interesting that the Labour government won after the war and then pretty quickly they were replaced by the Conservatives as people thought this was what we really need, order not revolution.

There was nothing else around at the time that was absurd in the way the Goons were. You could have jokes about this, that and the other, and there was a lot of sexual innuendo – you've only got to listen to a George Formby song for something like that – but to

'Jazz didn't really impinge much on my life but the coming of Elvis was a great epiphany. Rather like the Goons were to comedy, Elvis was to pop music for me, and 'Heartbreak Hotel', as many people have said, had extraordinary impact when it came out.'

suggest that life is absurd, meaningless and pointless and people are completely daft, well *The Goon Show* was the first programme to put that across to me. I felt they were saying look behind everything, don't take anything at face value.

I first heard a recording of *Beyond the Fringe* in my last year at school, in summer 1961. It was funny for a start, incredibly funny, and also quite daring. There was an underground cult following of people who listened to *Beyond the Fringe*, and I listened to it together with another album that I'd been given a couple of years before that, which was by Tom Lehrer. I remember listening to his songs, and again there was an edge to them which was quite different to a lot of the comedy I'd grown up with, which was basically friendly, domestic and jolly. The Goons had been surreal and absurd, but these ones had real attack in them, like Alan Bennett's impersonation of a vicar – it was one of those things that once you'd heard it, you couldn't listen to sermons ever again in quite the same way. They were clever. I felt they were a bit out of my league, very metropolitan, especially Peter Cook who was so amazingly elegant and confident, and I felt a million miles from them, but then living in Sheffield you felt a million miles from most things.

My other great obsession at that age was pop music. We all listened to Radio Luxembourg, that's where we heard a lot of the songs. That's where you could get pop music shows, you couldn't hear them anywhere else. You couldn't actually hear them that well on Radio Luxembourg either, as its frequency was quite weak and the signal kept fading in and out. You had shows with some pop music in them on the BBC, but it was mixed with a lot of standards, Max Bygraves, Vera Lynn and things. Or you had jazz, which was ploughing a different furrow. Jazz didn't really impinge much on my life but the coming of Elvis was a great epiphany. Rather like the Goons were to comedy, Elvis was to pop music for me, and 'Heartbreak Hotel', as many people have said, had extraordinary impact when it came out. Again, it was one of those things which made my father think that the wireless set had actually broken, because he'd come in on the bit, 'Well, since my baby left me', and he couldn't understand why this man was singing as if he was being suffocated. Odd, really, because he was singing almost with a stammer, and the one time stammerers don't stammer is when they sing, which of course I knew from my father's own experience. But I couldn't really explain to my father or my mother why I liked Elvis, so it was my own thing and it was magic.

At that time there were suddenly more things on the market you could actually buy quite cheaply. I remember buying my first record player. It was a blue and white Emerson, which cost about £7.50 or something like that, and that was an enormous freedom for me to have my own record-player, because I had no portable radio either. There was this huge family set we had in the sitting room, a great Ekco, so in order for me to listen to it in my room, I would have to unplug it, take it upstairs, put it in my room and my father wasn't too keen on that. So, there wasn't really much chance to listen to anything new and different. Then, in the mid-'50s, along came a little bit more prosperity and a few more consumer goods on the market, including records themselves. So we bought seventy-eights, and then of course forty-fives came out, which were absolutely brilliant, a wonderful invention. Graham and I, largely I think with Graham's money because he always seemed to have more than I did, kept up with most of the new releases and we'd go and buy a record a week, sometimes more. There were British artists like Billy Fury and Cliff Richard, but it was largely American pop music that we were in to – Duane Eddy, Eddie Cochrane and Bobby Darin who I loved. Connie Francis was my earliest real crush. And there was Elvis of course, always.

In 1959, when I was sixteen, we went on a family holiday to Southwold which is a small, genteel holiday town on the Suffolk coast which my father had decreed would be the place that we would go to for our holidays, having exhausted the delights of Sheringham, in Norfolk, where we'd been going for the previous ten years. We were in a very old-fashioned guest house (which eventually became a source for a location in *East of Ipswich*, a film I did for the BBC recreating my experiences much later on). Across the road was this bungalow which was being rented by a family and every morning at 8 o'clock this tall, athletic man with blonde hair went across the road and down the beach in all weathers with this bevy of girls behind him. You could tell he was keen to swim and the rest of them were gradually less keen. There were a couple of girls at the back who were rather giggly and one of them sort of took my eye. Later that week my friend and I saw them on the beach sitting there and we were in the sea. I wasn't very good at how you introduced yourself to women, it was just something we weren't really taught. But one of the girls was a bit more worldly about it. She and this girl called Helen were throwing a ball around and she said to Helen, 'If you want to meet him, just throw the ball a little harder and it'll go into the sea and then you'll have to talk to them.' The ball was thrown and we had to stumble out of the sea and retrieve it and that's how I first got talking to Helen Gibbins (whom I later married). The trouble was that there were two girls and I think the one I really fancied was the other one. But I don't think we'd have got on at all well, whereas Helen and I got on very well.

So that turned into a holiday romance really, more based on humour, shared humour. There was a bit of lust involved, but it was something that sort of lasted maybe a week or so, then she went off. But then the next year she was back in the same place and we went back to the same place, so in a sense my father's obsession with regularity and predictability paid off and I kept seeing Helen each year.

It was a romance that began in August and ended in August. Then two years after I'd met her she wasn't there at the same time as me and I was really truly mortified and heartbroken. That's when I knew I must have been in love because I used to sit and listen to these pop songs about people driving their cars into the sea and feel somehow they applied to me. I was a terrible lovelorn thing and life would never be the same again. And of course life ticked on. She wrote a few letters to me at school, actually quite a lot of letters, but then there was a gap and it was much later on that I got a card from Helen saying, 'I hear you got into university', and she included some rude joke about 'obviously they're lowering standards', and I got in touch and said 'Yes' and 'I thought we might meet up some time'.

'So that turned into a holiday romance really, more based on humour, shared humour.'

Then the most curious element of the whole story was that in my first term at Brasenose College in Oxford I got talking to another student named Robert Hewison, again we had again a similar interest in jokes, but he was from London, very metropolitan, rather more suave and sophisticated than me. He said that his girlfriend was at this teacher's training institute in Roehampton called the Froebel Institute, that she was coming up to visit and that she knew someone who knew me. And that someone was Helen Gibbins, whom I'd met on those holidays. So it was just impossible to evade fate. Helen came up with Heather and from that moment on we saw each other fairly regularly. I was nineteen. So between sixteen and nineteen it blossomed and by nineteen it was meant to be.

As I've said, my father was a man of regular habits, and I think he would ideally have liked me to replicate his career, which is what you did then. He wanted me to go to Clare College, Cambridge, if the storybook of life worked out. I took an exam and they said no, they couldn't take me, because English was very over-subscribed that year and if I had chosen to read forestry or something like that, I probably would have got in. Too late by then to go back and say, 'Oh yes, I want to be a lumberjack.'

I had a very inspirational history teacher at Shrewsbury called Michael Hart and he said, 'Don't worry if you can't get into Clare, try for Oxford. They've got some exams on 12 December, that's a couple of months time, I'll just write off, get the papers and you can go and sit those.' He said, 'You'll sit for a scholarship and then if you don't get it, it's a good sign that you've tried the scholarship and they'll probably give you an entrance place anyway.' I think he knew full well that I wasn't going to get a scholarship.

So I went off and duly did exams at Trinity College, Oxford, and failed those. I didn't even get a commoner's place. So he said, 'Oh, try somewhere else', and I went to Oxford, and had some very wonderfully embarrassing interviews there. At some of them I was going to do history and at others I was going to do English. Worcester College was one of my English attempts and the master interviewing me said, 'Who are your favourite authors?' So I rolled out all these people, including Graham Greene who I'd done a lot of mugging up on and really knew absolutely backwards, and he said, 'No, Graham Greene doesn't come into the English course because the course ends in 1900.' No one had told me that. So I stumbled out some other names, and he said, 'Anything else you like?' And I said, 'I love poetry, I'm very fond of poetry.' So he said, 'Right, name me six poets.' I think he must have sussed out that I was obviously a fraud. My mind was suddenly a complete blank, but I did come up with Wordsworth. So then he relentlessly pressed on, 'Name me six poems of Wordsworth.' Eventually I got 'Michael' for obvious reasons. 'Michael, yes, that's one!' Then 'Daffodils' and that was it. I just wished the whole sofa could open up and I'd slide beneath the smoky old beams into the refectory below.

Then I tried for Magdalen College and I can remember some wonderful gaffes on one of the papers. They had a question about Le Corbusier: 'A house is a machine for living in – Le Corbusier. Discuss.' I didn't know who Le Corbusier was. I assumed he was French. I began it by saying, 'Well, of course, it was all very well for Le Corbusier in the days when he lived …', and I wrote this whole thing about the days before the Black Death. They must have had fun reading it and laughing at me. My earliest comedy scripts must have been my exam papers.

Finally Michael Hart looked down the list and said, 'I can see one coming up in April, Brasenose College, I know a jolly good chap there, I'll ring up.' And I got in.

John Cleese

' I was never in the slightest bit

interested in doing the big school play,

which was in the summer term,

because that was the cricket season.

Anyway, when I did the house plays

there was never any sense of doing it

for anything other than fun. **I liked the experience
of being part of a team.'**

My family name was originally Cheese. Dad was Reginald Francis Cheese, his father was John Edwin Cheese, and when my dad went into the army in 1915 he changed the 'H' to an 'L' to avoid being teased. When he came out of the army he changed it legally by what is known as deed poll. I had an aunt who had not changed her name. She remained Dorothy Cheese and lived near us, and I was very fond of her.

Years later I was at the Edinburgh Festival and there was a man in a kilt – what else! – sitting at a table halfway up the hotel staircase and I went up to him and said, 'May I ask what you're doing?' because he looked so incongruous, even in Edinburgh. He said he traced people's family names, so I got him to trace Cheese and he traced it to Norwich in 1273.

I do have mild regrets about the name change. I think it would have been much better to have been Cheese. Before I became well known, people could never make out what my surname was and I always had to spell it. My wife Alyce Faye has always called me Jack, and I liked the idea of being called Jack Cheese.

My mother was called Muriel and she was born in Weston-super-Mare in 1899. She married my dad in 1923. They were married for thirteen and a half years before I was born on 27 October 1939. My mother never earned a living; she was a housewife, as most women were in those days. She played the piano, a bit, but there were no other artistic interests in our family.

Dad was born in 1893 so he was six years older than my mum and he lived in Bristol. He left school at sixteen. He was good at mental arithmetic and went into insurance and did a few clerk-ish kinds of jobs, until he went off in 1915 to fight in the First World War. He was injured but re-enlisted when he recovered.

After 1918 he got to know some posh people who encouraged him to go off to India. He started to work in marine underwriting in Bombay and moved on to several other places in the Far East. Then after a few years he came back to England and not long afterwards started to court my mother. All his life he worked in insurance and in the '50s – I used to go with him in the summer holidays – he would be driving around Somerset, South Gloucestershire, North Devon, selling different types of insurance. And people thought he was a decent, honourable sort of fellow and were happy to recommend him to each other. So he always did well. He worked for the Guardian Assurance Co. all the way through until the mid-'50s. He was pissed off with them by the mid-'50s and only about two years away from retirement. So he said, 'I'm out of here,' and he left.

He and mother always moved home a lot and it wasn't connected to his job. They simply kept moving and it became a family joke. They were in Weston-super-Mare when I was born. They moved eight more times before they moved back in 1948 so that I could go to St Peter's Preparatory School, and they then moved to Bristol so I could go to Clifton and not have to board there, which they couldn't afford. Then eventually they moved back to Weston because it was my mother's home and my father had spent so much time there. When he used to live in Bristol as a young man, he'd come down to Weston with his friends because it was the nearest seaside resort.

After I'd gone to Clifton for five years, I came back to Weston and taught at the same prep school I'd attended as a boy. Weston was very decent, unimaginative, kind, friendly, unthreatening and completely unartistic – with the single exception that my mother's best friend was married to a violinist who had played professionally at one stage. When I knew him, he managed a shoe store, but he'd once been musical director of a touring company.

My parents had me very late in their marriage, and I was overprotected by them as a result. I never had a bike as a child! When I was teaching I noticed a pattern that parents who were older tended to produce children who were physically more careful, didn't throw themselves into the hurly-burly and often watched what was going on much more thoughtfully. But I enjoyed sports, provided it was never anything too physical. I hated rugby, which seemed to be a nasty, rough game; I couldn't see the point of it. What I always intensely admired was physical skill, always have and always did. So I loved the skilful footballers, the Len Shackletons, and I hated the ones who clobbered the skilful ones. I felt fiercely that I wanted the skilful ones to thrive. And cricket was just terrific. It was soccer and cricket that I loved by far the most. I really enjoyed playing them, but my extreme height and thinness meant I struggled to take part in anything that required strength.

When I first turned up at prep school, the first term, it all felt very strange and unfamiliar. Suddenly you were in a big, big school with dozens of boys, all of whom were looking at you because you were one of the new kids and you didn't know how anything worked or how you were supposed to behave. Also, being an only child didn't help. But I think I adapted OK, if a bit slowly.

It probably took me two years and by then my social skills were quite average and I had some good friends. But I was 6 foot tall by the time I was twelve, which felt awkward at times, and that feeling went on for years and years. I still notice sometimes when I walk into a room, I have a desire not to be noticed – ironic that I should go into television.

I have very specific memories of making the classroom laugh soon after I'd got to prep school, and gaining popularity and acceptance by being funny. I learnt that when you make people laugh it's a nice feeling. People only laugh if they basically like you and accept you. I think that was my way of becoming more popular, given that, as an only child of older parents, my social skills were poor to begin with.

I was very happy at school overall. Two or three of my very closest friendships at Clifton were very much about laughing together. In a funny kind of way, I was closer to one or two of those guys at Clifton in my mid-teens than I was to the people at Cambridge later on. You're probably less self-conscious with friends when you're fifteen, and more self-conscious when you're twenty-one or twenty-two.

I think I've always had an orderly mind in the sense that logical thought comes very easily to me, although I'm not good at mechanical things. I've also always had a lot of trouble with poetry in the sense that I don't know what it's about; I don't know what they're trying to say. I didn't come from an educated family. It was not an illiterate family; it was literate, but not educated. By that I mean they spoke and wrote very correct English, but they wouldn't have had any idea who Henry VIII was, they would know he had six wives and that was it. If you had asked them which century he ruled in, they wouldn't have known. So when I went to St Peter's, at the age of eight, I had no academic framework in my head. But I discovered that each fortnight, you were ranked in your class first to fifteenth or so. And I noticed that there were

said, 'Yes, sir, three bags full, sir.' Consequently, I appeared at the end of that period holding a piece of paper with three science A Levels on it. But there had never been a choice, there had never been a moment when I thought I wanted to do that, I simply went along with the suggestions.

When I decided to apply for Cambridge, dad had no notion I might go there. It was a complete surprise when I mentioned it to him. He assumed that I would go to Clifton until I was sixteen and then go into accounting. No one in my family had ever been to university. But dad was really kind, he let me stay on for A Levels, and I got accepted to study science. But because of the recent abolition of National Service, Cambridge couldn't take me for two years. This news somehow got back to Geoffrey Tolson, who ran St Peter's, my old prep school, and Geoffrey said, 'Well if you have a gap, why don't you come and teach?'

So I left Clifton in the summer of '58 and by the middle of September I was back at St Peter's in Weston-super-Mare, this time teaching boys of eight to thirteen. When I look back on it, it was remarkably unadventurous. Although my father had been quite a traveller, that option didn't occur to me. And I had an enormous affection for St Peter's. I also must have thought I could teach quite

more points given for maths and Latin than there were for French and English, so, not having any particular sense of these things, I realised that maths and Latin must be important if they were given the most points. Luckily I found them relatively easy, whereas French seemed to me tremendously difficult, because it wasn't pronounced anything like how it was spelt, which I found bewildering. So because I was reasonably good at maths and Latin, I did OK, although I was bad or pretty bad at everything else. My essays were never ever picked out as having any talent at all, I hated history and I hated the Old Testament, but my maths and Latin got me through. I was put into the Clifton scholarship exam by the Latin teacher and in fact was awarded a minor scholarship on my maths, so when I got to Clifton, they said, 'If you're good at maths, you'll be doing physics and chemistry as your optional subjects, won't you?' And I said, 'Yes, sir, three bags full, sir.' So when I emerged two years later with my O Levels, including physics and chemistry, they said, 'Well you'll be doing science A Levels won't you?' and I

well. Also I guess that at an unconscious level, I knew it would keep me in all the circumstances that were familiar to me. In retrospect, I should have gone somewhere and learned a language, particularly in the second year. But in the first year the teaching was quite interesting, and I was having to learn so I could keep one page ahead of the kids, because I was teaching subjects I knew nothing about, like history, geography and English. To be perfectly honest, it was a time when I educated myself a little. And I enjoyed all the other teachers, who were bright and rather learned and very kind. So I finished teaching in summer 1960, knowing what a semi-colon was, and the difference between a phrase and a clause, which I didn't have a clue about when I'd finished at Clifton at the age of eighteen; liking history, which I'd hated before; and knowing where countries were, and how big their populations were. Useful stuff, which almost repaired my Clifton education.

My parents had the same interest in entertainment that two people in the lower middle class would have had – they watched a lot of television, things like *What's My Line?* And we would watch certain comedy shows. Tony Hancock was the high point of the week. We also watched a lot of Americans shows like Jack Benny, Amos and Andy, Phil Silvers, George Burns and Gracie Allen.

More significant, though, by my teens I was obsessed with the Goons in the same way that people were later obsessed by Python – so I understood their behaviour! And I remember writing down jokes people told me, God knows for what reason, in various notebooks. Subsequently, I did do a few house entertainments, though I never went to those books for inspiration. I just wrote these jokes down. I couldn't have begun to define what made me laugh or why it did, but I knew I didn't want to forget it. When I listened to *The Goon Show*, there would be so much laughter in the studio, you missed jokes, and then there was a repeat two or three days later and I would lie on the bed with a cushion over one ear, and the other glued to the radio, to try and get the three jokes I had missed. Why? It was as though there was a small, but very intense, part of me that was tremendously interested. But if anyone had said to me at that time, 'Are you thinking of going into show business?' I would not have known what they were talking about. My fantasy was to play soccer for Bristol City or cricket for Somerset. The whole idea of show business was not an option – like wanting to be an astronaut. I always felt later with Python that there were some people who got it very early on, just as something in me responded to the Goons. I was very pleased to find Clifton friends who liked it as well. But it appealed to something very deep in me and I still feel great affection for everything to do with the Goons.

I somehow began acting at St Peter's. When I was twelve, I played Malvolio. Quite a big part, and I can still remember chunks of it because I had no idea what any of it meant. Anytime you've got to remember something that is more or less meaningless, the memory trace is much stronger. So the Reverend Dolman asked me to do Malvolio and I have no recollection why I said yes. I remember not having any idea of what I was doing. No idea at all. Consequently nobody thought I had any real talent, quite correctly. When I got to Clifton, I got involved in the house plays, which I thoroughly enjoyed. They were done in the spring term. I was never in the slightest bit interested in doing the big school play, which was in the summer term, because that was the cricket season. Anyway, when I did the house plays there was never any sense of doing it for anything other than fun. I liked the experience of being part of a team.

I didn't feel I was acting in any meaningful sense of the word. The different houses at Clifton often did plays that had been quite successful in the West End in the near past, and the first thing I did at Clifton was a comedy called *Seagulls over Sorrento*. I played the part of a character called Lofty and, again, it was full of lines that I didn't know the meaning of, but I learned them and said them. I don't think anybody had the slightest idea what they were doing really. But it was OK. The next year, I was seventeen, I was in a play by Tartuffe, and that one I understood a tiny bit more. In my final year, for some extraordinary reason, we did Marlowe's *Faust* – a very shortened version – and I played Lucifer, appallingly I think; there was a young fellow called Philip Mair playing Faust, and everyone agreed that he was a good and very promising actor. I certainly wasn't, though. Again I think we were all pretty terrible because nobody ever talked to us about how we were performing, nobody ever explained what you were supposed to be doing when you're acting.

It's like so much of life, nobody actually stops to explain what the purpose of it is. If you ask people about their job and say, 'What do you do?', they start saying, 'Well I get there at 8.15 and I make the coffee …' If you actually say to them, 'What's the purpose of your job?' they actually can't tell you. They've learned a certain number of actions, but they don't actually know what's underlying it all. Probably the reasons I've been successful at my kind of acting is that I'm almost entirely self-taught. Everyone in America assumes that the Pythons were all at drama school or studying theatre at university, whereas not a single one of us has ever had a lesson.

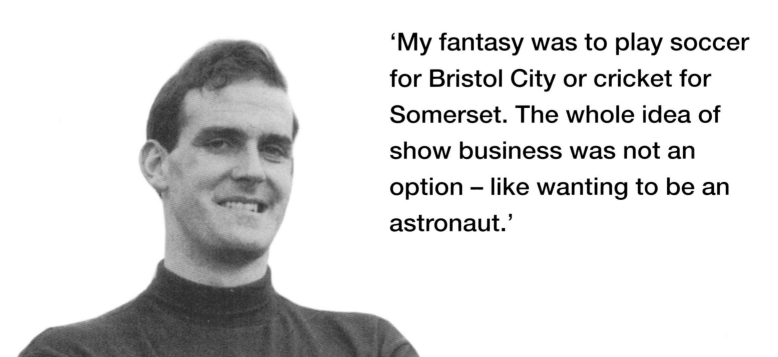

'My fantasy was to play soccer for Bristol City or cricket for Somerset. The whole idea of show business was not an option – like wanting to be an astronaut.'

Terry Jones

'Another school essay I wrote when I was seven

mapped out my future in no uncertain terms.

I wrote: "I am *hopping* to be an actor."

Well, I'm still *hopping*. But whatever I wrote

in my essay, I knew really that I wanted to write.

I'd never had any particular interest in comedy.

Humour was just something that came

with everything as far as my brother

and I were concerned. **Why should you ban laughter**

from any aspect of life?'

Terry Jones and brother Nigel at home in Claygate

I was born right bang slap in the middle of World War Two, in Colwyn Bay, North Wales, on 1 February 1942. My dad, Alick, was Welsh although he was born in Streatham. He was living in Ruthin and working as a bank clerk in Denbigh. I'm not sure how he met my mum – it was the kind of thing that wasn't really talked about in those days – but she was living with her parents in Colwyn Bay. Her parents were teachers, and in their spare time they indulged in amateur dramatics and opera. In fact they ran the Colwyn Bay Amateur Operatic Society or at least I got the impression they ran it. They certainly used to put on a Gilbert & Sullivan operetta twice a year at the end of the pier. My gran (whom I always called 'La-La' because that's how she used to sing to me when I was little) taught music I think, and my grandfather was – for some unaccountable reason – a conductor in the Australian Navy. It's one of those 'facts' you grow up with but can't really believe the older you get. Nevertheless there were these pictures of him on the deck of some ship standing in full dress uniform in front of an orchestra. So maybe it was true. And of course, there was the 'ceremonial sword'. That was the clincher. It was an elaborate dress sword for special occasions, with W.G. Newnes engraved on it. Occasionally we were allowed to slip it out of its sheath and gaze at the elaborately engraved blade with the groove down one side 'for the blood to run out', as we were told …

When I was born my dad was in the RAF and stationed up in Scotland. I suppose they must have been guarding the grouse,

I remember meeting my dad for the first time: going up to the railway station at Colwyn Bay and walking up the steps and over the bridge. In those days they had enamel plates on every step with the names of exotic destinations like Rhyl, Bangor and Llandudno Junction. In those days of steam, trains and stations had a very particular smell and atmosphere, a smell of coal and soot and long mysterious journeys to far-off destinations like Chester and Wolverhampton.

Well, we stand on that platform and a train pulls in with clouds of smoke and steam and people pour off it. And my mum's getting beside herself with nerves and anxiety and why not? She hasn't seen

although he used to say later that they were testing out this new-fangled stuff called RADAR. He came and saw me when I was a week old, and was immediately posted to India. I would be four before he saw me again.

My memories of those first years in Colwyn Bay are still vivid in my mind, sometimes more vivid than what happened yesterday: riding in the charabanc, changing on the beach, Eirais Park and Fairy Glen, a tank rumbling up our dusty road between the high hedgerows, my mum drawing back the curtains before we went to bed to magically reveal amazing shafts of light striding through the night like vast fingers – I think they must have been searchlights celebrating VE Day.

I have a clear memory of my brother and I getting up very early one day to go into the field opposite to collect mushrooms. I guess we must have been all of a combined age of six years – me two and him four. I was pretty scared. We got across the road (in those days roads didn't have traffic on them) and ventured into the field carrying our basket … How scary can things get eh? I was quaking in my little white socks. Then my brother – who always had an eye for the dramatic – pointed to the brook at the far end of the field and told me about the bear that lived there. That was it. I was out of that field, back across the road and safe back in La-La's kitchen before he had a chance to roar.

this man for four and a half years! I've seen photos of my dad – one of him with a mate, sticking their heads out of some large drainage pipes, another with a golf club and his shirt-tails out, teeing off a candle in a candle-stick. I knew from those photos that my dad had a sense of humour.

Eventually all these people flood off the platform and now my mum's getting anxious because he might not be on the train … but suddenly there's a figure at the far end of the platform in RAF uniform with a forage cap on his head and a kit bag slung over his shoulder. That's him! We run up and it's all hugs and kisses … but I'm not so sure, and when I'm finally picked up and kissed by this strange man I'm definitely off the whole idea! Wait a minute! He's got a 'strange and prickly moustache' (as I describe it in one of my later seven-year-old essays). This isn't in the bargain. I'm used to being kissed by women. Moustaches aren't my cup of tea at all.

I guess life changed when my dad arrived home. A certain amount of tension entered the family life and I started to hear stern words for the first time in my life. I realise now that it must have been terrible for him; he'd been shipped off to India and missed his family growing up at the most important stage. He'd left behind a two-year-old and a one-week-old baby and arrived back to find a four and a half-year-old and a six-year-old. And his youngest son

Terry Jones at play with friends and neighbours, Malcolm and Brian Coles

Old Colwyn was the only one I'd known, and now where was I? Where had the seaside gone? The Pier? The Prom? Where was Fairy Glen? Where was the Donkey Path or the Golf Links? The only bright spot in this new place seemed to be a brass coal scuttle that had eighteenth-century coaching scenes stamped on the lid.

I spent the next twenty years insisting that I was Welsh and that I didn't fit in where I now found myself. I never felt I belonged there. The whole period of living in Claygate, from five to nineteen, was like an interruption to real life. Maybe I shut myself away in my own world – back in Wales or up in my room writing poems or back in some happier time without a grumpy father and strict new rules about not putting your elbows on the table. Wales still feels

'I spent the next twenty years insisting that I was Welsh and that I didn't fit in where I now found myself. I never felt I belonged there. The whole period of living in Claygate, from five to nineteen, was like an interruption to real life.'

doesn't really want much to do with this stranger – doesn't like him kissing him even! Must have been hard.

And I suppose the truth is that subconsciously I regarded him as a bit of an intruder … or an outsider. I suppose I also knew – deep down – that he couldn't reach me at all, except that I felt sorry for him. I had bonded with my mum so strongly that no relationship could ever be as real as that for me. Poor dad. I learned later in life that he was a caring, gentle, humorous man, just like he appeared in those photos, but something was wrong when he came home. Maybe he and mum couldn't re-find whatever it was they had in the first place. Maybe mum resented his return. I don't really know. But whatever it was, it turned him into a small home tyrant, who could only communicate with us boys by telling us off or yelling at us.

A few months after my dad turned up on the scene there was another major disruption in my life: we moved from North Wales down to the Home Counties to a place called Clay-gate – right in the heart of stockbroker Surrey, on the very fringe of the London suburbs. It was for me a small disaster. The home in

like home but a home that is somehow far away and untouchable and still partly a memory.

Dad worked in 'The Bank'. As a kid I didn't really know what 'The Bank' was except that my dad didn't seem to enjoy it very much and really wished he was working in anything else. He was better with his hands than his brain and wasn't even that interested in money. He'd wanted to become a joiner or carpenter, but when he'd left school in the late '20s/early '30s that wasn't the sort of career that was considered respectable. The bank was a bit like going into the Church: you stood the chance of becoming middle class or even – dare one say it – upper middle class. But he hated it. He wasn't management material and he knew it.

I can remember he once went up for an interview at head office – he was particularly nervous and probably told us off more than usual – and then it didn't really work out. No promotion. The odd thing is that now my memories of my dad are of him smiling and joking, the same as I remember my mum as this always available source of love and reassurance.

Life was a continual struggle for my parents. Working in the bank may have been extremely 'respectable' but you had to live on almost starvation wages. There was a whole raft of experiences that we never had – like holidays. Apart from going back to Colwyn Bay in the early years to stay with La-La when she was alive, the nearest we ever got to a holiday was a day's coach trip to Worthing. I remember writing a school essay when I was seven about Christmas and saying that I was going to give my dad some new underwear because 'his was all in tatters' – an expression I must have got off my poor mum, who probably never lived down the public humiliations of her son's shock-horror revelations in his school work.

Another school essay I wrote when I was seven mapped out my future in no uncertain terms. I wrote: 'I am *hopping* to be an actor.' Well, I'm still *hopping*. But whatever I wrote in my essay, I knew really that I wanted to write. I'd never had any particular interest in comedy. Humour was just something that came with everything as far as my brother and I were concerned. Why should you ban laughter from any aspect of life?

I can actually remember my first joke. We were in Colwyn Bay so I guess it must have happened before I was four. We were sitting round the table in 'Bodhwyl' (as our house was called – 'House-in-A-Whirl' my mother used to say). I guess we were having what was known as 'High Tea'. We'd just had our pudding and La-La asked if anyone wanted seconds of custard. Suddenly my three- or four-year-old mind saw the opportunity for a bit of humour. So I raised my hand but instead of passing up my plate, I passed up my table mat. I watched with bated breath in delighted disbelief as the joke went like clockwork. I'd expected someone who passed the mat on to notice what they were passing but no one did. Then La-La

plunged the ladle into the custard and – bliss! – ladled out a good dollop of custard onto the mat. Well! I sat back and waited for the laughter and applause. A career in showbiz suddenly opened up ahead of me. I saw my name in lights on the London Palladium … Well, I would have done if I'd ever heard of the London Palladium. But then it all seemed to go wrong. Instead of the laughter and the applause, all I heard was a chorus of abuse: 'You stupid boy! What did you do that for? Look what you've done!' Nobody turned on my gran and said, 'Why don't you look where you're pouring the custard!' or on the person in between who'd passed the mat along.

It was at that moment that I realised comedy is a dangerous business. If people find something funny you're OK. But the moment you do something that's meant to be funny and someone doesn't find it funny, they become angry. It's almost as if they resent the fact that you tried to make them laugh and failed. Nobody comes out of a mediocre performance of *Hamlet* seething with rage because it didn't make them cry. But just listen to people coming out of a comedy that didn't make them laugh.

My first school was Esher Church of England Primary School. The headmistress was – to my slight concern – a 'Miss Terry', but I quickly realised there was nothing significant about this. The walls of the school were hung with fading pictures of Jesus in the carpenter's shop, Jesus walking amongst the flowers, other pictures of lambs and springtime and a small child with a shepherd's crook praying. We were packed into the schoolrooms forty to a class.

I suppose I was around five and my brother must have been seven and a half. But in those days even a five-year-old and a seven-year-old could be reasonably independent. We'd walk quarter of a mile down the road to the bus stop at the Swan (a pub), catch the bus to

Esher a mile away, get off at the Windsor Arms (another pub) and then walk round the corner to the school. We were let out of school at 3 o'clock and either caught the bus back outside the Bear (why were bus-stops always pubs in those days?) or else walked home the mile and a half along Esher Park Avenue, an unmettled road with vast houses set back amidst acres of lawns and shrubbery. I don't suppose there are many five-year-olds today who have that sort of freedom.

In those days I suppose I had a secret life. It was somewhere inside my head. My gran had got me reading poetry – 'The Brook' – by the mysteriously named Alfred Lord Tennyson. And I was pretty much into writing poetry. I knew that's what I was going to be. A poet. Simple. I had a role in life already. That made everything much easier.

Actually I suppose I didn't mind what I made so long as I was able to make something. It could have been poetry or it could have been writing novels if I'd known about such things – or making chairs. If anyone asked me what I was going to do when I grew up, I'd reply, 'Something creative'. Little clever-dick.

The radio played an important role in family life in those days. Crowding round the speaker to listen to *Children's Hour* – Larry the Lamb, Uncle Mac and Monty and Peckham. The main listening, apart from *In Town Tonight* and the Palm Court Orchestra, would be Sunday lunchtime when we'd eat lunch to the accompaniment of *The Billy Cotton Band Show*, followed by *ITMA* in the early days, then *Up the Pole* with Jimmy Jewel and Ben Warris, *Beyond Our Ken*, *Raise a Laugh*, *Take it from Here* with Jimmy Edwards, *Hancock's Half-Hour* and of course *The Goon Show*. It was a good time of the week – feeling the whole family together, spying out of the window to see if Mr Elias was coming back from the Swan with a couple of bottles of brown ale in a bag so we could all tut-tut about the dissolute ways of our neighbours. For a moment you could feel really Welsh. The Goons of course were my favourite. It was the surreality of the imagery and the speed of the comedy that I loved – the way they broke up the conventions of radio and played with the very nature of the medium.

My elder brother, Nigel, was my guru in all things cultural. He formed my tastes. Told me what I could listen to and what I should avoid. Taught me about the wonders of Traditional Jazz and the evil snares of modern Big Band music, which lacked any sort of improvisation. Popular songs he scorned with a deep and sincere

disrespect. I didn't dare let him catch me humming 'Pyramids Along The Nile' or 'How Much Is That Doggy In The Window'. The only time he cracked was when he took a liking to Kay Starr, and then suddenly I was allowed a certain limited repertoire of pop music. Otherwise I was to stick to Bessie Smith, Ottilie Patterson and Muddy Waters.

One day he announced, to my consternation, that I was going to have to listen to a radio drama that was going on that very night and would last for an hour and a half. I was slightly won over by the fact that it was written by a Welshman and it was about life in Wales. And so that evening we sat in the dining room – well I crawled under the dining-room table – to listen to the first performance of Dylan Thomas's *Under Milk Wood*, narrated by Richard Burton. I don't think I realised at the time what a tremendous influence Dylan Thomas was going to have on me and on my whole attitude to poetry. I think I gave up in the end because how could I ever write stuff as magical as he had.

Television was, for a long time, something that happened down the road at my friend John Campion's house. His parents, who were more affluent than mine, were the proud owners of a 7-inch Pye. We used to rush home from school to catch the 4 o'clock cowboy film: *Hopalong Cassidy* or *Riders of the Range*. On Saturday mornings we would sit and watch the test card for ages, waiting for something to happen, because in those days there was very little in the way of daytime television. Even evening programmes didn't start till 9 pm or perhaps 8 pm. Sometime in the morning, however, they would put out the BBC test film. Apparently this was designed so that television salesmen could demonstrate television to potential customers. Perhaps it was to fool them into thinking there were actual programmes on at all times of the day. The demonstration film was an hour long and it was always the same. It had a snatch of drama, a bit of news and – for some strange reason – a haunting bit of Victorian footage of some poor man attempting to fly from the Eiffel Tower and actually falling to his death. This was the bit we ghouls all waited for with horror and fascination. The moment where he hesitates … he's not going to jump … but then someone pushes him forward and must say something like: 'You can't let us all down! Look at the crowds!' And so he jumps … into oblivion and history at the same time.

But television was never really my thing. In those days the image was only 425 lines and a rather murky purple colour. I couldn't really see the attraction. By the time my family could afford a set, they'd sit downstairs watching it and I would be up in my bedroom making up poetry. There were things that occasionally tempted me downstairs like Michael Bentine's *It's a Square World* but generally I preferred generating my own amusement.

I seemed to take the 11-plus exam in my stride, although I thought I'd really failed because I didn't get into my first choice: King's College, Wimbledon. That was a public school and they'd been hoping I'd win a scholarship there but I didn't. So I found myself going to the Royal Grammar School, Guildford.

Jones starts his performing career –
the common room, Guildford Royal Grammar School

My brother, who was highly intelligent, did not have an exam-friendly constitution. He got so worked up about exams that he'd failed both the 11-plus and the 12-plus. But at the same time I got into Guildford, he managed to get the 13-plus and assumed he was all set to come to the Royal Grammar School with me. Then to our dismay we learnt that the grammar school wasn't taking him but

that they'd given him a place in the grammar stream of the secondary modern next door, Pewley School. It was a cruel bit of bureaucracy. My dad did his best to complain and to point out to the exam authorities what a terrible effect this would have on my brother's attitude to school and on his self-respect and everything, with his little brother swanning off to the grammar school while he caught the same train to the second best. But the authorities were deaf to reason and my dad was not really good at that sort of confrontation. I don't think my brother ever forgave the system for the daily humiliation it must have forced upon him.

Looking back at school I must have been absolutely stupid. I

'But television was never really my thing. In those days the image was only 425 lines and a rather murky purple colour. I couldn't really see the attraction. By the time my family could afford a set, they'd sit downstairs watching it and I would be up in my bedroom making up poetry.'

ROYAL GRAMMAR SCHOOL
GUILDFORD

Full Name   *Terence Graham Parry Jones*

Address   *28, Ryde Rd., Claygate, Esher, Surrey*

	Day	Month	Year
Date of Birth	1st	February	1942
Date of Admission	11th	September	1953
Date of Leaving	28th	July	1961

Age on leaving *19 yrs 6 months*

OFFICES HELD IN SCHOOL   *School Prefect 1959–61*
School Captain 1960–61
House Captain 1959–61

RECORD OF GAMES AND OTHER OUT-OF-SCHOOL ACTIVITIES

PHYSICAL REPORT

RECORD IN PUBLIC EXAMINATIONS
G.C.E. "O" Level 1958   Eng. Lang. 71%   Eng. Lit. 57%   History 74%   French 60%   Spanish 61%   Latin 66%   Maths 57%   Art 57%
G.C.E. "A" Level 1960   English Lit. grade 2   History grade 3

SPECIAL APTITUDES

Jones and early girlfriend Rosemary Surrey

stayed on and was made head boy and I was always a bit surprised when people kept on leaving school and thinking, 'Oh, so and so's just left school.' But it never occurred to me that I could have left school after I got into university. By the end I was beginning to feel a bit isolated because everybody else had left by the last term, but I was still there and head boy, always having to run various things. As head boy you had to run assembly, for example, you organised it all and made sure everybody was there.

I really wanted to write, but in those days that wasn't at all the sort of thing a grammar school could encourage. Primary school had been quite different, and they'd really taken an interest in my poetry, but the grammar school took the attitude that you can't ever make a living out of writing so stop thinking about it. The best you can hope for is to become a teacher. There was one master, Mr Martin, who encouraged me; he used to read my essays out to the class, and that really helped me get through – feeling somebody appreciated the kind of things I wrote. But otherwise I had a feeling that grammar school was like being fitted out with a straightjacket. It certainly fitted and was very practical but you couldn't expect to do anything in it.

All my early plans to grow up and 'do something creative' seemed to be being thrown out of the window as I progressed through grammar school. It seemed as if the possibilities were closing down rather than opening up. I certainly shouldn't ever imagine I could make a living out of writing or anything like that. The most I could hope for was to become a teacher, like them, or – as an outside chance – a university lecturer. It was a strange feeling, putting your head down to slog away working hard to attain something you didn't really want to do.

I also wanted to act, but there again the Royal Grammar School, Guildford, was not exactly the place to foster the dreams of a young thespian. The nearest we got to drama lessons was in divinity classes, when the headmaster would advise us that all actors were homosexuals and you could tell because they wore green suede shoes. He also warned us that the BBC was run by Communists and that Tom Driberg was a 'bugger'. We had no idea who Tom Driberg was and even less idea of what the implication of being a 'bugger' was – except for the fact that the headmaster used to shudder as he said it – so we knew it was pretty bad. Innocent days. I learned later that Tom Driberg was a life-long and strident critic of Moral Rearmament. He was also homosexual, so the headmaster may not have been entirely mistaken.

The headmaster was a constant embarrassment to us schoolboys. You just never knew what he was going to say in our divinity classes. He occasionally would inform us that he and his wife had not had sex for four years and that they were really happy. Of course we always used to whisper, 'Have you seen his wife!' Actually she was a very nice lady. In any case we scarcely knew what 'having sex' entailed, so there wasn't much point in his warning us off it.

But somehow, and we were never quite sure how, the evils of sex put the idea of acting or performing on the stage right outside the remit of the school. The nearest we could get to the experience of theatre was once a year at the Christmas Party, when the prefects would put on a little show. I can remember in my last year getting together 'the Chicken Chorus' — we all assembled on stage and I conducted the choir who all made chicken noises. It was a bit surreal but unfortunately didn't really have an end. My friends Simon Oxley and Richard Rampton joined me for 'The Delegate Noir Geological Sextet', in which we shared one dinner jacket suit between the three of us, sang 'Wiggle Your Knees' and ended up using the instruments as rackets in a game of badminton. Clive Nightingale also joined us for some serious blues and Leadbelly songs.

However, I did finally do some acting shortly after I left school. Another of my school chums, Chris Robinson, was involved in his local amateur dramatic association in East Horsley and he asked me to do this piece *Time Remembered* by Jean Anouilh. So I did the play with a lovely lady called Ruth. I had no idea what it was about really.

I guess by this time I was just going through the hoops – doing what was expected of me as well as I could. I applied to Oxford and Cambridge and by a stroke of bad luck was eventually offered places at both universities. I'd done so badly at A Level (owing to misreading the exam paper) that not a single provincial university would even look at me. Nowadays I wouldn't have got into university at all. But in those days Oxford and Cambridge had their own exams and systems and I got in under the net. I really wanted to go and study modern poetry at Cambridge, but St Edmund Hall, Oxford, offered me a place and I accepted. A week later Gonville and Caius, Cambridge, who had put me on a waiting list, offered me a place. The Royal Grammar School said I couldn't change because it might put them in bad odour with Oxford. I thought, well, what do I know? I *think* I want to go to Cambridge but who knows really? In the end I decided to stick with Oxford.

Lucky, really, looking back on it. If I'd gone to Cambridge I'd never have joined the Footlights (too organised for me) and so I'd never have done any revue or comedy. Also I wouldn't have met either Mike Palin or Geoffrey Chaucer – and without those two meetings the rest of my life would have been quite different.

'The nearest we got to drama lessons was in divinity classes, when the headmaster would advise us that all actors were homosexuals and you could tell because they wore green suede shoes.'

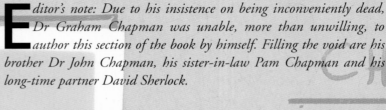

Editor's note: Due to his insistence on being inconveniently dead, Dr Graham Chapman was unable, more than unwilling, to author this section of the book by himself. Filling the void are his brother Dr John Chapman, his sister-in-law Pam Chapman and his long-time partner David Sherlock.

GRAHAM CHAPMAN: My parents, Tim and Beryl, sorry, Tim and Betty, were outraged when I arrived because they'd been expecting a heterosexual, black Jew with several rather amusing birth deformities as they needed the problems. They lived in an enormous Gothic castle in the South of France called Dundrinkingginand-slimlinetonicwithicebutnolemonin, which was originally built by Marco Polo for himself and a few friends he wanted to invite round to his place after the pub closed.[4]

JOHN CHAPMAN: We were living in Wigston Fields, south of Leicester, just outside the city boundary and my father was then a police constable in the Leicestershire constabulary. Graham was born on 8 January 1941. I was four years of age when he was born. I can't remember him as a little tiny baby; I begin to remember him really when he was about two and old enough to be a nuisance to me. Our mother's name was Edith and our father's name was Walter.

DAVID SHERLOCK: His father was a copper. Before he decided to become a policeman in the '30s, he had been trained as a French polisher for a coffin-makers and therefore he knew about wood. He was one of those self-sufficient men who was a good gardener and, when he retired, he was constantly bringing us presents of little things he'd made. I've still got a shoe-cleaning box and various little bird boxes he made us. He was a wonderful man, but dedication to the job in hand was absolutely paramount. Graham was very much like that.

Graham Chapman

'When the time came at school to think about the future – I was thinking of medicine merely because my brother was at medical school – I saw a piece of the Cambridge Footlights Revue televised, so I thought, **"I'd like to go to Cambridge!"'**

JOHN CHAPMAN: I'm not aware of my father turning down promotions but I'm aware of him being offered various job opportunities abroad which might have meant much more rapid promotion. The Bahamas was one place he was thinking of going to, but in the end he decided against it and would stay where he was. I don't think he ever turned down promotion, but he actually turned down the idea of going into the colonial service, as it were, which would certainly have meant much more rapid promotion.

DAVID SHERLOCK: 'Gray' always said he had an extremely poor upbringing. His parents had very much dragged themselves up by their bootstraps. His mother's father died in the First World War and her mother only had a small widow's pension and a large family of seven children, so everyone had to help out. Graham's mum and dad were very dedicated to duty, which is an extremely old-fashioned word but I think it is something which both Graham and his brother were very much aware of. Graham has memories of blacking the soles of his shoes as a child to go to primary school, having put a piece of cardboard in the sole, because there were holes and they couldn't afford to mend the shoes.

JOHN CHAPMAN: I think my parents were actually very generous and did without things themselves so that Graham and I could have things we wanted. But we weren't well off. My father used to make toys for us rather than buy them. That was partly because there weren't many toys in the shops in those days during and just after the Second World War. But I don't think we ever lacked for shoes. We may have worn them a bit longer than our growing feet would have required normally, but I don't think we were quite ever into that level of penury, as it were. My mother sacrificed for us, though. She never visited a hairdresser in her life, that sort of thing.

PAM CHAPMAN: She wanted the boys to have whatever they needed. She prided herself that she never visited a hairdresser.

JOHN CHAPMAN: And they sacrificed quite a lot to allow Graham and me to stay at various schools that we were at when they moved around, and they put us through university.

certify that the person
card is the person whose
affixed hereto.

.G.A. Brewster.

eadmaster

RESULTS OF G.C.E. 1957

NAME ...Chapman G............ Index No.....52.......

Ordinary Level – .. Pail Advanced Level. – Pail

45 – 99 Pass – Pass at Ordinary Level.

– Pass at Advanced Level.

Distinction: –

ENGLISH LANG.	57	ART		BIOLOGY	82
ENGLISH LIT.	65	MATHS.	61	GEN.SC.	
LATIN	67	ADD.MATHS.		COOKERY	
FRENCH	64	APP.MATHS		NEEDLEWK	
SPANISH		PURE MATHS		HUMAN BIO.	
HISTORY		CERT.PR.ARITH.		BOTANY	
GEOGRAPHY		PHYSICS	71	ZOOLOGY	
MUSIC.		CHEMISTRY.	80	DOM.SC.	

B.G.R.Brewler.

DAVID SHERLOCK: Graham's mother once dealt with a man with an axe who'd just attacked someone. She was the only one at the police station, everyone else was out, and she single-handedly talked to the man and got him to put the axe down. He'd come to own up. These were early formative things. Another thing was the police station had a dog pound and it broke Graham's heart that he was never allowed to have a dog because his father moved around such a lot.

JOHN CHAPMAN: Being in the Leicester County Constabulary, my parents lived in Wigston until 1947, moved to Braunston, another part of Leicester suburbs, on my father's promotion to sergeant, then back to Wigston on his promotion to inspector in 1951, to Melton Mowbray for a period of some years, where Graham went to school, and then to Syston. As an officer you had to live virtually on the job as it were. So we had to move home with each new place. You had to have a telephone there so that you could be called out and get to any problems in a fairly short time. I suppose, before I left home, we lived in five different houses. Then my father was eventually promoted to chief inspector and that's the rank at which he retired. That was while Graham was at Cambridge.

Graham and I led different lives because our age group was different. We were never at the same school at the same time. Our friends were different and I was always off playing football or cricket or something like that. When I was close to him, when I played with him, I usually got into trouble. I remember one famous occasion when we were playing with home-made bows and arrows and it was arranged that Graham would poke a hat on a stick round the corner of the house and I would shoot at it with a bow and arrow. The silly devil poked his head round to see if I was ready, and I was! I got a hell of a leathering for hitting him in the corner of the eye. I was quite frequently in trouble for not exactly looking after him, but dominating him and trying to bend him to my way of thinking.

He was certainly quite keen on the Goons and particularly on

R SCHOOL'S RODUCTION HE TOPS"

aditional end-of-term school play. ly written by the immortal bard — stumbled and finally lost the power r" — probably one of the finest pro- Melton Grammar School have ever

Another who showed a high standard of dramatic talent was Elizabeth Chamberlain, who played Portia, wife of Brutus. She showed commendable ability during the emotional scene where Portia begged her worried husband to tell her of his doubts and fears. Her sense of timing was perfect in a difficult role for one so young and inexperienced.

But the plaudits must go to the 44-strong cast as a whole. This was not just another 'school' play. They brought to life one of the most critical and exciting periods in the history of our world. For that alone they must be highly commended.

...arcus Brutus played his part as if he were, truly, the man who changed the course of the Roman Empire by thrusting a dagger into the breast of his idol and friend.

THE STAR

The brightest star, however, was Graham Chapman. As Mark Anthony, Caesar's greatest friend and chief lieutenant, Graham showed an aptitude for Shakespearean acting rarely witnessed behind the amateur footlights.

He combined fine diction with an impressive appearance and brought to life the great Mark Anthony in a performance which will long be remembered by Melton audiences.

He completely dominated the stage and enthralled the audience during the final scene as he made his famous oration over the corpse of Brutus...

Frankie Howerd, I remember. That would have been 1950/51. Frankie Howerd was later on. Before that, around the age of seven, he was into *Dick Barton Special Agent*, *Journey into Space* and things like that.

It was 1944 or 1945, I'm not sure which, but there was a Polish-manned RAF aeroplane, I think it was a Dakota, that crashed during the day in the grounds of Long Street Modern School in Wigston. I remember the acrid smell following this aeroplane crash, which had happened on my way back to school after lunch. This thing had come down and my father had been called out to it. They said there were originally eight Polish airmen on the plane when it crashed. But it had exploded and bits were found all over the place, in trees, a boot with a foot in it and that sort of thing, a bit of a torso on a parachute harness up in a tree somewhere. I remember that the back garden of our house was used as a reception area for bits of the bodies that had been brought in. They were all put into sacks at the side. And I remember there being a tremendous kerfuffle when it was learned that one of the people who was said to be on the plane had reported sick that morning and wasn't on the plane, so they suddenly had to reduce eight body bags to seven and they weren't quite sure who was who. But they were all laid out in the back garden of our house, which was the police house nearest to the site of the crash. They disappeared fairly rapidly those bags, that evening. That was obviously something which made some impression on Graham as well.

GRAHAM CHAPMAN: A street in Wigston Magna 1944. There has just been an explosion in an aircraft in which nine free Polish airmen had been flying. The force of the explosion has reduced them to their component parts and one can see clearly a lung hanging down from the lower branches of a chestnut tree, a leg on a front lawn, and a hole in the roof of a semi-d, which was later explained by a lady who came out of the house carrying a bucket with what looked like liver in it. The three-year-old boy is not particularly worried because he is holding his mummy's hand, and his daddy is in charge, and being very efficient about trying to sort out bits of

THE DESERTED HOUSE

A play in three acts by T. B. Morris

The play takes place in a room of a deserted house in France, during its occupation by German troops in May 1944. The French Resistance movement is trying to discover the whereabouts of a secret German factory, so that it may be bombed by the Allies.

CAST

Antoinette (Toni)	Ruth Pannell
Pierre	Mayes
Henri	Vurley
Marie	Pierre's sisters — Elizabeth Chamberlain
Jeanne	Rosemary Saunders
Kathy	Rowena Drewry
Delphine	Brenda Cross
Georges	Foster
Lt. Keller	Kite
Cpl. Tieck	Wood
Pte. Doppel	Brown
Capt. Weiner	Chapman

There will be an interval between each act. Coffee will be served in the dining hall during the second interval.

Set designed by Mr. Barnard: decor by Mr. Jackson: properties by Miss Unsworth, Gillian Brewster, Hilary Maskell: firearms by Mr. Partington: special effects by Luce and Stevens: prompter Valerie Maskell.

Production by Mr. Frank Bridges.

The Producer gratefully acknowledges the help of all those who have assisted him in producing this play.

PRINTED by the SCHOOL PRESS

Melton Mowbray Grammar School Middle School Dramatic Society

THE DESERTED HOUSE

Graham treads some early boards

human flesh into at least nine different sacks. Unfortunately there seem to be only eight heads and no other suspicious roof-holes.

Mummy calls out to daddy, 'Walter …'

'Sorry dear, I'm busy. Hey you, that sack's already got two legs in it.'

Reflecting on this I go 'Waaaaagggh' inwardly, and am just thinking of going 'Waaaaagggh' outwardly when my mother grabs my hand.

'Walter dear, we're just out shopping and I thought that Graham might like …'

'Look dear, I'll see you later. Has anyone found that head yet? Hey! Has anyone in the street found a head? Come on, someone must have it, I know this street, you'd whip anything … I mean, what the bloody hell are you going to do with a head?'

'Well dear, perhaps we'll go and get your tea.'

'What? Oh yes, eggs on toast please. Left arm here, anyone missing a left arm?'

'We haven't got any eggs. There's a war on.'

'Ask Harold. Something's bound to have fallen off the back of a lorry.'

'All right dear. Come on, Graham, stop staring at all that blood, it won't do you any good.'

'Oh come on, mum, this must be one of my major formative experiences. Waaaaaaggggghhhhhh….!'[4]

DAVID SHERLOCK: Graham followed in his brother's footsteps really, he wanted to be a doctor too. He was already showing signs of being darn good at chemistry; he also did Latin at Melton Mowbray Grammar. He was one of their brightest pupils ever, potentially a real high-flyer.

JOHN CHAPMAN: I think Graham probably followed me into medicine. I went into medicine really on the advice of my headmaster. There wasn't a lot of careers advice in those days and I had to decide

what I would want to do at the very tender age of fourteen because I was quite young to be taking O Levels. My headmaster asked me what I wanted to do and I was thinking of going into the navy, because we still had some battleships at that time and a few aircraft carriers and things, or going to do forestry or something like that. Farming I would have quite liked to do but there was no prospect of me ever being able to afford to buy a farm, so that was counted out. So it was my headmaster who suggested medicine and I thought, 'That sounds interesting, perhaps I'll try that,' so we decided at the age of fourteen what A Levels I would take to get university entrance and matriculation exemption, and I think Graham simply followed on after my decision because I was obviously enjoying my undergraduate medical career.

I had to give up quite a few O Levels to be able to go on and do A Levels at the same time, so I dropped Latin at O Level which meant that I couldn't get entry into Oxford or Cambridge, because that was a necessity for entrance at Cambridge. But when it was

time for Graham to go to university, I felt going to Cambridge would be an advantage to him, because I saw people coming down to London to do clinical medicine with me who had had a proper university education rather than a medical school education. And he had his Latin O Level. Graham, by that stage, had got entry into a London medical school, St Bart's, which was my school. But I had suggested to him that he try for Oxford or Cambridge, the only

good piece of advice I ever gave him! Everything else in his career followed on from that decision of his.

GRAHAM CHAPMAN: When the time came at school to think about the future – I was thinking of medicine merely because my brother was at medical school – I saw a piece of the Cambridge Footlights Revue televised, so I thought 'I'd like to go to Cambridge!' I hadn't realised that had entered my thinking – it had subconsciously – so I found out how to get to Cambridge … so that's where I went to do my medicine rather than straight to a London hospital.[5]

JOHN CHAPMAN: I honestly don't know whether he had any great knowledge of the Footlights before he went to Cambridge. I know he was involved at school in amateur dramatics and found it something very much to his liking and he was, I think, acknowledged as being a good actor for someone of his age. That was at Melton Mowbray Grammar School.

I went to a different school and boarded with relatives. Graham was then living at home and he had a lot of friends. He got particularly involved with amateur dramatics at the grammar school and was very much encouraged. That's when I first realised that he had any talent of any sort at all – for acting, but not for original thought and writing comedy and that sort of thing, not at that stage.

I suppose being small-town people in the lower middle class, as it were, our horizons were fairly limited in those days and we didn't realise what we might be capable of, and the ultimate seemed to be to have a profession and make a good honest living out of working hard.

PAM CHAPMAN: For parents it showed that they had done their very best for you in the eyes of the community, and in the eyes of their own family. Two very bright sons, both becoming doctors.

DAVID SHERLOCK: Graham's parents tended to declare that they would be coming to visit and it was nearly always on a Sunday. They would drive down from Leicestershire and they'd arrive at Highgate and we'd have a roast dinner ready for them. However busy Graham was, that day would be set aside as soon as he knew they were going to come. I think he was closer to his father. His

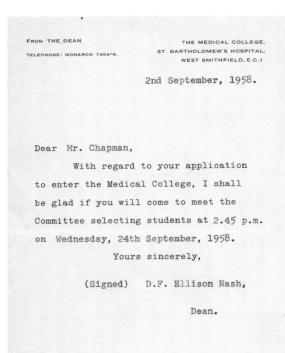

Graham with his niece (above) and as best man at his brother John's wedding (right)

mother, at times, could be extremely stern. But then she'd grown up as a country policeman's wife. His father had trained as a policeman in the '30s. There were no decent jobs to be held down with any prospects for the future and there looked to be much more financial safety in being a copper than anything else.

JOHN CHAPMAN: We certainly shared a sense of humour, appreciating that sort of thing. If we were at home together, we would always listen to *The Goon Show* whenever it was on, we were certainly both very fond of Goon-type humour. We would do the silly voices and things like that, all that sort of silly thing.

DAVID SHERLOCK: Graham was such a dedicated sportsman. He was very good at athletics, and he was a good rugby player. Also he was tall at an early age. At around the age of fifteen he was asked to join the local rugby club and he was thrilled. But of course, after rugby and they'd all cleaned and showered up, it was a Saturday afternoon, so they piled into the pub. Graham told me that if you were going to go into a pub as a fifteen-year-old

in those days, when your father's a copper, you'd better damn well look older. So he then took to smoking a pipe which gave him much more gravitas than smoking cigarettes, which he never really liked, and he also took to drinking pints of beer, along with the rest of the boys. So that's the earliest link I can find, looking back to how Graham started his boozing tradition.

PAM CHAPMAN: He was really quite shy.

JOHN CHAPMAN: But he could lose the shyness in two ways. One was by playing somebody else on stage and the other was through the bottle. But that was later on.

DAVID SHERLOCK: Graham's father had a much broader view of the world and there's the famous story of Graham telling his mother that he was gay, that he was living with me, and she said, 'Don't tell your father, it'll kill him.' And, of course, Graham's father said in passing on the telephone some months later, 'I've been awfully worried about your mother. It's been bugging me what's wrong with her, but eventually she told me.' And then he said to Graham, 'Don't you worry, women don't understand these things.' And that's all there was to be said.

GRAHAM CHAPMAN: Quite a lot happened over the next few years, a disastrous sexual experiment with Rita Blake; my first love affair with another boy; stuffing snails into a gatepost with Annette Hoy; the hen-stealing nuns; Pigshit Freeman; Miss Chamberlain's three consecutive head-girls pregnant; my questions about ejaculation to a biology master; Anthony Blond and a book called *Health and Hygiene for Secondary Schoolgirls*, written by myself and my brother; Albert the groundsman; me holding hands with Mark Collins in a maths class; the couple copulating in the French library; Painting John Wilder black; 'Who knows Eskimo Nell?'; M'sieur le bog va pooh; purple smoke; little boys' eardrums; 'This is a raid'; and elderly spinsters wanking off birthday cakes – but such trivia need no elaboration. One childhood is much like another.[4]

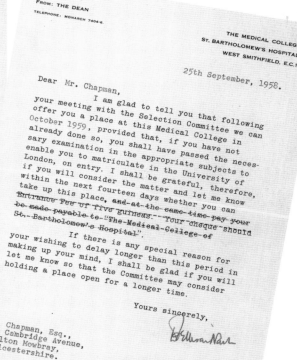

FROM THE DEAN

TELEPHONE: MONARCH 7404-6.

THE MEDICAL COLLEGE,
ST. BARTHOLOMEW'S HOSPITAL,
WEST SMITHFIELD, E.C.1

2nd September, 1958.

Dear Mr. Chapman,

With regard to your application to enter the Medical College, I shall be glad if you will come to meet the Committee selecting students at 2.45 p.m. on Wednesday, 24th September, 1958.

Yours sincerely,

(Signed)   D.F. Ellison Nash,

Dean.

G. Chapman, Esq.,
26 Cambridge Avenue,
Melton Mowbray,
Leicestershire.

FROM: THE DEAN

TELEPHONE: MONARCH 7404-6.

THE MEDICAL COLLEGE,
ST. BARTHOLOMEW'S HOSPITAL,
WEST SMITHFIELD, E.C.1.

25th September, 1958.

Dear Mr. Chapman,

I am glad to tell you that following your meeting with the Selection Committee we can offer you a place at this Medical College in October 1959, provided that, if you have not already done so, you shall have passed the necessary examination in the appropriate subjects to enable you to matriculate in the University of London, on entry. I shall be grateful, therefore, if you will consider the matter and let me know within the next fourteen days whether you can take up this place, and at the same time pay your Entrance Fee of Five Guineas. Your cheque should be made payable to "The Medical College of St. Bartholomew's Hospital".

If there is any special reason for your wishing to delay longer than this period in making up your mind, I shall be glad if you will let me know so that the Committee may consider holding a place open for a longer time.

Yours sincerely,

Terry Gilliam

'The first time I ever won a prize for art was in school. I must have been nine or ten. We had gone to the zoo and we came back and I was supposed to draw an animal from memory, and I cheated. I had a book in my lap with a picture of a bear, so I drew this really good picture of a bear and I got a box of crayons as my reward.

. . . . . So my art career began by cheating .

I was born on 22 November 1940 in Minneapolis, Minnesota, but we soon moved to a small community in the country outside of Minneapolis called Medicine Lake. I'm a country boy basically. My childhood was a Tom Sawyer-esque existence. We lived on a dirt road, a couple of blocks from the lake. Across the road was a swamp and behind the house was a big wood where we played. It was actually more rolling countryside than flat. Mainly Scandinavians lived round there. The community was made up of what had been summer cottages which people had begun living in all year round.

My dad fixed ours up, insulated it, made it habitable for the winter. He was a carpenter. My mother's maiden name was Beatrice Vance, but she was known as 'Bea'. They basically provided whatever we needed. I never seemed to want anything. But our needs were simple. There was a real Christian morality surrounding the household. You didn't want to disappoint your parents, it was as simple as that.

I always felt I was the favoured one, but perhaps that was my ego speaking. I was the first born of three. I was the brightest. I had the most talent. My brother has always thought he was left behind because he was ten years younger. He has always felt he has had to live in the shadow of this successful brother and I believe it was difficult for him. But ten years is a big gap. My sister is a couple of years younger than me and, looking back at it, a lot of the time I behaved badly towards her because she had invaded my little world run by these two wonderful parents and was now occupying their time and energy. In the end I felt I was just ploughing my own furrow and the others were just there, or in my way. Privately I was an incredibly selfish little bastard. I'm not sure if the others noticed. My mother still swears I was a perfect, polite, generous child with impeccable table manners.

What I remember most about Minnesota is the freedom of living in the country. Across the road from our house dozens of large trees had been cut down and dumped into the swamp. They were horizontal and damp. They formed great labyrinths and caves and hiding places, all carpeted with moss. Behind the house in another direction, in two minutes you were in a forest. Over the hill to the west you'd be in a cornfield with ranks of cornstalks as high as Rogers and Hammerstein's 'elephant's eye'. In the other direction was the lake. That was the world we played in. It was a fantastic world – the innocent America that Spielberg keeps trying to put in his movies but only knows from the movies he's seen, and from Norman Rockwell's illustrations. Ever so slowly, my memory of it is becoming like that as well.

But, the fact was, people were nicer and there was a real sense of community. I always felt my childhood was full of communities which I abandoned because I felt trapped by them; now I wistfully long for them. Maybe making films is a way for me to work within a temporary community – where I'm the mayor!

For years we only had an outdoor toilet – in a wooden lean-to at the bottom of the garden. Strangely, I have no sense memory of what it felt like when it was 40 degrees below zero in the winter and I had to go out for a dump in the 'biffy', as it was called. It must have been painful, but I don't remember it. But I do remember when we finally got an indoor toilet. We dismantled the biffy and we used the wood to build me a three-storey-high tree house. In the winter we would build caves in the man-high snow-drifts and leap from the top of the tree house trying to grab the electricity wires on the way down before disappearing into the deep snow. Luckily we always managed to miss the wires. It was that kind of world – paper routes, ice fishing, tornadoes, haunted houses – all that. This temperature thing really bothers me because you think somewhere there'd be some sense memory of it but there isn't. The winter was the winter. Freezing cold was normality.

Years before I came along, my dad had served in the last mounted cavalry unit of the US army. It was only later that I discovered this. A lot of the time I seem to discover things about my family long after the event. That romantic-seeming

Gilliam with younger brother and sister, having relocated to California at age eleven

which I think I've done ever since . . .'

period was all finished by the time I was a kid. The thing I do remember is him working on the Alaskan Highway. He was away from home a lot during the building of it. After that he was a coffee salesman, so again he was away. He ended up as a carpenter, a very good one. My only real disappointment was that for years after we moved to Los Angeles I wanted him to get a job in one of the film studios but he never did. He had enough connections, he knew enough people, but he never did. That was a shame because he ended up not really using his skills to their fullest in his day-to-day job – putting up pre-fab partitions in office blocks. Work on our house was the real outlet for his craft.

The first time I ever won a prize for art was in school. I must have been nine or ten. We had gone to the zoo and we came back and I was supposed to draw an animal from memory, and I cheated. I had a book in my lap with a picture of a bear, so I drew this really good picture of a bear and I got a box of crayons as my reward. So my art career began by cheating, which I think I've done ever since. Besides drawing I was very keen on learning to perform magic tricks and my dad built me a beautiful cabinet that I used for my shows. Unfortunately, they always ended up being more comic than amazing.

It was a very simple existence in the country. Because we didn't have television, radio was our home entertainment. I just loved radio. I had to invent all the visuals in my head. I'd sit there and imagine the faces and costumes and sets. I actually think radio is the best training for a visual sensibility. There was *Let's Pretend* which took place in a fairy-tale world. There was *The Green Hornet*. There was *The FBI at Peace and War*. *The Fat Man* was always mysterious – he tipped the scales at 300 pounds and announced his presence in the perpetual fog with echoing footsteps and a whistled tune. *The Shadow* was a particularly smart idea for a radio show. Lamont Johnson, the hero, had learned in the mystic East the power to cloud men's minds, and as he battled crime, laughing his signature laugh, the evil-doers, like the listeners, were unable to see him, fantastic stuff. *Johnny Lujack*, who was a Catholic quarterback from Notre Dame, was another favourite … but, in retrospect, I suspect it was the work of Opus Dei trying to cloud my innocent Protestant mind. I've always thought you can create more atmosphere with radio than with film or with any other form because it's all shadow, so it's all imagination on the listener's part. You are exercising your creative and imagination muscles when you listen to radio, which you don't have to do when you watch television. With TV it's all done for you, it's all served up. Just lay back and get dulled down and fat.

I remember when some neighbours up the road actually got a television – I was around ten at the time. This was the first television I had ever seen and the first shows I remember were Sid Caesar's *Your Show of Shows* and Ernie Kovacs. Comedy shows. Kovacs' shows were totally surreal. It was the first time I'd bumped into surrealism, or surrealistic comedy. He'd do these extraordinary sound effect gags – libraries with noise-making books: when he opened a copy of Camille, a consumptive cough would be heard. Dutch Master Cigars were his only sponsor and they allowed him to do their ads as gags. My favourite was two gunfighters having this big shoot-up. One of them falls down dead. The victor goes up

to the bar, lights a cigar, takes a big drag, and smoke pours out of a hundred holes in his body as he collapses to the floor.

My first serious reading seemed to be mainly about dogs – Lassie and Scottish books about loyal highland dogs written by someone named Albert Payson Terhune. Later, along came *The Hardy Boys*. And always there were comic books. There used to be a series called 'Classics Illustrated' that re-told classic stories – *Moby Dick*, *Treasure Island*, *Master of Ballantrae* – but in comic book form.

I always drew. But, in terms of my being exposed to art, it was only through cartoons and comic books. I'd already started altering the world when I drew it, turning household appliances into extraterrestrials – Martians that looked like vacuum cleaners. That's what my mind was doing then, turning the extraordinary and alien into useful things around the house. I could always entertain people with my drawings. With cartoons you get immediate feedback. You draw something, people instantly go 'Wow!' You write something and it's never recognised as a special skill. People are always impressed that you can draw well and I enjoyed showing off all the time. It's nice to have people say, 'Aren't you talented! Clever boy.'

When I was eleven years old we moved from Minnesota out to California. My sister's health wasn't great. She had had a couple of bouts of pneumonia. Living in Minnesota was tough and she was somewhat less than tough. And my father was finally tired of shovelling snow. California was the place that offered new opportunities. My memories are of the excitement of going out West where cowboys and Indians roamed. We moved to the San Fernando Valley to a new development called Panorama City where the sun shone all the time and the heat was permanent too, but there were no cowboys or Indians. However, there *was* a panorama – of beautiful mountains, but within a few years they were gone, lost in a soup of stinging smog.

We lived in a new suburban house, like the ones in *Edward Scissorhands* – your choice of one of five designs. About three years before we arrived, the place had been orange groves and sheep farms, just like in *Chinatown* when Jack Nicholson drives out to the valley – that was our valley. But Henry J. Kaiser, of Kaiser Aluminium, tore them all down and built this huge tract instead.

Even at an early age I was obsessed with knights and tales of chivalry. With my father's help we'd make great big wooden shields.

'I always drew. But, in terms of my being exposed to art, it was only through cartoons and comic books. I'd already started altering the world when I drew it, turning household appliances into extraterrestrials – Martians that looked like vacuum cleaners.'

'I'd always been thrilled by circuses and particularly side-shows, mesmerised by the extraordinary and impossible tricks nature can perform with the human physique . . .'

I'd paint them with colourful heraldic designs. My friends and I would gather thick eucalyptus branches for swords, put five-gallon ice cream containers on our heads for helmets, and then go out and bash each other senseless.

Clyde Beatty was a famous lion-tamer with his own circus. Each year they would appear in a field near our home that would soon be the Panorama Shopping Mall. One year, when I was old enough, I got a job working with the circus. It was only for one day, and my job was helping raise the tent for the freak show. I'd always been thrilled by circuses and particularly side-shows, mesmerised by the extraordinary and impossible tricks nature can perform with the human physique especially in the most mysterious and untamed parts of the planet: rubber men from Borneo, half-man/half-alligator people from the Congo, Pin Heads from Siam, Sealo the Seal Boy from the Arctic. The hoardings were exotic, sexy and terrifying and on that day I took my first trip through the looking glass. Back stage was not magical at all, it was utterly mundane – having got the tent up, I was able to wander around before the crowds arrived meeting the strangely shaped people who made their livings as freaks. Although they didn't look normal, they were

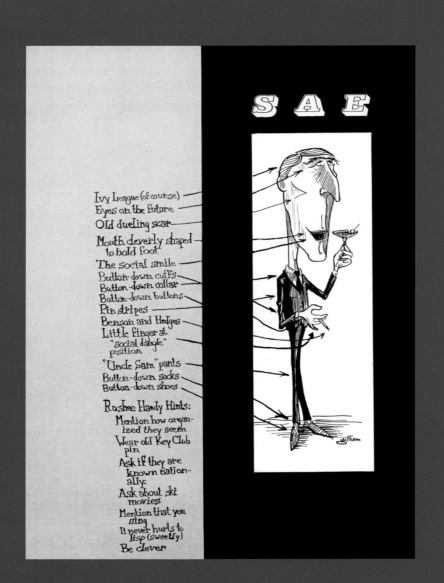

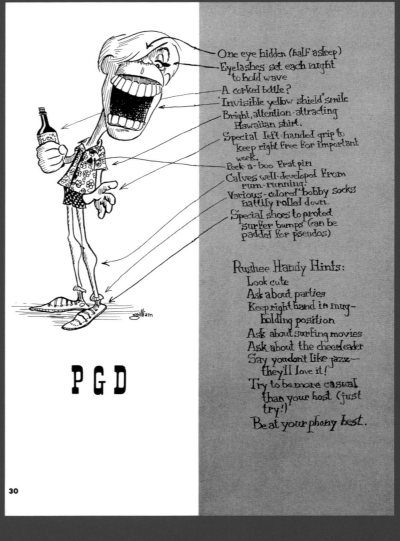

behaving utterly and disappointingly boringly normally, sitting around playing cards, washing clothes, smoking, belly-aching about the weather – behaving just like the ordinary people I had to live with day in and day out. They were not at all the wondrous, bizarre, magical monsters painted on the front-of-house hoardings. I was confused, struggling to deal with my desperate desire for the exotic and my relief at discovering that humanity and normalcy are probably king. Ever since, I have been torn between wanting to fly high on the magic carpet of the extraordinary and, at the same time, trying to demystify it and drag it back down to dusty banality.

My education was very straightforward, utterly normal. I did read a lot, but it was always casual and it came easy. So it was with movies. I never thought of them as anything I wanted to make. I just wanted to be transported by them, to escape: King Kong, Westerns, Roman epics, Ivanhoe, pirate films – other worlds. I remember when Disneyland was built … I was actually back East visiting my grandparents in Arkansas when the park opened – an event which glued me to the television. I was just fascinated by the idea of Disneyland, a real, solid, touchable fantasy world. It was my first chance to see a real castle. Of course it wasn't real – it was Disneyland! But when years later I came to Europe and saw real castles, I stayed. The

Middle Ages have always interested me, especially when it comes to films. Like a Western, you have a very clear hierarchy and structure you can play within: kings, sheriffs; knights, cowboys; maidens, gals.

I became aware of animation when I first saw *Snow White*. The early Disney features were just great. The craftsmanship was so wonderful, the detail, the backgrounds. Those were the ones I loved. Tex Avery and Chuck Jones cartoons weren't the same. They were funnier and they were zippier. I loved them but I never knew who Chuck Jones was, or who Tex Avery was – these names didn't mean anything. I was just a normal kid in the sense that Disney was the only name you knew if you were talking about animation. Everything else was just cartoons. I remember seeing *Pinocchio* again a few years ago, and I was stunned. It's a really short, tight little film. I remember it as this huge canvas and landscape that I travelled through, but in fact everything is very contained, it's a very tight bit of storytelling. But somehow it just opens up your imagination. I think *Pinocchio* is probably my favourite. But *Snow White* is also wonderful, particularly the personalities of the dwarves. For better or worse what Disney always did with Grimm's fairy tales was fill them with really well-drawn characters. Unlike some of his later

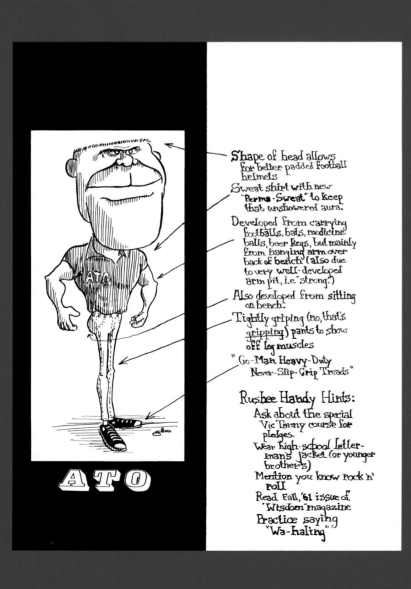

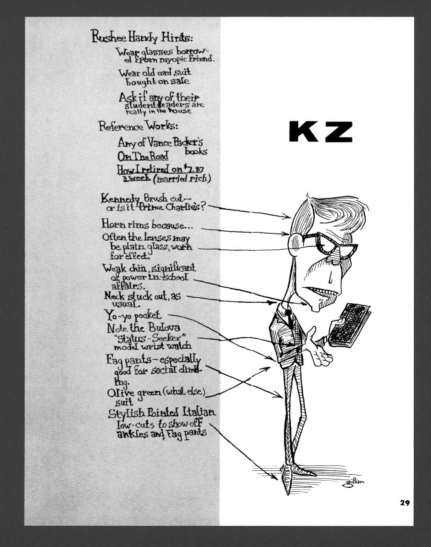

Judy Seder
Girls' Vice-President

Mike Gettleman
Boys' Vice-President

Pat Dooley
Secretary

Nancy Becker
Treasurer

Terry Gilliam
Student Body President

VALLEY TIMES SECOND SECTION

VALLEY TIMES, MONDAY, NOVEMBER 25, 1957 • 15

SCIENCE STUDENTS, FOR NOW AT LEAST — These Birmingham High School seniors are typical youngsters who load up on science and math courses, but often branch to other fields in college. Left to right are Mary Kay Worden, Mickey Burns, Diane Strauser and Terry Gilliam—Valley Times photo.

EXOTIC ADVERTISERS INC.
Present...
the Fang Little Players in....
QUICK, HENRY, THE FLIT!!
or ...BUG BOMBS REVISITED
by Gilliam

films, Disney's early tales were as frightening as they should be. Fairy tales should confront real fears. They're a part of growing up.

The church was also very big in my childhood. We were church-goers – Lutherans in Minnesota and Presbyterians in LA. My grandfather was a Baptist minister and I went to college on a Presbyterian scholarship. At one point I was going to be a missionary. I was leader of the church youth group – a regular little zealot. Ultimately I became disenchanted because of the hypocrisy and pomposity of too many of the church-goers who didn't share my sense of humour about God. I said to them, 'What kind of God is this that you need to protect from my cheap jokes? If He can't take them, He certainly isn't worth worshipping.' There were two good things about my church days: first, and once again, the sense of community; and secondly, having to read the Bible – a seriously good book. My kids have been raised with no religion as such and I keep thinking it's a pity because the stories and poetry of the Bible are extraordinarily powerful and they don't know them. So I keep thinking maybe I've deprived my children of something very important. The sense of morality and responsibility I learned in church always rears its head in my films, that and the sense I get of feeling I'm serving a higher good when I commit myself to creating a film that has something to say to the world. Talk of pomposity!

'I was constantly surprised by the way the world saw me. One day, out of the blue, two girls – high-powered student politicos – showed up and said they'd like me to run for student body president.'

'My early abandoned modelling career'

MUNROE'S MENS & BOYS SHOP
8416 VAN NUYS BLVD.
PANORAMA CITY, CALIF.
OPEN MON., THURS. & FRIDAY TILL 9 P.M.

BULK RATE
U. S. POSTAGE
PAID
Permit No. 123
Van Nuys, Calif.

Mrs. J. H. Gilliam
Van Nuys, Calif.

Rolling Out 1960 Campus Favorites

In school I was always overly ambitious with my extracurricular schemes and dreams. I would start projects and discover too late that I was not going to be able to pull them off in time. If I was designing and building sets for a play or a huge castle for a school dance, I would invariably run out of time. With only hours left before the curtain going up, wood, nails, big sheets of cardboard, glue, paint and brushes would be spread out over our backyard and there would be my mother and dad helping me, doing as much work as I did – saving my ass.

School was easy for me. In high school I concentrated on getting good grades, goofed around, played mediocre sports, but always totally focused, thinking that I had a pretty good picture of who I was and what I was doing. But I was invariably wrong. I was constantly surprised by the way the world saw me. One day, out of the blue, two girls – high-powered student politicos – showed up and said they'd like me to run for student body president. This was a total shock to me. I had no political ambitions or any idea that anybody thought that I was capable, much less electable. Their enthusiasm was hard to resist, so I said yes. Somehow I was elected and became student body president without a clue how to run a council meeting or behave with the necessary gravitas. It all seemed rather dreamlike. Then I was chosen king of the senior prom. That was an even greater surprise because it was a popularity contest and I had never striven for popularity. Somehow, by the time I graduated, I had been student body president, valedictorian, king of the senior prom, head cheerleader, a letter man in track – all with no understanding of how any of it came about. Most of my subsequent life has carried on in the same manner.

'...Life doesn't happen like that. You don't sit and think, "I'm going to have a career now." Things just happen...'

IN WHICH
WE
PRETEND
TO GROW UP

'When people say it's undergraduate humour I think they're wrong, it's postgraduate humour. By the time we're writing Python we've all been through Cambridge or Oxford.'

TERRY GILLIAM: To me college was wonderful. It was like being in this safe secure world where everybody's intelligent and you can start the jokes at a certain level already.

GRAHAM CHAPMAN: Cambridge. A university town built in a featureless flat landscape – so featureless and flat you wonder why anyone chose it as a location for anything. 'The magnificence of St John's,

the noteworthy splendour of Trinity, the sheer pauntliness of "The Backs" … and gazing at the magnificent, noteworthy, sheer splendour of the pauntley King's College Chapel, it would be a world weary traveller indeed who did not pause to think "Why the fuck didn't they build the whole town two inches to the right?"'[4]

ERIC IDLE: The only good news about my school was that it got me to Cambridge, which was totally unexpected. People didn't go to university from our school, let alone Cambridge. My history master got me into Cambridge. He was a lovely man, he was ex-RAF and I loved history very much. And he'd been at Pembroke. The great thing about Pembroke was that I was interviewed by an Arabist, a mathematician and the Dean. If I'd been interviewed by somebody in the English department I'd never have got in. All we could talk about was the West End. I'd been to see all the plays in the West

End, and they'd been to see the plays, so we could discuss plays, and they figured I was right for English Literature. That got me in, I just had to learn Latin. That was my quest for my last year at school. I had to learn Latin in a year and pass O Level and then I got in.

It was like going into chrysalis form and going from a grub to a butterfly. Suddenly you went to this beautiful place and it was amazing, you didn't have to do anything, you could go and be with whoever you wanted. I went to lectures for half the first term and then I realised that I could achieve far more by reading in an hour anything somebody could tell you in ten hours of lectures.

MICHAEL PALIN: I'd enjoyed what acting I'd done at school and in between leaving school and going to university I spent what would now be called a gap year, working in the publicity department of the steelworks where my father was employed in Sheffield and I met someone there who invited me to join an amateur dramatics group. Sheffield had a number of quite good amateur dramatic companies and I joined this one which was called at that time, rather heftily, the 'Brightside and Carbrooke Co-operative Players'. By the time you've said that, it's the end of the evening. They'd put on two or three plays and I think they discovered I was quite good because they gave me quite meaty roles to do from the start. These were not comedies, these were quite serious dramatic roles. I felt I'd been rather frustrated at school in not being able to act in any of the big productions because my father was very much against acting: he thought it was a waste of time and didn't really want me to get distracted too much by that. I had the feeling that at Oxford I would get the opportunity to do some acting, so I joined up pretty quickly with the Oxford University Dramatic Society.

GRAHAM CHAPMAN: It is the year 1958. A Ford Anglia is juddering south along the A604, containing Chief Inspector and Mrs Chapman and a rather spotty figure, precociously dressed in the kind of suit that he thinks doctors might wear. He also has on a rugby club tie and is busy reading the Daily Telegraph, trying to catch up on current affairs – a mistake he's never made since. 'What', he thinks, 'will the Master of Emmanuel College ask him [me]? His [my] headmaster has told me [him (me)] to let him [not I (him)] do the talking, agree with him most of the time, but to disagree strongly on a few points to show that I [he (that is me)] have one or two brain cells. If he asks me questions about English grammar I'll be up shit creek …

So I left two quivering parents and attempt to saunter past a lot of very important looking people in gowns, and stared round the courtyard. I could see no sign of a Master's Lodge. Overawed by the paunty magnificence of the groups of overtly musing academics, I asked an old gardener where it was … I knocked on the door and was greeted by the gardener who asked me to come through to his study.

I said 'Yes' quite a lot and nodded, particularly when he was talking about the history of coal mining and the Industrial Revolution. But when asked whether I was going to pass my A-levels I gave a definite 'No' to physics. He was clearly impressed by this and at last sensing a possible argument, thrust forward his head, raised his eyebrows to the point of nearly covering his bald patch…

'Let me put it another way. Are you going to fail?'

'No.'

'Good, then we'll see you next October.'

I left and stood for a moment in the corridor, trying to work out whether he had said 'yes' or 'no.' I decided that it amounted to an almost definite 'yes,' walked back through the courtyard feeling that it was mine already, and was rather annoyed that no-one was staring at me.[4]

TERRY JONES: I went up to Oxford ready to be intimidated by everything and everybody. I expected everyone to be incredibly clever and incredibly high-faluting. In a way it was a lesson in how things aren't what you expect them to be. I don't remember being very happy there either. I wasn't really used to people being *that* competitive. The first two years were like that but by the third year you're top of the pile anyway and I'd done this revue at the Phoenix Theatre in London. So when I came back, I and others had been on the West End stage, and suddenly I was in demand.

TERRY GILLIAM: Occidental College was a small California college. There were 1200 to 1500 students and it was a really fine college, but unlike UCLA [University of California at Los Angeles], which was like a huge city basically, this was a little village, though the standard was very high. A lot of the kids came from really wealthy families, so it was a privileged college in that sense, and practical jokes were still very much alive in the late '50s. There were several guys in the dorms who were very funny people, so pranks would be done. Simple ones like you'd fill a person's room with wadded up newspaper; or you'd take the pins out of the door hinges and you'd lock the door, but before you

did this you'd tie a rope to the handle and hang the bed out of the window, so when he comes along and puts the key in the lock the whole door goes flying across the room and smashes against the window. One time they actually got a car disassembled and put it back together in the person's room with the engine running. It took incredible strategy and planning to pull these off. That was the spirit of the time and you just got involved in different ways. And I got more and more interested in extracurricular things like that.

JOHN CHAPMAN: Graham had been accepted into a London Medical School – Bart's. But once I suggested to him that he try to get into Oxford or Cambridge, he went along to discuss it with his headmaster who, a few days later, was entertaining the Master of Emmanuel to dinner. So Graham was interviewed by the Master of Emmanuel at Melton Mowbray and not at Cambridge, and was offered a place on the basis of his headmaster's recommendation.

ERIC IDLE: Life at Cambridge was different beyond belief for me. At school every second of your day was organised, and you did this at this time, and you did that at that time. Suddenly you were in charge of your life, and you could stay up all night. You'd have a tutorial once a week. You'd have to turn in an essay once a week. The rest of the time was entirely up to you. That sense of freedom is unbelievable and really profound, and the good news is the privilege was not having to earn a living, the privilege was having that time to find out who you were or what you wanted to be in an environment of other people all of the same age. That's when I first met public school people, who were completely different from my kind. We were lower middle-class oiks. We could barely scrape through. Grammar schools are what we dreamed of trying to get to if we could escape from the orphanage. I found a guy in LA recently who was there at the same time as me, and I said, 'How bad was it?' and he said, 'It was fucking grim, a nightmare.' But my mum had to work, that's what she had to do. There was no money, we were broke. It wasn't a picnic and it certainly wasn't a public school. I used to bridle when people used to describe us all as 'public school' - it's not true. Graham was Leicester Grammar, Terry was grammar, I was this nightmare school and Michael was Shrewsbury, which is a public school, and John was at Clifton, also a public school. That's two out of six.

JOHN CLEESE: Pembroke was my first choice of college at Cambridge but I didn't get in there. I got into Downing and I didn't particularly like Downing. Pembroke was smaller, older and cosier. It was full of nooks and crannies, little staircases and friendly little rooms. You'd walk down one flight of stairs and you'd come out and there'd be a lovely lawn there with a croquet match set up. And it was quite warm and cosy, which was saying quite a lot in Cambridge. Whereas Downing was built much later and consisted of these buildings on three sides of a rectangle of grass which was absolutely flat. There was a tremendous bleakness about it. The buildings were vaguely Georgian but very spare, and the thing about Cambridge was this raw wind that came in from the east. You spent an awful

YORK FESTIVAL 1963

THE 1963 FOOTLIGHTS REVUE

'A Clump of Plinths'

lot of time wrapping up with sweaters and scarves and walking round with your head down.

I never felt particularly welcome in Downing. In the three years I was there, I met the College Master just twice – once for sherry on my first day and once for sherry on my last day, in the two and a half years in between I never set eyes on him. Whereas I knew some of the teachers at Pembroke and I knew and liked people who lived there, like Tim Brooke-Taylor and Bill Oddie, and we spent a lot of time together. I used to have dinner there all the time and the porters thought I was a member of the College, so I was never challenged. It was also much closer to the centre of town and my digs, so I could get to Pembroke in about five minutes whereas Downing was quite a way.

ERIC IDLE: John had done two years teaching. I often wonder why he went back to his old school and taught. Wild horses wouldn't have dragged me back to my school. That's a huge gap at that age, two years. In an odd way he always still looks on us as if we're still just junior people coming around. The rest of us are annoying and get in the way and get on his wick. But of course at this age it's really good to be four years younger than John.

MICHAEL PALIN: Robert Hewison and I met on the first day at Brasenose. I was chatting away and Robert was this slightly bumptious, confident boy from London and I liked and disliked him at the same time. I felt rather provincial and slightly clumsier than he was in dealing with life. He was full of jokes and all that sort of thing. But we actually struck up a pretty good relationship, and of all the people there in my history set, he was keen on comedy. He loved the Goon shows and loved what Spike had done since then. We had an album called *Milligan Preserved* that was quite important then. In a way, while *Beyond the Fringe* was happening, I was still quite interested in the characters that Milligan created in a more odd and imaginative world. *Beyond the Fringe* was fine, that was Satire with a capital S, men in suits and all that. I didn't feel as close to that as to some of the things I was hearing on the Milligan album. Some of the earliest things that Robert and I wrote when we were at

ABOVE The *Beyond The Fringe* team of (from left)
Jonathan Miller, Peter Cook, Alan Bennett and Dudley Moore.

OPPOSITE The team behind *That Was The Week That Was*,
with David Frost on the left

Oxford were these sub-Spike style characters, very much based around Milligan's ideas, like the 'Cougher Royal', the man who coughs for the Royal Family – I found that just wonderful. It was a love of something that was nonsensical but seemed just true …

I'm not quite sure I went to Oxford knowing that this was going to be the world of the people who wrote *Beyond the Fringe*. I just felt *Beyond the Fringe* was more London than Oxford, in fact it was actually put together after they'd all left university.

JOHN CLEESE: *Beyond the Fringe* had had a huge impact on me, but not the impact it had in London. The press in London

FOOTLIGHTS 1962

DOUBLE TAKE

OXFORD PLAYHOUSE
THE UNIVERSITY THEATRE

Monday June 25th 1962 for one week

THE CAMBRIDGE ARTS THEATRE TRUST
presents

CAMBRIDGE FOOTLIGHTS

ROBERT ATKINS   GRAHAM CHAPMAN
HUMPHREY BARCLAY   JOHN CLEESE
TIM BROOKE-TAYLOR   ALAN GEORGE
NIGEL BROWN   TONY HENDRA

MIRIAM MARGOLYES

in

DOUBLE TAKE

Directed by TREVOR NUNN
Music by HUGH MacDONALD
Décor by ANN JASPER

in Wolverhampton and then in the holidays everybody scatters, so you don't have friends in the holidays, they've all gone off. So I arrived very much isolated, very much 'Please sir, where do I put my bags?' You're marching through the gates of Cambridge; it's a totally different world. But of course being in a boarding school, you can adapt to almost any situation because that's one thing you've become used to. You're adaptive. I'll put my bags here, I'll put my shoes here. That was the first thing at school, when you had to go out into the playground, you had to change from your indoor shoes to your outdoor shoes, then you go outside. Then when you come in you have to change from your outdoor shoes, put your outdoor shoes on the rack, get your indoor shoes, put them on. When you go upstairs you put on your carpet slippers, put your indoor shoes by the outdoor shoes. I mean that was life! You didn't have to wear shoes at Cambridge. So I didn't know about the comedy there, I lucked into it.

When you make an audience laugh they love you, they really do love you, and that's one of the nicest things about being a comedian. When you make people laugh, usually you've touched them at a time when they needed some kind of reassurance or they wanted something or they were feeling depressed and then you made them feel better. So there is a sort of healing thing to it.

I stumbled into performing at Cambridge. That's the first time I ever became a comedy performer. My first ever performance was playing Second Fieldmouse in *Wind in the Willows* at my school and I chose the Second Fieldmouse because he had one more line than First Fieldmouse. That made it two lines he had. I think there's something very seductive about the glamour of dressing up and playing somebody else, and that comes from a sadness. I think I only became any good eventually through Python by being disguised and by being other people and it was only latterly in my life that I have been able to be funny as myself or be confident. I don't have to put on a disguise or wear a wig now but that's what I used to do.

Joining the Footlights was very important for me because it was a learning club. You would have to write and perform and so you would learn by doing. In Cambridge that was my life, really, from

Eric in the Footlights –
from left, clockwise: Christy Davies,
John Grillo, Clive James, Eric Idle,
John Cameron

about the middle of 1963, right through until I became big Grand President and changed the laws and admitted women, and I've been admitting women ever since!

TERRY GILLIAM: I was head cheerleader in college, but I didn't wear a short little skirt or falsies. There were all the girls and then there were three guys and they were the leaders of this thing. The girls were just the backing group. I had been head cheerleader in high school as well, so I had this whole history of standing in front of this huge crowd of people at the football games, and leading the cheers. We didn't have pom poms or jiggle our tits, we did manly jumps in the air. In college I got into this whole thing of getting people to shout silly words – 'Give me a Cromety Silk' and they'd all say 'Cromety Silk'. And one day I said, 'Give me a fleck', and of course with me and my bad enunciation, thousands of people shout 'FUCK!' and that was a word you didn't use publicly in 1960. Everybody stopped and went 'What did he say?' and there was a gasp from the other side of the field.

TERRY JONES: One day at university I was just sitting there in the Bodleian Library, watching everyone else writing, and at the time I was getting very worked up about what somebody had written about what somebody else had written about what Wordsworth or Milton had written, and I suddenly thought, 'Why I am getting so emotionally outraged by what someone else has written about what someone else has written about what someone else originally wrote? I'd rather do the original writing in the first place.' So I was suddenly hit with a blinding flash that I didn't want to spend my life being an English academic and commentator, and I wanted to do what I always wanted to do really. I wanted to make things and write the raw material.

MICHAEL PALIN: There was a lot of comedy about in both Oxford and Cambridge: 40 to 50 per cent of people who went to Oxford brought with them a public school influence for a start. I came from public school to Oxford and there was a great deal of humour, a lot of it a very dark humour, that came from boarding school, because that was a closed institution. In order to survive it and not go under, you really had to have a healthy sense of humour and a

'When I did the Pembroke Smoker, it was John's last year and my first year, I was a freshman, so I had a few sketches, not much material.'

lot of the people I knew and met at school were always making jokes to survive. Also we had masters who would use jokes in order to either put you down or encourage you, or show that they were independent spirits who had a voice of their own. There was a lot of reaction to the idea of it being an institution and much of that reaction came in humour. Shrewsbury was where the entire team who invented *Private Eye* was educated and they were influenced by this one teacher, a man called Laurence Ducaine, who had a very enlightened attitude. They spent a lot of time with him – at boarding school you do, you spend a lot of time with the same people – and they created their own little world which depended a lot on comedy, on looking at the world as something quite absurd and ridiculous. They founded a magazine called *Mesopotamia* at Shrewsbury, which developed later into *Private Eye*.

So humour was important at school, it didn't just start at university, it transferred on. There was a certain added element, which was that both Oxford and Cambridge, and I assume other universities as well, had revue traditions. Cambridge, particularly, with the Footlights. That was the place where people came and did funny, witty sketches and it had quite a lot of status in the university. It was approved of to make jokes and sketches and be funny about the world, and I think Oxford had the same sort of thing, though not perhaps in quite such a formal way. Nonetheless, it did exist. So there was a conduit for humour and humour was expected to be part of the mix. It tended to be people involved in languages, history or the arts. Very few people I knew from the science side made jokes, they just went on splitting the atom instead of splitting their sides.

Also things were loosening up. After Suez in '56 the whole idea of empire seemed suddenly absurd and it was all being given away. The severe, stern face of conservative Britain seemed to be gone, and into this slight limbo afterwards came the young comedians.

ERIC IDLE: I passed the audition and they wanted me in the Smoker. In the show there was Bill Oddie, Tim Brooke-Taylor, myself, Jonathan Lynn and a girl or two, and it was performed for four nights in this very small old library area. People would just get plastered and you'd just do comedy. That was my first real revue experience.

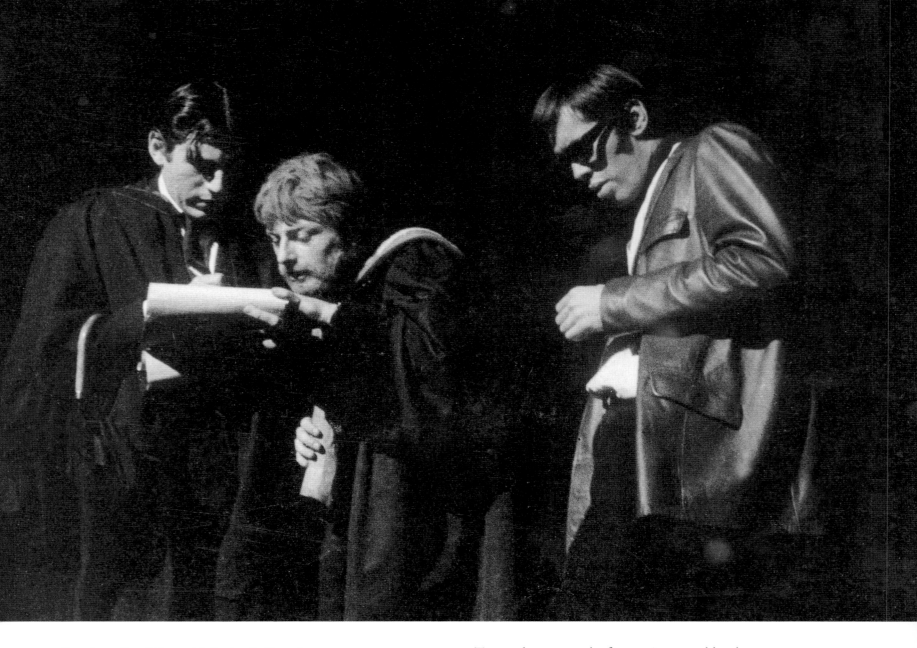

Terry Jones, Doug Fisher and Jo Durden-Smith on stage

When I did the Pembroke Smoker, it was John's last year and my first year, I was a freshman, so I had a few sketches, not much material. So for the rest of it we performed stuff that they'd come up with, and I did a sketch that John had written with Bill Oddie. From that they said, 'Oh you'll have to audition for the Footlights,' and I said, 'What's the Footlights?' So Johnny Lynn and I auditioned for the Footlights together the next term with a piece of material I'd written for the Pembroke Smoker, which was based on a commercial for guards who kept passing each other; every time they passed they would say something and you'd have to wait for the next line as you marched up and down.

TERRY JONES: It was Michael Rudman who got me doing comedy. There was a great intake at Teddy [St Edmund] Hall in my first year and Teddy Hall was very much a rugger playing/sporting/ rowing college, a big sports college. There was a joke that if you went in for an interview at Teddy Hall, they'd throw a rugger ball at you and if you caught it you were in. But this particular year, our year, it was kind of different. We went along to the Dramatic Society and it was absolutely packed – everybody wanted to be in it. There were two people, Michael Rudman, a very soft-spoken

Texan who was maybe five or six years older than us, a mature student, and David Aukin, who was doing law. They took over the society and in that first year Michael Rudman did a production of Turgenev's *A Month in the Country*, which we did in a very unusual way because he took it very, very seriously. Normally you'd work on something for the term and then do it at the end of the term, but Michael started it in the autumn, we did two terms of rehearsals, and basically he gave us a drama course. We didn't start learning the play, we started doing exercises, all the sort of things you do to learn about technique. Then we stayed up at college for awhile in the vacation and came back early before the next term and did some more. We spent weeks doing this. It was actually during one of the improvisations that Michael said to me, 'You should take up comedy.' That was it. Then we rehearsed all through that last term and then finally we did this production of *A Month in the Country* and it was very successful. David Aukin played the lead and I was playing a character called Bolshinsov who appears for about two minutes in the middle of the play and then goes off again, but it was a comedy turn, so it was quite nice to do because everybody's very pleased to have this comic character come in. It did mean an awful lot of sitting around in the dressing room. It was such a success, we were invited to do it at the Playhouse in Oxford during the vacation.

MICHAEL PALIN: We'd listened to Milligan and things like that and we'd just improvise ideas of our own and laugh a lot. Then, at some point, someone said, 'You should write that down, that's very funny.' And that's as far as it went. We wrote little jokes and the idea was to send them into a university newspaper. It was quite early on that Robert said there's money to be made from this, because he knew about things like cabaret. I didn't know what cabaret really meant, I just associated it with something German or middle European, dancing girls and all that. He said that we could make some money from this by hiring ourselves out as an act for various parties, people always wanted a cabaret. Robert had the great ability to network. He would talk to anybody, brazenly, people I would never dream of asking – 'Do you want a booking? We do cabaret.' He would just get in and talk to people and he got us our first booking at the Oxford University Psychology Department's Christmas Party. Not much laughter but great analysis. We'd also play the Oxford Union cellars, which were these cavern-like bowels beneath the famous union building. There wasn't any money involved to start with. We would just go on and try out our thirty-minute act in the break when the band went off to have a few more beers.

TERRY JONES: For me writing and performing really were the things – both of equal importance. It's the same as making things really.

ERIC IDLE: I always felt when I did the first performance, at the Pembroke Smoker, that I was fortunate to be with people who were accustomed to being funny. Bill Oddie and Tim Brooke-Taylor had already done the Smoker, so I'm the new guy, but they're supporting you and it's like being in the football team. You're sixteen and you've just got into the team but there's twenty-seven-year-olds around who've played it a long time so they're helping you to do well, and that's the same with the Footlights. You get in and they see that you've got talent and they help you and encourage you to do it. And don't forget when I joined the Footlights Cleese was there performing and he was remarkable. There was nobody like him. He was utterly remarkable.

TERRY GILLIAM: One of the things I always did in high school was build sets. My dad installed these big partitions and they were in these 4 by 8 corrugated cardboard boxes. And he'd bring them home and I'd cut them up and make sets, for dances and things like that. And that went on in college, too, so there was always that kind of design work going on in the back of everything. And the cartooning just carried on. My art professor used to be a bit pissed off at me because he thought I had a bit more talent than just being a cartoonist, he thought I could be a decent artist.

MICHAEL PALIN: We were known as the Seedy Entertainers. Robert had this very old car, an Austin 7, and we would take our props and drive off into the countryside to wherever the event was that we were performing at. And we just invented this song called Seedy Entertainers as we went along. At that time some of the parties and dinners we went to were quite smart. I remember the Conservative Party Ball at Blenheim Palace for which we were the cabaret. When we arrived they showed us into the coat cupboard and that was where we were based. They didn't want us to be seen in the party until it was our time to go on and then we'd be raked out, perform, do our bit, everyone would roar with laughter, 'Oh jolly good', then they'd go off and dance and we'd be chucked out again. It was after that that the name Seedy Entertainers seemed to just delightfully sum up our work.

We were always playing characters. That was the fun of it really, always putting on a different voice. A lot of them were the television interview programme set-up, and then some of the Spike kind of characters. I enjoyed playing characters because it was quite awkward being yourself, it didn't seem to be what people wanted.

I was probably more into characters and Robert was more into concepts, if you want to roughly split it. One of Robert's pieces was a song called 'I Hope We Never Go Beyond the Fringe'; that was a canny song really. Not surprisingly, Robert is now a theatre critic.

'One of the things I always did in high school was build sets . . . for dances and things like that. And that went on in college, too, so there was always that kind of design work going on in the back of everything. And the cartooning just carried on.'

He was always particularly aware of developments; for example, because he was a Londoner, he knew about the Establishment Club, he'd been there. The sort of people he met in London were all talking about what was fashionable, and I just felt that his terms of reference were slightly more current than my own. I just loved the pleasure of performing and creating roles for comic characters that were there lurking in my head, whereas Robert was aware somehow that this was all a tide and a trend and quite deliberately set out to go with that flow and, if possible, help to determine its course.

TERRY GILLIAM: At college we used to get rolls of butcher paper and every night we'd make huge posters and signs and cover them with cartoons. In the morning people would come down

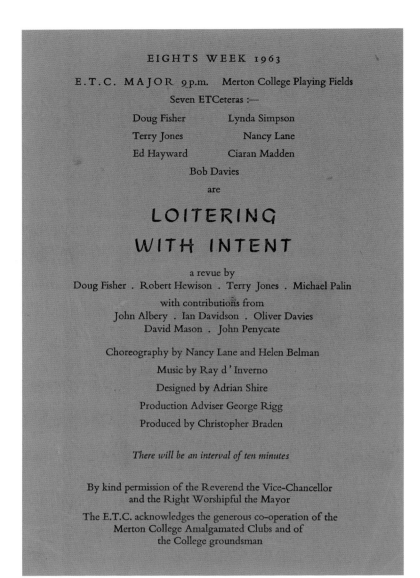

EIGHTS WEEK 1963

E.T.C. MAJOR 9 p.m.   Merton College Playing Fields

Seven ETCeteras :—

Doug Fisher   Lynda Simpson

Terry Jones   Nancy Lane

Ed Hayward   Ciaran Madden

Bob Davies

are

LOITERING

WITH INTENT

a revue by

Doug Fisher . Robert Hewison . Terry Jones . Michael Palin

with contributions from

John Albery . Ian Davidson . Oliver Davies

David Mason . John Penycate

Choreography by Nancy Lane and Helen Belman

Music by Ray d'Inverno

Designed by Adrian Shire

Production Adviser George Rigg

Produced by Christopher Braden

There will be an interval of ten minutes

By kind permission of the Reverend the Vice-Chancellor
and the Right Worshipful the Mayor

The E.T.C. acknowledges the generous co-operation of the
Merton College Amalgamated Clubs and of
the College groundsman

TERRY JONES: The first revue I did was called *Loitering with Intent*, in the Easter term of my second year. Chris Braden, was directing it, and he suggested a lecture about slapstick, but a very serious lecture with all the actions being demonstrated. Michael Bentine claimed it was his idea later, which it may well have been. He may well have done it and Bernard Braden had mentioned it to his son. Anyway, wherever the idea came from, Mike Palin and I and Robert Hewison worked it out; then I wrote the lecture and we did that in *Loitering with Intent*. I also had a series of quickies in that revue, and all I can remember is I used to creep across the stage and nothing ever happened, I would just creep across the stage rather slowly. It was called *Loitering with Intent* because it was done in a tent.

MICHAEL PALIN: *Loitering with Intent* was a revue in my first year. I wasn't in that, but Terry Jones and myself and Robert Hewison worked together on some of the material, and one of those sketches was the 'Custard Pie' lecture sketch, which we eventually ended up doing in the Python stage shows. The monologue was written by Terry.

JOHN CLEESE: There was another piece I wrote for my first revue which was a series of news items, and that was the sketch that finished up in the revue. Humphrey Barclay performed that. One piece of it, which people thought was all about the British addiction to animals, was about a dog that had got trapped somewhere and people were killed in their hundreds trying to rescue it.

RIGHT Bill Oddie, Tim Brooke-Taylor
and Jonathan Lynn perform the
Terry Jones-penned 'Custard Pie' sketch

from the dorms and see all this stuff on the walls. And this became a regular thing, we just did it. It had been started before, but myself and a couple of other people who were cartoonists did it non-stop and we just loved it. We became a kind of entertainment for everybody.

Then there was this thing called the Bengal Board, which I got voted on to. The Bengal Board was in charge of school spirit. That was in my third year. That whole school spirit thing was interesting because it was close to Goebbels' 3 new pix work and I thought 'What is a school spirit? You can do anything with this.'

So we invented whole initiation ceremonies. The school had initiations for freshmen but we upped the ante. There was a Greek amphitheatre in the college and we started these huge torch-lit rallies for all the freshmen and they'd have to come up and be indoctrinated in all these school traditions that we'd read off. And they were totally made up, total lies. What was interesting was that by the end of the year, even the seniors who'd been there for three years believed our lies. It was one of those moments when you realise how dangerous lies are, and how gullible people are. They wanted to hear this stuff, so we invented a whole world and they believed it. And I thought in other hands, like Goebbels', things could go very wrong, but we were just having a good time.

MICHAEL PALIN: Robert Hewison and I would rehearse our thirty minutes. We would take along a bucket because there was a whole rather conceptual sketch of us looking into a bucket that emptied and we saw different things in the bucket. There was a sketch about being obsessed with eating bananas and I would have to take along a bunch of bananas. And there was a thing called 'Tide', which was just a quick sketch involving a big packet of Tide and me doing a German voice, extolling the virtues of Tide

VARSITY STRIP-TEASE

ON Merton Sports Ground on Tuesday of fifth week, undegraduate stars will present "Loitering Within Tent," an ETC revue directed by Chris Braden (Wadham).

One of the stars is 22 years old Canadian graduate Nancy Lane (LMH). Beautiful Nancy told me, "in one sketch I have to strip with the assistance of four gentlemen."

BOGGLED

My mind, which had began to boggle, and think of Proctors, was eased by Terry Jones (SEH), who from the bottom of his green and white football socks said, "It's not a complete strip, it's what we call a political strip." Scriptwriter Hewison warned "How far she goes depends on the sale of tickets."

The scriptwriters of "Loitering Within Tent," Michael Palin and Robert Hewison (both BNC), went to great lengths to point out that their work was not satirical. "We're trying to create the humour from with-

'The Braden Beat' ●

in the sketch." Lynda Simpson (St. Hilda's) explained this by whispering, "The whole point is that we have not got David Frost."

The shape of the revue has still not been decided, and the material is still being written and added to. Braden summed it up. "We began last vac with 14 sketches. Now we have six, one for each member of the cast and a girl left over for me."

the washing powder, which ended with me tipping some Tide into a cereal bowl and eating it. The amazing thing was we always did it with real Tide, we never used a substitute. We were real purists, people could tell if it was rice or cocaine or whatever. Robert was rather good at understanding theatre and the dramatic shape of it and interested in exploring the concept of comedy and all that, which I was less interested in. But I could see it made us a bit different from the others.'

JOHN CLEESE: In my first few years in this business I always felt that sitting down to write with someone was a bit like dating, that your ego was, to some extent, at stake. You didn't want them to turn down too many of your ideas or think that they weren't funny, and similarly you were fairly careful and tactful if they came up with something you didn't like. We had no experience, we had no confidence. It was like two fairly inexperienced people dating, and I think most people found it like that. Many turned into long-term relationships, like Marty Feldman and Barry Took, Galton and Simpson. A lot of people describe writing partnerships as being quite like marriages, because you spend their seven or eight hours a day with this guy which is actually longer than you spent with your wife.

MICHAEL PALIN: We discussed everything together, but like any

writing relationship that I've ever known, at times you'd just go off and write one whole thing yourself, other things we'd write in collaboration. We spent quite a bit of time on our cabaret, but then we had time, because it was my first year. The reason was that I had a more traditional view of university, and I was thinking I should play football and sport, a kind of extension of what I'd been doing at Shrewsbury. But Robert saw that as wasted time and was quite instrumental in my giving up that side of things. Without those things to do, there was a little bit more time in the afternoons and evenings. I suppose Robert was, in a way, quite deliberately manipulative. He could sense that we were onto a good thing and so he made quite sure that he organised my life around doing these shows. Once we'd done a few of course, I got an appetite for them and enjoyed it and just forgot about the football.

The first paid job we had was to do the cabaret for the Oxford University Psychology Department Christmas Party. There was complete silence through most of it and at the end they applauded and said it was wonderful, in Freudian terms.

ERIC IDLE: The level of comedy around at Cambridge was of such a high standard because Cook had been through there, Miller had been through there. You have to be really funny, and you have to get these huge laughs. There is a tradition of this, you've got to be good. I don't think the subject matter is so important. It opened up a box where you weren't afraid to write sketches about Proust, but of course you don't have to know Proust to enjoy the 'Summarise Proust Competition'. It's just a wider range of subject matter. You can deal with philosophers, but as piss artists. I don't think there's anything in it that you can't understand if you haven't been to university. It's not important in that way.

TERRY JONES: I was never comfortable when I started performing. I never knew what I was doing really! Maybe I'm exaggerating, but I had so little experience, and with a lot of plays I had no idea what they were going on about. I was always a big worrier as well. I remember playing the role in *Professor Taranne*. Somebody had got a wig for me, it had been sent up from London and I hadn't tried it and just before going on stage I was trying this wig on and it was just terrible. I didn't know how to put it on. Eventually I abandoned it and had to do it without the wig.

I enjoyed doing comedy. But what I found so mysterious with plays was I had no idea what the audience was thinking. We would be doing pieces, mostly two-handers, very intimate plays, with a lot

SIGMA ALPHA EPSILON

SPRING 1960

of dialogue. I enjoyed it but I would just wonder what the audience thought all the time. In comedy you'll get a reaction so you know where you are, so it's much more reassuring.

TERRY GILLIAM: I did some acting on stage in college, such as Chekhov's *The Three Sisters*. I played one of the old comical retainers. And I designed the sets. Then at the fraternities – I was a member of Sigma Alpha Epsilon – every year there would be the Fraternity Sing, a battle between the four fraternities. After joining the fraternity, I decided I didn't want to be in it. But they still allowed me to come to all the good events, like the Homecoming Parade where I built a float which took the form of a giant chicken. It was always the making of things that got me going. For the Sing we would put on comic sketches.

ERIC IDLE: I wouldn't describe myself as self-confident, I was just totally ignorant. I fell into a play and they said, 'Well, there's a party …' What's interesting for me is why I decided to perform cabaret at this party. That's really an interesting move at the end of my first term. I don't understand that – why? It was held in somebody's room downstairs, and somebody must have said, 'Oh well, do some entertainment.'

The Way of the Lion

Cal Epsilon of Sigma Alpha Epsilon

Performing's a good way of hiding. I equate it as more like hiding in the spotlight. Putting a cap on and going out. Sometimes you feel more comfortable being in that spotlight world than you do off-stage. I'm a very instinctive performer. I don't think too much about it. I just find myself able to do it and I don't know what that is or where exactly that comes from. I really don't. I'm not being disingenuous. I remember doing it in the junior school, there was this woman who came in and did voice classes and acting, and I remember people looking at me and going 'God!' I must have thrown myself into a character or something and I just remember their reaction afterwards, going 'Whoa'. So I don't know what that is. I can't tell. I wouldn't necessarily describe it as confidence.

MICHAEL PALIN: I didn't seem to have too much problem with performing. I think I'd gained a certain amount of confidence from doing these three or four plays in Sheffield, which were done before quite big audiences at the Library Theatre. Of course I had the usual few nerves before you go on. But once I was there, I so enjoyed performing that that took care of any nerves. The actual delivery of the material justified any slight collywobbles you might have. My feeling was always 'Why me? Why should these people come and look at me?' Robert didn't seem to share that, he always felt that people were quite happy to come and see him. But I always felt, 'What is this?' Once you have established that you are a comedy act and people know you for that, then I found that was much easier and I'd just deliver what we were expected to deliver at endless balls and parties and often university do's.

ERIC IDLE: In my final year, I was suddenly the President of the Footlights where you get this awful pink jacket. So I decided that we'd have to have women in the revue. I said 'This is really stupid,' and insisted on changing the rules and admitting women. So my Footlights was really bustling and then I also introduced associate membership so we

could have girls for lunch and things, because the Footlights had its own club room, it was fantastic. We had a bar, we'd open after 11, we could stay up all night if we wanted, drinking, it was a fantastic world. We had it really well organised, absolutely brilliant.

TERRY JONES: In my third year I had what was more or less the lead in a show called *Hang Down Your Head and Die*. That was done by two guys called Braham Murray and David Wright. It was in the style of Joan Littlewood's *Oh What a Lovely War!*, based on the idea of doing 'total theatre'. The subject matter dealt with capital punishment and again we spent two terms on that one, so we did it at the end of my Easter term. We improvised things, taking the subject to the cast to generate their own material, and the idea was that David Wright would then take it off and compile it all. I was playing the condemned man. I'd been asked to do some Shakespeare for OUDS, but I chose to do *Hang Down Your Head and Die* instead because I thought it sounded more interesting. It seemed like an odd thing because somebody offering you a part in *the* big Shakespeare production of the year was a big thing.

It was all very interesting, but nobody really knew what they were doing in a way. There was this bit we'd come to in the rehearsal and they said, 'Oh that's when you do your dance sequence, Terry.' And I said 'What's it going to be?' and they said, 'Helen's going to show you, Helen's the choreographer.' But I never seemed to get together with Helen. Eventually we sat down but Helen didn't seem to have any idea, and I had no idea either. In the end I said 'Maybe I should treat it as a mime.'

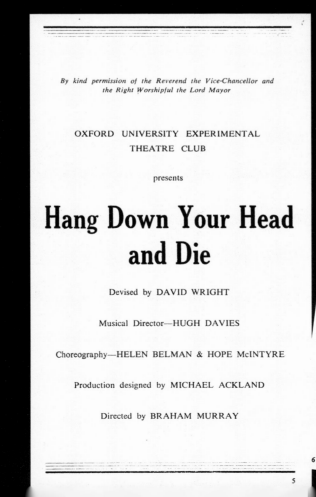

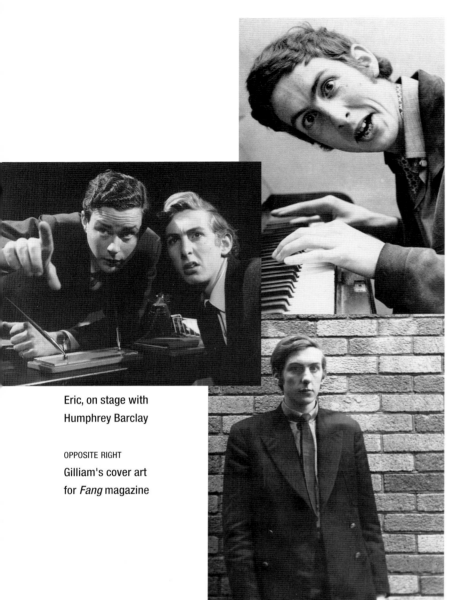

Eric, on stage with
Humphrey Barclay

OPPOSITE RIGHT
Gilliam's cover art
for *Fang* magazine

MICHAEL PALIN: *Hang Down Your Head and Die* was in my second year in the spring term, or the Hilary Term as they call it, and that was an Experimental Theatre Club production, in which myself, Robert Hewison and Terry Jones were all part of a quite large cast. We also wrote material for that.

TERRY JONES: Mike was still writing with Robert Hewison at the time, but obviously we were doing a bit because we'd worked on the slapstick lecture together. We did *Hang Down Your Head and Die* in Oxford and it was a big success. But it was a nightmare doing it because the script seemed to me like a total mess. Mike and Robert Hewison were in it doing various funny turns, and I remember the three of us sitting up all night once because we were so worried about it – it must have been just a week or two before we were opening the show and we stayed up all night trying to make some shape out of it. Then we went to Braham and David saying, 'We think you should do this.' And they didn't take any notice of us, so when we did the first full rehearsal it was three hours long. So then they pushed it back a bit more into the shape

we were talking about. Michael York was in it, his name was Michael Johnson then, he was a ringmaster, and the whole thing was done as a circus.

MICHAEL PALIN: The show was a big success and was brought into the West End by a producer called Michael Codron and we did six weeks at the Comedy Theatre during the holidays in 1964. That was my first real introduction to London. I stayed with Robert and it was really quite exciting. We were in a West End theatre, and had very good reviews, so we also had a bit of confidence going there and it was quite a hard-hitting show to do. There was comedy in it, but there was also some quite dramatic and serious material, sequences where we would just sit on stage in a long line all in our clown outfits looking at the audience without saying anything. Ethel and Julius Rosenberg had been killed for spying, and we just sat there for the length of time it took for them to die from cyanide. It was only about 55 seconds before she was actually pronounced dead and that's how long we sat there for, but it was an incredibly powerful moment. All the noise of London outside and the underground rattling through and we were just absolutely silent on stage. So it was good strong stuff. And we were getting paid reasonably, but even then I didn't really feel that this was going to lead to a career because it was acting and my parents' attitude was that acting was just about OK provided you did your work. Basically it was a dangerous irrelevance to the rest of life and they had successfully brainwashed me into thinking that I couldn't become an actor. I didn't know if I would ever be able to justify it and they would cut off what little money they gave me anyway.

TERRY JONES: We were at the Comedy Theatre during the vacation before my finals and my family was a bit alarmed at this, as I should have been studying. I couldn't bear the thought of going home because I thought they'd just be so worried about me, so what I did instead was rent a terribly small room in Earls Court. We did six weeks at the Comedy Theatre, so it was my first taste of living in London. I don't know what my parents thought of me being on stage really. I'd always jumped through the hoops for them and at this point I really didn't let them influence me much.

ERIC IDLE: I wrote a song at Cambridge called 'I'm too Old to Be a Popular Star', which is one of the first songs I ever wrote. Obviously, pop music had a huge influence on us at school. It provided us with a focus and an identity outside of our school and the context in which we were. We could identify with it and it was our music. As one got a bit older, one got into jazz music, and jazz was really hip and cool. Then, when you got to Cambridge, suddenly the Beatles came through in my first year and everything changed again. The whole of England was altered; there was a big change in England brought about by the Beatles. Where everybody had been wearing tweed jackets with leather elbows, suddenly we were wearing leather jackets, and it was cool and you'd discuss your favourite George solo and things like that. That really made a difference and that kept going throughout the '60s until glam rock, at which point you went 'Oh, fuck off'. You'd think 'I don't have to keep buying these records any more', because that used to be an event for us. Going down and buying the new Beatles album was something I did with Tim Brooke-Taylor. We were quite mature men but still excited to go and buy the new Beatles album, even when we'd left Cambridge and were working for the BBC.

TERRY GILLIAM: In my senior year we took over what was the college's literary magazine and turned it into a humour magazine called *Fang*. Where before they maybe got three issues out a year, we got six issues out and they were packed with funny stuff. I was inspired by Harvey Kurtzman and *Mad* comic, which had been my favourite comic book. *Mad* was in the early '50s; that's really when I started drawing cartoons more seriously, because the cartoonists in *Mad* were brilliant – Wally Wood, Jack Davis and Willie Elder, these were the guys. I was saying, 'I want to draw like that.' Around the time I was in college Harvey quit *Mad* after a big fight with the publishers, and *Mad Magazine* continued as what it is today. Harvey started *Help*, which was the only national humour magazine going.

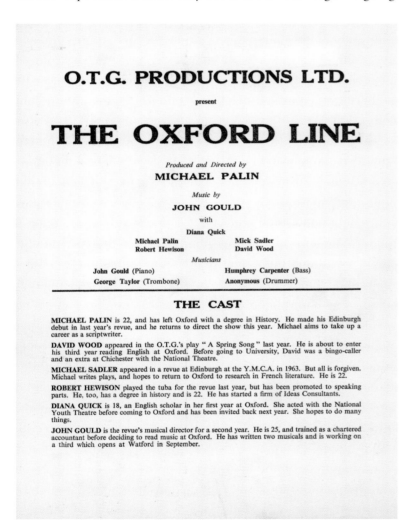

They gave us this huge house in Edinburgh, which somebody had willed or left to Edinburgh University, and there was nothing in it except a bathroom with taps that actually had water coming out of them. We all slept on inflatable plastic things with dirty sheets and had a great time. The show was very successful with audiences. We were packed every night.

MICHAEL PALIN: There was a very important outfit at university called the Oxford Theatre Group, which was actually started by my brother-in-law and another mad gentleman in the 1950s specifically to finance and produce work for the Edinburgh Festival. Robert helped found an offshoot group, the Oxford Revue Group, to take a revue up to the Edinburgh Fringe.

TERRY JONES: Ian Davidson was running the Experimental Theatre Club Revue, and used to do these wonderful cabarets with Robin

Suddenly, there was *Mad*, but that was for kids, *Help* was a much more intelligent, sophisticated thing. We always thought it was great and we tried to emulate it when we could. So I started sending copies of *Fang* off to Harvey in New York, and he wrote back saying, 'It's a really nice magazine, blah blah …' That was the beginning of my connection with that.

JOHN CLEESE: The next show I did with Footlights was the first time we went up to the Edinburgh Fringe. It was a very good experience.

Grove-White and Doug Fisher. They were the kings of comedy in Oxford at that time and they were doing the Oxford Revue up in Edinburgh, called the '****' show. The fourth member of the cast was Paul McDowel who was then singing with a band called the Temperance Seven. They'd just had a top hit with 'You're Driving Me Crazy', which had got to number one, so Paul suddenly had to go off to do this. Obviously he was making money and he was much in demand, so he fell out of the revue. Ian had seen me in *Loitering with Intent* and during that vacation he rang me up and asked if I would come and take Paul's place. So it was Paul McDowel who really got me into revue. By default.

Being drafted in at the last minute made it quite difficult really because they'd done it the year before with another guy, and they were always telling me how Tim used to do it. I was trying to be somebody else, although we did do the slapstick lecture in that show, which was one of mine.

Doug, Mike, Robert and I wrote the next one. It was the Oxford Revue, which was the last one I did.

MICHAEL PALIN: That's what I was asked to do in the summer of 1964.

TERRY JONES: The Oxford Revue felt different to what we'd done before. I wasn't writing with Mike at that point. I was writing with Miles Kington, and Miles and I had three or four sketches in the revue. But we felt our revue was different, because whereas the other ones had been very much satire, the Oxford Revue was very much more fantasy, much more off the wall, and it was hugely successful in Edinburgh.

What always interested me in comedy was when it became conceptual as well, when it had ideas that were contained in the humour, and the way it played around with the form. One of the most influential sketches for me was in the first cabaret I ever went to and I saw Doug Fisher, Ian Davidson and Robin Grove-White doing a sketch called 'Tennis'. It was just two people standing each side of the stage and Ian Davidson came and sat on the back of the chair in the middle. Robin says, 'Didn't see you at Margaret's party last night', and Doug says, 'No, I wasn't invited.' Then Ian says

'"What do you do?" We said, "We do jokes and sketches." He said, "You got anything blue?" We said, "Well, not really. They're just sort of funny ideas and that." His eyes rolled heavenwards and he delivered us like Christians to the lions as we went out there. That was the last time we did a full cabaret.'

'15-Love', and they have this conversation like a tennis match and it was just one of those wonderful things. When I saw it I thought, 'That's such a brilliant conceptual idea.' So that became something I wanted to emulate.

MICHAEL PALIN: In a pub called the King's Head a man called Doug Fisher, who was an absolutely brilliant performer and hero-worshipped by most of us at that time, asked me if I would be one of the team at the Edinburgh Festival and I was a bit embarrassed because clearly he hadn't asked Robert. I said, 'Well I work in a team, there's two of us,' and Doug said, 'There's only really one place because we've got the others.' Terry Jones was doing it, and we both knew Terry and highly respected him. I had really mixed feelings because I was terribly excited and flattered to be asked and then a bit worried about what it would do for our writing relationship and our friendship, which was quite close. In the end Robert came up and played the tuba in the orchestra and watched it from the sidelines, and I think was probably a bit hurt that he wasn't part of it. But our relationship survived and we still see each other, so it was OK. However, that was quite a turning point. Being in that revue was probably the single most important career move I made at university.

TERRY JONES: The revue had transferred to London, but we were a bit disappointed because the only offer we got was to play at the Establishment Club. It was Willie Donaldson who organised it.

JOHN CLEESE: Some critics did make mention of the fact that there were what they referred to as certain sadistic elements in our show, but I had learned something just from audience reaction. You see, when you're with friends you often make quite hard-edged jokes because your friends know you don't really mean it. It's more like a conceit than something that you mean and so we all say these wicked things, like when the Challenger shuttle exploded with seven people on board. Within a week I remember somebody said, 'Do you know what NASA stands for? – Need Another Seven Astronauts.' People will always make those kind of jokes. But you don't make them in public. What I discovered was sometimes that when Graham and I were writing, a funny hard line would come along and I would think, 'Well, it's only the Footlights, let's try it,' because even if I don't know them all, it was a friendly place, and these lines would get the biggest laughs. So more and more I would put what I call these harder lines in and more and more I was rewarded with the biggest laughs. So I learned that it was OK and that what I would laugh at with Chapman, in fact the audience would laugh at too. In England round about this time, after *Beyond the Fringe*, we were beginning to put much harder humour in, because after all you couldn't get much harder than *Beyond the Fringe* and nobody fainted because of that, it was the biggest show in London.

MICHAEL PALIN: By my third and final year, Robert and I had done a lot of work getting together a group called the Et Ceteras which was designed to be an Oxford version of the Footlights. And in my last year, although I had to work for exams, Robert and I put together a show called *Keep This to Yourself*, which was on at the Playhouse in Oxford.

My last appearance with Robert as a double act was at a holiday camp in Pagham, which is a fairly nondescript place somewhere on the south coast. That's when we realised that Oxford cabaret didn't really have an extended life outside Oxford. It might have been OK in the centre of London but it wasn't particularly good in a holiday camp on the south coast. It was the last night there, so there was a lot of drinking going on at the bar and not many people could hear it. We gathered together in the kitchen before going on – you had to go through the kitchen onto the stage – and the compère looked at us sadly and said, 'What do you do?' We said, 'We do jokes and sketches.' He said, 'You got anything blue?' We said, 'Well, not really. They're just sort of funny ideas and that.' His eyes rolled heavenwards and he delivered us like Christians to the lions as we went out there. That was the last time we did a full cabaret.

MICHAEL PALIN: It was different writing with Terry because he and Robert were just very different people really. In a sense Terry was less driven than Robert was, but Terry, like me, was interested in building up characters, not really so interested in the world outside or seeing comedy as something fashionable, if you like. So our approach together was slightly different. Terry was particularly keen on little films and he would have his 8mm camera, and we used to shoot little films in the back garden of his house in Claygate and rush around moving the chairs in different directions, so when he put it together, the chairs would appear to whiz around. Also, Terry was more of an actor than Robert. Robert was sharp, he was incisive, he was clever. But Terry was very sympathetic on stage, and also a very good straight actor and a very good physical actor as well. There was probably more of an actor's relationship between the two of us as we were writing. I felt with Robert, in a sense, I was trying to write to some standard that he wanted; with Terry it wasn't like that. We were a meeting of minds and what we thought was funny together was something altogether more simple and, in a sense, a touch less contrived. It just seemed to happen.

JOHN CHAPMAN: Graham was in the Footlights along with people like Cleese, David Hatch, Humphrey Barclay, Bill Oddie and Tim Brooke-Taylor, they were all involved at that time. I think he regarded himself as being a bit of a dilettante in the world of revue, show business and that sort of thing. But his primary concern was don't give up the day job, the medicine.

PAM CHAPMAN: He didn't have to work very hard at medicine.

JOHN CHAPMAN: He was always bloody bright. He was a lot brighter than me.

PAM CHAPMAN: He was extremely bright, he wasn't a slogger. He didn't have to swot for exams and that sort of thing, he was one of those annoying people!

JOHN CHAPMAN: Despite the time he spent with the Footlights, he did not neglect his studies, certainly at that stage. He was able to take that in his stride and do much more.

GRAHAM CHAPMAN: The Footlights' final examination took place over two weeks in June at the Cambridge Arts Theatre, and if you earned a distinction, you would be offered postgraduate work at the Oxford Playhouse and the Traverse, Edinburgh; picking up a Ph.D. at the Lyric Theatre, Shaftesbury Avenue; followed by a lecture tour of New Zealand and culminating in a Full Doctorate on Broadway. Our exams were open to public scrutiny, they were rigorous and cruelly fair. If you got laughs, you passed – if not, you failed. Compared to these, the university exams were about as reliable a guide to a student's ability as the width of his mother's kneecaps, and I treated them with the nonchalance they deserved.[4]

TERRY JONES: I think education was a very big factor in Python in a way, because I think that's partly what got us interested in comedy, in that it was a kind of literate comedy. You knew *Beyond the Fringe* had come from a kind of literate thing. It had sparked this whole satire movement, which was about something because it was making fun of the government. It actually had targets, so you could see that comedy wasn't just something that was simply funny ha-ha. It now seemed to have more importance than it had done in the past. Not only did it make fun of topical people and events but it informed you about them as well. Realising that you could have a literate form of comedy, an informed comedy, was influential in making it something you felt was worth doing. All the revues we did were very much modelled on *Beyond the Fringe*, even though we hadn't seen it. Certainly a show like '****' was modelled on it.

JOHN CLEESE: I don't think education was very important, but I think intelligence played an enormous part. For example, two of the brightest people I ever met were Frank Muir and Denis Norden. I don't think they had vast formal education. They were hugely intelligent. On the whole, in those days, I think you could say that the most intelligent people had been to university, but I think intelligence was very important and education was secondary. After all, if you're intelligent, you can always educate yourself later on. It was 90 per cent intelligence, 10 per cent education.

ERIC IDLE: I think history played a big part in Python. Terry did history, Mike did history, I did history up to A level. When people say it's undergraduate humour I think they're wrong, it's postgraduate humour. By the time we're writing Python we've all been through Cambridge or Oxford.

the performers afterwards. He didn't actually talk to me much, he shook my hand and all that, but he talked to Doug and that's when I realised that it's about writing as well. That's why this man who represented one of the funniest and most successful modern television shows, *That Was The Week That Was*, was in our midst, because he wanted writers and performers. There was a little glimpse then when he came up: yes, he's recruiting people for paid work after university and it's not just about acting, it's about revue and it's about what Robert and I had been doing for three or four years; it's about writing and playing characters and being ahead of the game and not just doing Shakespeare plays or even modern theatrical documentaries like *Hang Down Your Head and Die*. So that was when I suddenly felt: yes, this was where you could make the bridge, and of course eventually that was the bridge we crossed when Frost, two years later, recruited us for this new series, *The Frost Report*. He got in touch with Terry and myself who were then struggling to write something called *The Love Show* and said, 'Would you come in as writers on this new series?' I was able to present that to my parents and the world generally as being something quite respectable. I was working with David Frost in a new BBC programme. As long as it had BBC on the end of it, it was fine.

ERIC IDLE: Life doesn't happen like that. You don't sit and think, 'I'm going to have a career now.' Things just happen.

GRAHAM CHAPMAN: I left Cambridge with a BA in Natural Sciences (lower second class), several bottles of the college sherry and a Ph.D. in Claret.[4]

JOHN CLEESE: I hadn't the slightest intention of leaving the law. It never occurred to me for a moment that I would go into show business. That's one of those things, like the importance of money or the old culture of deference, that has changed so much. Now it's very hard for anyone to realise what it was like before the British became so interested in money. They were always competitive with status symbols, but not money itself. To go out and get money was considered slightly vulgar. It really was. It's utterly changed.

No one had ever thought you even could go into show business as a possible career until our year. The people who'd done it before, Richard Murdock, Jimmy Edwards, Peter Cook, were absolute exceptions and it never occurred to me to go into show business until I was approached by the BBC and suddenly thought, 'Why not?' It was the BBC, and there was a pension plan, so my parents were much less worried by it.

MICHAEL PALIN: Funnily enough, when we did the Oxford Revue in Edinburgh, David Frost came up to a performance and mingled with

TERRY GILLIAM: I started college as a physics major. Science and maths at that time were being pushed. Within a few weeks I realised that was a big mistake. Then I became an art major but I couldn't stand the art history professor, it bored me, I just wanted to get on and paint and draw and sculpt. So I quit that one and then became a political science major because it had the least number of required courses. So I could take oriental philosophy, I could take drama, and I basically got a very liberal education which I thought was more intelligent than everybody else, who were all becoming specific and focused.

Earlier on in my junior year I wanted to be an architect, but that didn't last very long. I went to work in an architect's office one summer and just hated it. When I saw the way the architecture office worked and how the designs were constantly being compromised by the clients, I thought it was disgusting. This firm was a very successful one in LA and they were very good at bending over backwards to the demands of the clients rather than fighting for good designs. That's probably why they were successful, because they appeased. So I dropped that and then I didn't really know what I was going to do. After graduating everybody was going off to do what they wanted to do and I really didn't have a clue what I wanted to do.

JOHN CLEESE: When I was at Cambridge I had a number of people that I got on with very well, but I don't think I had any idea of how to open up in such a way that any of my friendships were based on anything that was all that real. In other words they were social relationships rather than anything deeper.

TERRY JONES: I started sharing a flat with Noel Picarda, who had been President of the Union and had a place in Goodge Street. I lived there for about six months and Noel was an outrageous man. Then I moved to Lambeth and I was living there with Nigel Walmsey, who now runs Carlton Television, and we had a place we rented for £4 a week in Black Prince Road, just south of the river. It was a great location, next to Lambeth Walk, it's all been knocked down now. That Christmas I appeared in something Noel was responsible for, called *The Carrierbaggers*. It was a Christmas pantomime at the Poor Millionaire Club, a take-off of Harold Robbins's *The Carpetbaggers*, which was a big Hollywood movie. We used to do our version, but as a pantomime. It was so embarrassing! We'd do it to these few dozen Japanese businessmen who'd been conned into coming into this wretched nightclub. They thought they were going to get some sexy girls and instead they got me, Sandra Carron (who was Alma Cogan's sister) and Richard Stilgoe. That was fun. Then Willie Donaldson commissioned me to write *The Love Show* and I brought Michael in. Miles didn't want to do it. I'd written one version of it for which Willie Donaldson paid me £50 and then I brought Michael in to do a new draft.

MICHAEL PALIN: At the end of my time at Oxford, I had a lot of acting offers and things like that. By that time I had worked with Terry on the Oxford revue, and acting with Terry, there were certain things we did together which seemed to work awfully well and awfully easily and there was a rapport between us. Terry had gone down a year before, and then he called and asked would I come and write this project called *The Love Show*. That was it really. I think he just wanted me to work on it, not me and Robert, partly because Robert had very strong ideas of what he wanted to do, and this was Terry's project and he wanted to stay in control. He probably saw me as a little more malleable than Robert and once I'd agreed that, I got the first pay cheque I ever received in my professional life. It was for £50 signed by Willie Donaldson in a pub in Sloane Square. Once I'd agreed to do it, I was then spending a lot of time with Terry, and Robert got the message, as it were and, besides, he had other things to do. Robert was quite keen on teaching and went to work at Ravensbourne Art College and taught about television there. It was a fairly natural parting. We both realised this wasn't going to be something that could go on and on. Once I'd started doing *The Love Show*, then that led to a writing relationship with Terry, rather than with Robert, and so when David Frost came along, it was Terry and myself that he was after. We were a team.

GRAHAM CHAPMAN: Whatever the failings of the Footlights it was in fact more important than Cambridge University. Invisible to the outside world, but painfully obvious when you went for your first fitting, the University wore rose-coloured contact lenses. All it could offer was three years of dull and pointless work, with no hope of a job at the end of it, while Footlights had a much more practical and enjoyable syllabus, ending with a very good chance of achieving what every human being really wants: fame.[4]

Terry Jones hits London –
Michael Palin hits Edinburgh

JOHN CLEESE: Two of the sketches that I wrote for the '61 Footlights Revue were later done on *That Was The Week That Was* because David Frost knew about them. He got me jolly good payments, too, something like £30, more money than I'd ever seen in my life. I'd taught for £5 a week, so to get £30 a sketch was unbelievable. They did it by inflating the length of the sketches, which was very nice, pretending I'd written a five-minute sketch, when really it was three minutes. You got £6 a minute.

GRAHAM CHAPMAN: To supplement my meagre student grant I decided to do some cabaret. Full of confidence, being ex-Footlights, Tony Hendra and myself went along to the Blue Angel nightclub for an audition. We chose the Blue Angel because it was one of the best nightclub spots for revue and we'd read in the *Stage* – in an advertisement that sounded like whistling in the dark – how David

LIFE BEFORE THE CIRCUS

'That's why Python

isn't like this huge thing

that comes out of nowhere,

it's this froth of ongoing

shows, a bubble

that got bigger . . .'

Frost had recently been retained there for a 'second glorious month'. However, we were accepted at the audition and in two weeks' time found ourselves top of the bill, which meant that we didn't start our act until any time from 2 to 2.30 a.m., meaning that I didn't get back to College until 3.30, having to get up again at 8.30 in time for a ward round at 9. I found this routine too gruelling after five more weeks and we left the Blue Angel, to be followed by a promising newcomer called Dave Allen.[4]

JOHN CLEESE: I wasn't going to the BBC as a performer, I was going as a writer who was theoretically going to be trained as a producer, although that never happened. This offer came during the two weeks that *Cambridge Circus* was playing at the Arts Theatre, before it moved onto the West End. The first thing I had to do was to extract myself from the firm of lawyers I was lined up to work for.

They were fairly astonished but very nice about it. The second thing was to do this little flurry of extra engagements that came up before we went in the West End; the third thing was to get into the West End and start performing; and then the fourth thing was, after a little bit of time, to start work at the BBC, which felt like a very good place to be.

ERIC IDLE: Humphrey Barclay who had directed *Clump of Plinths*, sent me a telegram when I was on holiday in Germany saying 'Come immediately, need you to perform in Edinburgh,' and I came back home and went straight into rehearsal for the Edinburgh Festival. It was myself, Richard Eyre, Graeme Garden and Humphrey Barclay. And we did the material from the *Clump of Plinths* show, which was now *Cambridge Circus*. I did most of the Oddie songs and some bits of material that I'd already done in the Pembroke Smoker in '63, like 'BBC BC', and it was a really amazing show. We got rave notices because it was good material. The first rave notice I ever had said 'they attract admiration as effortlessly as the sun attracts the flowers'.

TERRY JONES: After college, one of the ITV companies paid me £200 to write a TV play called *The Present*. I think it may have been based on something Miles and I had written, but instead of writing this thing with Miles I'd decided to write it on my own for some reason. Maybe I thought I couldn't live on half of £200.

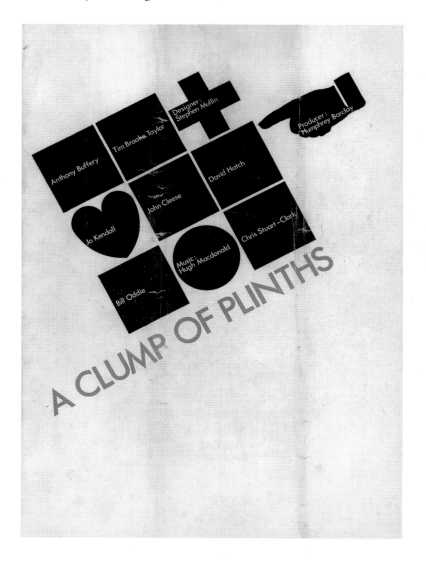

JOHN
THE PROSECUTING COUNSEL

After the '****' revue, I spent a week with Miles in London. He was living in Addison Road with his girlfriend Nancy and he had a lovely big room. They had a big bed at one end of the room and I slept in a sleeping bag at the other end. We spent a week and we wrote three radio shows, one for Max Bygraves and a couple for somebody else. We wrote those radio shows on spec and nothing ever happened to them. Then, after I came down, Miles didn't want to write *The Love Show*. Mike got involved, and after he'd finished *Now!* I said to Mike, 'They want some continuity scripts for *The Billy Cotton Band Show*, do you want to come and do that?' So Mike and I started writing continuity scripts for *Kathy Kirby* and *The Billy Cotton Band Show* and stuff like that.

MICHAEL PALIN: I had to have some money after I left university, especially if I was going to stay down in London, and I did odd jobs for my sister who was working at the BBC then. She got me a job as a DJ in a thing called *Roundabout*, a 5 to 6 o'clock programme. The first half-hour was middle of the road, young-audience orientated, then the last half-hour you could be slightly more risqué. I did that and made a bit of money, and I was also greatly helped by a man called Teddy Warrick. He got me little jobs here and there. Then a girl I'd known at Oxford called Jan Elsom put me in touch with these two writers called Joe Steeples and Michael Wale, who were looking for presenters for a new television pop show based in Bristol. At that time comedy had suffused everything, even pop

shows, so instead of having lots of pop groups, you would have vaguely satirical presenters who would comment on them and do a little joke and a sketch in between the songs. Then you'd have a fashion section where you'd show the latest Mary Quant fashions and all that, so pop had become a kind of magaziney thing.

Anyway, they'd invented this format called *Now!* and I passed the audition to be one of the four presenters. In the end they got rid of the other three and I remained the sole presenter and it gave me six months of quite well-paid work. It was £35 a week minimum and £5 if I went up the day before.

TERRY JONES: When Mike left Oxford, he immediately went off to the West Country, to Wales, to do *Now!*. It was only when he came back from *Now!* that he decided not to work with Robert. Doing *The Love Show* with me was his way of breaking his writing partnership with Robert, because there was a period when he wasn't around and when he came back I'd got into the BBC.

MICHAEL PALIN: On *Now!* I did sketches and presented these various groups. Some of the groups we had on were very good – The Yardbirds, The Animals, Them, John Mayall's Bluesbreakers – some of them were very bad. In fact, most of them were very bad, but that show gave me a financial cushion which ran from October/November '65 until it finally petered out in May/June of '66. That gave me enough money to be able to work with Terry for very little, develop a few ideas of my own for the BBC, get married, which I did in April of '66, and generally feel the world was OK. I was in television. I never could tell my parents what I was doing; fortunately they couldn't see *Now!* in Sheffield. The thing I enjoyed most about *Now!* was actually doing the sketches and having some input into them. I didn't write them, Michael and Joe wrote them, but it was the performing that was the best thing, me being in a studio. I wasn't being marketed as Michael Palin particularly, I was just this guy who happened to do a lot of the sketches and could do a few funny voices. Stardom didn't really come into it, to be honest. Sadly no one said, 'Hey, Michael, you're getting a big following here', because the show's ratings sunk slowly. Can you have exponential droop as well as an exponential curve? Anyway, it failed exponentially.

TERRY GILLIAM: I'd given up summer work completely. In my second year I quit working on the

Chevrolet assembly line. I worked nights and I said fuck this, I am never going to work for money ever again in my life. So I quit and I got a job in a children's theatre where I made sets, and painted myself green and played the ogre. I was reading Moss Hart's autobiography, *Act One*, all about this bare-foot boy with cheek coming down to New York and meeting up with George Kaufman, and then suddenly they're Kaufman and Hart writing all these great plays. I thought I've got to go to New York. So I wrote to Harvey Kurtzman at *Help* magazine and said I'm coming to New York and he wrote me a letter saying, 'Don't bother, there's nothing here for you kid.' But I just went to New York. I didn't have any plans other than I wanted to go to New York and meet Harvey. I met him in the Algonquin Hotel, which was great, especially after reading Moss Hart's autobiography and all those tales of the Algonquin round table. Harvey had taken a suite upstairs and stuffed all his cartoonists in there and they were working on this thing. There were all my heroes in this room – fantastic. It turned out that Chuck Alverson, whom I wrote *Jabberwocky* with, who was then the assistant editor on the magazine, was quitting and they needed somebody to take his job. And I walked right into it.

I was thinking, 'This isn't supposed to happen like this.' But it happened to Moss Hart and it happened to me just like that. It's very weird because it's almost like you're willing something to happen; having read the story and knowing this can happen, I was going to go and see. But the luck involved in this was great. So for three years in New York Harvey and I did the magazine. There was him, me and a guy named Harry Chester, who was the production

guy, and that was the magazine. And it was this amazing focus for people because it was before *National Lampoon* was created, so all the guys who became the great underground comic artists, Bob Crumb, Gilbert Shelton, Jay Lynch, all these guys had their stuff in *Help*. I knew 'em all, they usually stayed at my place.

GRAHAM CHAPMAN: John Cleese, who had just finished his finals in Cambridge, getting a rather snotty upper second, wanted somewhere to stay in London while he wrote for BBC Radio such things as *Yule Be Surprised*, a Christmas show for Dick Emery. I was very friendly with the junior warden, Buzz Mangrove, and had managed to find a passkey to all of the rooms in the hall of residence (on the black market), and I knew that there were several empty ones. I gave John the key and suggested he should stay in the room normally occupied by a person called Nick Spratt. He returned to England rather sooner than expected to find his room filled with a sleeping John Cleese. But, being a gentleman, he came in and said 'Um, um, yup … er, sorry!' and went out, and slept the rest of the night in the bath.[4]

ERIC IDLE: The thing about our generation at Cambridge was we went straight into television. When we were at Cambridge *That Was The Week That Was* was on and that was all of the people who'd previously been at Cambridge; Frosty and people were writing for it and that's what you did, you aspired to do late-night BBC comedy. That was a possible escape route into something interesting, funny and creative. There was a link there. Natural recruitment. They came looking for you at Cambridge. The same as MI5 or Russian Intelligence came looking. You searched the crop of the universities for the next lot of people. That was a whole new breakout because light entertainment was totally changing, it was no longer these terrible *Billy Cotton Band Show*-type, end of the pier-style shows. What happened was *Beyond the Fringe* went to New York and there was this vacuum; David Frost came in and said, 'Hello, I'll have that vacuum, thank you very much,' and then they did TW3 which was a life-changing show. People were very offended and very upset that they were being mocked. In fact they took it off during the '64 election because it was considered that it would bring down the government, which came down anyway. That's quite an impact for a television show to have.

TERRY JONES: I was in Lambeth and writing *The Love Show*. I even had a London agent who wanted to meet up with me but I was so shy they decided against taking me on, as a performer. That came about because I'd had a big picture in the *Observer* in a review by Bamber Gascoigne of *Hang Down Your Head and Die*. The review said what a wonderful show it was, and had gone on about how wonderful I was with this mime and everything. The only thing was he got the wrong name, because there was no way of knowing who anybody was in the cast. He'd said another cast member was me, so there was a big picture of me and underneath it had somebody else's name. It was 1965 by now and Willie Donaldson had said that the idea of this show, *The Love Show*, was to do something like *Hang Down Your Head and Die*, which made a big impression on people. Willie wouldn't give me anything more definite than

doesn't really want me to be there and what am I going to do, I'm just banging my head against a brick wall. In any case it's not a question of sorting things out with her, I've got to sort things out with myself.' It was one of those moments in life, I was just watching the river going underneath and thinking I've got to sort myself out; so instead of going to Oxford, I turned round and went back to the flat and started trying to get jobs, phoning people up, and the first bite I got was from Anglia Television.

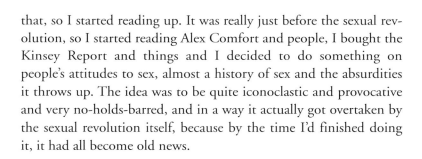

I went up to Norwich and they interviewed me and seemed to be rather impressed that *Cambridge Circus* had done the 'Custard Pie' sketch in New York. I'd rather cheekily taken the credit for it on the grounds that I'd written the text, so I got a good review in the New York Times. 'Who is this Jones? Comedy has need of him,' I think it said. So Anglia Television seemed rather impressed. I've never quite understood why actually. Anyway I was offered a job as a copywriter in Norwich. I was slightly heavy-hearted that I was going into copywriting. Then suddenly I got a phone call from Frank Muir's secretary, who said would I come along and talk to Frank at the BBC. I'd obviously sent a letter to Frank Muir. So I went along to Frank Muir's office, and he said, 'We couldn't offer you very much, only £20 a week, but you'll come into the BBC, see what's going on, you'll have an office, and get to know television from the inside.' It was an amazing offer and so I welched on Anglia Television and took this BBC job. It was actually a very odd brief. I could just hang around, go to all the meetings and see what happened. I was there when they were discussing *Till Death Us Do Part* and whether to put in with Johnny Speight or not. And I was sitting in on the departmental meetings whether to have *The Frost Report* – 'What are we going to do with David Frost?' I was right there on the inside track really.

that, so I started reading up. It was really just before the sexual revolution, so I started reading Alex Comfort and people, I bought the Kinsey Report and things and I decided to do something on people's attitudes to sex, almost a history of sex and the absurdities it throws up. The idea was to be quite iconoclastic and provocative and very no-holds-barred, and in a way it actually got overtaken by the sexual revolution itself, because by the time I'd finished doing it, it had all become old news.

MICHAEL PALIN: *The Love Show* was Terry's idea. He wanted to do a theatrical documentary about attitudes to sex using similar techniques that we'd used in *Hang Down Your Head and Die*. Terry had done an enormous amount of work about attitudes to sex through the ages, the way it had been open in some societies and repressed in others, and the way people had been tortured for licentiousness and others paid well for it. It was a rich area to go into. But how to put it on stage and how to make it work as a narrative, that's what Terry wanted me to work with him on.

TERRY JONES: I'd been down for awhile and I had a Siamese girlfriend, who was giving me a very hard time on the phone and I was getting very angry and one day it seemed to me like it was all over. I can't remember what we were having an argument about, but we were having these terrible phone conversations and after one of them I decided I had to go off to Oxford to see her and be near her. I was halfway over Lambeth Bridge and I suddenly thought, 'What am I doing? Why am I going up to Oxford to be near Oey? She

'Terry had done an enormous amount of work about attitudes to sex through the ages, the way it had been open in some societies and repressed in others, and the way people had been tortured for licentiousness and others paid well for it.'

LEFT TO RIGHT: Bill Oddie, John Cleese, David Hatch, Jo Kendall, Graham Chapman, Jonathan Lynn, Tim Brooke-Taylor.

This is a drawing (made especially for this celebration edition of *Varsity*) of the London-New York cast of "Cambridge Circus" by their director Humphrey Barclay. This was the record-breaking Footlights Revue of 1963, which spawned a group of comedians who have made an enormous mark on the entertainment scene since then. Between them they have created BBC Radio's "I'm Sorry, I'll Read That Again", BBC TV's "Twice A Fortnight", and Rediffusion's "At Last The 1948 Show" and "Do Not Adjust Your Set", four comedy shows which have broken completely new ground. Humphrey Barclay used to draw for *Varsity* and is now a TV producer (with Rediffusion).

I had an office with two typewriters and four telephones, which was rather confusing, on the fourth floor of the TV Centre. The other writer there was John Law, who was writing the Roy Hudd shows. He was a kind of resident comedy writer. This is when the BBC was full of creative people. Richard Waring was in the next office, he was writing *Marriage Lines* with a bottle of whisky under the table, and Robert Gray, who used to write *Pinky & Perky*, was in the next office. I did a lot of script reading and vetting of scripts, tried to write the odd thing and started contributing a few odd jokes. The first one was for Ken Dodd, who was very big then. I'd written these jokes for him and I had to go and show them to him. I went up to this tiny little office on the sixth floor and showed him one visual joke, and that went in. I didn't get a credit for it, when you're BBC staff you don't. But they used it in the *Review of the Year*, it was Ken Dodd's year and they used that clip – my joke!

JOHN CLEESE: At that stage I was just writing sketches and links for a magazine programme. I was perfectly happy, getting paid £30 a week. And enjoying writing scripts. The first thing I ever did was a Christmas special called *Yule Be Surprised*. Then I went on to write for Dick Emery. We used to send the script to him through the post, and he would always turn up at rehearsal and open the envelope for the first time. I was pretty relaxed, happy to be in London and of course I had more money than I ever thought was conceivable at £30 a week. I was able to go and have curries whenever I wanted to, go to the Baker Street Classic Cinema and see all the Marx Brothers movies. It was a good time. Surprisingly, it didn't seem to matter at all that I wasn't performing, though during that time at the BBC two or three shows were created out of the material that we were doing in the West End and all the same performers did them. So I was doing a little bit of performing. But I didn't miss it.

JOHN CHAPMAN: My parents had put a lot into Graham's education and they were a bit against his being over-adventurous in the show-business world. At that time Graham was President of the Students' Union at Bart's and there was an end of term jamboree which involved the Queen Mother coming to visit Bart's. And, being the president, Graham was asked to join her table at tea. He was just making conversation with her, and she asked what his interests were and things like that. When he mentioned that they'd been offered the chance of taking *Cambridge Circus* over to New Zealand, the Queen Mother called over the Dean of the medical school and said, 'You must let him go.' So she put in a good word.

He went off and did an eight-week tour of New Zealand, at which point they got an offer to do a Broadway run in New York. By then my parents were beginning to feel, 'Well maybe there is something to this. Maybe it's an opportunity that shouldn't be missed. He's got so far with his medical career now, it's not going to be completely lost. It can be retrieved later on, why not take the opportunity.'

PAM CHAPMAN: I can remember feeling at the time that it was something that was great fun and everything, and it probably wouldn't last. It was a risky thing to do, go onto the stage, because it wasn't regarded as a proper profession, unless you'd gone to RADA or something like that.

GRAHAM CHAPMAN: March 1964. The new Biochemistry and Physiology Block of St Swithin's Hospital was being opened by Her Majesty the Queen Mother. At the time, being Secretary of the Students' Union, I was invited to join Her Majesty for tea with other representatives of the student body after her tour of the new premises. The Queen Mother had an excellent complexion and was extremely charming. I was very pleased to find out that she had asked to come to tea with the students and not with a lot of old gits in red gowns and stupid floppy hats.

During tea I explained to Her Majesty that I'd had the offer of going to New Zealand as a member of the cast of *Cambridge Circus*, a revue, but that this would mean taking six months off medicine, and my parents had yelped strongly against this. The Royal Person said, 'It's a beautiful place, you must go.' I used this remark on my parents as if it were a royal command, and it worked. My mother was now able to go into the butcher's shop and say, 'Oh, the Queen Mother said he must go.'

Ten minutes later, I was on a plane to Christchurch. John Cleese had a shower in Karachi, lost his watch and held up the plane for an hour while he looked for it. I didn't particularly mind the delay, because I was sitting next to a rather nice looking Commonwealth sailor.[4]

Graham with *Clump of Plinths* co-star David Hatch

JOHN CLEESE: At the beginning of the summer of that year, suddenly somebody starts saying, 'Well, hey guys, what about coming to New Zealand and probably going on to Broadway?' Of course at that age, I don't think anyone was married or thinking about getting married, so you think, 'Why not? It sounds a lot of fun.' So we all met up again and we rehearsed for a couple of months, got on a plane and flew thirty-six hours to New Zealand and arrived in this strange time-warp place that felt like 'England, 1923, South Coast'. It had that feeling about it. Nonetheless we had a hilarious six weeks with a great deal of laughter, a lot of it at the expense of the New Zealanders.

GRAHAM CHAPMAN: Breakfast was served from eight to nine in the morning in a damp room the size of a moist barn. We all gathered together at our table only to be told that we had to sit at a table which was appropriate to our room number or we would not be served. That meant that the nine of us sat at separate tables dotted around the room. There were only two other residents. We shouted at each other across the room, saying that if things didn't improve we'd move out.[4]

JOHN CLEESE: I don't remember spending a great deal of time with Graham when we were in New York or even when we were travelling in New Zealand.

There was a time when I stayed at Barts Hospital. Various people would go on holiday and I was usually able to find a bed in Barts. I stayed for several weeks when I first came to London to work for the BBC. One guy would be out for the week so I'd stay in his room and he'd come back and someone else would go.

When I first went to London to do my job for the BBC I roomed with Brooke-Taylor, Chapman and a medical colleague of Graham's from Hong Kong called Benny Chi Ping Lee, and the four of us had a place in Manchester Street. I didn't see much of Graham, as he would go off to medical school early in the morning. I'd go into the BBC, usually walked in and did a full day's work, and I might see him in the evening. My recollection is that he seemed to me to have very extreme views on selfishness. I remember him going on about how selfish the Buddhists were. He had an ideal of a perfect unselfishness, and one time when I praised the Buddhists or certain aspects of Buddhism to him, he was very dismissive of them and thought they were very selfish, presumably because they took time to themselves and meditated and did things like that. I remember having a couple of arguments with him. I also noticed that he got much more aggressive when he was drinking, whereas when he wasn't drinking, he was very eloquent. That was something

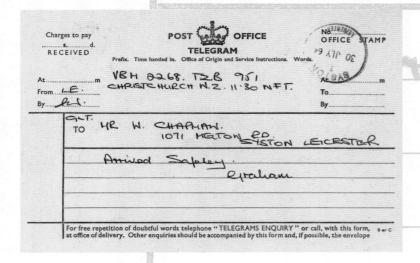

Graham arrives safely on the New Zealand leg of the *Cambridge Circus* tour

that I became much more aware of later on. It was as though his aggression could only come out when he'd been drinking. He found it very hard to assert himself. It ties up psychologically, some kind of over-idealised view of unselfishness with an inability to assert himself.

GRAHAM CHAPMAN: John Cleese and myself decided to have lunch at the hotel because we were performing in the theatre that afternoon and evening, and it didn't seem like that we would get a meal. I asked for a three-egg omelette. The waitress was astonished and said 'What?' I said 'A three-egg omelette' and pointed to the words on

was a pause and then this guy standing behind me saying, 'Hello Eric, going well is it?' I said, 'Yeah', and he said, 'Do you mind joining me on stage?' There was complete silence in the theatre, and I realised at that point that my future was probably more in writing than acting. I'd missed my cue, but he'd been on stage a long time before he'd figured out who was missing and then was very cool coming back to the dressing room and standing behind me.

TERRY GILLIAM: All through college I wanted to make films, but I had no idea how you got there. Growing up in LA, there were all kinds of friends whose parents were in the business, writers, editors,

The open-mouthed cast
of *I'm Sorry, I'll Read That Again*

the menu saying 'three-egg omelette'. She said 'A three-igg omlut?' and I said 'Yis', pointing again. Five minutes later she returned with a large omelette with three fried eggs on top. Even people three tables away threw up.[4]

ERIC IDLE: I was coming down from university and John Cameron and I were supposed to become a kind of Peter and Gordon act. We were going to be this rock 'n' roll comedy thing, but that never led anywhere. The first thing after Cambridge, I went into rep at Leicester. Richard Eyre, who was a friend of mine from the Footlights – we were contemporaries – directed *Oh What a Lovely War!*, so I went off to Leicester and did that. Then I realised I could never be an actor, and I started to write for *I'm Sorry, I'll Read That Again*, sending them scripts, and then Frosty. The long tentacles of Frosty came and picked me up from there. In *Oh What a Lovely War!*, though, you get to play everything, all the parts, but one of the things Richard got me to do was write a scene. I'd never written scenes for a proper play before, but he made me write one. That was really good for me and then they kept me on at Leicester Rep for *One for the Pot*, a dreadful farce, which I hated. I was so bad at it that I would spend my time backstage writing sketches for *I'm Sorry, I'll Read That Again*. I was there writing a sketch one day and there

all that. And then at these summer camps, where I worked during my last two years in college, there were kids from Beverly Hills, like Danny Kaye's daughter, Heddy Lamarr's son, Burt Lancaster's daughter. I was around these people and going to their houses and being astonished by all these Beverly Hills places, but I didn't know how you got to make films. I was really close to the whole thing but frustrated. I knew I didn't want to work my way up through the business. I didn't want to be a tea boy. Again, it was this pact I'd made with myself never to work for money, but also to only do work I had some control over. I made these rules for myself and I stuck by them. I said that's the way I'm going to approach life. Working for *Help*, I was being paid two dollars less than I would have been paid on the dole. But I was doing great work and having a great time. And it allowed me to do other things, like going to film night school, which I only lasted a month because I hated it. I then got a job in a studio that did stop motion animation, dancing cigarette packets and things. I worked there for free. They said we've got no money. I said let me just work, I'll sweep up, whatever – but I was in a place with real cameras and real lights. That was far better than the film school, which I thought was a load of wanking really. I've never learned how to make films, I just watched them.

Then I saved enough money to buy my first Bolex camera and a tape recorder. There were three of us living in this flat and on weekends we'd write a little movie, then go out and shoot it. Just to do this stuff and to play at the business of making movies. We were always stealing film from trash cans and drawing on it. We'd animate right on the clear film and do things like that. So we were constantly doing the beginnings of filmmaking. We never finished anything, we'd get it halfway there, maybe it would be edited and the sound would just be on this tape recorder.

ERIC IDLE: I then worked briefly on a late night show called *Twice a Fortnight*. That was my title. That's about all I wrote for it! Tony Palmer, who was a friend of mine from Cambridge, was in charge of it. He produced Jonathan Miller's *Alice in Wonderland* and Ken Russell's *Isadora*, where he cast me in a brief role alongside Mike and Terry. We were writing for anybody, we were TV writers. I wrote a few minutes for Tommy Cooper. That's what we were doing.

JOHN CHAPMAN: He had quite a marked example from both my father and myself, who smoked pipes, and we both smoked fairly heavily, so I suppose it was almost inevitable.

JOHN CLEESE: Many years later we were filming for the show on the Yorkshire moors. When you're filming you just hang around for hours and there are times when I find I'm going almost crazy with boredom. You can't sit anywhere and read because there's nowhere comfortable to sit, you can't do anything, and so you play all sorts of games. And on this particular occasion I saw Graham put his pipe down. What I did was very silly, but it was because I lacked the insight to understand the meaning of what I was doing: I took his pipe and I popped it in my pocket, and when he turned round and found his pipe was gone, he became so agitated that I realised after quite a short time that something was going on that I didn't understand. So I told him that I'd taken it for a joke and handed it to him, at which point he stepped towards me and literally kneed me in the groin. Fortunately he did not hit the testicles, he hit the bone which hurt a bit but not a lot, and I remember afterwards thinking, 'What on earth was that about?' And then I began to see that that pipe meant a great deal more to Graham symbolically than just being a pipe. And when I was absent from the publicity for *The Holy Grail*, apparently Graham told the *Daily Mirror* a

story which appeared duly the next day about how I had taken his pipe while we were in the studio in London, and how he had pursued me across the studio, ruggertackled me and then sat on my head, and I thought to myself, he really has lost any kind of connection with reality.

TERRY JONES: I had this job and I didn't know quite what it was, script editor, consultant or whatever, and after about six months Frank Muir said, 'Would you like to go on a director's course?' So I went on this directing course. It was great. The best thing I remember was David Attenborough, who was then Controller of BBC2, and Huw Weldon, who was Controller of 1, giving us these brilliant talks about how the BBC worked. Huw Weldon said: 'What the BBC tries to do is keep just one step ahead of public opinion, so we're just pushing the boundaries slightly and not just conforming to the lowest common denominator.' You were supposed to finish the course by doing a little set piece. I was going to do one with Mike. We wrote it together, it was called 'The Body', based on a character of his. We were rehearsing it and I was plotting how we were going to shoot it and everything. Then just before I was supposed to be filming it, I got peritonitis and was rushed off to hospital, so I missed the chance for it. I never made my demonstration film. They had a day in which you had an hour to do your film and then it was somebody else's turn, so that day of a free studio, I just lost it. After that I didn't get any directing work, because I didn't finish the course, but I was taken on as a PA and floor assistant which I was hopeless at. I just got yelled at (quite rightly) by hysterical directors.

TERRY JONES: I was very unhappy being a PA, so eventually the Light Entertainment Department and I kind of mutually agreed to part. Frank said that Rowan Ayres, who ran a show called *Late Night Line Up*, needed somebody to get a funny version of the show together

Michael Palin with his wife Helen interrupts their honeymoon to host the music show *Now!* – that week's guests: Manfred Mann, Pete and Dud, and Paul Jones.

MICHAEL PALIN: Terry was on a director's course at the BBC, and everyone had to produce their own little piece of material and Terry and I wrote a thing called 'The World of Charlie Legs', featuring a character I'd done in revue, a slightly Walter Mitty-esque character. We hoped to get the actress Sarah Miles, who was then the girlfriend of Willie Donaldson, to be in it and she told Terry she wouldn't dream of being in it, which slightly fractured his ego. It was all set in a little flat in which this man Legs lives next door to this wonderful girl and it was all about him thinking she was rather a nice girl and doing everything he could to make himself attractive to her. She rather liked him, but he was never in because he was at bodybuilding classes or something like that in order to make himself into this perfect man, but she just liked him for what he was, so it was one of these non-communication things.

TERRY JONES: Then I was seconded as a comedy adviser/researcher onto a show with Lance Percival, who used to sing calypsos on TW3. I was doing little film bits for him and it was then I found the problems with editing. There was a sequence, which I think I'd written, when we used old footage, put together with some silly commentary. I'd put this together but the editor had no comedy timing at all, so I'd spend ages with the editor trying to get him to re-cut it and eventually got bawled out by the director for interfering, because obviously the editor had complained to him and so it wasn't a very happy time.

MICHAEL PALIN: Then they decided that *Late Night Line Up*, which was a very serious programme, should be lightened up and should have some humour in it.

on Friday nights, so why didn't I go and see him? Again I involved Mike in that and we wrote stuff for it. You wouldn't have an audience, the shows were made in this tiny presentation studio. We would do these little sketches and everybody in the control room would laugh. Then on the sixth week we noticed nobody was laughing and we didn't quite know what was going on. Then it suddenly came to Dennis Potter being interviewed by Michael Dean and Dennis Potter saying, 'Look, before we start this interview I want to say I didn't come all the way down from Gloucestershire to appear on a show with rubbish like we've seen just now' – end of our career with *Late Night Line Up*, although I did hang on for a bit, writing little funny bits for them. Eventually I decided that wasn't going anywhere and so I said, 'I think I'd better leave the BBC.'

JOHN CLEESE: It was some years before I realised that Graham didn't work properly because he was essentially very clever. He had a very good mind. And I think it was only slowly that I began to see how disconnected he was emotionally. But in those days male friendships in my experience were rather old-fashioned. It was all people in brogues and sports jackets calling each other by their last names, those kind of relationships. Graham and I always laughed together and at moments when we laughed there was a genuine contact between us. But after the moments of laughter, there was a kind of retreat.

TERRY JONES: In those days we (Mike and I) started off writing as two people sitting together in a room, and we were writing like that for quite a while. I'm not sure at what point we stopped writing like that, but I was always getting in the car and driving across London and usually writing at his place in Belsize Park. Writing links for *The Billy Cotton Band Show* was just things like 'Wakey, wakey', 'Right we've got a great show for you tonight, ladies and gentlemen, Russ Conway' and 'Hello, Russ'. I think Mike's one was 'Have you just come back from holiday? Where'd you go?' 'Costa Brava.' 'No, Costa Fiver.' I remember going to the recording of that show, Russ Conway doing his piece and being stopped and having to do it about six times because he couldn't get it right.

JOHN CLEESE: Then towards the end of the New Zealand run [of *Cambridge Circus*], we were told, 'Yes, you are going to be doing it in New York.'

voice to the back of these big theatres; you could play at a much more naturalistic level, which suited me better. We did it there for some months and then we put together a second revue and it was during the time one or two people left. Graham left because he felt he should get on with his medicine. One night Tommy Steele was in the audience and the next thing I knew I was invited to audition for *Half a Sixpence* and to my astonishment, they gave the part to me.

TERRY GILLIAM: I was working for this magazine and doing these *fumettis*, which was exactly the same as making a movie, except nothing moved. You had to get sets, locations, actors, costumes, write the thing, and I was in charge of doing that. That's where I met all sorts

Cambridge Circus and Sammy Davis Jr. – together at last!

We flew back to England briefly for about three or four days and then flew on to New York and started rehearsing. At first there was a vague panic when they decided they didn't like some of the material. We all felt, 'Do we want to change this show and put in new material three nights before we open on Broadway?' But we opened and got very, very good notices from the *Post* and the *Tribune* and a bad review in the *New York Times*. And of course the *New York Times* was so important that that killed us. We played for three weeks, and we couldn't understand why they didn't publicise it. Somebody later told me the producers were after a tax loss.

But then a couple of guys from a place on Washington Square called Square East asked us if we wanted to come and do the show in this supper club. I loved it there because you could be rather lazy really. There were only about 200 people in the audience and it was a nice room so you didn't have to knock yourself out getting your

of people – Henry Jaglom was in one, and I had a friend who was a folk singer and she said can I bring my boyfriend, and her boyfriend was Woody Allen, so Woody Allen is in one. That's where I then met John Cleese because *Cambridge Circus* was playing in New York on the coat-tails of *Beyond the Fringe* except they failed and ended up down in the village. Then I decided to head off to Europe, and he ended up going to Chicago and working on *Newsweek*.

JOHN CLEESE: When I came out of *Half A Sixpence* I had a brief stint as a journalist for *Newsweek* magazine where I failed to make the grade. I realised that they were going to let me go and, as I liked the main editor, I wrote a resignation letter so he didn't have to fire me. I was always interested in journalism, even before I got the job at *Newsweek*.

This is where people always get my profile wrong. It's as though people think, 'But he was Basil Fawlty, why did he suddenly acquire all these strange new interests?' Well, the strange new interests have been there since I was fifteen. I remember when I did law, the only thing that I really, really liked was international law and jurisprudence which was more philosophical. I got a first in international law and I think I was rather drawn to the idea of travelling round the world. So, when I got this opportunity at *Newsweek* through a fellow I met on the subway station, literally, who happened to work there and we got to know each other, and then he suggested me to the editor because he felt I could write the lighter pieces, I thought this is a way of doing something that's seriously interesting.

It's just a fact that I don't think I ever believed that my soul really was in show business. It was an extremely nice way of making money, and there have been many moments which have been very enjoyable, but it's never felt to me like a whole life. Of course people who first got to know me in Python or as Basil Fawlty think, 'Well, that's the person he is. Why on earth is he getting interested in psychology and spoiling it for us?' And I understand the thinking, but the interest in psychology I can date back to black and white TV programmes I remember seeing on the BBC probably when I was fourteen.

TERRY GILLIAM: I went off to Europe, hitchhiking around for six months, and I fell in love with Europe. It was that sudden thing of getting out of that cocoon of America and American thinking. What was funny was I was very anti-American, I was against the war and everything. And I was doing a lot of cartoons for political magazines and things. But then I was travelling outside America

and in Spain somebody would start giving me trouble for being an American. I'd get really angry and start defending America. It was frightening to find myself sounding like this terrible right-winger. It was like I can criticise, but nobody else can.

I worked for *Pilote* which was edited in Paris by René Garsine, the creator of Astérix and Obélix, and when I was travelling in Europe I was also getting a little bit of money by doing things for *Esquire* magazine. I remember coming to London and going up to the *Private Eye* offices with my cartoons and nobody was interested. The whole front cover of *Private Eye* with the speech balloons was taken from *Help* magazine, *Help* did it first.

Then what happened was I got as far as Turkey and all my money was gone, so I got back to Paris and I went to René and he said, I can give you a couple of pages, you can do something on snowmen. So I earned enough money doing that to get myself back to New York. Then I moved into Harvey's attic for a couple of months.

One way to avoid the draft was to join the National Guard, which meant you went on weekly meetings and summer camp. And you went to basic training same as the regular army but after that you just played at being soldiers for the next few years. Again the cartooning came in useful, because at the end of bootcamp when everybody's out on their belly in the mud, under machine gun fire and barb wire, I'm sitting in the barracks drawing portraits of my CO and his bride to be. What you learn in the army is to malinger. Which I hate. I hated being in the army.

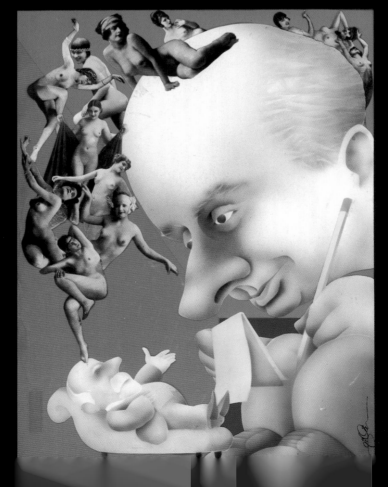

'I worked for *Pilote* which was edited in Paris by René Garsine, the creator of Astérix and Obélix, and when I was travelling in Europe I was also getting a little bit of money by doing things for *Esquire* magazine. I remember coming to London and going up to the *Private Eye* offices with my cartoons and nobody was interested. The whole front cover of *Private Eye* with the speech balloons was taken from *Help* magazine, *Help* did it first.'

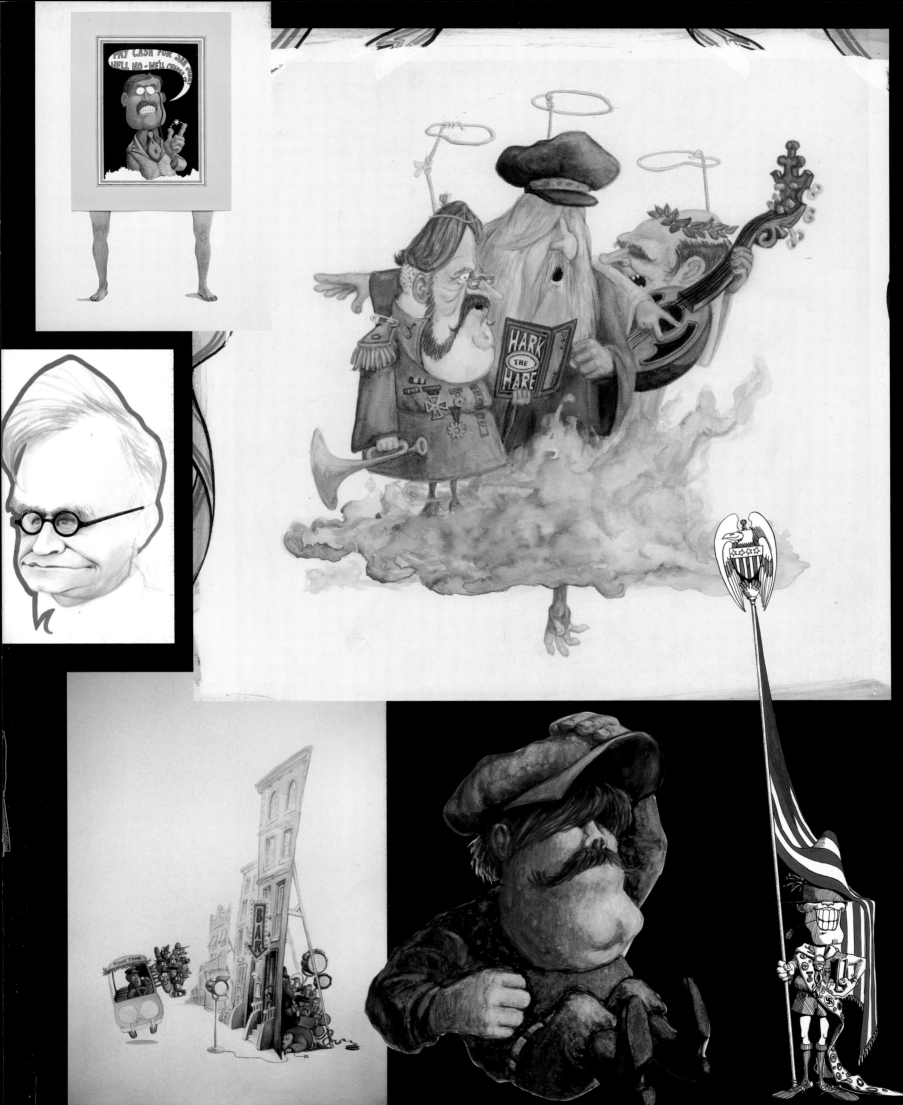

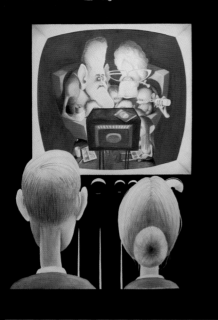

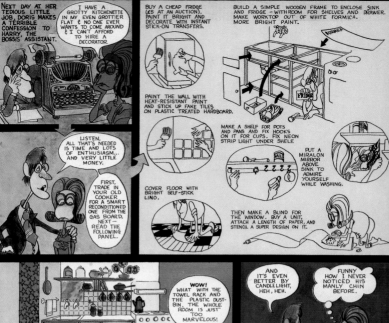

'Again the cartooning came in useful, because at the end of bootcamp when everybody's out on their belly in the mud, under machine gun fire and barb wire, I'm sitting in the barracks drawing portraits of my CO and his bride to be.'

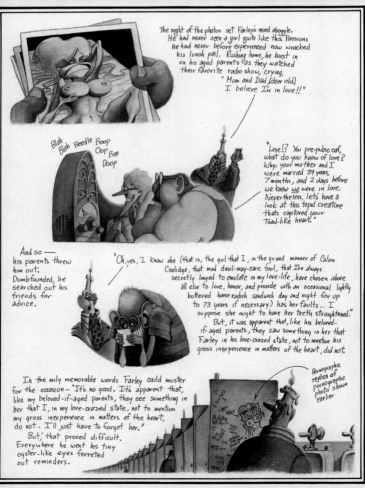

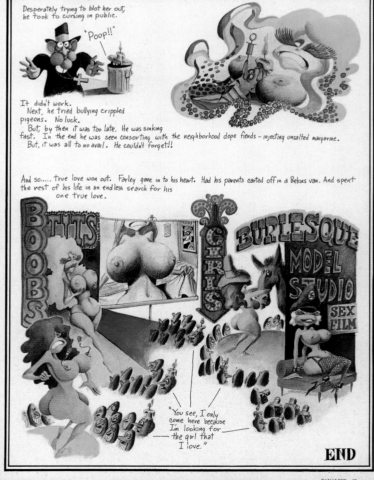

'I used to regard it as wonderful practice. It was like warming up in the nets before you go out to the middle to play cricket. It was great, but you knew that this was not as important as live television, peak hour, but it was tremendously useful and it gave me a chance to play off the audience.'

JOHN CLEESE: Almost immediately after I left *Newsweek*, I was catapulted, through a friend, into a show that was going to Chicago and Washington. That was the show that had come over from Peter Cook's London club, the Establishment, and one of the guys in it, Peter Bellwood, had been President of the Footlights in my first year. So he and I and two other people went on the road and did the Establishment sketches for a number of weeks. It was a good show, funny material. I was playing characters rather different from what I'd played before but that was all to the good, particularly as I had several weeks doing them so you had time to get better. When I was in Chicago doing the Establishment Show, we were asked to do publicity for it and one day I found myself in a radio studio, and Jack Palance came in. We were just there publicising the show, and Palance was nice and offered us a

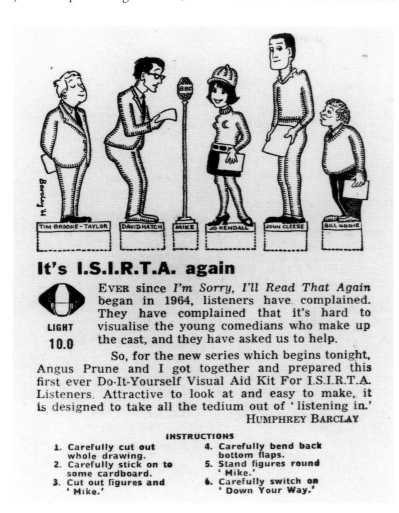

It's I.S.I.R.T.A. again

LIGHT

10.0

EVER since *I'm Sorry, I'll Read That Again* began in 1964, listeners have complained. They have complained that it's hard to visualise the young comedians who make up the cast, and they have asked us to help.

So, for the new series which begins tonight, Angus Prune and I got together and prepared this first ever Do-It-Yourself Visual Aid Kit For I.S.I.R.T.A. Listeners. Attractive to look at and easy to make, it is designed to take all the tedium out of 'listening in.'

HUMPHREY BARCLAY

INSTRUCTIONS

1. Carefully cut out whole drawing.
2. Carefully stick on to some cardboard.
3. Cut out figures and ' Mike.'
4. Carefully bend back bottom flaps.
5. Stand figures round ' Mike.'
6. Carefully switch on ' Down Your Way.'

couple of matinée tickets to the show that he was doing, *Heaven Can Wait*. We went along and when we went to say hello afterwards, he told me he loved to play light comedy, but he was always being offered these villains, Mexican bandit chiefs and so on …

While I was in New York, the others all got back to England and started doing *I'm Sorry, I'll Read That Again* on BBC radio, based around the *Cambridge Circus* group, but without me because I was still in America. They brought Graeme Garden in, and when I got back to England, they were happy to add me to the cast.

ERIC IDLE: It was two years of the previous generation, the *Cambridge Circus* people, who were all doing that show. They'd come back from America now and they had this radio show. And they

needed material, so you could submit anything. They'd done some of my material in New York. I wrote a thing called 'I Want To Hold Your Handle', an early Beatles parody which we'd done. People were always looking for material and Humphrey Barclay stayed in touch, always saying, 'If you've got anything, we need material. They're doing a radio show now, do you want to come see it, do you want to write something?' And they would give me 3 guineas a minute for that, so that was great.

JOHN CLEESE: I did that show for a long time, at the same time as I was doing *Frost*. I used to regard it as wonderful practice. It was like warming up in the nets before you go out to the middle to play cricket. It was great, but you knew that this was not as important as live television, peak hour, but it was tremendously useful and it gave me a chance to play off the audience. If you do a hundred shows, you learn a bit in that time in terms of technique. Eventually, the audience became so much an integral part of the programme, and being a bit of a purist, as I certainly was in those days, I got fed up with the fact that so much was based on pun, which I did think was the lowest form of wit.

TERRY JONES: I knew what was going on within the Beeb. I knew, for instance, *The Frost Report* wanted film inserts and everything, and I knew the director, Jimmy Gilbert.

ERIC IDLE: Mike, Terry and I were all on the roof of a hearse in Ken Russell's *Isadora*, but that was because we knew Tony Palmer, who cast us all for a day. It had never been part of my ambition to be an actor, but I found myself in rep. Then I thought that I could earn some money writing for radio, because I obviously had a facility for writing scripts, which had developed from doing cabaret at Cambridge every weekend. So I earned quite a good living during my last two years at Cambridge. They'd book the Footlights, you'd go up in your dinner jacket and you'd do half-an-hour cabaret. They'd all squat down in their ball frocks and you'd get £25 – £5 each and £5 for the driver. That was a lot of money in those days. So I was doing quite well and I'd even done TV. At the end of my first year when I did Footlights '63, we were on TV several times at the festival. We did sketches on television, so suddenly you've got television experience.

But afterwards I still had no idea what I wanted to do, and it was only in '66, when I did Jonathan Miller's production of *Alice In Wonderland*, there was some filming in that and I got to meet Alan Bennett and go bowling with him and Jonathan and it was hilarious – the commentary between the two of them. I was in seventh heaven because they were my idols and I was bowling with them. Alan had his own series then called *On the Margin*, which was absolutely brilliant, except the BBC kindly wiped it so it looks like Python came out of nowhere. Most of our precursor shows were carefully wiped: there's hardly any of *Not Only But Also*, which was on before Python came out; there's hardly any of *On the Margin*, which was really funny Alan Bennett stuff. These things usually turn up in New Zealand or somewhere on telecine. That's the great saviour of all these things.

MICHAEL PALIN: Then in the middle of writing *The Love Show*, along comes the call. I remember very vividly being down in Terry's parents' house and hearing from Jimmy Gilbert, who was the producer of *The Frost Report*, asking us to come on board as writers. That started in about May '66. What had happened was we got a booking at the Royal Court. We were invited to go and do a few nights there in their Rehearsal Room Club and we went along and did our revue. Sometimes we'd outnumber the audience. But on one night David Frost was there and I have to really hand it to David, looking back now, he was incredibly good at looking out for new talent and at that time he was very much the risen star of television and the modern new satirical comedy. So it was quite something for him to come along. Then, another night, Paul McCartney and Jane Asher were there at a table. We were told that Paul McCartney would like to come and meet us, and I think he probably meant meet us all, but for some reason I said, 'I'll go and meet him, he won't want too many people around, I'd better just go on my own,' so I went round and toadied up to Paul. We had a very high calibre audience, compared to numbers; out of probably twenty-five people who saw us, two were megastars and one was David Frost. David has this amazing memory and he remembered the Oxford Revue and the characters I'd played then. It was the first time he'd really talked to me.

JOHN CLEESE: I was definitely returning to England. And I was also coming back with Connie Booth to get married. I came back safe in the knowledge that Mr Frost wanted me to join these two people called Ronnie Barker and Ronnie Corbett, neither of whom I'd ever heard of. If you include the New Zealand trip, I'd been away from England for eighteen months and suddenly, within two and a half months of coming back, I've got a flat in Earls Court with my oldest friend, Alan Hutchison. Then two weeks later, there I was in the rehearsal room and suddenly I was in show business properly.

ERIC IDLE: Tim Brooke-Taylor came to me and said, 'Why don't we write something for *The Frost Report*?' So we went to Lord's

cricket ground and we sat at Lord's trying to write material. You could either write sketches which were harder to get in the show, or you could write what Frost called the CDM, which stood for 'continually developing monologue', which I think John and Graham called OJARIL — old jokes and ridiculously irrelevant links. *The Frost Report* was nice, really, because what it did was take a subject every week, then Anthony Jay would write a two-page essay on it, you'd all meet as writers, listen to the essay on, say, 'education', then you'd all go away and write stuff. I didn't stay writing with Tim Brooke-Taylor for very long. We started to write together really early on, but then I got a joke on the air. There's that wonderful moment when Frosty does a joke and wow, it gets a laugh and you think 'I wrote that'. It was 10 guineas a minute for TV and they guaranteed you 3 minutes a week, so you're guaranteed 30 guineas a week. Then you'd write all that stuff and they'd send a taxi to pick up your material. A taxi would come for your jokes, and then you'd have to take the tube for the meeting, it was hilarious.

'But on one night David Frost was there and I have to really hand it to David, looking back now, he was incredibly good at looking out for new talent and at that time he was very much the risen star of television and the modern new satirical comedy.'

TERRY JONES: Jimmy Gilbert wanted some little film inserts and said, 'Why don't you do it?' So Mike and I used to write these little film bits, like 'What judges do on their lunch break', where we put all these people in judge's robes and had them in a kiddies playground. We were getting paid 7 guineas a minute, but that's a minute of stuff that goes on air. We'd be lucky if we got two minutes of material on a week, so we weren't really getting enough to keep us together, so Jimmy gave us performing parts for which we'd get paid £20, so that was much better. We were doing these filmed pieces but also writing piles of stuff for the CDM, not that much got in.

MICHAEL PALIN: Generally speaking they were always looking for one-liners for David Frost, which were very much appreciated. Terry and I gradually wrote slightly longer material, usually films, because no one was writing that stuff and the sketch market was largely taken over by these two, Cleese and Chapman, and they just used to write such good sketches every week that everyone was floored. Cleese and Chapman were kings of the sketches, and Terry and I made this little niche for ourselves doing short film pieces. Then gradually we got a bit more confidence and wrote more sketches, and in the second series we weren't equal to Cleese and Chapman, but we were certainly consistent in terms of the sketches we were producing, as well as the little films.

ERIC IDLE: What was good was I renewed my acquaintance with Mike and Terry, who were also writing on the show. There were a lot of very good people, Dick Vosburgh, Barry Cryer, very funny nice people, so you're part of a team creating this show which was live and going on the air and was really funny. Then pretty early on we won the Golden Rose award at Montreux, and one of my jokes was on the clip they showed on the BBC news. I thought to myself, 'I got a joke on the news.' How brilliant was that, fucking great! The boy's going places.

MICHAEL PALIN: What would happen on *Frost* is they would choose the various themes and the first one was 'authority' or something like that – a big idea for a comedy show at that time. Tony Jay, who was the keeper of the flame as it were, would write a theme script which would go out to people. We'd have a look at that and then there would be a meeting of the writers which was held in Crawford Street in Paddington in a room that was part of a church hall. I remember the very first meeting there. Terry couldn't go along for some reason. Terry was always senior to me in a sense, he was a year older than me, and Terry knew people in the BBC much better than I did. I still felt very much on the fringes. These were the major scriptwriters in the country, and I felt very much like a new boy at school. Two people, one was Barry Cryer and the other was Marty Feldman, went out of their way to come up and ask who I was and welcome me in and introduce me to people, which is something I've always remembered. Then the meeting would start, you would be told what to do and after that you would be asked to bring in material and read out a bit, which was quite intimidating at the beginning.

DAVID SHERLOCK: Graham still thought of himself as a writer and part of his writing career was working for both Cilla Black and writing links for Petula Clark. There was an awful lot of time when Graham was working on his own, particularly in the early days. He

was writing for Roy Hudd, and the BBC asked him to write the links for Petula Clark and whatever. Some of those jobs came from hanging round the BBC bar.

ERIC IDLE: Later on when Frost moved to ITV and he was actually interviewing people, I was brought in because Frosty needed ad libs. I think that's rather sensible. You're on a live show and you've got to get from A to B, why not have six lines by Barry Cryer, Eric Idle and Dick Vosburgh up your sleeve? Smart boy.

I think my mother thought I was supposed to get a proper job, but she was never really in my life in a big way after Cambridge. I guess she was proud of it – you're on air, your name's flashing up at the end of the credits, it's like you're doing something useful. But it was a good time to be part of the BBC and what was nice about it was being part of a team creating comedy. We were all writers together, because normally writers are very solitary people, yet with *The Frost Report* you'd have at least two meetings, where you all got to meet every week, have a laugh, go to the pub and hear everybody else's material. Comedy's done best when it's an anarchic conspiracy with people communicating and encouraging and egging each other on, and that was a very good example of that early on.

TERRY GILLIAM: I was a huge Anglophile when it came to film. The Goon shows and all the Ealing comedies I loved. I just loved English films and in New York at that time foreign films were really big, so you're getting Fellini, Antonioni, Buñuel. I knew all these works on film, so it wasn't like I was walking out not knowing where I was going. I had very strong preconceptions of what it was going to be like. I was usually wrong, but you always manage to find enough things to patch it together to make it look like the movie you saw. I remember coming to London, spending all my time trying to find the locations for *Blow Up*. I went up to Hampton Court one day and walked from Hampton Court to Shepperton Studios. I got there and there was the gate and I walked around and I climbed over the wall. I walked around the whole studio on my own, through the *Oliver* set, everything. I would walk into editing rooms; all the doors were unlocked. It was my studio. Then I walked out the front gate passed the guards. And then years later I made *Jabberwocky* there.

JOHN CLEESE: In many ways Graham's great value was that even though he didn't say much, what he was so good at was throwing in a completely new angle. My weakness is that I get so interested in the logic that I can disappear into a logical vortex trying to get everything to fit in a mathematical way. Graham was great at suddenly taking the sketch off in an unexpected direction which would give it great new energy.

DAVID SHERLOCK: Cleese has no perception of the fact that, for many years, Graham wanted to keep open the ability to return to medicine. That meant keeping a damn good check on the people who still worked at Bart's and could give him a houseman's job, because he would only ever have started again as a houseman and gone back into having to work his way up. He was constantly deeply unsure as to whether he would always be a writer, even though he'd made that decision.

JOHN CLEESE: Chapman, firstly, was always a little bit in a world of his own and secondly he was lazy. His main way of earning money was to go from one writing group to another to another. So he'd leave me and go to work with Barry Cryer and then go and work with someone else. Thus, without making a major contribution in any group, he would be getting one third or one half of the fees for three different shows. But he was worth it for two reasons. He was the greatest sounding board that I've ever had. He was extraordinary in the sense that if Graham thought something was funny, then it almost certainly was funny. You cannot believe how invaluable that is. I think that's why we tended to write in pairs, because it would have been too scary writing on your own, to know whether you were doing something funny or not. Whereas I discovered that if Chapman thought something was funny it almost always was. I knew it from very early on. And I think at the beginning, while he was still more in the swing of being at Cambridge and training as a doctor, he was more focused than he was later on and made a bigger contribution.

ERIC IDLE: To be twenty-three and on *The Frost Report* was really cool.

TERRY JONES: It was exciting being part of the *Frost* programme, but I think it was also interesting seeing ideas done well and not done well. Jimmy Gilbert was very keen to take our ideas about how to do these film pieces. He asked us very closely about what we meant, how do we see this and how do we do that, so that made us think quite rigorously about the visual side of it. I remember him ringing us up once because we'd written one piece that had twenty-four people on motor lawnmowers coming to the rescue, like the cavalry. He rang up and said, 'We've only got half a dozen, is that enough, do you think that will do?' Then we said, 'I think we'll need a few more than half a dozen to be the cavalry.' And in the same scene, just to frighten Jimmy because he was always scared, we'd put in '100 Zulus come over the skyline' or something, and Jimmy rang up and said, 'Do we need 100 Zulus?' We got him on that one.

JOHN CLEESE: It was terrifying because *Frost* was live. I was surrounded by entirely nice people who were friendly, supportive, cheerful, helpful, couldn't have been nicer. I think I learned a little bit particularly from Ronnie Corbett, which might surprise people because Barker is a great actor, but Corbett had moments of timing that were absolutely

Humphrey Barclay's interpretation of David Frost

uncanny. Ronnie Barker could play anyone or anything; Ronnie Corbett had a narrower range but his timing sometimes was extraordinary. I was able to sit around with Barry Cryer, Dick Vosburgh and all these people who knew show business, and I loved being part of that. It felt as though I was learning. I immediately saw that Eric was writing solos, normally for Ronnie Barker, and then Mike and Terry were writing the filmed item each week. And I suddenly found people taking an interest in me as a performer for the first time.

MICHAEL PALIN: I didn't see John that often because John was contracted mainly as an actor. He was one of the stars of the programme, with the two Ronnies. John and Graham would write their own stuff separately; they had a different conduit through to *Frost*. Graham would occasionally come to the meetings. So I would see them on recording days and on rehearsal days. I saw much more of Eric.

ERIC IDLE: I much prefer writing alone, but it's very hard. It's ten times harder than being in a team, because who do you make laugh? Who's laughing? I don't like working with other people, I find it exhausting. I like to write out of my own mind and I find that much more useful. You learn more about yourself, you become your own critic and that's the thing you learn much later on in life. I know I can be funny, I'm not concerned about that. I know I can hold my own with Robin Williams and it doesn't scare me anymore. I don't have to be the same or better than him, but if I'm with Robin and he starts to be funny, whenever he pauses for breath, I can get in there and say something funny and then he's off again. I don't feel I have any anxieties any more about being funny.

TERRY JONES: It was at that time that Marty Feldman and Barry Took invited us to go over to Marty's place. Barry said, 'You two really do some good stuff,' and I think both Mike and I felt for the first time that there was a career in comedy and in script writing. So Barry's encouragement, and Marty's too, was rather key for us. It helped to keep us going.

MICHAEL PALIN: The first time I appeared on television with Terry was in December '66 when we did something for a programme called *The Late Show*. It was a piece written by Ian Davidson and Ian asked Terry and myself to be in it. I remember I had just moved my parents from Sheffield into this house in Suffolk, near Southwold, and I had to get up very early one frozen December morning, in order to drive down to Ealing Studios in London. The traffic was awful and it took me hours and hours to get across

London. Eventually I got there and did this. It was a take-off of a Samurai film with Terry, myself and Ian. That was the first time I can remember appearing on the television screen and having something transmitted, apart from *Now!*, and obviously *Now!* wasn't going to lead to anything, but *The Late Show* I thought would. This was the BBC.

ERIC IDLE: I didn't perform on the BBC *Frost*; I think I got on once or twice in the ITV one, but not in any big way.

MICHAEL PALIN: Performing was very much part of the equation, as far as I was concerned. I wasn't really interested in just being a writer and I was writing material which I felt often only I could bring to life, to be honest, and I think Terry and Eric probably felt the same way. That was because we could all act, we were all interested in theatre work and we had kind of been conditioned at Oxford and Cambridge into the notion of both writing and performing. The process of writing was really the first part of what I wanted to do; the second part was delivering that material myself. So when we would be at script meetings, we'd perform our material. Other people would read their material, we'd perform ours, it just added a certain extra. And they'd think, 'Oh God, here we go,' and that became a very important part of the Python process eventually. When you read the material, you had a very strong chance of getting that part for yourself if you did it well. So writing and acting were very much interlocked.

DAVID SHERLOCK: He was always around people who drank, the Bart's connection continued for many years after he left. He went back to see ward shows; after all he and Alan Bailey had founded the bar for the students at Bart's and he kept an eye on that, and where else, at 11 at night, could you get a cheque changed. So Graham would often say, 'Sorry folks, gotta go change a cheque,' and he'd be off to Bart's students bar where he could change a cheque at any time of the day or night, if it was open. He used to drive Cleese barmy.

MICHAEL PALIN: I soon discovered that my parents' disapproval was a very inchoate thing. It really boiled down to the fact that my father didn't have enough money to support me after university. He was just desperately worried that I would end up, rather as my sister did, trying to get into theatre, and it not working out, coming home and having to live at home, or he'd have to

John Cleese and Ronnie Corbett –
The Rise and Rise of Michael Rimmer

finance me. He just couldn't do it, he just wasn't making enough money. That's what it boiled down to with him. Once I was making money, he didn't really look too closely at whether I was making money by low comedy performances or smashing up pianos on *Now!* with Arthur Mullard, so long as the money was coming in. My mother really didn't mind at all. She was very supportive of my acting ambitions anyway and she was quite proud of the fact I could act. She came along to shows I did in Sheffield and all that. My father was never really like that. Once I was actually earning money and doing programmes, and on the front of the *TV Times*, then my parents were quite happy about it. They were never star-struck by me at all; I think they always thought this was on the way to something more serious.

GRAHAM CHAPMAN: John and I had written a lot of sketches for David Frost ... in consideration for our services Mr Frost wisely chose to pay us the kind of pittance that we would think a fortune to write a film ... After my final examinations the prospect of three months writing a film on a Mediterranean island appealed to me more than six months of looking into ears, noses and throats.[4]

JOHN CLEESE: When Graham and I were writing for *The Frost Report* it was a much, much more equal operation, and later it became almost progressively more unequal with the alcohol exacerbating that tendency anyway. But I remember when we were writing *The Rise and Rise of Michael Rimmer* in Ibiza in 1966, which was just after he'd met David Sherlock but before he'd told anyone about the relationship, I remember I was sitting inside in the shade at a table writing and he was on the balcony sunning himself and we were talking through the door – that's a clear image that I have of those days.

TERRY GILLIAM: The Vietnam war was beginning to heat up, and these guys wanted to go. Training sergeants couldn't wait to get out there; they were raring to go. It was madness. They didn't want to serve their country; they wanted to have a good bash is what they wanted. They found it exciting. And at the same time I'm drawing anti-government cartoons against the war. When I finally come back to Europe, I managed to get an honourable discharge from the US Army because I'd done this really bizarre thing. When I did my first trip to Europe my ex-roommate was actually living in Rhodes so he became my mailing address. I got out of the National Guard when I said I was going to Europe. So I was put into a control group which was based in Germany but I was claiming to be living on this island in Greece. Eventually I came back to America and this ridiculous communication was going on when the army would write to me. They would basically write from St Louis, Missouri, to Germany; then it would be sent from Germany to Greece, then from Greece to New York and eventually, when I went back, from New York to LA. I would respond to it, seal it in an envelope inside an envelope and send that to my friend in Greece, who'd then mail it from Rhodes to Germany where it would be sent back to St Louis. This went on for years.

When I finally moved to England, the war was getting really hot and they were closing down all these control groups and insisting everybody return to America. By then I was getting everybody – the BBC, Humphrey Barclay, the *Sunday Times* magazine, everybody that I was working for – to write letters saying I was essential to the continuation of their companies. I got a lawyer here in England to say that if I went back to the States I would be indigent, there'd be no way of supporting myself, and I got an honourable discharge from the US army for behaving so dishonourably.

DAVID SHERLOCK: When I met Graham, he was still very much a man who preferred to drink pints of bitter than anything else. And it wasn't until after he'd been in Ibiza, writing, that he decided that gin and tonic was a much better bet for all occasions.

I'd gone to Ibiza to meet somebody else; it didn't work out as holiday romances from the year before often don't, but I met Graham. It was the only place I'd ever been where people didn't seem to bother as to whether you were gay or not. I had noticed Graham in the street, he's fairly striking and it was the 14th of July, Bastille Day. And as these people were streaming out of the campsite, I, slightly tanked up, would look them up and down and say goodnight in whatever language I thought they might be. Suddenly behind me I could hear this very English voice saying 'Good evening', which turned out to be Graham, and I said 'Good evening'. I was aware of the fact that this could be a pick-up; at the same time here was a man who always looked so straight and with the sort of gravitas you do not expect from your average poofter, in those days anyway. He behaved just like any ordinary straight man. He had his pipe and he said, 'Do you want to go and have a drink at the bar?' So on top of a meal and a jug of sangria, we suddenly found ourselves at the bar surrounded by lots of French people who were jumping in the pool dressed in banana leaves or whatever they'd managed to make into fancy dress for their fabulous Bastille Day celebrations. Of course, I've always joked that Graham and I got together on a day like the fall of the Bastille, it has a certain ring to it. So we had several drinks at the bar, and I found out that he was a writer. Then came the famous moment when Graham casually said, 'Are you camping here? Can I come and see your tent?' So I said, 'Yeah, all right.'

I knew by then that he had worked for *The Frost Report*, which I thought was very senior, and also that he knew John Cleese and was working with him. Of course John Cleese was one of the names that I knew from *The Frost Report* but at that time I had never seen Graham as a performer. So we went to the tent and I suddenly found myself swept off my feet and into a clinch. I thought, 'Oh, that is what he's up to,' and at that point I really didn't know, because his manner was just so correct and so straight.

Then he decided he would like to spend the night, in a tiny tent which was really meant for one. Graham's feet must have stuck out of the end. All night long these pissed French people were falling across the tent, tripping on every guy rope, but my favourite moment was in the morning, very early, when Graham had to creep back home. The large Alsatian camp guard dog sniffed Graham, realised he was not a member of the campsite and he was chased down the road with this dog snapping at his heels! So it was quite a meeting really.

JOHN CHAPMAN: I'm not sure that Graham was aware of his homosexuality until he went off to Ibiza, to do some writing. Prior to that there had certainly been some heterosexual relationships.

PAM CHAPMAN: Whilst he was at Bart's, he actually asked someone to marry him and she'd turned him down because she knew that things weren't quite right.

JOHN CHAPMAN: My mother was always aware of it and was unhappy with it, always feeling, 'Where did I go wrong, it must be my fault somehow.' And I'm not sure that she ever properly came to terms with it.

PAM CHAPMAN: I think her viewpoint was that if he hadn't gone to Cambridge it would never have happened. That was how she coped with it.

GRAHAM CHAPMAN: In the course of David Frost's One-Day Holiday in Ibiza he checked up that John and I had actually been doing some writing and even 'squawked' at it, which we took for laughter (but he pointedly looked forward to reading more than ten pages); said that he thought it'd be a good idea if John Cleese, Tim Brooke-Taylor, Marty Feldman and myself did a TV comedy show together; and added that he was looking for something for Ronnie Corbett to do, remarking, 'Perhaps you, Graham and Barry Cryer would like to have a go at writing it – a kind of middle-class situation comedy – there hasn't really been one.'

That all sounded very good to me. Although I knew him, I'd never written with Barry before. 'How would it be if Eric Idle, Barry and myself were to write a pilot programme for the series?'

'Super,' said David, 'Super,' and went off to frolic in the shallow waters.

And so what was to become *The Rise and Rise of Michael Rimmer*, later re-written with Peter Cook; *At Last The 1948 Show* (very much a progenitor of Python); and several series of Ronnie Corbett's *No That's Me Over There* would never have happened if it hadn't been for forty-five minutes of David Frost's enthusiasm and confidence prior to paddling.[4]

JOHN CLEESE: I took a break in the summer. David Frost had approached Tim Brooke-Taylor and me to do a show. I think he meant for us to do two separate shows but we said we wanted to do it together, and we immediately roped Graham in. Then we decided we wanted to use Marty because I'd got very friendly with Marty during *The Frost Report*, and I thought he would be a terrific performer. Then he was only known as a writer, he was the head writer on *Frost* but not a performer. So that was *At Last The 1948 Show*.

Eric's way of doing things, whilst Terry and myself were quite happy with a fairly plain and simple lifestyle. But we all got on.

ERIC IDLE: Humphrey Barclay knew me as a performer from Cambridge. Then he made the move from radio to TV. He was trying to put together a TV show, and he had got a brief to do a kid's show at 5.25. So he came to me and he had some ideas which were rather good; he got the Bonzo Dog Band. He discovered David Jason, who was not too shabby, and we made this rather funny show for its time slot. It was a kid's show that wasn't condescending. The first thing we said was 'We're going to do exactly what we usually do. We're not going to write down for kids, we're not going to change what we do, we're just going to keep any filth out,' which is also a very good discipline. And we caught a very nice audience, we caught people returning from work, so we got a young audience and we got adults too. Even though it meant leaving *Frost*, moving to childrens' TV was a step up for us, because we were performing. Now we were on television, before then we were just writers, watching and waving goodbye to our jokes in a cab. Now we were getting our own Carnaby Street suits, we were filming, we were down in the TV studios and we were using all the equipment.

MICHAEL PALIN: Comedy was the great leveller because we all laughed together. With *Do Not Adjust Your Set* we wrote collaboratively, with Eric, Terry and myself; we'd sit round and put things together. The shows were credited as written by the three of us, plus David Jason and Denise Coffey who wrote Captain Fantastic.

ERIC IDLE: I would write with them very infrequently. Captain Fantastic, which was a superhero sketch every week for David Jason to do, we wrote together and we'd write link material together. We'd meet and say, 'What have you got? Oh, I've got this. Let's put this together.' And that's when the editing would come in.

For us, what was odd about the show was the fact that there were the three of us who wrote it and were clearly in charge of it, and then there were the two who were just the two actors, David Jason and Denise Coffey. Obviously it was difficult for them because we were the writers, so anything that was good, we were going to get first dibs on casting. So we developed Captain Fantastic to give David something to do that was his own and he and Denise could go off and film that.

TERRY JONES: I didn't have any doubts, I thought it would be really interesting because I thought we'd just do what we wanted to do and make it a funny show for us. Our agent was full of doubts and was very against us doing it. He said, 'It's ridiculous doing a children's TV show, it would be much better to write a stage show for Dora Bryan, that would make much more money!' But we were quite determined we were going to do it. For us it was a chance to act as well.

MICHAEL PALIN: We had no doubts about moving from *Frost* into children's television. It seemed like promotion in a sense because it was our own show and we could set the parameters for it. No one

was saying it's got to be like this or it's got to be like that. Basically Humphrey's brief was very broad – write a really funny, scatty, wacky show for children. We knew that it wouldn't be something that would talk down to children, and in a sense we didn't worry too much about the children's audience. Certainly getting the Bonzo Dog Band on board with all their strange druggy songs that

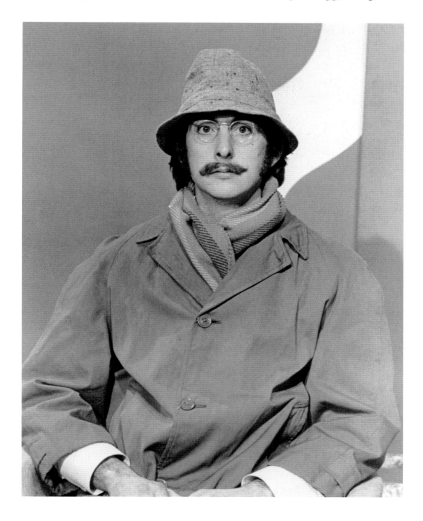

nobody ever seemed to know were about drugs gave us a pretty broad palette, so I don't think we really thought this was a step down at all. Personally, I felt it was quite a step forward. At last we were given the chance to write our own television comedy show, be innovative, do different things, look at things in different ways and take risks and all that stuff. It would have been lovely if it had gone out in the evening, but that's the way it was and I don't think any of us felt it was anything less than a very good test bed for things we wanted to do later on.

TERRY JONES: We'd spend the whole week doing it really. We were working quite continuously. There were several days when we spent the whole time together, either at his place or at my place, usually his, especially around the time of *Complete and Utter History of Britain* and *Do Not Adjust Your Set*, because we were working so hard. There was one time when we were writing *Complete and Utter History of Britain* in the morning, rehearsing *Do Not Adjust Your Set* in the afternoon and then going back to one of our places and writing a pantomime for Watford Palace Theatre in the evening, so we were obviously still working together then continuously. It was much later that we started writing separately, maybe in Python times, but even then we would get together afterwards and sort things out. Certainly most of Python was written quite separately.

MICHAEL PALIN: The key thing really was that *Do Not Adjust Your Set* from '67 onwards really had established Terry Jones, myself and Eric as writer-performers, so people had seen what we could do. But still you didn't know which way your life was going to go at that time and by October '68 I had a son to support, so you still took work wherever it came from. So if we were asked by *Twice a Fortnight* to submit material, we would submit material to *Twice a Fortnight*, and we'd take pride in being able to write for certain different groups, like *The Two Ronnies*. We wrote quite a lot of material for them.

TERRY GILLIAM: I'd literally just started working as an illustrator and cartoonist and Glenys, the girl I was living with, got a job as the

editor on the *Londoner* magazine and I became art director on that. It was just magazine work for the first year and I was getting frustrated with it. Then I made contact with John somewhere along the line and he was doing *The Frost Report* and becoming very well known on television. I asked him if there was any way of using me in television and he gave me Humphrey Barclay's name. What I've always been able to do is carry around a portfolio of my work. That's the great thing about cartoons, you can carry them around. Humphrey was an amateur cartoonist and he loved the sketches. I also had a few written sketches that I'd done and he bought a couple of them from me, and forced them on Mike, Terry and Eric, much to their chagrin, and they didn't even do one of them well, which pissed me off.

ERIC IDLE: He was trying to write sketches. I don't know whether we did one or two of them or not.

MICHAEL PALIN: I met Terry Gilliam in the Rediffusion bar. Humphrey Barclay said, 'I'm going to bring along this man from

America called Terry Gilliam who does cartoons. It would be great to have cartoons in the show.' I remember thinking, 'Well, where would they fit in?' and 'Americans – what do they know about this kind of humour?' and having this general feeling of mild doubt about the whole process. This increased when Gilliam was brought in. There he was. He looked like a showbiz character with a great long fur coat down to the ground and a glamorous blonde girlfriend and I thought, 'God, this is all we need, it's not going to work.' I don't know how long that lasted, maybe ten minutes of resentment and then we became bosom buddies. Or maybe it was two months, but as soon as Terry produced his first animation, we knew this man was exceptional and that this was an enormous bonus for the show and could he please do some more next week. So there were no problems there. But to start with, noses were put slightly out of joint by this added ingredient. But good for Humphrey Barclay. Humphrey was an odd mixture, being ultraconservative but also quite open-minded in who he got together, quite pioneering in this way. You'd have thought that Humphrey

would have wanted a much more conservative show, but he went along with what *Do Not Adjust Your Set* had become, could see it was quite loose, saw a gap for this person that John Cleese had recommended, slotted him in and the rest is history, as they say.

TERRY JONES: Gilliam had been mooching around wanting to write for us and I think Mike and I had been a bit hostile. Eric was very welcoming. Eventually he said he could do these little animated bits and he'd done one for *We Have Ways of Making You Laugh*. Then Terry came on and did a couple of things. He did the 'Postcard' one first and then 'Elephants', which was really the grain of Python.

TERRY GILLIAM: I met Mike, Terry and Eric on that show but I was really just around the edge. Then Humphrey started this show with Frank Muir, *We Have Ways of Making You Laugh*, London Weekend TV's first comedy show, and Humphrey got me on drawing cartoons of the guests. I was doing that for several weeks, and Dick Vosburgh, who was on the show, had collected three months' worth of Jimmy Young's punning links between the records and they were awful. But nobody knew what to do with this stuff. They knew it was really funny but they didn't know what to do with it. So I said, let me make an animated film of it. I had £400 and two weeks to do it in, so the only thing I could do was cut-outs. I got pictures of Jimmy Young, cut his head out, drew other bits and pieces, and started moving the stuff around, wiggling his mouth. I knew everything and nothing. We had always done flip-books so I knew that. It was like somebody who picks up a guitar and can just play it. I could just do it. And in New York in the early '60s I'd seen this underground film of cut-out animation, and the thing I remember

Eric on *We Have Ways of Making You Laugh*

'Nobody had ever seen anything on television like it and I was an animator. Just like that.'

from it was Nixon's head and suddenly a foot in his mouth as he tried to talk. They were just crude cut-outs and suddenly I thought that's what I'll do. I'll have to do it that way. I even think I had Jimmy Young put his foot in his mouth. And I did this thing and it went out on television and it's the power of television because suddenly 10 million people saw it. Nobody had ever seen anything on television like it and I was an animator. Just like that.

ERIC IDLE: *We Have Ways of Making You Laugh* was actually supposed to be the first show that aired on London Weekend Television. We did the whole show, and it was hilarious, the audience laughed and laughed and laughed. Humphrey Barclay, who was the producer, came and said, 'It was brilliant, it was really funny, but it didn't go out. The unions pulled the plugs at the beginning, it was never taped.' The show fell apart from that point, it was like 'Oh, fuck'. We'd just done this live comedy show and there was a union dispute, as any union would when there's a whole new station going on the air. It's a good time to have a dispute. So that

EIGHTPENCE   LONDON Feb 17-Feb 23

TV TIMES

Charles Tingwell hits out □ **Pat Phoenix at home**
PAGES 2-5   PAGES 8-9

DO NOT ADJUST YOUR SET
Thursdays, 5.25 p.m.

was the first unseen show that never went out on London Week-end Television.

TERRY JONES: It was awful watching the very first *Do Not Adjust Your Set*. I was at my parents' home in Claygate, and it came on and Rediffusion got the wrong tape. For some reason the tape they'd put on to broadcast hadn't got the adverts spliced into it, so it went on and then there was a blank patch for about three minutes where the ads were supposed to be. It was terribly embarrassing.

MICHAEL PALIN: The great thing about *Do Not Adjust Your Set* was that nothing had to relate to anything else, it didn't have a theme like *The Frost Report* did. There were certain characters that we quite liked so we'd put them in again and Captain Fantastic was a good character. So what with that and the band, plus the ad break, it wasn't that much. Eighteen minutes of material was all we had to get each week. So it wasn't arduous work.

TERRY JONES: We were hoping to do something fresh and different with *Do Not Adjust Your Set* and we thought, 'Well, it's a kid's show but we're not doing it for kids, we're just doing it for us really.' Then you began hearing that people were coming home from work early so they could catch *Do Not Adjust Your Set*. Then we did the second series and it went out at its normal time, 5.30, and then they put it out again at 7 o'clock or 6.30 so adults could catch it.

TERRY GILLIAM: My animation style came out of necessity, nothing more. I had to do something quick and fast and all I could do was

'There were certain characters that we quite liked so we'd put them in again and Captain Fantastic was a good character. So what with that and the band, plus the ad break, it wasn't that much. Eighteen minutes of material was all we had to get each week. So it wasn't arduous work.'

THURSDAY

5.25 CHILDREN'S TELEVISION
**Do Not Adjust
Your Set**
The Longest Running Show of 1968
WITH
DENISE COFFEY
ERIC IDLE
DAVID JASON
TERRY JONES
MICHAEL PALIN
FEATURING
Bonzo Dog Doo-Dah Band
AND THE INCREDIBLE
Captain Fantastic

WRITTEN BY ERIC IDLE, TERRY JONES
AND MICHAEL PALIN
DESIGNED BY
SYLVA NADOLNY
PRODUCED BY
HUMPHREY BARCLAY
DIRECTED BY
DAPHNE SHADWELL

Terry Jones, Michael Palin, Denise Coffey,
Eric Idle and David Jason say Do Not
Adjust Your Set. Find out why at 5.25

TV Times January 4th 1968

cut out things. Before, when I'd done animation, I hadn't used cut-outs. I would draw nice frame after frame animation but I didn't have time to do that. I think it was the crudeness and the outrageousness of it that worked. Then they had me do one about whoopee cushions. I was always looking for free things, so I'd go to the library. There are a lot of dead painters, a lot of dead engravers, so we could use that stuff. Then you start playing with it and I guess my art education has come from that. With the whoopee cushion piece, I went down to the Tate and they've got a huge collection of Victorian Christmas cards so I went through the collection and photocopied things and started moving them around. So the style just developed out of that rather than any planning being involved. I never analysed the stuff, I just did it the quickest, easiest way. And I could use images that I really loved.

I only did a couple of animations for *Do Not Adjust Your Set*. The Christmas card thing and the elephant thing. That was the first real stream-of-consciousness thing I did which Terry Jones grabbed onto when we started to do Python. He always kept referring back to that cartoon, and its stream-of-consciousness approach. Terry kept arguing as we were starting up Python that we've got to keep working in that style.

ERIC IDLE: 'Christmas Cards' was for *Do Not Adjust Your Set*. 'Elephants' was for that as well. Gilliam was always such a last-minute person, you'd always be just about to do a show and Gilliam would be just finishing off and getting his stuff in, so you don't see it and go 'Oh, that's brilliant.' It's more like he's got his stuff, you've got your stuff, you're about to go. So it's all in a general panic.

TERRY JONES: After he'd seen 'The Battle of Hastings' short film we did for this programme called *The Late Show*, my brother Nigel said, 'Why don't you do a whole show like that? A silly version of history. Why not the whole history of Britain?'

MICHAEL PALIN: *The Complete and Utter History of Britain* came from all sorts of roots. Obviously, it was a fusion of the academic side of our upbringing and the comedy side: how you look at the world and make sense of it by turning it on its head. The two things came together. Suddenly it seemed a very easy idea that we should treat history as if it had always been covered by modern media and communications, so you could have cameras at the Battle of Hastings and so on and so forth. From then on it was just looking through the rich sweep of history, taking things out and deciding how we could play them, how we could make them funny. So there'd be the invention of a chair, which is like sitting on the ground only higher up: 'We've got this device for sitting on the ground higher up,' which is Terry's great line. And things like the Battle of Hastings being done like an interview in the showers afterwards, like it had been a football game, and then they talk about the arrow: 'Oh it was very sad that, you know, we're all very sad about that, good army, and we had a go, someone sent one up, Harold 'appened to be looking up at the time, there it was, back of the eye, lucky for us, bad luck for him, you know we're not crowing over it, that's the thing that 'appens.' So you could write a very modern satirical show, but it would all appear to be about history.

That was the attraction of the *Complete and Utter History*. But Humphrey Barclay was very important in that one, because he was producing it and Humphrey was seen then as our friend. He guided us through a few *Do Not Adjust Your Sets* and our destiny was very much tied in with what deal Humphrey could get for us, because despite *Do Not Adjust Your Set*, I don't think there were any television companies rushing along saying we're going to offer you a series.

There were various things going on. Barry Took, I know, was very interested in Terry and myself as writers and wanted us to write *Comedy Playhouse*-type half-hours, but in the end we didn't go in that direction because we felt that things were changing and we had to reflect that change. Things were changing in the country, in music, fashion, all these tastes were suddenly up for grabs and I think we wanted to change the way comedy was done. I think that was quite important to us and so *Complete and Utter History* seemed to be doing that. But there were certain compromises we made in casting and I think we would have liked to have done more of the characters ourselves, but we got various people in and with one or two exceptions they weren't very good, to be honest. We couldn't have played all the characters ourselves. It would have been too much to do, and people didn't really do that that often. Dick Emery did all the parts in his show, but Dick Emery was a big star. We needed a repertory company around us, it was just that in many of the actual performances, something was wrong. We knew it wasn't working so from our point of view many of the ideas of *Complete and Utter History* were very good but the execution wasn't that great.

Looking back on it now, it needed the Python team in it, that's exactly what it needed. A lot of the stuff was like *The Holy Grail*. There was a scene where there was one very tall Norman, so the Anglo-Saxons would come along with ladders, and they'd lay their ladder against this person, climb up, hit him on the head, go down again, take the ladder away, and he'd fall over. Trying to explain this to the actor who was being hit on the head was absolutely impossible, whereas if you'd have done it in Python it would have been hilarious. So that was the weakness of *Complete and Utter History*. It was the way we wanted to go and the way we did go in Python, but we didn't really have the clout, or the strength of our own convictions perhaps, to insist that we should do it ourselves. Having said that, I don't think anyone would have given us the money for that.

TERRY JONES: I think it suffers from slightly lugubrious performances sometimes. Colin Gordon, who did the introductions, was a little bit too severe. And Roddy Maude-Roxby would never learn the lines for some reason and always improvise things and miss the jokes. It was very frustrating. But it was through doing *Do Not Adjust Your Set* and *Complete and Utter Histories* that I really felt it became crucial to get involved in the production as well, it wasn't enough just to act and write it, you had to get involved in the direction somehow. We turned up once to shoot a big battle scene, and the idea was it was meant to be done like a Western spoof with the Indians appearing on the bluff, but when you go closer they're actually Frenchmen with berets and onions and bicycles, and they have a secret weapon, the accordionist! And they'd come and breathe garlic on the English troops. But when we got to the location we found we were in this rolling countryside and I said to the director, Maurice Murphy, 'Where's the cliff? It's meant to be a Western.' I was really furious about that. And that was the moment when I thought, 'I've got to go on location reccies and check up on where they're sending us in future.'

MICHAEL PALIN: We watched *The 1948 Show* and they seemed to us like senior boys at school. They were going out at peak time. Later it turned out that John had been keeping an eye on *Do Not Adjust Your Set* and certainly *Complete and Utter History*. There was that famous call when he rang me after *History* finished and said, 'Well you obviously won't be doing any more of them!'

We never heard about ratings for *Do Not Adjust Your Set*, no one ever told us those, they wouldn't anyway, that was for executives. But it was certainly doing well and Rediffusion were very pleased with it and so we assumed there must be people watching it. The only people I ever knew who watched it were waiters. I judged our status by the restaurants we were asked to have lunch in. Humphrey got us together at La Terazza, in Ramillies Street, run by these two guys, Mario and Franco. And it was at restaurants like this that people would come up and suddenly recognise us and say, 'That programme is so good, so funny,' because they had to work all night long, so they'd get up about midday, have their lunch and then they'd have a couple of hours before going off to work and during those couple of hours they'd watch television. *Do Not Adjust Your Set* came along and they all thought it was wonderful: 'I like your programme, you very funny' and all that. We were getting quite good feedback.

We'd also got into this area of taking control of the show much more, and after the first series Daphne Shadwell, who'd been the director, was gently – she probably wouldn't say gently, rather brutally – removed. We got another director in because we didn't feel that Daphne's view of the show was particularly the way we wanted to go. That was the first time we thought, come on now, we've got a bit more strength, we ought to have a bit more say in how the programme's

From London Weekend Television

COMEDY

London Weekend makes television history with

THE COMPLETE AND UTTER HISTORY OF BRITAIN

the show with a distinctly hysterical view of historical fact, which throws new light upon some of the un-answered questions of history, by bringing you the facts as they "really" happened!

London Weekend cameras turn back the clock to bring you action-packed high-lights of some of the most gruelling battles ever fought AND exclusive interviews with famous figures in British history, including (from left to right) : KING CANUTE, WILLIAM THE CONQUEROR, QUEEN ELIZABETH I, OLIVER CROMWELL

and many, many more.

further details from
Richard Price, RPTA Ltd., 25 Berkeley House, Hay Hill, London, W.1.
Phone: 01-493-1339   Cables: TeeVeeFilm, London

done. Daphne had strong ideas about how we were all presented – I was 'Pretty Palin', Eric was 'Idle Jack' and Terry was 'Terry Jones'. And it was all slightly school mistress-ish, so we got another director for the second series, a man called Adrian Cooper. Then the whole thing began to go much more towards what we were looking for, which was a much more experimental off-the-wall kind of show. We pushed *Do Not Adjust Your Set* as far as we could go with it really.

ERIC IDLE: I don't think there is an Oxford/Cambridge divide within Python. I don't buy this at all. This is bullshit because Terry G did not go to Oxford. Occidental doesn't count as Oxford. Terry's from a completely different world. He's from a different alien planet so it doesn't count at all. But Michael and Terry are from Oxford, that is different from John, me and Graham being from Cambridge, but it didn't mean the group fell into that. The group, as I see it, breaks down much more easily into those who are from *Do Not Adjust Your Set* and those who are not, because we were together so much longer; practically from post-university we were writers on *The Frost Report*. So I think that's the way it breaks down much more satisfactorily.

The *Do Not Adjust Your Set* gang are very affectionate and we go back to being boys in a gang together. We were doing a kid's show, this wasn't even grown-up television. And John and Graham were from a slightly older tradition. They were the older pipe-smoking members of the RAF. So I think that's the dichotomy right there, I don't fall for the Oxford and Cambridge argument.

TERRY JONES: I think Eric would have liked to carry on with *Do Not Adjust Your Set,* but Mike and I thought we wanted to do something else. There were so many elements that were not going like I thought they ought to go and our opinion was being ignored slightly, so we felt we didn't really want to go on.

MICHAEL PALIN: We'd just come to a natural end. David and Denise, I think, wanted to take it in a slightly different direction and wanted to do more writing and be more involved in it. The way they were thinking about it was different from the way the three of us were seeing it. We were probably quite selfish, we were thinking about what we wanted the show to be, forgetting that they were this great strong popular centre of the show. So it seemed as though it was something that had run its natural course.

And if we did want to try something new and different, we had to go on to a different group really.

'It's...'

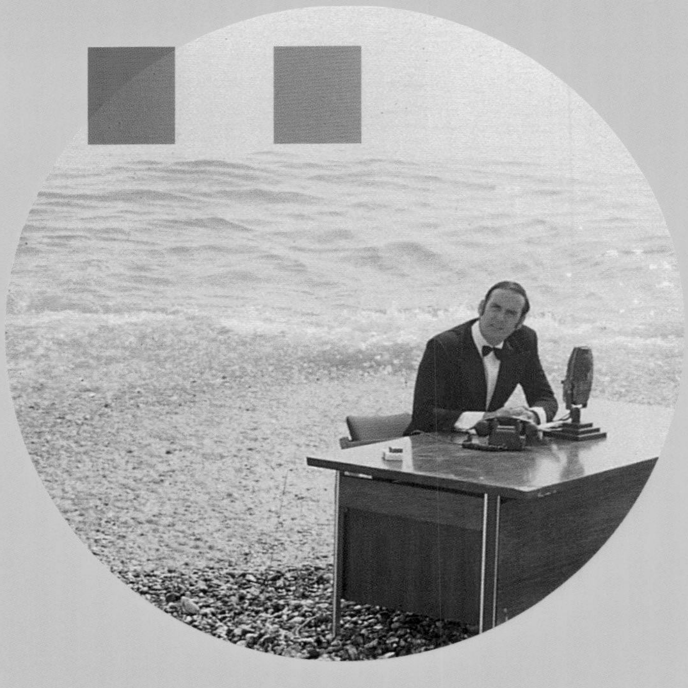

'… The first thing that was shot was the 'It's …' man down in Poole Harbour coming out of the sea. We liked the idea of the show being called 'It's …' and then not having a title at all. Then this idea came from somewhere to have it said by this terrible castaway, a man who with the last breaths of his life, just gets the title out. That went down very well and that's when the 'It's …' man was born …'

MONTY PYTHON'S FLYING CIRCUS

MONTY PYTHON
SOUNDS LIKE SOME
SORT OF NASTY
SNAKE TO ME!

'Did the 'Death of Genghis Khan', and two men carrying a donkey past a Butlins redcoat who later gets hit on the head with a raw chicken by the man from the previous sketch. All this in 18 degrees of sunshine beside the sea at Shell Bay with a small crowd of holidaymakers watching, what an extraordinary life.'

JOHN CLEESE: Graham and I used to watch *Do Not Adjust Your Set*. It was our treat on a Thursday afternoon. We would finish early and watch that because it was the funniest thing on television. I said to Graham, 'Why don't we ring the guys and see if they want to do a show with us?'

MICHAEL PALIN: The point of the phone call was that John wanted to work with Terry and myself because he liked our material. That included Eric too, because he was referring to *Do Not Adjust Your Set* as well as *Complete and Utter History*.

JOHN CLEESE: We talked to them direct, and they weren't very keen because they'd just had an offer from Philip Jones at Thames Television. For a couple of weeks they were wondering whether to go with Philip Jones, and I think that if they had accepted his offer, they wouldn't have gone with Graham and me. But after a couple of weeks they came back and said, 'OK, we've given up on that, let's do it together.'

ERIC IDLE: We had the offer from Thames on the table for Mike, Terry and me to do this thing, but they couldn't get us a studio for another year or eighteen months, so I thought, 'Hell, great – good news, bad news.' Then Mike and Terry said, 'John's got this offer from the BBC.' Mike had done *How to Irritate People* with John. I never went to the tapings of that because it was a nightmare, it went on forever. The only choice was whether we went to ITV or whether we went to John and I think, for me, John was so brilliant that it was a no-brainer really.

MICHAEL PALIN: *How to Irritate People* was the show which John asked me to do with him in '68. That was important because it was

the first time I'd ever worked with John and Graham as an actor and a writer and it was very much like a mini-Python except that I wasn't writing with Terry. I was an actor with their material, but we changed it a little bit in rehearsal. We really enjoyed doing that even though the end result had not been very successful largely due to technical problems with the recording itself. That was David Frost getting myself, John and Graham, Marty and Tim Brooke-Taylor together in one go.

At that time John was being pursued by David Frost who'd started this company, Paradine Productions, and John and Graham were already committed to write films for Paradine Productions. John tried to distance himself from David in some way and this was confirmed by a later call I got from David Frost in which he was quite upset, the first time I'd really heard David upset.

From the diary of Michael Palin, April 1969: Frost rang in the evening, all he really wanted to know was whether people were turning against him or did we still love him. It was slightly embarrassing, for the first time David seemed really out of control. How are the mighty falling, I thought, and sank back to watch a two-and-a-half-hour programme on the violent universe.

TERRY JONES: David Frost wanted to produce it. He wanted it to be a Paradine Production. Frosty rang Mike up one day and said, 'Hello Mikey, what's all this I hear about you don't want this to be a Paradine Production?' And Mike said, 'We just don't.' It was just John who was supposedly contractually bound to do Paradine stuff and John said, 'Well, he'll look a fool if he sues me.' So John just went ahead and ignored it. There was never a question that John wouldn't do the show. The idea of doing a show together really came from John and John didn't want to do it for Paradine.

ERIC IDLE: Frosty wanted to spin off people. And he was always trying to host Python. He'd call up and say, 'Can't I just introduce it?' And we'd say, 'No! Fuck off David!'

Early writing sessions in
Terry Jones's house/back garden

MICHAEL PALIN: Barry Took had talked to Terry Jones and myself over a period of a year about writing *Comedy Playhouse* things or writing a series of our own. Being a writer himself, Barry saw something in our writing that he liked and felt he should encourage. But he also could see that between me and John there was a sort of chemistry in performing and he always thought it would be very good to get the two of us together.

ERIC IDLE: Barry Took was working as a consultant for the BBC and he approached John. I think John said he didn't want to do it on his own and we came into the frame then. John always had his eye on Michael because he'd worked with him, and I think that what Barry did was instrumental in getting it sold to the BBC or getting them excited.

DAVID SHERLOCK: Once it was decided they were going to do it, someone had the bright idea of having a picnic. We drove down to the Thames, somewhere like Eel Pie Island, and we had a celebratory picnic with Python's wives and partners in various forms. They were the writers and I don't know whether Terry Gilliam was there or not.

TERRY GILLIAM: The meeting in the park was somewhere out near Hampton Court.

ERIC IDLE: The only thing I ever remember is a meeting in a park somewhere, where we sat and talked about it with John and it

seemed like a good idea. The initial meeting in the park was to see if we all wanted to do it and would it work. Then we went to the BBC to show them what we were going to do, which was basically, we didn't know! And I think that convinced them. We were all pros, you could rely on us, we'd got a body of work behind us that was quite imposing at that stage, one way or another.

TERRY JONES: I don't remember a meeting in the park.

A newly married Terry Jones
with wife, Alison

Writing and lazing in
Terry Jones's back garden

JOHN CLEESE: My recollection is that Barry Took somehow got involved at some point and was very useful. I think we had a couple of discussions at his flat and then we went to see Michael Mills at the BBC. We gave a very poor account of ourselves with him asking if we were going to have guest stars and music and film. We weren't able to give him a satisfactory answer to anything he asked.

TERRY GILLIAM: Barry got this job as Head of Comedy, whatever that was, and he was trying to justify his existence because the job had been created. The BBC had offered John the chance to do whatever he wanted to do whenever he wanted to do it, and he took advantage of that by bringing Mike and Mike's friends along.

From the diary of Michael Palin, 17 April 1969: There have been negotiations and murmurs of murmurs of negotiations on behalf of the '5' Show … It's a time when there's no work to do, I've been, for the first time since July last year, free from script deadlines, rehearsals, filming, recording, et al and Terry Jones is away in Crete, Eric is in his playboy paradise somewhere near Spain and I'm waiting here in London to leave for Locarno.

MICHAEL PALIN: I think calling it 'The 5 Show' was just the way it was discussed. That just meant we were the writers and performers and Gilliam obviously would come in on the sideline and not as a writer/performer.

ERIC IDLE: I'm pretty sure Gilliam was involved with us in the ITV offer. So whether we were preparing to shaft him I don't know. I hope so, but I don't think so. Mike and Terry were always trying to drop him, sexual jealousy.

JOHN CLEESE: We came out of Michael Mills's office, after we'd said, 'All right, we'll make thirteen programmes,' which I think will go down as one of the great executive decisions of all time and something that really wouldn't happen for a split second today. But we didn't really know what we were doing. Jonesy confirms this: we both happened to watch Spike Milligan's Q5, and one or the other of us phoned up and said kind of jokingly but also rather anxiously, 'I thought that's what we were supposed to be doing?' And the other one said, 'That's what I thought too.' We felt that Spike had got to where we were trying to get to, but if you'd asked us the previous day, we couldn't have described very well what that was. However, when we saw it on the screen we recognised it, and in a way the fact that Spike had gone there probably enabled us to go a little bit further than we would have otherwise gone.

ERIC IDLE: That came pretty quickly from Michael Mills: 'I'll give you thirteen, you're on air in October, but that's all I can give you, night-night. Now go away and get on with it!' Whoa, OK.

From the diary of Michael Palin, 23 May: We lunched at the BBC with Barry Took. It was the first time since a lunch at the Light of Kashmir at Fleet Road earlier in the month that the six of us, Cleese, Chapman, Eric, Terry G, Terry J and myself had met together. Barry bought us drinks in the BBC Club which seemed fuller than ever. It was not really since our work on *A Series of Birds* that we'd worked regularly at the BBC. Now we were about to start again, only this time we would be solely involved in one show and that's the first time we've been able to afford that luxury. We had a very convivial lunch and afterwards retired to a conference room where Barry talked to us for a while about what he was offering us and what we wanted and what he hoped would result from the show. The name of George Schlatter, the American producer of *Laugh-In*, was mentioned with a little hint of awe by Barry. He seems to be the man through whom Barry hopes to sell English comedy to the States and our show is high on Barry's list of American sales hopes. As to the question of whether we took the BBC's first option, recorded seven shows and then break for a month, then six further shows or thirteen in succession without a break, we agreed after much discussion with T. Jones, the only dissenting voice, to do seven and six. Then the door burst open and small, bearded Michael Mills, Frank Muir's successor as Head of Comedy, burst in to tell us that we were doing thirteen on the trot, our time slot was

'Barry got this job as Head of Comedy, whatever that was, and he was trying to justify his existence because the job had been created. The BBC had offered John the chance to do whatever he wanted to do whenever he wanted to do it, and he took advantage of that by bringing Mike and Mike's friends along.'

to be Saturday evenings after *Match of the Day*, the old *TW3* slot in fact, this had been agreed to by Paul Fox, wasn't it all wonderful, goodbye, and with that the dreadful little Michael Mills left. Not wanting to appear ungrateful … After he left, everyone seemed to accept his new specification for the series just like that. Barry obviously has very little bargaining power once it gets to the actual scheduling. Graham Chapman disappeared for a week in Ibiza and the remainder of us began talking about the show. It was a very useful and inspiring discussion, some good material had been written on all and what was more important the Jones, Gilliam, Palin idea of a sort of stream of consciousness way of putting the material together was accepted enthusiastically, by John at any rate. So at six we left the BBC feeling a lot better.

JOHN CLEESE: It was like somebody inviting you into a field of flowers that you have never been in before, no one has ever been in. You open the gate and you suddenly walk in and they're all there just to be picked, and there's so many you don't know where you want to start picking.

GRAHAM CHAPMAN: Our biggest thing really was getting rid of the punchline. For years people had been doing a punchline, and we had to do it too as writers. The producer would look quite blank if there wasn't a punchline because how can he end if he can't cue the audience to applaud, you've got to have something there. Well, we don't worry about the audience particularly, let them get on with it.[6]

JOHN CLEESE: There was a lovely producer/director on *Frost* called Jimmy Gilbert. We'd say something and people would shriek with laughter, and Jimmy, who had a lovely sense of humour, would smile and say, 'Yes, but they won't understand it in Bradford.' What happened with Python was that we went off and did all the stuff

that we were not allowed to do in the other shows like *The Frost Report*, and enough of the audience *did* understand it in Bradford.

From the diary of Michael Palin, 7 May: After playing squash with Terry we drove back to my place to watch episode 12 of *Do Not Adjust* which I thought was a good one. Then off in Terry's car to John Cleese's flat in Knightsbridge for some talks about the projected show which now has dates, 24 August for thirteen episodes and what could be a title – 'It's Not'.

From the diary of Michael Palin, 11 May: We really must get ourselves organised, with six people planning and writing the show it seems that 80 per cent of the time is being taken up by arranging where to meet.

ERIC IDLE: We discussed it in the spring. I know because we started shooting in July '69, and I got married on 7 July and they all came to my wedding and party. Then they went off shooting and I went for a week to France. So we must have written it in the three

months previously. We must have written at least five before we went filming, because I missed that first week's filming.

From the diary of Michael Palin, 27 May: Five of us, less Graham Chapman worked in a room at the BBC putting a prototype show together. A good day's work we continue tomorrow at Eric's.

From the diary of Michael Palin, Tuesday, 3 June: We gave up the attempts at emulating Monday's progress and drove up to Graham Chapman's via a bookshop in Hampstead. Graham, very brown from a week in Ibiza, treated us to his usual generous portions of scotch and was very appreciative of the writing we'd done during the week he was away. He was particularly enthusiastic about the continuity of the show.

TERRY JONES: Terry G said, 'I've got this thing, "Elephants", I don't know what it is really, it's just a train of consciousness sort of thing.' So when we were trying to get a form for Python, I thought of that. I'd just seen Spike Milligan's *Q5* series and I thought, 'Ah he's done it, he's done something new.' He'd done all these sketches that didn't have beginnings or ends. They'd just stop or they'd turn into a different sketch or something and he just didn't care. I was thinking, 'How can we do that, how can we use that breakthrough that Milligan's got there?' I was just walking up the stairs in my parents' house in Claygate and I suddenly remembered Terry's 'Elephants' cartoon and the way that went from one thing to another. I thought, 'Maybe we could do that for the whole show.' So I rang up Terry and Mike and they said 'Yeah, great idea.' Then we put the idea to the others at the next script meeting and they weren't interested. So the first series was a bit of a struggle, with Terry, me and Mike trying to get this chain of consciousness going. We had this flow and the others were still really writing sketches with beginnings, middles and ends and punchlines and things.

ERIC IDLE: Jonesy was very obsessed with how it should be in structure, that was definitely his obsession and he loved Gilliam's stream of consciousness thing. When we saw *Q5* we thought, 'Oh fuck, he's done it,' because Spike broke the fourth wall. The other thing we were really worried about was *Laugh-In*, because that also came on the air and we went 'Oh fuck, they're doing what we wanted, this madness.' So Gilliam became the glue, he became the link thing. He's thinking in forms of structure whereas we're thinking in terms of material. I don't think there's any issue there, I think they're all overlapping things that somebody has to take care of.

JOHN CLEESE: There was a serious doubt about the feasibility of Terry doing animation. He had to sit down with one or two BBC people and really convince them that he could do the stuff on the sort of budget available; that was the problem. Also he was much less of a known quantity than the others, he was the one who had not been sitting with the other five at *The Frost Report* table.

TERRY JONES: Terry Gilliam must have been in it by the time I'd made the connection with 'Elephants'. I don't think he was brought in because of that. We always intended to bring Terry in, but the five of us met first just to talk about what the show was, because we didn't regard Terry as a writer at that time.

JOHN CLEESE: Jonesy saw how animation could give the show something very special and I don't think Chapman and I were that interested. We liked the idea of it, but we were excited by just doing completely different types of sketches and not obeying the formats that everyone had developed and seemed to think were necessary.

TERRY GILLIAM: Terry took on that whole stream of consciousness way of doing something. And that happened because very early on in Python one of the things we had noticed, having watched Peter Cook and Dudley Moore and all the sorts of programmes where there was a need for a traditional punchline, was that they would do these great sketches, all sorts of characters, but the punchline was often weak and left a bad taste in your mouth when the sketch was wonderful. So we decided OK let's get rid of the punchline and not worry about that, which fitted into the stream of consciousness

'So we decided OK let's get rid of the punchline and not worry about that, which fitted into the stream of consciousness idea.'

idea. We don't need punchlines. We'll keep it running until we think it's run out of steam then we'll pass onto something else. And that really freed us up.

JOHN CLEESE: We were never great theorisers. We discovered what we were going to do mainly by sitting down and seeing what came out on the sheets of paper at the end of the day, quite literally. Then another stage was when we all got together in the same room and were faced not with just writing three minutes of funny material, but how we put the different three minutes of funny material together. And I remember that that was exhilarating. We almost never met at the BBC, but they gave us some little underground room, and I just remember coming out of a script meeting and thinking 'This was real fun'. There was a tremendous liberation, this energising feeling when you break through stuff you felt constricted by and you suddenly sense all the possibilities around.

MICHAEL PALIN: We had no idea what was going to go in each show. We just assembled a great mound of material. Some of it obviously came from ideas we had when we were at John's flat, up at Graham's or at the Light of Kashmir or whatever. Ideas would be tossed around and other things would just have come on impulse when we were actually separately writing together. Throughout May material was being put together.

Cleese and Chapman were kings of the castle, as writers, and we rather liked Graham as a performer and John was just the best around really, so in a sense we were quite excited that John wanted to pitch in with all the rest of us in this experimental form of show. That's what seemed interesting, that we managed to persuade John and Graham, who probably had many more offers than we had, to do something that was quite off the wall. I remember a lot of discussion about the shape of the show, which was generally led by Terry J and Terry G. This idea of the stream of consciousness approach to continuity was definitely thought about, and at the various times that we met together there clearly wasn't any problem with the kind of material. There weren't any points where people said this is going the wrong way, let's not do it that way. We sound a remarkably united bunch. Although the old *Frost Report*

divisions were there in that Terry and I still wrote a lot of the material that needed to be filmed, we wrote with a visual sense which John and Graham didn't really bother about at all. They really weren't concerned, as far as I could tell, about where things were shot or what we were wearing, whereas Terry and I would begin a reading by setting the scene: 'A mountain side in Scotland, mist is drifting over.' And these became parodied amongst the group as we went along. As soon as I'd start reading something, 'Oh, here we go again – pan over idyllic countryside, the sun is shining' and all that. So mine and Terry's work was known as 'Pan Over Idyllic Countryside', but we had to set the scene sometimes and that was part of it.

ERIC IDLE: It was a writers' commune. The writers were in charge. That's very, very, very, very, very unique. There was no producer. There was no director or any power telling you what to do. There was almost no network. So we were the creators. And we never cast until after we'd written everything and there was a certain sense of fair play in it. I think there was definitely ego involved, but it was odd in the formation of that group. Put together we formed almost one completely mad person. Everybody was mad, but in a slightly different way, each had his own element of madness. But together we made this perfectly mad person. So there wasn't a lot of clash of temperament, although there was a big clash between John and Terry Jones – huge, huge, all the time.

JOHN CLEESE: There were sometimes tremendous fights about material but the strange thing was it was always about material, it was never about who was going to act what material. We always instinctively knew as actors who was going to make anything work best and that's the way it was. If you had a light week, you thought, 'Well that's fine, did a light week this week.' There was a great sense of we were all in it together. If the shows were funny we all benefited and if they weren't we didn't, and it didn't matter particularly who got the laughs, it really didn't. But there were catfights about the material. I remember once we got into a terrible fight about whether a candelabra should be made out of a goat or a sheep. We knew that there was going to be a light bulb screwed into each of its four feet but there was this almost vitri-

olic fight, three against three, insulting each other: 'Fucking sheep! What do you mean a sheep? It has got to be a goat.' I remember halfway through thinking, 'This is absolutely insane.' So there were always a lot of arguments about whether material should go in the show, whether it was good enough whether it was not good enough. There was a high degree of energy expended on that. Jones and I expended more energy than the others. Michael was the natural peacemaker. Graham was happy to put a word in but didn't argue, although he cared. Sort of. Graham was never quite there. He would come in, say something marvellous and then drift off in his own mind, so he wouldn't have a point most of the time.

'I remember halfway through thinking, "This is absolutely insane." '

GRAHAM CHAPMAN: John's bigger than the rest of us. I can be fairly fierce, but I don't think there is any friction in that way. I find I tend to align with John as far as choice of material is concerned, we have a much more aligned sense of humour and Mike and Terry tend to go along the same way, and Eric, poor thing, is on his own. I think we've now reached a point where we can be fairly honest with each other about what we think of something, I can say I think that's rubbish or that's good and nobody gets hurt. I think when we started off in the first series, we were a little bit conscious of 'Oh, we've got to use him for something', but now I don't think that applies.[6]

TERRY JONES: It was always meant to be an equal group and it was on that basis that we entered it. I remember right at the beginning, the first meeting, John saying, 'We don't want any of this personality stuff and, we're not going to put our names up at the end of the show with our faces and who we are.' And we all went along with that. It kind of went up and down a bit, John was a dominating personality, but in terms of artistically, I don't think anybody did dominate really. Nobody had the final say or anything like that.

ERIC IDLE: That's how we did it on *Do Not Adjust Your Set* – we'd write and then we'd meet and read out the material. So on Python we met and then said, 'Let's split up and meet again in two weeks.' That's when it turned into a creative meeting, we'd spend a whole day down at Jonesy's and read it all out. I think that's what Python was really good at, what we got really good at, which was reading our own material, editing it and saying, 'Why don't you just cut it there, that's when it stops being funny, and put that next to that and do this.' We all got good at editing.

TERRY JONES: A lot of the time we'd meet in my front room and talk about the kind of things we'd want to do and then we'd disappear and write for a couple of weeks. By that time I think Mike and I were writing separately, but together. So he and I would write for a couple of days and then we'd get together, read out what we'd got, vet it and say, 'That is funny, that isn't.' Then we'd change over stuff, maybe write a little bit together, but we hardly ever wrote much together – we'd just swap over material and then go back and vamp it up again. Then after a couple of weeks we'd all meet together round the table at my house and have the read-through. That was the best bit of Python really, you'd look forward to the read-throughs because you knew you were going to hear something silly.

MICHAEL PALIN: It's very difficult with something that makes you laugh because you can't fabricate a response. It either makes you laugh or it doesn't. And you could tell around the table whether it's been funny or not. It's not like reading out a report on something so people at the end can nod and say, yes, very good points there, well argued. You will have provoked a gurgling noise at the back of the throat from people around the table or you won't.

It was a very good process and very generous because for all of us it was the first time we'd put all our material together and yet we were admirers of each other's material. We knew stuff that Eric wrote which cracked us up, Eric knew stuff that Graham and John had written which cracked him up and so it went round. On a good day it was a real treat, fine material from six people who all shared a similar sense of humour. If that sketch hit the target it was a delight, that would go through and that would put us all in a very good mood, which we wanted to be in.

It was all rather exciting at the beginning. I don't think anyone wanted to be over-critical, but at the same time people were aware that it had to be a good show and we had to get the stuff through, but generally it was a feeling of great elation and exhilaration at the sort of material that was coming up.

ERIC IDLE: We brought in some material. I know I had brought in material because I'd been writing for the ITV *Frost*. I'd written 'Nudge, Nudge' for that show for Ronnie Barker. They'd rejected it, and if you look at it, there are no jokes on the page, so you can see exactly why they turned it down. I read it to the Pythons and I remember them falling about laughing and saying, 'Well that's in!' And it's one of the earliest things that I did. So we had material around which we read out to each other and then we went away and started to write more stuff. There was a bottom drawer of stuff because we were current writers. 'What have you got at the moment?' 'Well I've got this and I've got that – now let's get on with it.'

MICHAEL PALIN: As far as I remember, our stuff was written absolutely from scratch, because we didn't have any good stuff in the bottom drawer. We'd sold it, all that was left there was absolute crap really.

TERRY JONES: I know John had a bottom drawer of scripts because he had the 'sheep nesting in the trees' script they'd written for *The Frost Report*. Jimmy Gilbert, the producer, had said, 'Oh no, that's too way out, we can't do that, that's silly,' and John was feeling, 'Well, I want a show where I can do really silly things, like the sheep nesting.' So that was the first sketch that we filmed for Python.

TERRY GILLIAM: Everyone would start off by going off in his separate group. And then we'd come back and read the stuff out. And I always had certain ideas that I wanted to do that I had worked out in my head. The problem with me was that I couldn't read them, I'd describe them, but that's not the same thing and the others would look aghast.

JOHN CLEESE: I remember writing in the script quite carefully that you'd end a sketch, and then we would send a message to Gilliam saying something like, 'We need 45 seconds of animation here Terry, starting with the end of this sketch and taking us into the next sketch which is set in a pet shop.' Once he'd got the script, we never saw what he did until he came in on the afternoon of the day we recorded. And then we would sit back, usually in the afternoon, and watch his stuff on the monitors and it was a great treat. And it gave the show something truly unique.

go and in the end that was the trade-off. We would be allowed to have our own name that came before it, but we had to keep 'Flying Circus'. It was the only sort of real attempt by the BBC to try and keep us in order at that time, apart from cutting off funds and generally treating us tightly.

TERRY JONES: Finding the right title was very important, and it was a bit of a nightmare because we just couldn't agree on the title and it seemed like we never would. Until you had the title you couldn't really say what it was in a funny way. We knew it was going to be a funny show but I was a bit alarmed because I didn't like 'Bunn, Wackett, Buzzard, Stubble and Boot', which was the title that was decided on, but I was outvoted on that. So I was rather pleased when the BBC came back and said that was too silly and we had to think of a more sensible title.

They'd been calling it 'Barry Took's Circus' or something, so we had to call it something else and we said 'Flying Circus' definitely. Then there was the 'Gwen Dibley' suggestion quite early on and so we went back to that, but thought, 'Mmm, not quite right'. We were sitting round and Eric said, 'Shouldn't it be some sort of seedy showbiz agent? Something like Monty?' Then John said, 'How about something nasty like a python,' and we said, 'Monty Python'. We said, 'Yeah, spot on.' I went back home and told my brother, 'We've got a title for the show, we're going to call it *Monty Python's Flying Circus*.' And he said, 'It'll never catch on.' My brother had a good sense for these things, but not that time.

From the diary of Michael Palin, 1 August 1969: The show has been renamed *Monty Python's Flying Circus*.

From the diary of Michael Palin, 10 June 1969: We met our directors for the autumn show. One was Ian MacNaughton, director of

the Spike Milligan *Q5* series which we all thought was one of the best comedy shows on TV and certainly the most far ahead …

MICHAEL PALIN: John was very keen on John Howard Davies as director of the show and Terry and myself were very keen to get Ian MacNaughton because of *Q5* and the work he'd done there – we liked his slightly madcap irreverent approach. He seemed to really respond to the silly ideas we had and John didn't like that because John liked things to be fairly organised, he liked order and I think he saw Ian as somebody who was chaotic and disorganised. It was a bit of a risk going with Ian MacNaughton in some ways, but there was no question in the minds of Terry and myself and Terry G, this was just what the series needed. This was part of the process of getting rid of the old approach to comedy and going with somebody who would be a soulmate. John Howard Davies, the nice, very likeable man that he was, to us represented the old BBC, wanting to bring it back to something that was less adventurous, whereas with Ian it was sailing off on a great adventure, we knew not where it would go, but that's what it felt like. But Ian was away on holiday, so John Howard Davies directed the first few shows until Ian came back.

JOHN CLEESE: I personally liked working with John because I thought he was much better at casting and he gave me good acting notes, which Ian seldom did. I also thought John was more straightforward to work with. I sometimes had to take what Ian was telling me about rushes with a pinch of salt. I discovered at one point that when he went on about how good the rushes were, there was usually something slightly wrong with them. Whereas with John, I found him very much more straightforward. John was not very good with his film camera. I think he was fine with the studio cameras, but I think Ian was much better with his cameras than John was. So it was a kind of swings and roundabouts: which do you think is more important, the cameras or the performance?

'It was a bit of a risk going with Ian MacNaughton in some ways, but there was no question in the minds of Terry and myself and Terry G, this was just what the series needed. This was part of the process of getting rid of the old approach to comedy and going with somebody who would be a soulmate.'

'Of course, Ian didn't want to use Carol, he wanted to bring in various bits of totty, so we had a string of people who weren't as good as Carol. Eventually we started pushing for Carol and said, "We must have Carol for this."'

MICHAEL PALIN: The first thing that was shot was the 'It's ...' man down in Poole Harbour coming out of the sea. We liked the idea of the show being called 'It's ...' and then not having a title at all. Then this idea came from somewhere to have it said by this terrible castaway, a man who with the last breaths of his life, just gets the title out. That went down very well and that's when the 'It's ...' man was born. It was quite an uncomfortable part and Terry J and myself were quite happy to do uncomfortable things, though John wasn't really very interested. Graham was OK about those kind of things, but not really. We were good for anything mucky. I thought up the 'It's ...' man, the character of him, and if someone got a really good bead on a character, he was told, 'Right, go off, you know what to do, work out the make-up and all that.' There'd be a lot of trust. People wouldn't say, 'We've all got to see what the "It's ..." man looks like before he does it.' You didn't have to audition every costume or anything like that.

JOHN CLEESE: There was such an integration of writing and performing in Python, that to have had somebody in the show on a regular or occasional basis playing large parts who had nothing to do with the writing of the show would have changed the nature of the programme.

But in the first show there was a sketch in which a sexy girl was required and that's the moment when we thought, well, we can play the pepperpots and we can play various other forms of hags, but we really can't play a sexy girl because it changes the joke. It becomes a Python playing a sexy girl instead of being a sexy girl and is no longer a sketch about men revolving around a sexy girl, so it changes the joke. John Howard Davies cast Carol Cleveland and we thought that she was very good, so from then on whenever we wanted someone who was a real woman, in the sense that sexually she was female and attractive, we almost always asked Carol to do it.

TERRY JONES: He brought Carol in, and we didn't really approve somehow, but then she was so good. Of course, Ian didn't want to use Carol, he wanted to bring in various bits of totty, so we had a string of people who weren't as good as Carol. Eventually we started pushing for Carol and said, 'We must have Carol for this.'

From the diary of Michael Palin, 7 August 1969: We arrived at Cleese's for an evening script meeting to put Show 7 together. 'Them' is the biggest item and was read and approved in total. All 20 minutes 24 seconds of it. I hope it is a good idea and not just a

private anti-professional fantasy. However, it puts us all in high spirits and at 9 o'clock we went for a celebratory Indian meal at the Khyber Pass in Bute Street, South Ken. Very spicy, tasty, well served meal, with a smack of authenticity about it which caused me traditional curry repercussions in the night.

MICHAEL PALIN: Our early location filming involved going up to Bradford and doing stuff in a working man's club up there and I can remember being up in Bradford and doing the 'Hermits' sketch and the 'Batley Townswomen's Guild Recreation of the Battle of Pearl Harbour' in a muddy field, also up in Yorkshire. That was very early stuff that we did.

ERIC IDLE: I remember the stripper in Bradford! Oh God, that was wild. I remember it very, very well. Ian MacNaughton insisted on filming this stripper in Bradford, and we said, 'But Ian we haven't written a stripper sketch.' 'Oh, I promised her a part, it's great, and she'll be great.' So we said, 'Oh right, we'll be undertakers.' We might have written the thing about the undertakers and we probably said, 'They're sitting there watching a stripper.' So we have to sit and watch this stripper and I find strip shows offensive. They're

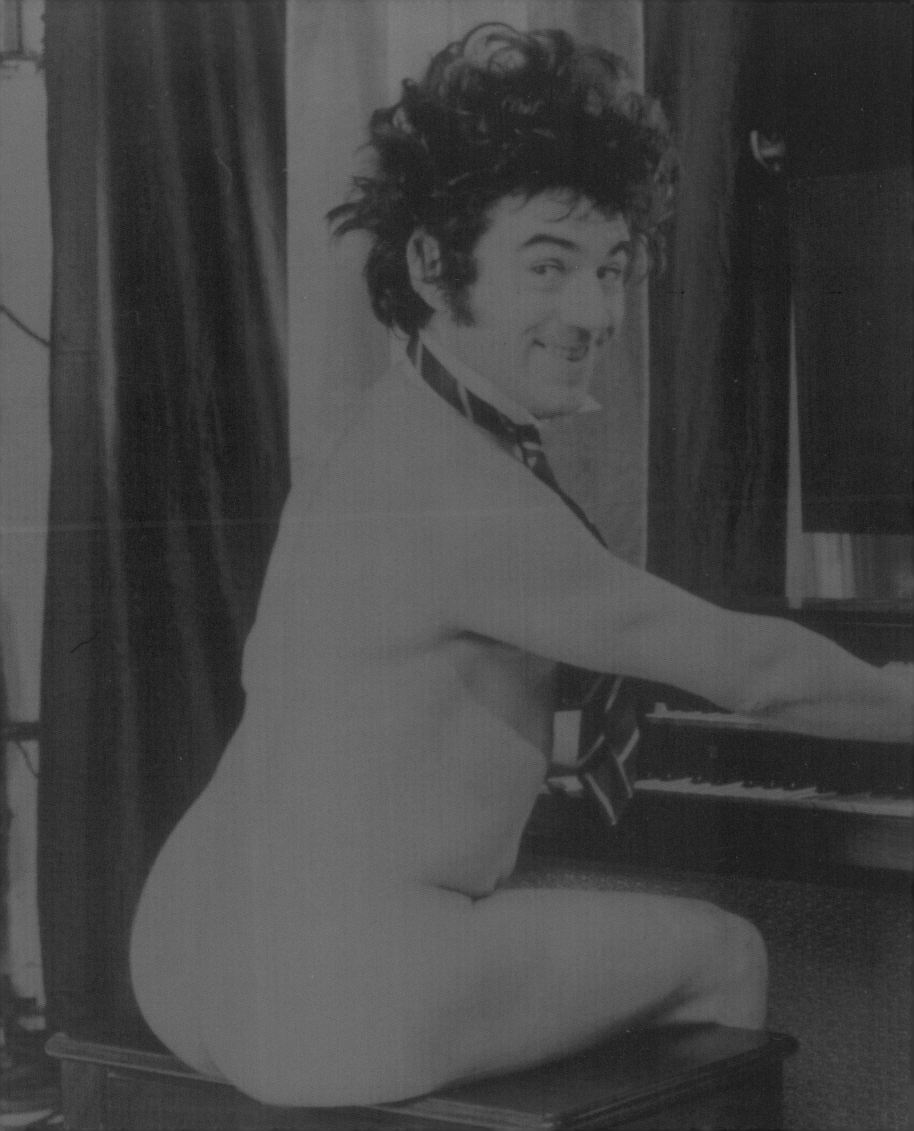

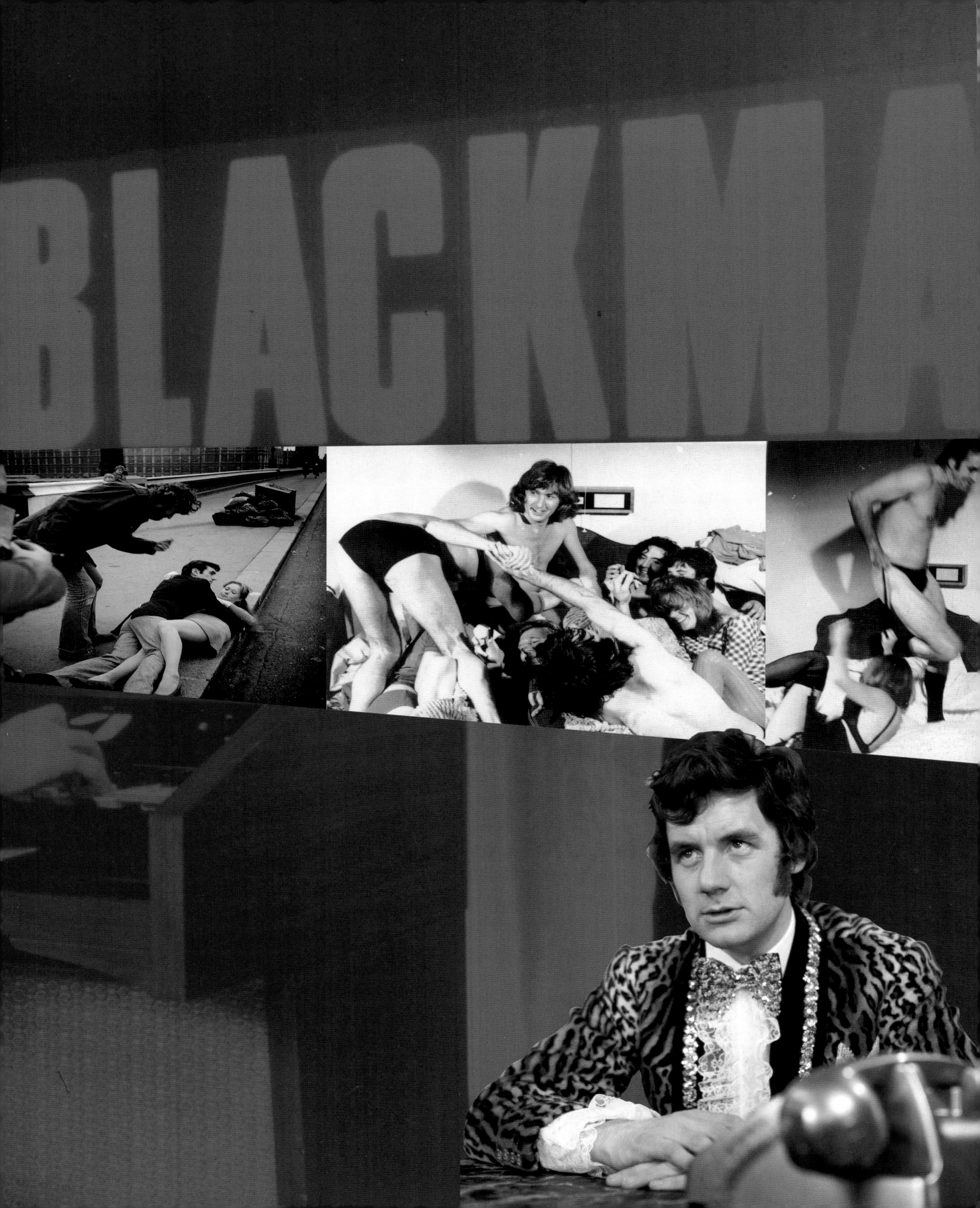
BLACKMA

Palin, Jones and costume designer Hazel Pethig gear up for 'The Cycling Tour'

aggressive and women who do it are very aggressive, it's not at all sexy or erotic. She was a bit of a scrubber and she did this thing and I remember going, 'Oh, fucking hell.'

TERRY JONES: I remember the stripper coming along because we had this bit in the 'Dull Day of a Chartered Accountant'. He goes into a newsagent and we had a topless newsagent, so this stripper was brought along to be the topless newsagent. That was quite brave, bare breasts hadn't been seen on the BBC before.

From the diary of Michael Palin, Friday, 11 July 1969: Did the 'Death of Genghis Khan', and two men carrying a donkey past a Butlins redcoat who later gets hit on the head with a raw chicken by the man from the previous sketch. All this in 18 degrees of sunshine beside the sea at Shell Bay with a small crowd of holidaymakers watching, what an extraordinary life.

MICHAEL PALIN: For the next week we filmed in bars around London and Walton-on-Thames for the Picasso cycling race. I don't know if we had to have any permission for shooting on location, but we used members of the public, we never screened off anywhere really. We had to maximise all the time we had. We felt that 29 minutes 50 seconds – the contracted length of each show – was never enough. So on the filming what you looked like, what you were dressed in, where it was shot, how it was done, were all of crucial importance. We'd go around with this coach and we'd have a props bus. Then we'd come to a place and sort things out. For instance, 'The Gumby' was created in Suffolk. I remember that, because we went to film quite near where my parents lived, and they were in it at a certain point. With 'The Gumby' I'd written this character and John had to play him. We found this little stream running by and John decided to play it standing in the water, so he wore the gumboots and that's how the Gumby outfit was created. We said it was someone with a knotted handkerchief on his head, but the rest of it, the gumboots and so on, were created on that day, obviously with a lot of help from Hazel Pethig, our costume lady, who would always be suggesting things.

TERRY JONES: When Ian came back from his holiday, Tom Sloane, who was Head of Light Entertainment, called Ian up and said, 'Look, you've got to do something about this show. It just isn't funny. There's nothing funny about a man coming out of the sea, walking up to camera and saying, "It's …"' Ian came on and the main thing he changed was to have the credits going horizontal across the bottom at the end instead of going up and down on a roller. So Ian was in a bit of a state when he arrived.

ERIC IDLE: Ian's alcoholism was progressive and was more evident during location filming, where sometimes he wouldn't appear after lunch, he'd go in the pub and that would be it, so we'd finish the shooting ourselves. You can't not appear for the afternoon – that's a bit bad – and expect to remain a director. Graham's was much more invidious and much more hidden and something that nobody really noticed. I remember noticing at *The '48 Show* backstage that he was shaking and had to have a drink, and I thought, 'That's a bit weird.' With Python, if we were doing a show, they'd go to the bar. I'd always have a bath and relax and run through my words and get ready to do the show. I couldn't do all that up in the bar and see friends and then do a show. But they would only be having a jar or two.

MICHAEL PALIN: Filming gave you a certain amount of latitude, you could experiment a little with that. Any improvisation was mainly done during the writing process around the table, the ideas on a good day just sort of flowed very fast, and it was all you could do to get it all written down. Beyond that there was a second stage when you were filming, when you had time to say, 'Oh, I've just seen something in the van, a particular prop maybe, let's try that.' Or something like the brief 'Come back to my Place' sketch, where I proposition John as a policeman. That was just done on the spot! I think John had got this outfit on for some other character he was playing, probably in the sketch about the Piranha Brothers, and we just played around with that. So a certain amount was improvised on film. Where we couldn't really improvise of course was on the recording day because we only had ninety minutes of studio time. That had to be very thoroughly and efficiently worked out because that was our only chance. The BBC wouldn't give us an extra half-hour, so we couldn't fool around and try things. By that time, all the improvisation had to be done, so the cameras knew what was going on. There was no point doing a funny movement if you hadn't told the cameraman or the director and it was missed.

GRAHAM CHAPMAN: We have lots of people on Python saying 'It's amazing how you ad-lib that well' and not a single word of it is ad-libbed, never – it's rehearsed throughout the whole week, it has to be otherwise you'd never get camera angles on it … People think we make it up on the spur of the moment, they think David Frost made it up on the spur of the moment, while there's only fifteen people in the room at the back of him.[6]

JOHN CLEESE: Oddly enough it didn't seem particularly daunting at the start. What was daunting was whether it was going to be funny or not. But somehow we all agreed it was, and there was a kind of 'What the hell!' attitude. I mean, nobody was taking any notice of us, you have to remember that.

MICHAEL PALIN: We rehearsed the week before we recorded. The first programme was broadcast 5 October 1969, so the rehearsal process would have been the end of September 1969. That was the first time we got together to rehearse having shot the various film inserts and knowing that Terry Gilliam was going to be doing things that would fit in, so we'd be rehearsing twenty-three to thirty-four minutes a week. We rehearsed in Old Oak Common Lane, at the Acton Working Men's Club. It was a working men's club with a bar where a lot of old blokes had a pint at midday and probably had a bit of a knees-up in the evening with a darts board and all that. There was this big room where they had their get-togethers and meetings and dances and whatever and on the wall I seem to remember some strange Venetian motif, a kind of mural. It was all a little bit shabby and down at heel, just off the A40, and there was a little estate of small, brick council houses around and you'd approach through that to get to the club. We rehearsed 9 to 5, but probably what it

would usually be was 9.30 or 10 till lunchtime, then we might do a bit after lunch. People would watch each other doing the sketches and say, 'Wouldn't it be funny if you did this?' So a lot was actually honed and created during the rehearsal period, especially earlier on in the week. Then we would have a technical run-through on the Thursday. The lighting man from the BBC and maybe two or three cameramen would come down, and basically the studio staff would come and watch us doing it, which is really quite odd, because they would just stand there on one side of the room without any of their equipment or anything like that.

The assistant stage manager would have actually marked out the sets so we would know exactly what room we had to move in for each set and then we would do the performance for them. A lot of it, of course, was knowing where you had to move to, and how much time you had in-between sketches to get changed. If you've only got thirty seconds and you've got to become a Viking and all that sort of stuff, you'd say, 'Well how about if Eric does his little monologue here, that gives you an extra minute, is that all right?' So you'd solve things like that. Basically it was to ensure that when we came to the recording on Saturday night it was a bit like a live show because there wasn't much time for re-takes.

From the diary of Michael Palin, Thursday, 28 August: This morning rehearsed in front of the technical boys, not an encouraging experience, I particularly felt rather too tense whilst going through it. At lunchtime Terry and I played squash for the second day running then returned to the centre to watch the final edited film for the first show. A most depressing viewing, Queen Victoria music was completely wrong and the Lochinvar film was wrong in almost every respect, editing and shooting most of all.

ERIC IDLE: We'd rehearse for three or four days in, first of all, the 'Old Soak Club'. There was an Irish club in Old Oak Common Lane, at the back of a pub, where there was a rehearsal room. We'd go in there, and I remember after the first few shows, Huw Weldon came down and said how great it was, which I thought was absolutely brilliant. He was head of the BBC and he came down. He'd seen the one about the gas cooker and he really identified with that one because he'd just ordered a new gas cooker. I thought, 'This is a good man, a man who comes all the way down to a shabby rehearsal room in Old Oak Common Lane, the back of Wormwood Scrubs.' But it was a pub, there was a bar just in the next room, so Ian MacNaughton and Graham would always be wandering in and getting another pint of something. Eventually we ended up in a very smart BBC rehearsal block somewhere out in East Acton, so rehearsing at the Beeb might have been a way to try and cut down on Ian's boozing and get a bit more useful time going, but it was really good for football, because they were smart new rooms and you could get really good goalposts. We always played good five-a-side indoor – whilst rehearsing.

From the diary of Michael Palin, Friday, 29 August: The strange depression which has been with me on and off since Wednesday, kind of nervous tension I suppose, reached a point at rehearsal where I really felt I had to stop, but it passed and the rehearsal passed and I played squash again.

TERRY GILLIAM: I would get down to the rehearsals maybe once a week, and there was a real separate life going on. They were going to pubs and restaurants all the time while I was locked up in my place cutting out pieces of paper and colouring. I always was the odd man out, there was no question about it, turning up on the

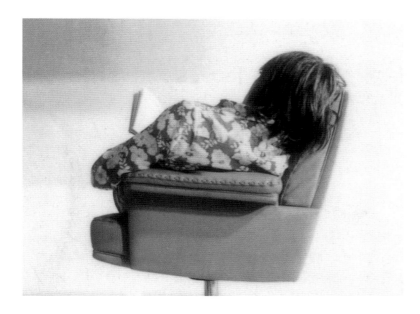

days of the shows with cans of film. I'd try to catch up because I wanted to be part of it. Then very patronisingly, graciously, they would allow me to put on an uncomfortable suit of armour and hit somebody with a rubber chicken.

ERIC IDLE: In Python we would hardly see him because he'd always be producing his stuff at the last minute to get it ready for the show. They'd only play it for the first time to the audience while you're off changing. We only had a day in the studio, so you were always belting around getting costume changes and everything ready. Sometimes they'd run a bit and you'd see it and it would be good. You'd watch them test it out, but you'd never see it in isolation like a viewer would.

From the diary of Michael Palin, Saturday, 23 August: In the afternoon, we went over to TV Centre for a dubbing session, everyone was there including Terry Gilliam who has animated some great titles, really encouraging, just right, and Ian MacNaughton, short haired and violent, he seems now to have dropped all diplomatic approval of John Howard Davies by roundly cursing him to the skies for not shooting all the film he was supposed to. I think this sounds a little harsh. And the weather was twice as bad with John than with Ian. Rehearsals began today at the Old Oak Club on Old Oak Common Lane, a club well endowed with bars, but as we only rehearse in the morning, the bar is only used by us. Rehearsal went well, but the projected work session in the afternoon fell apart after an excellent Chinese lunch at Li Wan in Earls Court Road. Arrived home to find that our front door had been used by the BBC for a science fiction series. I had five pounds to show for it.

MICHAEL PALIN: Obviously we were apprehensive, this was the first time we were actually going in front of an audience and John came up to me maybe thirty minutes before the show was due to go out and instead of slapping me on the back and saying right, good luck, and all that, said, 'Do you realise this could be the first comedy show to go out with absolutely no laughs at all.' Which of course was very good and cheered me up no end. No one really knew quite what to expect and I can remember really enjoying doing it. I suppose I was nervous, but I didn't feel like I was nervous, but the laughter wasn't raucous by any means. If you look at that first show, it's quite quiet, and at the end one didn't really quite know if it had worked. We were just so pleased that we'd done it, and we'd played all these silly characters and generally people felt our performances had been up to the mark. We'd done the best we could. Then I can remember certain reactions afterwards, among them our agent saying 'Really good but gotta dash!' and Humphrey Barclay, too, who clearly hadn't really liked it and felt uncomfortable with it.

I got a little nervous at this point. But then nobody, least of all us, knew quite what we were getting into, it wasn't as if we'd said, 'This

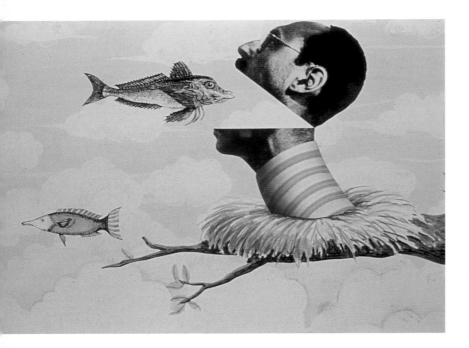

is going to be funny all the way through.' John wasn't quite joking when he said that this could be the first comedy show ever to go out with no laughs at all, because it might well have happened like that and that was a token of the fact that we weren't doing traditional material. I remember very few taglines in it and some of the ideas were very strange. Were they going to be funny ideas or were people just going to say, 'Oh, that's clever, but …'? So I remember it being a little awkward afterwards.

JOHN CLEESE: I was probably cocky enough to know that it wasn't going to be everyone's cup of tea and it absolutely wasn't. There's so much comedy people quite like, they don't hate it but they're not crazy about it, and Python really split people down the middle, they either loved it or hated it. I think that Michael is, oddly enough, despite the relaxation he has in front of an audience which is much greater than my own, in a funny way more sensitive to criticism than you might think. If you had to arrange the Pythons in order I think Michael might be the most sensitive of us.

MICHAEL PALIN: I think everybody was quite businesslike about the whole process. It wasn't sort of 'Oh wow, let's just get together and have some wacky ideas', it was pretty carefully worked out because we earned our living from this. I feel that all of us needed the experience of writing for other people, writing for television and watching how television shows were put together, both in a positive sense and in a negative sense of having something to work against, so that we could say, 'We've seen the way that's done, now we want to do it our way.' We just needed that kind of experience and certainly from '66 to '69 Terry and I did an awful lot of work on all sorts of shows, not just *Frost* but *Do Not Adjust Your Set* and *The Complete and Utter History of Britain*. We'd written twenty-six shows of *Do Not Adjust Your Set* and six shows of *Complete and Utter History*, we'd been script editors on *A Series of Birds* and *Marty* and worked on *How To Irritate People*, we'd done a ton of stuff, so in a very short period I suppose we'd learnt a lot, not just how the programmes are made but how they're set up, how they're produced, the money you have available and how you deal with people. I don't think we could have done Python any earlier, because we needed that experience. I think we'd have been a lot more hot-headed about five or six years previously.

ERIC IDLE: The first show is very weird, we did push it. If you look at the first show, it's the Vikings and the sheep and all that falling, it's very peculiar. There's a line where Gilliam says 'And now' and just says one word, it cuts straight through him and that's still bizarre for television, it's still weird. And I know there was a very weird response to the show, it was by no means a triumph. I used to play football in Hyde Park every Sunday and they'd go, 'That was a weird show of yours, that was bloody weird.' Then they'd go, 'That was bloody weird, I like it though,' and then, 'That's rather good, that bloody weird show.' It picked up, their responses, picked up as they got into it.

'I would have at least one all-nighter each week, maybe two. And I was working seven day weeks like a madman. It was all just stuff, paper, images.'

TERRY GILLIAM: I would have at least one all-nighter each week, maybe two. And I was working seven day weeks like a madman. It was all just stuff, paper, images. And at some point they start arranging themselves, which was very simple. They'd do it for me and I'd just be there to catch 'em. At three or four in the morning you get pretty funny.

MICHAEL PALIN: There would be breaks in the studio recordings, but as little as possible. If there were two sketches which involved all of us changing and there was just no one to spare to do anything in between, there'd just have to be a break and then we had people do warm-ups. Barry Cryer did warm-ups and told jokes, and there was a folk singer who'd come on if there was a gap. Inserts would be shot, usually on the morning of the day of recording when we had the studio there. If it was just a question of a quick one-liner or someone had to get dressed as a Viking and say 'And now …', those little inserts would be recorded in the morning. It was quite a tricky thing for them to do in the control room.

Eric Idle with dog Chelsea.
And some others

Python PA George Clarke – with large BBC camera!

'I'd take it all down to the BBC and use their rostrum cameras and shoot it. There would be a day of filming, I would prepare all the work before. I was working in a field of about 30 inches, which is big, because they're just pieces of paper. You'd be constantly trying to get rid of the shadows, packing things underneath the backgrounds. It's a really slow process, and the way I was doing the cut-outs was just inherently crude. The movements were always jerky.'

TERRY GILLIAM: I'd take it all down to the BBC and use their rostrum cameras and shoot it. There would be a day of filming, I would prepare all the work before. I was working in a field of about 30 inches, which is big, because they're just pieces of paper. You'd be constantly trying to get rid of the shadows, packing things underneath the backgrounds. It's a really slow process, and the way I was doing the cut-outs was just inherently crude. The movements were always jerky. Take something like lip synch – you'd normally get a lip synch chart and map out all the words. I wouldn't do it that way. I'd do four frames here, six frames here – OK, open, close. I'd shoot a lot of extra stuff with the mouth flapping away and then we'd fix it later in editing. It was really pretty free-form. I look back and I can't believe I was producing two to two and a half minutes a week. I don't know how I did it. Most of the time I was just working on my own. It was crazed. I listen to them now and the sound is so crude because I was doing it at home. The only sounds we had came from the BBC library of sound effects and the rest were generally just made by me sitting in a room with a blanket over my head and a microphone, making noises.

MICHAEL PALIN: The very first Python sketch I did in front of an audience would have been the flying sheep and the silly Frenchmen piece I did with John, although I think it was a Graham job. Pretty much sure from the language it would have been Graham and John, or John and Graham, or McCartney and Lennon, if you want to put it like that, and I can't really remember anything particularly about it. I just knew there was a certain point where they talk about the sheep flying, and the reaction was quite quiet from the studio audience. There were no great belly laughs in that first show; in fact if you listen to the soundtrack playbacks of a lot of the first few programmes, there were long silences. We had to do a re-shoot at the end and there were people who enjoyed it the first time but were a little bit baffled by it, so when we came to do a re-take they were all warmed up and we got a much better reaction.

JOHN CLEESE: I felt exhilarated after we recorded the first show, particularly after Michael and I had to re-shoot that silly sketch with the model of the sheep and us jumping up and down as Frenchmen talking nonsense French. Just occasionally in front of an audience when you know that you've succeeded, as on that particular evening, you get very loose and then it can be great fun. You just play around doing all sorts of things you hadn't planned and a lot of it's very funny as a result. So I felt very, very exhilarated after that reception by the studio audience, and I thought that if they liked it as much as that, we must be pretty safe.

MICHAEL PALIN: We usually had only one and a half hour's telecine time, that meant literally the time which you had to record the show and once that ran out that was that. Ninety minutes isn't much when you've got to do the whole show plus all the changes, some of them quite elaborate. That's why re-takes of any kind always added immeasurably to the tension. There were a lot of re-takes for technical reasons: a piece of scenery wasn't wheeled in,

'The very first Python sketch I did in front of an audience would have been the flying sheep and the silly Frenchmen piece I did with John, although I think it was a Graham job. Pretty much sure from the language it would have been Graham and John, or John and Graham, or McCartney and Lennon, if you want to put it like that, and I can't really remember anything particularly about it.'

film wasn't cued in at the right time and so on. We were always stopping and starting and you knew when you went into a show there were going to be all sorts of hold-ups, so if a show went by without a technical hold-up that was absolutely brilliant, but it was very rare.

TERRY GILLIAM: Ray Millichope was the editor of the show and I would just go down and say, 'Here it is, cut there, take that out there and there.' Editing has always been crucial in the films, whether I'm doing it myself or someone else is doing it. I just have to be there. I don't understand how films get made where you hand it over to the editor and they just go and do it. I think there's a lot of directors who don't have a sense of timing.

MICHAEL PALIN: There was no autocue – it was like a badge of courage. I don't think any autocue could have quite kept up with the pace of it somehow. My memory is that was a decision we all took. Again, that was traditional, it goes back to cabaret days when you would deliberately try and create something that was complicated to learn because that would be part of the performance, part of the skill of it.

TERRY GILLIAM: Airbrushing was not popular then. Airbrushing took off in the late '70s. But I just loved the fact that I could get very round things. It's this constant battle of only going so far and then saying, 'OK that's it, I've got to move on.' I don't know if I'm ever

capable of taking things to the utterly refined level that some people do because in the end I don't care that much. I care about the overall thing. And that's what happened with the cartoons, there's an overall effect with engravings, airbrushing and photographs – all these different techniques and media squeezed together into one thing. I found doing illustrations for magazines much tougher. I couldn't stay in one medium. When I was doing Python it freed me.

MICHAEL PALIN: I expressed a preference for some brass band music, which I'd always liked. Ian MacNaughton and our floor manager Roger Last, as far as I can recollect, got various LPs of brass band music out of the library. I seem to remember being in a room with Terry Jones and Ian listening to some of the music and at some point we decided that 'Liberty Bell' felt right. Who said it first I'm not absolutely sure.

TERRY JONES: My memory of it was Roger Last, who was our floor manager, came along with some brass band music and played us 'The Liberty Bell'. He said this was one he really liked and would be good. We all said, 'Yeah, that's great,' so it was his choice. I don't know why he was choosing the music. I think he was just coming up with suggestions.

ERIC IDLE: I think Gilliam found 'The Liberty Bell', that was a perfect signature tune. 'All right, you take care of that and I'll take care of this' – Python's always been good at that.

TERRY GILLIAM: The Python theme, 'The Liberty Bell', was my choice. We were going through material, that came up and I said 'That's it', because I could see myself animating to it. It did everything I wanted to do and boom that's it. Now you only think of it as the Python theme, nobody thinks of it as 'The Liberty Bell'. When I was in Philadelphia on Twelve Monkeys, we were checking out this huge department store that we used in the film. I had my video camera and just as we were going in this huge atrium, I started hearing 'The Liberty Bell'. I thought, it's a big joke, someone was setting me up. Then I remembered – Philadelphia – 'The Liberty Bell' – they play it everyday. Bingo.

TERRY JONES: The BBC took pride in not only not looking at the scripts, they didn't look at the shows before they went out. The heads of department would watch the shows when they went out and that was an essential part of their job really. If there was something they didn't approve of, then they would haul the producer over the coals, but it was an absolute point that they did not look at

BOROUGH OF MORECAMBE AND HEYSHAM
Publicity and Entertainments Department
TOWN HALL · MORECAMBE AND HEYSHAM

MISS GREAT BRITAIN

National Bathing Beauty Contest

TELEPHONE :- MORECAMBE 720 (7 lines)   G. THOMPSON, Publicity & Entertainments Manager

OUR REF.:   YOUR REF.:

Dear Miss Chapman,

We are writing to inform you that unfortunately you have not been selected for this year's contest.

Have you ever thought of a career in mudwrestling?

Yours apologetically,

Eric

TERRY JONES: We were very cross with the BBC and the Montreux television awards, because they wouldn't put us in for the first series, but it was shown out of competition, so the next year there were all these Python imitations from the continent. In fact the show that won the Golden Rose was an Austrian show called 'Somebody Somebody's Ladinsky's Flea Circus'. I don't think I ever saw it but everybody definitely said it was based on Python, so that won the Golden Rose and we won the Silver Rose.

Members of the cast of the B.B.C.'s "Monty Python's Flying Circus" which won the silver rose award at the Montreux television festival yesterday. The golden rose award went to "Lodynski's Flohmarkt Company" from Austria. Left to right in the photograph: Michael Palin, Terry Jones, John Cleese, Carol Cleveland, Graham Chapman and Terry Gilliam.

From the diary of Michael Palin, Monday, 4 August 1969: Worked at Eric's in Redcliffe Square to put Show 5 together, a good steady day.

From the diary of Michael Palin, Tuesday, 5 August 1969: John C. rang up in the morning to ask if I felt like working in the afternoon, so I ended up in Knightsbridge about 3 o'clock. It's funny but when one has written in partnership almost exclusively for the last three years as Terry and I have done and I suppose John and Graham as well, it requires quite an adjustment to write with somebody different. Terry and I know each other's ways of working so well now, exactly what each one does best, what each one thinks and what makes each of us laugh. When I sat down to write with John there was a moment's awkwardness, a slight embarrassment, but we soon loosened up and embarked on a saga about Hitler, von Ribbentrop and Himler Bimler being found in a seaside guest house. We do tend to laugh at the same things, and working with John is not difficult. There are still differences in our respective ways of thinking, not about comedy necessarily, which means the interchange of ideas was a little more cautious than it is with Terry. However by the time I left at about 7.15, we had almost four minutes of sketch written.

From the diary of Michael Palin: Yesterday we went further into negotiations about forming Python Productions Limited which now seems to be decided and next week we will set to work producing a film script for Victor Lownes.

ERIC IDLE: We were doing the stage tour and you needed some kind of management to deal with what you're doing or where you'll be. Somebody had to talk to us corporately as a sensible entity and make sure we turned up. Before that we had no real need. The deal with Python was always even money going in, which I think was very fair of John in those days because he could have commanded a huge amount of money, if we'd negotiated separately. So I think we just all got the same, that was always an agreement which made it all much simpler when we became a corporation because we just split everything. It feels so little like a business I don't even remember starting the company.

MICHAEL PALIN: Forming Python Productions was discussed because we quickly learned there were other interests beyond BBC Television. Methuen wanted to do a Python book, and we all felt that this is something we should own. There's no point in going to the BBC and doing it with them and indeed that wasn't the offer. It was a Methuen book and we were going to get paid some money for that. Similarly, Vic Lownes wanted to do this film with us and it would be much better if we were a body, a group which was also a limited company, because we'd get all sorts of tax and negotiating benefits. We were being offered things outside the BBC, which was quite interesting and quite unusual, because it was still a time when, if you were BBC stars – *The Two Ronnies*, Dick Emery, *Dad's Army* or whatever – you stayed with the BBC. Since a lot of us had done work for ITV companies prior to Python and John and Graham, for instance, were writing films and had experience of life outside the BBC, it was to our advantage to get ourselves organised as a production company. Eric was always the best businessman, the shrewdest one of the group.

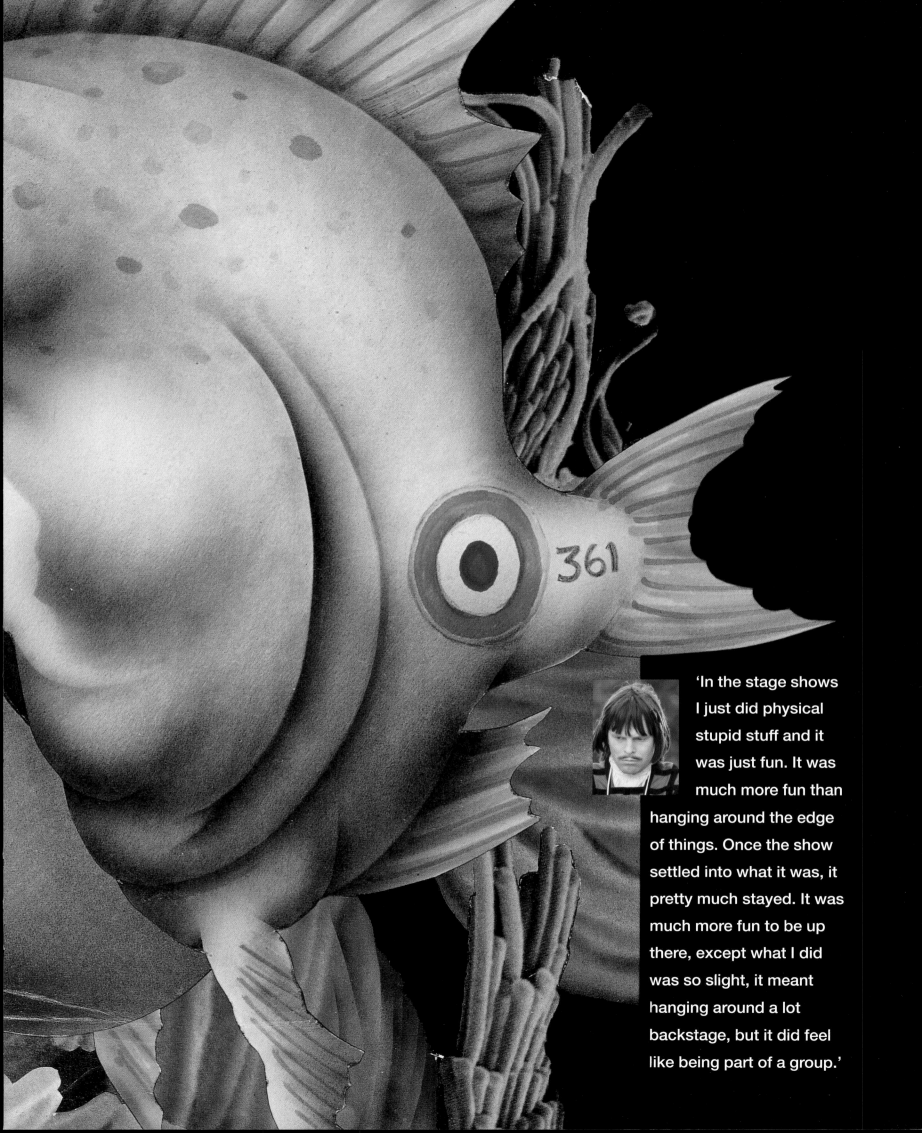

'In the stage shows I just did physical stupid stuff and it was just fun. It was much more fun than hanging around the edge of things. Once the show settled into what it was, it pretty much stayed. It was much more fun to be up there, except what I did was so slight, it meant hanging around a lot backstage, but it did feel like being part of a group.'

ERIC IDLE: I put together the live show. I assembled the list of material and I was very much instrumental in putting that on at the Belgrade Theatre. I was doing sketches in something called *Up Sunday*, and they asked us to do a Python show in Coventry. I put together the show from bits of the series, there was a lot of good material and I organised it with them. We'd all come from university revue and it wasn't that long ago since we'd done revue. We had this wealth of great material and then we found out that the audience preferred stuff they knew. That was when we first discovered it was like rock 'n' roll, they wanted the hits. You think that you have to give them new stuff – absolutely not. It was completely the opposite, the more familiar they were with the material the more they howled.

DAVID SHERLOCK: The audience reaction to their three nights at the Coventry Festival was very exciting. It was the first time they realised that people knew every word, which was a bit scary, because if anyone forgets their lines there's a whole front row who can prompt you immediately. So later when they went on tour in Britain they were being treated like pop celebrities.

ERIC IDLE: We didn't have very long to do it, two or three days rehearsal, then we went straight on. And it just went nuts, they were just crazy for it and we were going, 'Wow, this is interesting.' We had no idea of the wealth of love for Python or the depth of it, or the craziness or the fanaticism of it. I think it was our first real brush with our audience as such.

DAVID SHERLOCK: It was amazing when they went to Coventry. They were invited to the Lanchester Arts Festival and did Python live, where the audience reaction was stunning. The next day we went to visit J.B. Priestley, which was an extraordinary little outing. He was living just outside Stratford at the time and we all turned up and went to see him. Cleese, Chapman, myself, John Tomiczek and Barry Cryer. Barry virtually invited himself to tea and J.B. was so flummoxed and amazed that anyone should want to come and see him. It was an extraordinary thing because he was extremely shy and rather gruff but, because Graham smoked a pipe and so did Priestley, they struck up this sort of rapport, talking about the technical thing of tamping down the tobacco and what sort of mix and everything else. It broke the ice and he relaxed and talked a little bit about the politics of the day and how he thought it was a mess. He knew who Python were, which was quite extraordinary. Graham and I adopted the two white mice that were used on stage in the 'Mousaphone' sketch. They were real mice and we actually named them after Priestley and his wife, we called them Jack and Jacquetta: Priestley's wife was Jacquetta Hawkes. They had quite a good life with us.

JOHN CLEESE: When we did the first stage show in Southampton, I did the 'Ministry of Silly Walks' and it was a complete flop. The audience watched, it was profoundly embarrassing and when I got off the stage I said to the others, 'See! It's not funny!' Well, we did a deal. They said, 'Do it tomorrow night in Brighton, and if it doesn't work you can cut it.' And I did it the next night in Brighton and of

course everyone laughed and it's been in the show ever since. And when I was doing it on stage I used to say rude things to Michael because there was always so much noise they couldn't hear me anyway. I would say things like 'You know this sketch isn't very funny and you can't take much satisfaction in having written it'. I used to say this while I was silly-walking round him. It just never struck me as being that funny a sketch and to this day I still don't

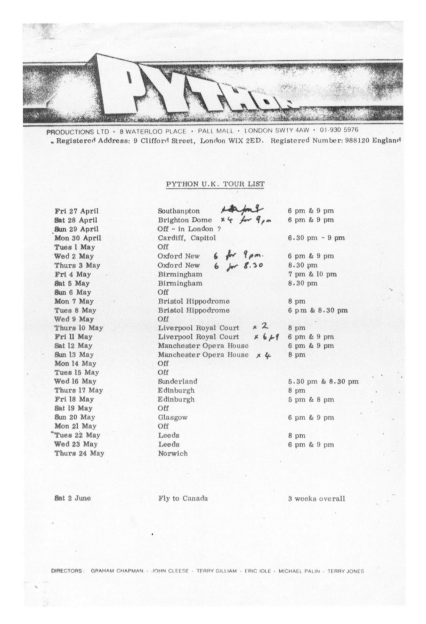

know quite why people love it as much as they do. Every night on stage it would be precisely the same, the same number of steps. It's like a tiny, tiny, tiny scaled-down bad version of Fred Astaire. Why not figure out exactly what you're going to do and do it perfectly? There's only one reason. No, there are two: one is laziness and the other is that you think you might think of something better on the night. Well it's statistically very unlikely. It's like the drunks who used to shout out at the stage every Saturday night. I always wanted to say to them, 'Look, friend, we've been doing this show a long time, we've tried an awful lot of different things and we've come to a conclusion, as a result of how audiences respond, about what is the funniest. And if you shout something out, particularly in your present state, it's statistically unlikely to be funnier than what we've come up with.' That's my attitude to it, and my attitude to improvisation is somewhat similar. I think it's something you do in rehearsal.

TERRY GILLIAM: In the stage shows I just did physical stupid stuff and it was just fun. It was much more fun than hanging around the edge of things. Once the show settled into what it was, it pretty much stayed. It was much more fun to be up there, except what I did was so slight, it meant hanging around a lot backstage, but it did feel like being part of a group.

ERIC IDLE: The BBC did the first album and we did it in a day in front of a live audience in Camden Town but they were a particularly dead audience. We didn't have much control over that, and then we decided to do a proper album. Terry and Mike were in charge.

TERRY JONES: We thought an album would be fun to do. It paid off because we became known in the States through the records first. We recorded that first album at the Camden Town Hall and we did it as a live performance. We weren't really sure it would work.

Mike and I produced the second one. We had this horrendous time because we were recording in this rather hippy recording studio which fortunately I can't remember the name of. We were recording everything and we'd never done any of this kind of thing before. We were very keen to use the stereo and everything, but what I hadn't realised was that the guy who was doing the recording, who I think was out of his head for most of the time, had not been making any notes. We'd end up with tapes and tapes of material with no idea of where anything was on the tapes. I suppose we should have been making the notes, but that was a bitter experience.

ERIC IDLE: Then there were the books. Methuen came to me and said, would we do a book, and nobody was very interested. So I took that on and I remember Gilliam was really against it, he said, 'Comics don't make any money.' He'd obviously done *Help Magazine* and had all that experience. He wanted nothing to do with it, he said, 'It won't make any money, it's dreadful.' So I had to send Katy Hepburn up to his house and we just stole a lot of stuff out of his drawers, all the cut-outs and animated drawings and things. I don't think anybody wrote anything for it hardly except me. I think we invented the Christmas book market. The first run was only 20,000, that was the first print run because we put the numbers in the inside, 'This is number 19,999'. I remember looking at that recently and it had got to be a huge number – 504,999, I believe.

TERRY JONES: Everybody was happy to let somebody else get on with it. If somebody else wanted to take on that role, it was good, like Eric took on the editing of the books, which was great. But I enjoyed the records. I came up with the idea for the cover for the *Another Monty Python Record*. That was quite funny because I said let's have a Bruegel painting, or something like that, but we'll have it all crossed out and our title scribbled over the top, so it looks like the wrong sleeve. Terry G got it immediately and designed it. We had a proof made of it and I remember showing this proof to people and saying, 'What do you think of this? It's the cover.' And they'd go, 'Oh yes, that's very good, but what's the cover going to look like?' And I said, 'No, no, this *is* the cover! Crossed out, that *is* the point'.

MICHAEL PALIN: The feeling amongst the group was that if we did an album or we did a book we should make them special; they should be different from the shows in the sense they shouldn't just be

...ese, Michael Palin, Grahame Chapman, Eric Idle, Terry Jones, Carol Cleveland
from the BBC Television Series

'We had a proof made of it and I remember showing this proof to people and saying, "What do you think of this? It's the cover."' And they'd go, '"Oh yes, that's very good, but what's the cover going to look like?" And I said, "No, no, this is the cover! Crossed out, that is the point."'

transcripts of material that already existed. And it really was a question of who had the time as well. John never had the time for either books or records. He had time to come along and record and maybe write a bit of material, but the editing, the conception and the design of the covers for both books and records were really done by other people: Terry and myself mainly for the records and Eric for the books. I'm not blaming John or even Graham for not taking part particularly; it was just that we wanted to do it and we felt it was important to do it in this way and money was adjusted accordingly. It was all quite fair, if you did production time on it, you were paid, but it was a slight source of stress sometimes when you were doing a lot of hours on it. You would occasionally say, 'Why aren't others helping out? Why do we have to do all this?' But we got into it in the first place, we were the ones who said we'd deliver it, so we got on with it.

It was a real sheepdog job. We had to round up people: could they write a bit here and there and when could they come in and record it? It was quite difficult to get two or three days when people would come in and do the material. If we did get everyone together it was usually very creative and it worked very well. Nobody arrived looking rather sullen because they'd been asked to come in on a day they didn't want to come in. In some cases you couldn't get much writing and shaping done on an album, but you could get people in for two or three days recording. So we would read material, people would select it, the input would come in and it was all very good. It was always very good when the six of us were together. It was just becoming more and more difficult to get the six people together on something that wasn't mainstream show material. In those days no one really knew whether the book would make money or whether it was just an irksome task or whether the albums would make any money or whether it was just cashing in. We had absolutely no idea that these were money-spinners. We had to prove that they were good enough and we had to prove that they were worth buying. It was generally self-directional: people would come and deliver a bit of material, and I think we all knew if we had done it well or not.

The Pythons were never lazy, in either writing or performance. Quite a high standard was demanded and people knew if they'd got it right or not.

ERIC IDLE: I produced *Contractual Obligation Album*. One of the ways to get people to do something new and different was to ask them to write silly songs and to encourage them to do mad things. That's always been a tradition ever since Cambridge certainly, and Oxford, both had funny songs, it's just there were more of them on the *Contractual Obligation Album*. Then I thought to myself, 'Oh, there's a great album to have, "Python Sings",' so I produced that and it sells like fifty times more than the sketch albums, because you can hear a song again, but you can't play a sketch over and over again. That's my favourite Python album because you can just play it, and it's completely bonkers and goes all over the place.

MICHAEL PALIN: Part of the tradition of Oxbridge cabaret and revue was that you had songs as well. A lot of people who couldn't sing very well would have to get up and sing, because that's the way it was. Eric was probably the most musical and was very gifted at writing these songs which were quite cabaret-like in their way, sort of Noel Coward, that kind of thing. And Terry J also liked songs. But Terry was odd because he wasn't supremely musical but he did love music, and I think he had a guitar and all that. I hope he won't mind me saying it, but he wasn't a natural, elegant, easy, gifted musician, though he did love music. So Terry and Eric were quite keen to do

songs, and the rest of us were not much good really. John was probably tone deaf, and I was just very shy of singing and it was one of those ridiculous things. I'm not a great one for going back to my schooldays and saying, 'Yeah, that's where I went wrong, that's where I became a sex maniac,' but I do remember going to a music class at school, and we all just sang jolly songs for three quarters of an hour. Mr Biltcliffe, who was our music master, said, 'Someone's singing flat over there,' and my good friend, whose sixtieth birthday I've just attended, pointed to me and said, 'It was Palin', as a bit of a laugh. We were only about ten and I had to go up and stand by the piano and do a scale. Of course I was very nervous and didn't do it very well, so Mr Biltcliffe said, 'You're right, you're sitting amongst the non-singers.' So there was this idea of a table full of non-singers, people who could not sing. That was it, there was no 'relax a bit and then we'll help you to sing, everyone has got music naturally in them'. No, you were a non-singer. And oddly enough I recollect having this conversation with John and the same thing happened to him when he was at school: he was told he was a non-singer in some way or another. So we were rather frightened of singing.

I knew I could sing, but doing the 'Lumberjack Song' was quite an ordeal for me because I didn't have the confidence of a powerful voice and I had to sing solo. So I got through it by being the character and slapping my leg a lot and doing lots of burly things and of course once it was taken up by the chorus it was fine and it was all very funny, but it didn't come easy to me.

I think the songs in Python gradually increased as we grew in confidence and in the films there's always a song somewhere there. Is there a song in the *Life of Brian*, I don't know? Oh yes, at the end. Sorry Eric.

ERIC IDLE: One of my latest songs is called 'Muff Diving', but you can't really do that on *Top of the Pops*, you know what I mean? Now in the States people are cutting my songs, and I'm going, 'Wait a

'We did a Harmony shampoo and a Birds Eye frozen pea thing. Those were always great fun. They were like a day's shoot and we'd just have fun. Jonesy always directed those. He was quick and fast and they were always quite silly and we'd always have fun writing them.'

minute, you should listen to Eminem for a minute or two before you start to try and cut my fucking lyrics!'

GRAHAM CHAPMAN (May 1973): Michael lives not far away from me so I see a fair bit of him. Terry lives further away and Terry Jones lives in Camberwell, a long, long way away. We've seen a lot less of each other socially recently. I've seen a lot less of John lately, but that's because I've been insulting him, I suppose, not publicly particularly, but privately, saying that he really shouldn't mess around with advertising.[6]

TERRY JONES: John was involved with the Labour Party before he got seduced by the dreadful Democrats, the SDP, so we did a little thing for the Labour Party. Then he asked us to do a promotional film for Birds Eye peas – it was a full twenty-five minutes – and as far as I was concerned it was an opportunity to try directing, to do a bit of filming without anyone else around or interfering.

ERIC IDLE: We did a Harmony shampoo and a Birds Eye frozen pea thing. Those were always great fun. They were like a day's shoot and we'd just have fun. Jonesy always directed those. He was quick and fast and they were always quite silly and we'd always have fun writing them.

They were promotional films. I don't think we were ever asked to endorse anything. Guinness once asked us to come in and throw out some ideas. But advertising is always very keen to use anybody who seems to be popular or successful; being basically a parasite industry, it's always trying to subvert current culture and use it for its own purposes. I wasn't against it and I think I actually got some nice money from doing the 'Nudge, Nudge' commercials for Breakaway chocolate bars, which were kind of fun for me. I was on the stage tour one night in Brighton, I would do the 'Nudge, Nudge' sketch and I'd pull out a Breakaway from my pocket and go, 'Urgh, Breakaway,' and throw it away and the audience would go nuts. Ronnie Corbett attacked me and said, 'That's disgusting, you shouldn't do a commercial and then abuse it,' and I thought, 'Why not?'

JOHN CLEESE: I would guess that the others were disapproving to a lesser or greater extent when I started doing corporate training films. I would think Eric probably less so, Terry Jones probably more so. But I'm guessing. I did them primarily because I liked Tony Jay so much. I started the Video Arts Company with him, because I wanted to spend time with Tony as I enjoyed working with him so much, and partly because I thought I could sell the company after three or four years and make some money to create space to do whatever I wanted to do at that time.

ERIC IDLE: John's always been older and he's always been much more into that world of corporate advertising. But I think there's very much of the teacher in John, he was a teacher and he is a teacher in many ways. He liked to teach people about business and to open them up to doing business better.

TERRY JONES: I thought Video Arts was a bit odd really. He seemed to be joining the sort of things that he otherwise made fun of. However, we didn't realise how successful it was going to be.

GRAHAM CHAPMAN: A lot of people, comedians in particular, really want not only the laughter from the crowd they also want a little bit of adulation. Obviously it's a necessary part of their makeup. I don't think we mind if we get contempt.[6]

TERRY JONES: We would occasionally still do cabarets, when the show was running. I remember one terrible one I did with John which was for Bart's medical school in London, and when we got there, it had been advertised as *Monty Python* and it was just me and John. We did things like the 'Pet Shop' and everything and we really got the bird because there were all these drunk medical students who were really pissed off that it wasn't the whole of Python.

Then we did this May Day show for Europe. It seems odd now, but in those days it was a new thing to be able to transmit live TV pictures to Germany. I can remember the first television pictures coming across the Channel. It's just so funny, it was like a little group of people at Calais waving and that was it: 'These are the first live television pictures across the Channel, isn't it amazing!' So that European link-up was quite a big thing and we'd done this chunk for the BBC, we were the English contribution to it.

The funny thing about the May Day show is that when we re-showed it on the 30th Anniversary night, we had to reconstitute the soundtrack because the BBC hadn't kept it. That material had been lost although a small TV station in Germany said they had their version of it, but of course they'd put their own soundtrack on in German. We did have a script of it, but it didn't quite fit the film. All we had was their German version of it, so we had that translated and then re-did it, but I don't know how close to the original soundtrack it was.

MICHAEL PALIN: The 'Fish Slapping Dance' was done for one of those odd little non-Python moments, it was not done within the shows. We were asked to contribute to this Euro Comedy May Day event and our contribution as Python was to write a whole lot of silly folk dances and sort of examine England and the whole idea of tradition and old customs. A rather jolly English voice chuckles away at the quaint ways of the foreigners while we show the British doing completely stupid things themselves, and so 'Fish Slapping Dance' is one

'A rather jolly English voice chuckles away at the quaint ways of the foreigners while we show the British doing completely stupid things themselves, and so 'Fish Slapping Dance' is one of those dances that we invented, but it's quite a funny section.'

of those dances that we invented, but it's quite a funny section. I always enjoy that one because it's one of those pieces of material which just works. You can't analyse it, you can't really break it down, you just look at it, it's fairly short and almost without exception when someone sees the end of it they roar with laughter. I always thought, well, if you really wanted to check for a sense of humour, the 'Fish Slapping Dance' is quite a good thing to show to somebody. While it was being rehearsed, the lock was full of water, but by the time it came to be performed the lock had emptied and I suddenly looked down and there was a 15-foot drop. But we still carried on and I just plunged in, and I must say it's one of the things I'm most proud of in my entire performing career. John is just a supreme master of bits of comic detail, that's what makes him such a genius, anyone could have hit me with the fish but John lines it up in a certain way and then thwack! Just a very clever bit of work. But that was a one-take shot, I wasn't going to do that again!

GRAHAM CHAPMAN: Everything in the programme comes from observations or experiences one or other of us has had. We might be achieving something and we might change peoples' minds sometimes. We don't feel clever enough to preach – all our views creep in around the edges. Like the sketch about the mortician's shop where John brings in the body of his mother in a sack and discusses with the mortician what to do with it. We wanted to point out that it is stupid to worry about death. They are cutting the sketch out of the repeat. I was so angry when I heard that, I kicked the studio door hard; unfortunately it didn't budge and broke two bones in my foot.[7]

ERIC IDLE: It never became more than just another show for many years actually. I don't recall it being culty for quite a long time. What I think we were grateful for is it annoyed people.

GRAHAM CHAPMAN: Actually, we have a very small budget compared with a lot of other shows. I think what is called above the line costs, that is, what is spent on writers, that stuff, on performers, that stuff,

on costumes, on make up, on filming, film crews and accommodation while we're filming, for each show we get about £4,500, which is remarkably little considering there are six members of the cast. We've also got to pay out of that extras, we've got to pay for any other artists that we want, which often is Carol Cleveland or someone else that we can persuade to come along for a pittance. I suppose an average show, something like the Dick Emery show, for instance, would get something like £6,000. They don't quite realise that we are not an average situation comedy or an average film quickie, the back-studio type show, it's very much an integral show. We have large sections of the show on film, sometimes we have almost the whole show on film. Filming is very expensive, and then at the end of the series they have the gall to complain that Ian MacNaughton is about £100 per show over budget. It's amazing that he's managed to juggle the figures and get things done. We've done quite well. We did a lot of filming in Jersey in the last series and quite a lot in Scotland, both very oppressed areas I must say. I got thrown out of the first hotel in Scotland. The manager let me in later, largely because I'd spoken to a group of mountaineers, because I used to do a lot of climbing. They were four pretty butch people, I'd been talking to them and found out, in fact, that I'd done rather more difficult climbing than they'd done, so I though right, here goes, as an experiment, 'Hey blokes I'm gay', and their reaction was fine. That's okay, that's all right, but meanwhile there was a very county-type girl over the other side of the bar who'd been eyeing me up for a long time that evening and after having made this revelation to these people and they're all thinking that it's fun and exchanging climbing stories, I think I stood on the table and told her to fuck off, or at least that's what I was told later that I'd done, because she wouldn't get anywhere with me darling, 'cos I was a poof. She called the manager and I got thrown out, and eventually the other people managed to persuade the manager that I wasn't totally insane and I could stay in the hotel and I was allowed back in and eventually ended up chatting with the man and he ended up giving me a cigar and a free drink. It was like I'd come in from a concentration camp or something … I suppose of that budget of £4,500 about half goes to us collectively, including Terry Gilliam, which makes the margin for filming and everything very much smaller obviously. I don't know exactly how much we do get per show, I suppose it must be something like £400 each, but that's for writing and performing, that's four weeks work …

It varies from week to week and Terry is slightly different because he has costs as well, like the bench camera work, but the other five of us, yes, it's split five ways. If I say four weeks, £400 for one show that's £100 a week which sounds a lot but then out of that you've got expenses yourself on filming, like enormous hotel bills, especially if you drink.[6]

MICHAEL PALIN: For some reason fish were very funny and we used fish quite a lot throughout Python, fish slapping or the 'Piranha Brothers'. Piscatorial images were very strong. We had an instinct that the word 'haddock' was quite funny or 'halibut', and we had my pet fish Eric and all that sort of stuff and I don't know why. Other animals came in now and again. Animal behaviour was something that was a staple diet of television programmes of the time. And we played with it just because it was funny. Take the

Palin, Cleese and wardrobe department on location

'Visitor' sketch where I come in as Ken Shabby. Why Ken Shabby had a goat with him when he came in for that sketch, I don't know, other than the fact that we liked the goat. A man with a goat is funny, I don't know why but there you are.

TERRY GILLIAM: That's the great thing I like about Python – it goes from being incredibly intelligent to incredibly infantile. What I think we're good at avoiding is the middle ground. We swing from really, really hip smart stuff to really childish stuff. We were always pushing it one way or the other. So we'd either fall flat on our face or fly high.

ERIC IDLE: I got a letter from a lady who said she'd heard that one of the members of Monty Python was a homosexual, and in the Bible in Leviticus it says if a man lives with another man, he shall be stoned. So I wrote back to her and thanked her, and said, 'We've found out who it was and we've taken him out and stoned him.'

MICHAEL PALIN: There was a very strong threat of violence and anger at times in Python, and I didn't really share that. I got very upset

about things as we all did: Nixon being elected president of the US was one thing. And Terry got very, very worked up and angry about things, but it all blew over quickly. But John certainly harboured a lot of anger and so did Graham. Because of his homosexuality, there was a lot of feeling that there were a lot of hypocrites out there really. I'm not absolutely certain, but I think that Graham really felt that we were all at the very least bisexual and most people were homosexual, if they'd just admit it and come round the back for a quick snog. That was it. All these comments and thoughts about gays and non-gays seem so run-of-the-mill now, but then it was still quite unusual

for someone to declare themselves openly to be homosexual. I think the word 'gay' had just about come in at that time. And I remember there was this party to which Graham invited everybody including his fiancée and announced that he was gay and he'd met David in Ibiza. Now I didn't go to that party, but that was quite a bold thing. I think Gray felt that people were hypocritical and they were judging him and, especially when he'd had a drink or two, he really could get very, very angry with people. He would attack people and he'd attack within the group. He'd attack John sometimes. He'd attack any of us if he felt in a certain mood. It wasn't really Graham at all. It certainly wasn't the Graham that I knew later on, but in those days he was fuelled by drink and a sort of anger at his own life and the way it was. That brought out some very intense feelings and the only times I've ever seen a real row about performances and behaviour within the group was when we did our stage tour and Graham was so drunk the first week he could hardly get through it. John publicly gave him a real big bollocking about that when we were in Brighton or somewhere like that: it was just not good enough and it was selfish. And so there were dark moments when people would get very upset and angry. But then a lot of it came out in the writing. John could express anger wonderfully, really, really brilliantly. I just remember the guy in 'Confuse a Cat' when he's sitting there in his awful tartan jacket and he's talking about Commies or something like that. He starts off a very reasonable man and develops this wonderful tirade – the way he raises his fist at the table, it's just brilliant, it's a marvellous image of somebody consumed with impotent anger, which of course is like him hitting the car with a branch on *Fawlty Towers*. It's an absolutely brilliant piece of observation. I do it myself now and I sort of accept that: when I get very angry I find myself shaking my fist at something. We do do silly things like that. But John used it extremely well and made it very funny somehow, which was interesting. It was quite frightening, but it was very funny in its context and then he'd snap out of it. But there was something in there and I think it was like having to prove something about yourself.

TERRY JONES: There was always a confidence, a sort of arrogance about the six of us. If we were agreed on something, then we thought that was pretty rock solid and we had very few TV executives who would stand up to us. A lot of that came from John. John was a great strength in that kind of way and John's arrogance helped to enthuse us all.

TERRY GILLIAM: There was no sort of crushing authority that made us all into this Fascist group who all had to agree on one thing. Everybody was very individual and fighting for their stuff and I really think that was the strength of it. Everybody respected each other as individuals and their ideas as individual things, and yet it all went together and ideas seemed to be more important than individual egos in the early days. Of course that's all changed now, because each one of us was solely responsible for the success of Python!

TERRY JONES: The way we parodied television was partly biting the hand that fed us. John and Eric liked doing that and it was also partly that we felt we were being mucked around. In retrospect the BBC was being very generous allowing us to do these shows and it was brilliant. No other organisation would have let us get away with it. But at the same time they were kind of mucking us up, the BBC didn't like the shows and they'd take us off and there was a lot of resentment about that. John had a lot of contempt for the programme planners as he called them, so there was quite a bit of deliberate goading of the Beeb, which was always fun.

ERIC IDLE: I think we were just at the right point. It's like being in the Beatles playing for four or five years in Hamburg. You've kept people awake and you've played every bloody song in the world and now you're ready. You've rehearsed, now's your chance to do whatever you want to do; that was our chance to do whatever we wanted to do, and I think that what was brave about it is we didn't know what we wanted to do, we just knew what we wanted to avoid. And that's a good way to start, if you just avoid and cut out anything that's familiar and anything that's a bit hackneyed or been done. I think for a while that was very, very creative. It was a good format and it was an instructive way to be and I think it had about the right length of life to it.

TERRY JONES: I think Python must be of its time. We weren't lampooning, we weren't actually tying it to people of the moment or events of the moment, so it was hopefully kind of zoning in on human nature more, but it was still defined by the society that we found ourselves in and rebelled against.

ERIC IDLE: I remember learning to act in that first series, because with filming I could get more and more make-up or get more and more into character. It was like learning how to become a character actor. The only thing was that we were mocking the light entertainment thing – that's why we had 'And now for something completely different', because that's what the entertainment announcers would say when they introduced the singer.

TERRY JONES: Mike and I had always been friends, then we became friends with Terry. Graham was always off in his own world anyway, and even when we were filming, Graham would disappear very quickly. He always had these books where he'd find the gay scene so he wouldn't participate after the filming. One of the nightmares of filming Python was always that I'd find myself organising the evening's entertainments. I'd be saying, 'Now who's coming to the restaurant? OK, one, two, three, now how many people are coming? Where shall we go? Oh, we'll go there.' So you'd end up with these huge numbers of people. John often opted out but Graham would eat very quickly, then he'd be looking in his little book about where to go and he'd disappear. Eric was a friend, but he always had his own friends as well, so I'd be having dinner with Mike and Helen or Terry Gilliam or something like that, but not often with Eric or John.

MICHAEL PALIN: There were egos, but I think the egos were reasonably intelligently informed by the fact that you needed to have some control over your own material and that what kind of suit you wore and how big your car was didn't matter one damn; what really mattered was the material itself and what you could produce. I suppose that in the few years between the mid-'60s and Python, various of us had worked with egos and had seen where things go wrong.

TERRY JONES: In a way it was easier coming back to write the second series because we were enjoying the idea of the flow again.

MICHAEL PALIN: Sitting down to write the second series, I can't remember it being different. I think there must have been a slight air of confidence.

GRAHAM CHAPMAN: There is a kind of mad linking process developing throughout even though there isn't necessarily a direct flow. One thing we started in the last series, which we hadn't done before, was to shoot off a few shots of people illustrating situations, saying 'And now' or 'And then he said' or whatever, so you could virtually go to anything just in case we got into difficulties with continuity later.[6]

TERRY JONES: We knew Graham drank a lot and we knew that his performance was a bit impaired in the TV shows because he did drink before. I'm sure I didn't drink before the TV shows, now I come to think of it! But suddenly he used to drink at lunchtime. I remember being round at John Cleese's place and drinking Carlsberg Special. John had cats so I'd have antihistamines and I'd drink a can of Carlsberg Special and wonder why I fell asleep in the script meeting!

We began a bit early for the drugs scene really. I left university in '64 and I wasn't really aware of it very much. We knew people who smoked pot a bit, but in Python nobody was particularly interested really. You needed to be on top of everything. That's why the drinking was interesting in a way. I couldn't write if I drank, although Mike and I, if we were writing together, we'd tend to go off and have a curry at lunchtime and drink, but I think we were beginning to realise then that it wiped out the afternoon. Certainly for performance you had to keep on the ball. It was probably learning from Graham and seeing Graham unable to get his words out. We certainly knew when we were filming the second series, Graham's performance would go down after lunch and Ian MacNaughton's as well. It would get to a stage where you knew the afternoon was going to be pretty slow going. There was an occasion when we were filming, and basically Ian had drunk himself into a stupor at lunchtime, so we sat him in the theatre and then we got on with shooting the day's filming.

Another time we were in Glencoe, Graham had got a long piece that he needed to do and Ian said, 'It's lunchtime, come on, break for lunch.' I grabbed Ian and said, 'Look Ian, we really ought to do Graham's piece now, because he won't get it after lunch,' and he said, 'Nah, it's lunchtime.' So we broke for lunch and of course he came back and he couldn't do it. Ian had had quite a lot to drink and just kept on making him do it. In the end we did about fifteen takes and it was not going to get anywhere. So I immediately did an interview scene with Graham, and put my script on a clipboard the

COMPLETELY DIFFERENT

campus cinemas and if we can get $1,000 a cinema, we'd have $2m.' I remember him saying that. He said, 'Do you think you can put this together.' I said, 'Let me talk to the others,' and the others were more or less agreed. I think I was a bit bossy, I probably started assembling the material a little bit as though I was in charge. I think I felt that it was a little bit my gig, and my recollection is that some of the others disagreed with some of my choice of material. Somehow we figured out it was going to cost £100,000 and Victor showed it to Roman Polanski, who said, 'This is not funny.' Victor got slightly cold feet and instead of bearing the full brunt of the £100,000 investment, he brought in another guy and they did £50,000 each. And Ian directed it.

TERRY JONES: I'd rather have done something original, but Vic was prepared to finance this film on the basis that he had seen people laughing at these scripts. I think very much he or John selected the sketches, so it was rather weighted to John's material, and also there tended to be rather a lot of stuff over desks. We all agreed that the material we were using was funny stuff, but I never particularly liked the film.

ERIC IDLE: Victor was a fan of the series. He wanted to take it to America. So a movie of the best sketches was mooted. I think there was an £80,000 budget, of which Victor put up 40 per cent and somebody else put up the rest, but then at the very last minute the other backer totally backed out. Victor was a good chap, he was just a fan early on. Gilliam always had a problem with him, but then Gilliam had a problem with everybody. He ran the London Playboy Club and it was the only one that made any money. When Hefner was foolish enough to buy him out, the whole empire collapsed. And in the end Hefner owns that movie, which is very interesting. It's a Playboy film, the only one we don't own. It meant we could always visit the Playboy Mansion, which at certain stages of life was a very, very interesting and fun thing to do. I actually went with my wife, so I did behave myself.

JOHN CLEESE: I don't remember Victor coming down to the set or anything. I became a pal of Victor's because he had these very wonderful weekend house parties: half the people there were terrific and the other half weren't, but you never knew who you were going to sit next to at dinner. I remember sitting next to the actor Stuart

Starring

GRAHAM CHAPMAN

JOHN CLEESE

TERRY GILLIAM

ERIC IDLE

TERRY JONES

MICHAEL PALIN

CAROLE CLEVELAND

COLUMBIA PICTURES PRESENTS
A VICTOR LOWNES
AND GSF ORGANISATION
PRESENTATION

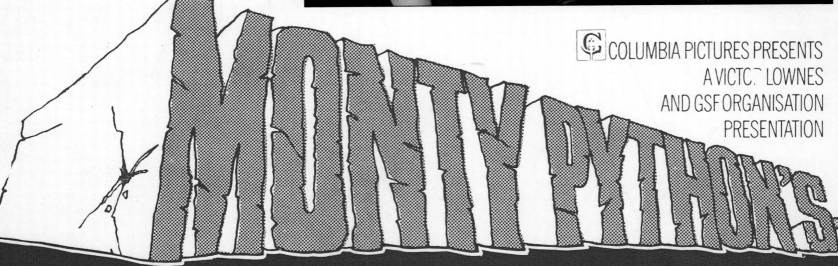

MONTY PYTHON'S

AND NOW FOR SOMETHING COMPLETELY DIFFERENT

STARRING AND WRITTEN BY **GRAHAM CHAPMAN** · JOHN CLEESE · **TERRY GILLIAM** · ERIC IDLE · **TERRY JONES** · MICHAEL PALIN
PRODUCED BY PATRICIA CASEY · DIRECTED BY IAN MACNAUGHTON · A KETTLEDRUM PYTHON PRODUCTIONS FILM · COLOUR

Whitman and the editor of the *New York Post*. Peter Cook was nearly always there. I got very fond of Victor who had a great record for booking unusual talent like Barbra Streisand, who he booked for the Playboy Clubs before she was known as an artist; he had a real impresario quality to him.

TERRY GILLIAM: With Vic Lownes it was the animation he kept talking about and not the rest of it. Then he became John's best friend, which I think meant access to Playmates – I don't want to say this, but it must have been. That's the part of America that John really aspires to, blondes with big tits.

TERRY JONES: I'd never really been interested in television really. It had always been in the back of my mind to do movies so I was very keen. Victor was a friend of John's and he'd approached John. The brief was to put on stuff he'd seen audiences laughing at and the idea was to do it for the States, which is why it was going to be called 'And Now For Something Completely Different'. So we were a bit pissed off when it didn't show in the States at all; it showed over here as *And Now For Something Completely Different* and it was all the old material. We didn't really want it to go out in this country. We thought it was the only way to get our stuff seen in America.

TERRY GILLIAM: I never wanted to be an animator. And as the films and everything else progressed, I just didn't want to be the guy doing the animation. I was into live action films. The first series is as good as anything. So when *And Now For Something Completely Different* came along, it was like 'Wow, films'. But it wasn't really like films because it was still the old thing.

TERRY JONES: I don't think the sketches were any better and we were filming in this strange dairy in North London somewhere, so it has a very strange, echoey sound to it.

ERIC IDLE: It was shot in a dairy that had gone bankrupt, so we were in there using all their offices and then we'd play five-a-side football in the huge area where they had all the milk trolleys. Quite fun.

MICHAEL PALIN: The film was shot in late October, November, December 1970, because my second son was born in the middle of it. On my day off, very obligingly. We had recorded the second series during that summer.

JOHN CLEESE: We shot it in Totteridge. It took six weeks. Every morning a car would pick us up and take us up there, pitch black, and we would never finish until it was pitch black. So I never saw Totteridge, except if I went out at lunch to cash a cheque, which I remember doing once dressed as a burglar, and of course nobody paid attention which is a typical English reaction. After four weeks I was so tired that I realised there was no point in my ever thinking about becoming a film director. Ian MacNaughton had been working at least an hour in the morning and an hour in the evening longer than I did, and I just wanted to go to sleep for a month. That's literally when I gave up any thought of directing, which I wasn't that interested in anyway.

TERRY GILLIAM: I re-shot all the animation for that film so it was all on 35mm. And that was a pain in the ass to do. They're pretty close to the original but they're better. There are new things in there as well. But that wasn't much fun. It's the same, the camera's just bigger. Better definition, better everything, but nothing changes as far as what I have to do.

TERRY JONES: I don't like to say it, but I don't think Ian was a natural film director. When it came to the film Ian made it quite clear that he didn't want any opinion from me, because in the TV shows I would say, 'Ian, I think we've got to move the camera a little bit

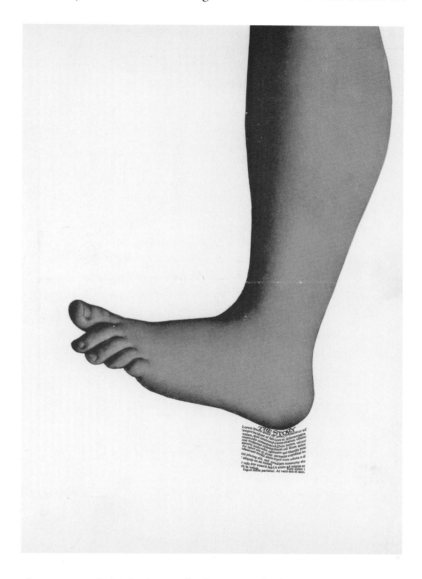

that way, or I think this is the better angle for this.' Ian was very hyped up for the film and didn't want *any* opinions coming out of you. I think I kept pretty quiet about it.

ERIC IDLE: I don't think we gave a shit about breaking America and I don't think it was anybody's ambition. What happened was fairly early on they came to us and asked to buy the format for Python, and we rolled about with laughter because we didn't have a format. Then we said, 'Wouldn't it be even funnier to say no?' So we did, we turned it down and I think that's when they started to make things like *The Marty Feldman Comedy Machine*. They were desperate to get Python onto American TV at that point.

TERRY GILLIAM: My being American probably did help because my simple crude, violent nature was a balance to their cleverness. Like in *And Now For Something Completely Different*, John would say we've got to say canned peaches for America. I would say, 'No, you've got to say *tinned* peaches. It's an English word and Americans will have to learn what tinned means. And they will learn and get excited by the idea of learning.' I would always throw back at them the time when the Beatles were doing 'Penny Lane' or any of those songs, I didn't know specifically what those songs were talking about, but I understood them and I wanted to learn, and I said that's what we should be doing. Not coming down to them, make them come up to us. So on one level I was very useful to them because John was always trying to understand the audience so he could control them. But that's what good about Python, it wasn't about compromise. Everybody got very passionate in the meetings and there was all this screaming and shouting but we all respected each other enough to scream and shout at each other. That's the way it should be.

JOHN CLEESE: However we edited the film, people got bored half way through because there was no story.

ERIC IDLE: There's only a certain amount of time you can laugh and then you have to put something else in. I'm always aware if I'm making something I'll try and put animation in or a song so you don't have to laugh. Those are the tricky areas to do in comedy. Better to stop!

MICHAEL PALIN: The editing was really incredibly difficult, it was where the crunch point came. Performance was usually fine, we could deal with that, but the editing was very important. Vic Lownes couldn't stand Ken Shabby. That was one bit of grossness too far, which is a shame because we all liked Ken Shabby and I think there was a general feeling that this was a soft decision. So that was taken out.

TERRY GILLIAM: It's somewhere about an hour in that you start running out of steam. And that's happened on all of them. After about an hour, somewhere in there, things aren't playing as well. You might as well not worry about it: just put a break in there, tootle along. Then pick up and have a good ending. I don't know why that is, it's probably just that laughing is physically tiring.

TERRY JONES: You do need a bit of a break at some point but I don't think you should be too rigid about it, but certainly things do change and it's not a question of how funny they are, but it's where they are and where they come.

JOHN CLEESE: Eventually we came up with an edit we all liked and it came out and did surprisingly good business in England where they'd seen it all anyway. Meanwhile, in America it was publicised with a Walt Disney-like poster of this happy little snake with a silly grin on its head and a funny pork pie hat. The people it was aimed at looked at it and thought, 'Oh, it's a kid's movie.' I believe we took less money in America than we spent on the prints and advertising. I think Victor got a reasonable offer quite early on and, because he was quite doubtful about the whole prospect, he jumped at the offer, which was money back and a bit of profit. The film slowly made a little bit of money here and a little bit of money there. I don't remember having difficulty with Victor, but Terry, who was much more involved in the editing, and also Terry Gilliam, who was involved in the titles front and back, had some kind of interference from him, which I imagine most producers would have regarded as entirely legitimate. But I think Gilliam, who loves kicking against the pricks, so far as any authority figure is concerned, put a joke title for him, for Victor, in the credits.

TERRY GILLIAM: I asked Vic what credit did he want on the front credits. And he said nothing. And at the end he went into a real snit, because he decided he wanted his name in lights. I said, 'It's done, I've done it, you told me you didn't care.' And he ended up getting Bob Godfrey to shoot his name in lights and they were cut in there in a later version of the film.

TERRY JONES: When we first showed the film in a big cinema up in North London we found that nobody laughed at the 'Dirty Fork' sketch, which was a mystery because it was the same as in the show. The only thing I could think was that Ian had put some muzak over it, because it's in a restaurant, so I suggested we should take the music off because maybe that's flattening it all out. So we took the music off and then people laughed at it again, so that was a good learning curve, to see what music does to comedy, how it just kills laughs if you have it on there.

TERRY GILLIAM: Something funny happened on that movie because basically we were taking our best sketches and re-doing them. This was going to be our big break in the American market because nobody thought we would ever get on television in America, so this was our way of breaking in and of course it was a complete disaster in America. That was partly because Columbia called us and said that nobody in America understands the 'Twit of the Year' sketch at the end. So we said, 'That's the end, that's how it ends.' They said, 'Well, if you leave this in we cannot guarantee the success of this film.' That was pretty obvious and then they sold it in some stupid way where it bombed. And in England where we didn't want it shown particularly because it was old material, it was a huge success. So this was us learning about the film business. But it was frustrating because Terry Jones and I were always in there wanting to be directing and it became more and more frustrating. Ian was lovely but he wasn't directing it the way we wanted it directed, and we were always saying, 'Oh, come on. Jesus, shoot it this way.' It didn't quite happen, so there was a certain frustration building up.

ERIC IDLE: It was quite fun filming because we had a lot more money than we did at the BBC and it was shot on 35mm as opposed to our usual 16mm, with James Balfour, 'The Prince of Darkness', who shot everything in the dark. Ian became completely alcoholic, I do remember he didn't turn up for the second part of 'Twit of the Year Show' after lunch and we just carried on shooting because we knew what we were doing. I think the pressure on Ian having the two Terrys over his shoulder was also one of the reasons he drank like crazy.

TERRY JONES: We'd already been doing the film inserts in Python and we were recording without an audience there, so in terms of filming without an audience there was no real difference in that way.

MICHAEL PALIN: Some things I quite enjoyed doing again, it was good to have another stab at them and do them without feeling the audience were there. It felt we could do it rather more properly and think about performance a bit more. 'Dead Parrot' was done with John not feeling very well, I can remember that. On the other hand, 'Lumberjack Song' I thought was rather good and 'Upper Class Twit of the Year' – it was great to be able to film that again in the proper place.

JOHN CLEESE: I don't think we thought there was the slightest chance of it being a huge hit. But we cared terribly that it was as good as it could be. I remember doing an enormous number of takes on something to get it absolutely perfect, and slowly discovering that that's not how you get the best film.

From the diary of Michael Palin, December 1970: On Monday we saw an assembly of the material so far and it was a little encouraging even without the cartoons and in black and white. It held the interest and kept up the laughs of our twenty-strong viewing audience through its ninety minutes … I think all of us were very glad it was finished. For six weeks it had been hard, concentrated work, rising in cold and darkness, doing maybe three costume and three make-up changes per day and arriving home twelve hours after setting out … At our luncheon, we talked about the future, it seems all of us are prepared to start work on another TV series next November except for John. John I find difficult to understand. He professes to dislike any pressure of work, yet he seemed to enjoy the added participation in the production of Python, which resulted in this pressure. He also claims to want a year off to read and absorb knowledge and possibly travel and generally improve his mind, and yet he has accepted a commission to write at least six of a new series of *Doctor in Love* for London Weekend, a series which has apparently plumbed new depths of ordinariness. So I have a feeling that John will be only too keen to write another series of *Monty Python* in twelve months' time. Graham will be writing some more shows for Ronnie Corbett. Eric is quite keen to work on the screenplay of a film idea suggested by Ian about bank robbers marooned on Skye, but I fear I may have dampened his spirits rather heavily, showing less than enthusiasm for it as a Python idea. Terry Gilliam is writing cartoons for 'Marty' and then, we hope, directing a half-hour script which Terry and I started work on on Tuesday morning.

'Some things I quite enjoyed doing again, it was good to have another stab at them and do them without feeling the audience were there. It felt we could do it rather more properly and think about performance a bit more. 'Dead Parrot' was done with John not feeling very well, I can remember that. On the other hand, 'Lumberjack Song' I thought was rather good and 'Upper Class Twit of the Year' – it was great to be able to film that again in the proper place.'

From the diary of Michael Palin, December 1970: BBC Light Entertainment Group party – it was a function Terry and I independently decided to avoid but for diplomatic reasons we accepted. The only remarkable thing about an evening which is really only any night in the BBC club with slightly better food was the attitude of the programme controllers. An article in *The Times* on 16 December had detailed, fairly prominently, the continuing saga of Python's mistreatment by the BBC programme planners. Stanley Reynolds was the author, Terry Jones his chief informant and about 80 per cent of his article was correct and true, which is high by journalistic standards. Whereas we'd all seen the article as good prestige publicity, differing from a lot of other pro-Python articles only in its greater length, it had struck the BBC planners rather hard. David Attenborough, who is I believe, assistant controller of programmes, edged his way over to me quite early in the evening and began some rather nervously jocose banter on the lines, 'I feel I ought to come and talk to you being one of those responsible for the repression of *Monty Python*.' But he made the point that the programme had done extremely well as a result of the BBC's treatment, which is an argument one cannot deny, and any altruistic feelings for the viewer in regions that don't get Python must always be tempered with the knowledge that we get assured repeats in the extra loop which accompanies them. Paul Fox, on the other hand, seemed genuinely aggrieved, not that he questioned our grounds for complaint, he seemed chiefly appalled that Stanley Reynolds had got the story, 'though drunken!, etc. etc.', muttered Fox, standing in the middle of a hospitality suite like a great wounded bear. But *The Times* article at least brought a positive reaction from the very top of the monolithic BBC organisation. The giant had been stung!

MICHAEL PALIN: There were usually slight tensions. Terry and I were working very hard on all sorts of things including doing scripts for *The Two Ronnies*, but also on albums, and Eric was working on a book. John was always slightly less involved. He would come in and do things and be fine, but one would have to arrange a time for him to come in. My Python work was mainly with Terry and Terry Gilliam and Eric and Gray. There was that slight feeling that the little Pythons were doing a lot of the work at that time, and the big

'The giant had been stung!'

'The actual philosophy of Python,

if you like, and what it ought to mean,

was always done by the shorter members.'

ones would come in and be very funny and go on and do whatever else they had to do. Perhaps that was just going back to previous pre-Python relationships anyway. Terry, Eric and myself had worked on *Do Not Adjust Your Set*, Gilliam had come into that, so that was a group which existed before Python; John and Graham came from a slightly different direction.

JOHN CLEESE: I can remember shooting some film for the television series and Graham was almost incapable. He couldn't get

two lines right, one after the other. And I remember in the third series we had to abandon a sketch because Graham couldn't get through it.

GRAHAM CHAPMAN: I remember one instance where the studio audience was so pleased when a particular line was got right that there was a cheer, so you had to cut that and do it again, by this time you're forgetting your lines like mad, and so then there's another cheer when you get it right.[6]

Palin and Jones relax on Ilkley Moor

TERRY JONES: There's one classic time when Graham had this bit and he just couldn't get it. I think we did about twenty-three takes or something and he finally gets it and the audience cheers. The thing had ceased to be funny but the audience actually cheers and you can't get it off the tape. You couldn't lose it and yet that was the only take that worked, so we had to use that.

JOHN CLEESE: I knew that when you wrote with him in the afternoon, he wouldn't remember what we'd written in the morning. That's when it was quite clear to me that there was something going on, but two or three of my friends have had drinking problems and it is the hardest thing in the world to know whether to do something and usually you chicken out.

JOHN CHAPMAN: Alcohol was a bit of a crutch and it became part of his life as a medical student, the ethic was always to acquire one's knowledge by stealth and only display it under the maximum provocation and to spend one's life at the bar.

GRAHAM CHAPMAN: … alcohol, yes. It seems to work for me.[6]

DAVID SHERLOCK: He was really burning the candle at both ends – the pressures of doing the show, doing a whole load of other things, and trying to learn lines at the last minute in a cab on the way to Shepherds Bush to rehearsals, for which he was invariably late, having had a night out the night before. Once he'd got the ability to earn extremely good money, he wanted to enjoy it and he certainly did. He loved good food, he was an excellent cook although a very slow one, so sometimes at a dinner party you'd perhaps start a meal at about 11.30 at night, but it would be excellent. He was never a morning person and of course to rehearse at the BBC one has to be, whether you like it or not. Plus of course he drank to give himself confidence and to allow himself to be the sort of social animal he would like to be, which was very difficult for him because of his shyness; however, lots of people never knew he was shy because he was always slightly inebriated.

'I knew that when you wrote with him in the afternoon, he wouldn't remember what we'd written in the morning. That's when it was quite clear to me that there was something going on, but two or three of my friends have had drinking problems and it is the hardest thing in the world to know whether to do something and usually you chicken out.'

ERIC IDLE: I was not really that close to him, as a pal, because he never revealed very much of himself, there was a lot hidden. It's hard to be friendly with somebody who's hidden.

JOHN CHAPMAN: He would always turn up late, he'd usually go to the pub beforehand.

PAM CHAPMAN: But he was a young guy and that's what young guys do.

ERIC IDLE: During the tour, particularly in Birmingham, Graham was so fucking drunk it was just horrible. He'd get very obstreperous and he'd always pick on me, he'd always have a go at me, I don't know why. And I'm not given to bullying, I don't like it, and I'm pretty spiky with it because I'm used to dealing with it. You don't let them bully you, so I'd always give him sharp tongue back. He'd get very angry because he was supposed to make a very quick

change as a Colonel and then he came on in the 'Ken Shabby' sketch. We used to go on before him and there'd be a silence and you'd realise that somebody was off, and it was Graham. So I'd go on for him and I think one night John and I both went on for him, we both appeared on opposite sides of the stage trying to fill in. We fell in behind each other and walked about together desperately trying to fill in. He was always furious if you filled in for him, saying, 'What are you fucking doing? I'm in the sketch!' On the tours he would always have either David or somebody topping him up with alcohol between bits. There was one time when we were filming up in Glencoe for the TV series – I came up, I'd been drinking on the train and I went to bed. I wasn't called first thing in the morning and I was so grateful as I had a huge hangover. So I staggered up, it was lunchtime and I met them all coming back. I said, 'What did you shoot?' Nobody would speak. Graham had had to do this one speech and he hadn't got it all morning. It took twenty-six takes, and they were all like 'Oh, fuck'. He'd been very

excessive the night before. I got off the train and I was drunk after drinking all the way up to Edinburgh, and he was thrilled to see me because I was more drunk than he was. It was one of those nights when he was crawling round the bar. So, sometimes it seemed to be fun and sometimes it was really quite serious.

JOHN CLEESE: I remember that during the shooting of *And Now For Something Completely Different* we went down one day to shoot the 'Upper Class Twits' and we couldn't find a script. Michael said, 'Oh, Graham's got one, I saw him put it in the case this morning.' He went to a little suitcase that Graham used to keep things in and opened it up and took a script out, and then did a double take and almost blanched. I think somebody said, 'What is it?' Michael looked at this bottle of vodka, which to my surprise was inside the case, and said, 'That was full this morning.' My recollection is that this was about 10 o'clock in the morning and there was a lot of vodka missing. That was the first time that I realised that something was going on over and above the fact that some people drink a bit too much.

DAVID SHERLOCK: The one person who had the guts to say anything about Graham's drinking was Humphrey Barclay who was working at the BBC at the time and mentioned it to Alan Bailey, the BBC doctor and an old friend of Graham's. Gray absolutely hit the roof and said, 'Nobody tells me what I should and shouldn't do, I'm a doctor myself and I know, I'll deal with it.' And it caused quite a lot of friction. The others would say something, but it was nearly always a comment to somebody else and not directly to Graham.

'It was some years before I realised that he didn't work properly, because he was essentially very clever. He had a very good mind. And I think it was only slowly that I began to see how disconnected he was emotionally.'

From the diary of Terry Jones:
Off to Munich.
Heathrow – April 26th.

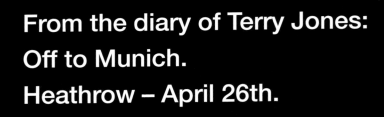

MICHAEL PALIN: Alfred Biolech was a producer with a German television station based in Munich, and he got in touch with us and said, 'I like your humour very much, I would like you to come over and do some shows in Germany.' I imagine his thinking was he'd love to buy the shows but no one will understand them, so get the Pythons to do them here. We all thought it was quite a strange idea to go off and do stuff in Germany, partly because the traditional view was that Germans had less of a sense of humour than ourselves.

JOHN CLEESE: It *was* a very unusual offer, which is what made it so interesting and so attractive. The first thing they did was they invited us to go and stay for two or three days in southern Germany just to discuss with them the sort of programme that we would be making. We had some ideas and as usual we came back to England and wrote completely different ideas.

From the diary of Terry Jones, 19 May 1971: Mike and Graham and John and Eric arrived about 10.30 and by 11 we had started working, reading through the Munich Show. This really took until lunch. Graham and I went off and bought cold meats and salad (and a charcoal grill for £2.50!) … After lunch, Mike and I went upstairs to start typing out our section. John and Graham stayed downstairs and Eric worked on the wording of the 'History of Comedy' sketch which we had previously worked out between the three of us (Eric, Mike and me). A certain tension between John and Graham. Also fights with me over letting Ian MacNaughton come along to a script meeting just to make him feel more part of it and also to actually put over what the script is meant to be. It's very unfair of us just handing Ian the written script and then expecting him to understand it completely.

ERIC IDLE: Alfred Biolech said this wonderful thing, 'Come to Germany and we'll do a recce to look at the places you might like to write sketches about.' And we thought, 'This is brilliant, a writing recce? Nobody's ever heard about that in the entire world.' That's a five-day visit to Germany. I bet John missed it too, because he always missed these good fun times. We get to Munich Airport and they're pouring huge steins of beer: 'Here come the Python boys!' And then they took us to straight to Dachau, and on the way we

got lost and it was rainy. We'd stop and ask the way and people would deny all knowledge of it. But we got there and it was really raining and it was late and they said they were closed, so Graham said, 'Tell them we're Jewish,' and they let us in. It was of course chilling.

GRAHAM CHAPMAN: The 'guards' were beginning to close the gates, it was due to close at 5.30. I shouted, 'But we're Jewish, let us in,' a jokey remark I wish I had never made.[4]

JOHN CLEESE: We wrote the script, polished it a bit and sent it off to the Germans, but they translated it into German, and then when we got back to Munich we would say, 'What word means what?'

ERIC IDLE: It was translated into German, we learnt it parrot-fashion, which was madness because what it must have sounded like, who knows, it was insane. But I can still remember most of my script because we had to learn it so hard. John and I wrote 'Eric the Half a Bee', sitting around in the Alps some time. A bit of schnapps was taken and everybody was in a really good mood. We did the 'Philosopher's Football', Germany vs the Greeks, and we shot that on the old Bayern München ground. I remember Cleesey crosses from the right and I scored a great diving header. I keep telling Gary Lineker, and he keeps promising he's going to show it in the best goals of the last millennium because it's not a bad header!

JOHN CLEESE: Once or twice they told me to emphasise a particular word and I was very, very puzzled because I spoke enough German to know what the word meant and it was quite clear to me that in English you would never have emphasised that particular word. But they said, 'No, in German you must emphasise that or it doesn't sound right.' So that was puzzling, but on the whole it was for me a very interesting challenge to learn it all.

TERRY JONES: The first thing we had to film was Mike being this Australian talking about a kangaroo's bum and you suddenly realised that not only did he have to do this in German, which he didn't understand, but he also had to do it with an Australian accent!

'There was a wonderful air of mutual bafflement and bewilderment throughout. We did 'Lumberjack Song' near Prince Ludwig's castle, and I had to sing it in German. I can remember every day learning a little bit more of it, parrot-fashion to coin a phrase, and that's exactly how I had to do it. I'd get one verse done each day, and at the end of two days I'd sing the whole thing through and then the next morning it was totally gone. I was wandering through the woods trying to remember the words and then on the morning I had to do it, suddenly it all came clear, and I've never really forgotten it since.'

MICHAEL PALIN: It fell to me to play this Australian with a hat with the corks on saying, 'I know as much about Dürer as I know about the inside of a kangaroo's bum.' This was dutifully translated into German, and whenever I say this to the rest of the Pythons they get rather irritated, but I said, 'Well, I thought we were going to do it in English and it would then be subtitled'. Then they say, 'No, of course, we were always going to do it in German.' But I do remember a sudden stark fear as I was being driven out to the mountains of Munich to do this Australian speaking German, which I didn't speak at the time apart from the basic things of saying 'Hello', 'I'm lost' and 'Have you a beer?'

In one sketch Eric Idle and I played two waiters, who are generally sending up these tourists in some Munich beer hall, and we'd say together, 'We are bringing you to the table, and sitting you here, in Bavaria, and scaring the shit out of you.' Which sounded OK when we did it in English but when we actually did it, there was an air of appalled, shocked disgust from all the technicians around. We later realised it translated literally as 'We are going to sit you down and cause you to involuntarily excrete on the chair', which is just not the same.

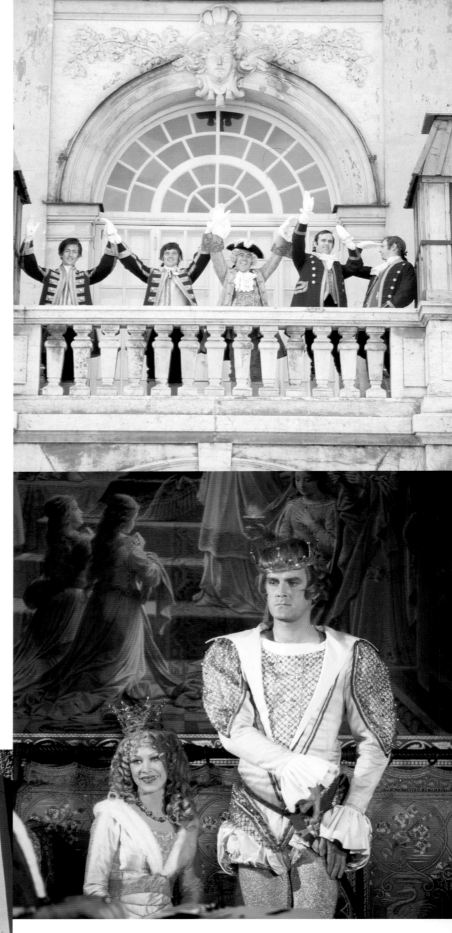

ERIC IDLE: We did it in October time, during Oktoberfest and I think Graham disappeared for days on end.

GRAHAM CHAPMAN: It was there that one afternoon I met a black American guy (it *was* during the Munich Bierfest) from the Munich cast of *Hair* whose eye caught mine and we whiled away an afternoon upstairs … My description of his anatomy to Michael Palin later earned him the title of the 'Boston Startler'. I certainly, with all my background of rugby clubs, hospital wards and other more personal experiences, had never seen anything like it.[4]

ERIC IDLE: We were put in this one rather middle-class hotel and the first morning Graham came down, the proprietress was shocked because there were a couple of German lads with him. She said, 'There are special hotels for zis here in Germany.' So Graham was discreetly moved off to this other extremely gay hotel and we never

heard from him again. I think he disappeared for actually two whole days of the shooting.

DAVID SHERLOCK: Four of us come down to breakfast rather than two in this nice little family hotel run by an extremely Munich-style Hausfrau and she was not amused, she was deeply tight-lipped. So the director said, 'I think you should go the German Oak, which is one of the places where dear Adolf and his gang used to go for drinks parties when they were actually forming the party.' They had dialect coaches every morning and Graham evolved a theory that German sentence construction is a little like Latin and because of that you can't have the subtlety of humour that you get in English.

I can remember Mike and myself commiserating over the fact that you could not get a salad for love or money. After two weeks of filming, one was dying for something fresh and green.

ERIC IDLE: We got to shoot at Ludwig II's castle in Bavaria. We went up there and the wolves were howling and it was great.

MICHAEL PALIN: There was a wonderful air of mutual bafflement and bewilderment throughout. We did the 'Lumberjack Song' near Prince Ludwig's castle, and I had to sing it in German. I can

remember every day learning a little bit more of it, parrot-fashion to coin a phrase, and that's exactly how I had to do it. I'd get one verse done each day, and at the end of two days I'd sing the whole thing through and then the next morning it was totally gone. I was wandering through the woods trying to remember the words and then on the morning I had to do it, suddenly it all came clear, and I've never really forgotten it since. There were slight translation problems though: they didn't have any equivalent for the Mounties of the Mountie Choir, and the Mountie Choir are quite an essential element to the 'Lumberjack Song'; and as for the

scarlet tunics and the big hats, there was something rather wonderfully, slightly, camply glamorous about them, but they said, 'The nearest we can get to that here is Austrian Border Guards.' So there was this group of people dressed as Austrian Border Guards with dark grey uniforms, little mossy green epaulettes and peaked hats, who just looked like how you expected middle European minor officials to look, so there was no feeling of style to it at all. John saw me and was very amused by my make-up because I had a little moustache on. He said, 'You look just like Mr Smith,' and this was the time when Ian Smith was very much in the news in Rhodesia. So I went into this short speech about 'We'll keep on singing white songs in a white way as long as we can' and all that sort of stuff, and John was saying, 'Cool it, cool it.' Actually what he meant by 'Mr Smith' was the name we always used in Germany when we talked about the war and Hitler, and I'd forgotten that, so I'd gone into what sounded like a very Hitlerian rant. I can remember John thinking this was extremely dangerous ground, so while I was doing Mr Ian Smith, John thought it was Hitler and God knows who they thought it was.

JOHN CLEESE: The show was transmitted and was reasonably successful, and the question of a second show arose. I was certainly keen, I think everyone was, because I don't remember any arguments. They said that they had no problem understanding Michael and me, but the others had accents that made it difficult for Germans to understand what they were saying, so wouldn't it be better this time to do it in English and they'd dub it. I was slightly disappointed. And we did the second show, but I don't think it was as successful as the first show and that was the end of it.

MICHAEL PALIN: Terry's mum died while we doing the Munich show and that was very sad because I was very fond of Terry's mum, she was just like Terry really. He had to fly back during that, but otherwise it was reasonably what we had expected, an unusual experience. But I think a good time was had by all because we were all together. I can remember having a great time and John got very silly – one evening John got quite tiddly and was chatting up the wardrobe mistress when we were having a little garden do. He leant against this hedge and he just fell into it because it wasn't as substantial as he thought. Then later in the evening he and I went off to try and find the red light district in Munich, and it was closed!

So it was a very good time and this was because the group was taken out of the home context and shipped off somewhere else. When we came back to England the groupings tended to split apart because people had different kinds of friends and different projects they wanted to do. The essence of Python, the Python style, what Python was and the form it took was actually always really Terry J's work and Terry G's and mine to a certain extent. John, Eric and Graham brought in material, but I don't remember them being

involved in the big debate about how the shows should look and all that. The actual philosophy of Python, if you like, and what it ought to mean, was always done by the shorter members.

JOHN CLEESE: Anybody who's a public service broadcaster has to worry a little bit about what's going in, for good reasons as opposed to commercial reasons. And I thought that the amount that the BBC interfered was absolutely minimal and on a couple of occasions I totally agreed with them. Eric wrote a sketch about urine, which I thought was tasteless. I found it embarrassing. I accepted that the others didn't. But if I found it embarrassing, then I thought it was absolutely fine for the BBC to interfere on that; and they interfered on an image of Christ nailed to a telegraph post on one of Terry Gilliam's animations. I don't mean that I necessarily personally agreed with them, although I did with the urine one, but what I mean is that someone who is in charge of a channel has to keep an eye on what's going on.

ERIC IDLE: John was upset, but that sketch was about snobbery, not wee wee.

MICHAEL PALIN: The BBC were noticing that they had this show. They pretty much let us have a free rein for the first two series, and were beginning to look at the material going a bit too far. We had the 'Summarise Proust Competition' sketch where the contestants had to give their hobbies and one of them was 'strangling animals, golf and masturbating'. The BBC got to hear about this after it had actually been recorded to an enormous roar of laughter and they insisted that 'masturbating' had to be removed. Ian had to forcibly go in and just chop it from the transmission tape just before transmission, so there's a horrible sort of gap and then 'golf', which got this huge laugh.

We all went to this one meeting with Duncan Wood at the BBC, six of us were sitting round there discussing masturbation and things like that. I remember Terry getting very worked up and saying, 'What's so silly about masturbation? I mean I masturbate, you masturbate, we all masturbate!' I thought, God, this meeting's going to turn into some sort of wanking competition, but of course at the time the whole idea of masturbating was a taboo subject. You really just didn't talk about it, you got on with it, you did it, but you didn't talk about it and you certainly didn't put it on television. So that was an issue. In the third series people like Bill Cotton, who had never been to a recording before, would suddenly come in the afternoon at rehearsal and check us out.

TERRY GILLIAM: There was something I think John was behind once. Ian MacNaughton got the blame for it but I think John was behind it. We were doing silly religions and there was a bit where some vicar was calling somebody else. Then we followed the wires and they went up to the next pole and there was the crucifixion of Christ with the telephone lines going through Jesus' arm. And that was the one thing that bothered John, I have no idea why. That was probably one of the few moments where he snuck behind our backs and got in there.

On the third series the BBC got interested and tried to censor stuff. What it proved to be was an indication of how sick their minds were, not ours. There was a scene where John thrusts his severed leg through a door to have it signed as a delivery for something. We had this meeting with BBC1 Controller Paul Fox and he was talking about this scene where a man pushes his giant penis through the door. What? It's a severed leg, but they saw a giant penis.

So we went through this whole thing and I think he was embarrassed by the end, because we were a terrible gang. I would hate to be the Controller and have the six of us walk into his office, like we did. Actually when the show went out as a repeat on BBC 2 they censored two things: the 'Summarise Proust Competition', where one contestant's hobbies were golf, strangling small mammals and masturbation, and they beeped masturbation. Then there was one of my cartoons where a prince has a spot on his face, he didn't tend to it and years later it turned into a cancer and he died – they changed cancer to gangrene, because cancer had become a word you couldn't make a joke about. What an extraordinary time, that in a repeat on BBC 2 you can't say cancer in a cartoon.

MICHAEL PALIN: John was absolutely in agreement with Bill Cotton and it was the first time ever that someone brought in an outsider. That would normally have been dealt with within the group, but that was quite significant. I think John brought Bill in because he felt it wasn't a good sketch and it wasn't working – it was abandoned in the end anyway – but there were many other small problems that we had during that third series. I think we all got the sense that not only was John not happy but the shows weren't as

Director Ian MacNaughton (right) and cameraman Alan Featherstone (below) on location in Jersey, filming 'The Cycling Tour'

Time Out

MONTY PYTHON'S LONDON GUIDE MAY 4 - 10 NO 167 · 15p

good as the shows we had done before, and it was quite hard to persevere in that atmosphere.

You can argue that it was more 'shock' funny in the third series than 'clever' funny; I think the problem was that some of the stuff in the third series wasn't quite as funny as it was in the first two series; not always, but often.

TERRY JONES: We always felt we were consuming a lot of material because we didn't want any padding. So we set a high pace. There was always the constant anxiety of can you get enough material and can it be funny enough? Always by the end of the series we'd be running out of material. So they tend to get more scatological towards the end of the series. I like it in the third series, when we really *were* running out of material and Mike and I offered what became 'Mr Pither's Holiday/The Cycling Tour', which we'd started writing as a half-hour show for ourselves to do outside Python. But we were getting short of material so we offered it to Python. That was good because it was half a show and John, Graham and Eric came in and took it on. I'd always hoped, if Python was going to do another series all together, that the way we'd go was to do half-hour narratives, which I suppose Mike and I did in *Ripping Yarns*. That would have been brilliant as a Python thing

JOHN CLEESE: I remember certain specific incidents and nights in the British tour, like listening to the show in Bristol when one of the matinée audiences hated it. I remember sitting there and

thinking, 'It isn't very good is it?' But that evening they were falling about and I remember thinking how fragile one's confidence is. If the audience doesn't laugh at it, then it's not funny. At least for those two hours that that audience isn't laughing, it's not funny.

From the diary of Michael Palin: Afterwards we had food laid on at the Dolphin, Lord Montagu had come backstage to meet us, a huge Daimler with a flagpole on the front swept us back to the hotel. Upstairs in the restaurant, ate salad and drank champagne, there was just enough to create the feeling of occasion. Graham and Eric reached a point of explosion and Eric threw down his napkin with a rather impetuous little flourish and left the restaurant. Later Graham, Eric and John had 'full and frank discussions' at which John told Graham straight out that he had performed very badly in both shows and if he went on like this every night there was no point in continuing on the tour. For my own part I feel that Graham's condition was the result of a colossal overcompensation for first night nerves and he's clearly gone too far in his attempt to relax. Maybe now the first night's over he will no longer feel so afraid.

ERIC IDLE: By the time we toured we actually were a rock 'n' roll tour. We were offered a lot of money to go on tour, a lot of money for us anyway. We weren't making big money from the BBC, the movie had only made us £1,000 each, considering we were writing and performing, and it wasn't like we were loaded. But the tour

looked like good easy money and that was when it became rock 'n' roll, because we were going up one side of England and coming down the other side of England and Bowie was going up one side of England and coming down the other. We crossed in Edinburgh and then you realised that this was like a rock 'n' roll tour.

DAVID SHERLOCK: There was of course the famous time when we went to a gay club and the table was double booked. We were at the table first and David Bowie and his dear wife, Angie, arrived at the same table. She said to Graham, 'Do you know who we are?' And Graham said, 'Do you know who I am?' I was kicking him under the table saying, 'It's David Bowie and Angie,' and he'd no idea who they were.

ERIC IDLE: I don't know whether it was enjoyable. I think it was madness. I think Graham was very drunk a lot of the time and

was aggressive in the hotels afterwards, John was weird and disappeared and had a series of secondary hotels he'd hire and do almost anything to avoid us. I don't remember it being a great time. Touring Canada was a great time but England was hard work, because we were on the road and it was almost one-night stands, which was rigorous to say the least.

JOHN CLEESE: One of the things I'd not felt comfortable about was that my wife Connie was not just in show business, and a very, very good dramatic actress, but was also a very funny actress. She always had funny ideas and funny lines and one of the effects of Python taking up so much of my time was that I didn't actually have much time to work with Connie, which I was looking forward to doing. Of course when I finished Python the first thing I did was go off and do *Fawlty Towers* with her. So this was the feeling, a lot of the time, that she was getting rather neglected, that my life was fine, I was out there being a Python, but there wasn't any space for her in my professional life.

GRAHAM CHAPMAN: We actually enjoy working together a lot, we also enjoy shouting at each other. The only danger is that there's a kind of feeling that John is getting a little bit conventional. He's not basically conventional, but he would, a lot of us feel, like to

settle down and just have a few nice investments and not have to do too much work. That's bad, because he's a very good creative mind and a very necessary part of the team and we couldn't really, the rest of us, do a show without him, just as probably no one would want to do a show without any of the others. So it does cut the whole thing up a little, but I think he'll come round in the end, he usually does … I mean, he's six foot five for a start and he's got a huge chin and he's a very strange shape altogether, therefore people tended to recognise John Cleese. The rest of us are a little amorphous as faces and do tend to wear beards or moustaches or drag or whatever. I personally like that, because you don't get pointed at in pubs or stared at or whatever and you can go in and have a drink somewhere. It's a bit awkward occasionally – you're going into a pub and somebody will say 'Mr Gumby' behind your back.[6]

ERIC IDLE: When we got to North America it was extraordinary to find that everybody assumed that we were totally stoned all the time while making it up. You had to point out to people that actually you can't write comedy when you're stoned, you can't find the typewriter, but a lot of people still say to this day, 'Oh when I was a college kid, man, we'd just get a joint and watch Python and we'd laugh and laugh.' And you think, 'Well, actually you didn't need Python, you could just look at the wallpaper!' Python has always been office hours, nine to five, even writing the movies we'd do that, we never wrote late or late nights. I don't know whether that's an influence of John's or whatever. But the audience, I think, were very stoned! Certainly in Canada.

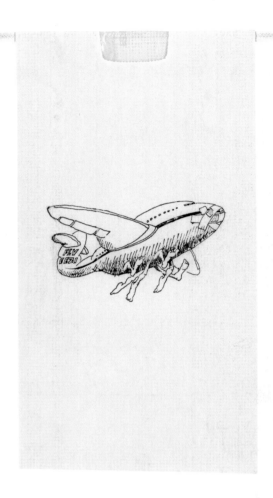

'Python has always been office hours, nine to five, even writing the movies we'd do that, we never wrote late or late nights.'

The viewers in Canada were our first loyal audience and the first ones to come out and demonstrate when CBC took it off the air. They came out and patrolled the streets, complaining, which was really great for us. That was the first time we knew we had some influence and people were prepared to come out and picket.

TERRY JONES: Canada was a bit hard because we were going round a lot of places doing one-night stands and that was a bit of a freaky

Eric Idle and Terry Jones on stage,
director Ian MacNaughton on location in Jersey,
and Michael Palin in San Francisco

JOHN CLEESE: Chapman was very possessive of me. He was very cross with me, that I went off and took work and wrote something without him. He felt that in a sense he owned me, I think, and that I was letting him down by going off. And that was what I found oppressive about Python. I was very happy to do the second series, although my enthusiasm was waning a bit because I felt we were repeating ourselves. But I was not keen to do the third series. My complaint is they never listened to the reasons for my not wanting to go along with ten months of the year being Python activity. When I finally decided that I didn't want to be involved any more and they were going to go ahead with the fourth series and not really hearing me at all, I said, 'OK, well fine, go ahead with my blessing. Graham and I have written some material.' It wasn't that I hated Python. What I hated was ten and a half months per year of Python.

At that point one of my real objections was that we were beginning to repeat ourselves. I didn't mind going out on stage and doing material that I thought was really good in a stage show, but I didn't want to spend two or three times as long as that producing shows that didn't strike me as being particularly original. So it wasn't that I hated the group or didn't want to see them, I just didn't want them completely taking my life over. There was a stage in the third series when I thought Graham and I only wrote two completely original sketches in the thirteen shows. Every sketch that came up I could point to two or three forebears in the first or second series, I could say, 'It's that sketch from the first series with a bit of that sketch from the second series and a little bit of that sketch from the last show of the first series.' I could see where it was all repeating. We got to the point where everything we did was beginning to derive itself from what we'd done at the start. I didn't see the point of doing that unless we were poor and needed the money.

TERRY JONES: It was getting more difficult to get people to meetings and there was an increased amount of 'I've got an appointment at 4 o'clock, so I'll have to leave'.

JOHN CLEESE: Some of the others were much happier with the almost sole identity of being a Python than I was. It had never occurred to me at the start that it was going to become an almost exclusive activity. What with the television, stage, records, books and films, we were probably giving up ten or eleven months a year to Python, which was much more than I'd ever wanted. I do like to do different things. I think that Graham, for example, loved being Python, because Graham was never in the engine room, Graham was always on the outside lobbing very good ideas and very good lines in, but he was not someone who could pick the ball up and run with it. You needed to have other people running it, then he would make a very useful contribution, so I think Graham was totally happy to be a Python. But the others, I think, once the initial excitement was over, wanted to go off and do other things. I think Michael did, I think certainly Eric did, and Terry J was more in the Graham camp. I think he felt really happy when he could be basically the director, the one who stayed on at the editing sessions

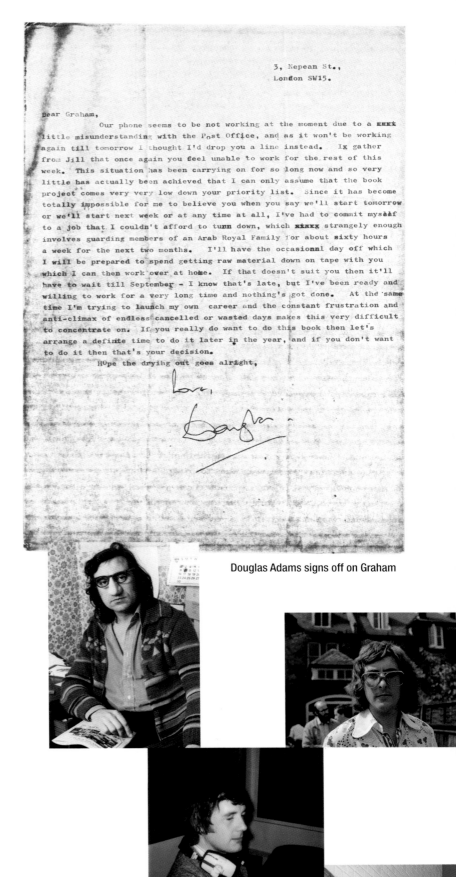

Douglas Adams signs off on Graham

after everyone else had gone. Because of his tremendous energy he was probably the most dominant figure in the creation of the programmes. I think that he and Graham were the ones who resented it most when I said I just didn't want to do it anymore, but I found it had taken my life over in a way that I hadn't anticipated. I think Terry referred to me in some kind of harsh way for letting the Pythons down, but I remember thinking, we were just going to do television together, we weren't getting married. I remember thinking that. It wasn't discussed for very long because I was not particularly effectual in those days. I had too much public school politeness.

ERIC IDLE: When I first met him, John had his own view. Everything John says is true for John, as everybody else's view is true for themselves. And, if you look at John's life, he'd done the BBC, he'd done *I'm Sorry, I'll Read That Again* with a bunch of Cambridge comics, he'd then done *The Frost Report* with a bunch of comics where he'd done sketches and he'd written sketches with Graham, then he'd done *The '48 Show* and then he'd done Python. He must have been in his early thirties by then, and he was just tired of writing sketches, I think, he just gets fed up with writing. So his dissatisfaction was more to do with writing and waiting for Graham, and Graham could take a lot of patience waiting for.

JOHN CLEESE: One of the other problems was as Graham got more and more into his alcoholism, the others wanted less and less to work with him.

TERRY GILLIAM: Some people had different skills at dealing with the group. That's why I think he probably got into this whole thing of learning to control other people, because he wanted to control the group. Unfortunately he got the wrong group!

JOHN CLEESE: One thing that characterises me, I think, is my genuine belief that people should, on the whole, do what they want to do. This is a revolutionary approach to human behaviour. It was how I felt about the stage tour, if there's somebody who doesn't want to do it, then let's not do it. And if the others all want to do another series without me, fine. It's only me that I'm trying to protect because the moment that something becomes successful there is a built-in momentum to keep doing the same thing. If, at any stage of your life, you really tried to change what you're doing, move in a different direction, you discover that there's a sort of system set up round you and everyone really wants you to go on doing the same thing. They will only pay you to go on doing the same thing and if you want to do something different you have to take a drop in salary. Which is what I took when I left Python. My income went down quite noticeably.

GRAHAM CHAPMAN: We all have more and more money to earn each year in order to keep up with things like VAT. We therefore tend to diversify, go off and write separate things and earn more money that way. But I think five of us would very much like to do another series of Python. John is reluctant, but then he always was. He didn't want to do the other three series that we've done and that I think is partly

'It's only me that I'm trying to protect because the moment that something becomes successful there is a built-in momentum basically to keep doing the same thing . . . you discover that there's a sort of system set up round you and everyone really wants you to go on doing the same thing.'

Idle and son Carey

a financial thing, partly he has this strange desire to go off and read lots of books before he's too old to be able to read easily, and he doesn't like filming very much because that means getting up terribly early in the morning. I think it's a very sensible worry, standing around all day with perhaps just one line to do. I think there was one example in the last series where John and I stood at the back of a crowd, the piece of filming took about half a day, and eventually on the screen you saw John's elbow and I think a bit of the spear I was carrying, and that for someone, you know, you regard yourself as someone who, perhaps, should be writing something instead of spending that time standing around in a cold situation, very likely raining, actually contributing nothing to the world around you because it could have been done by pieces of polystyrene, those particular parts. I think that eventually we'll reach some kind of compromise whereby we'll do another thirteen half-hours.[6]

ERIC IDLE: Everybody goes 'I'll take Graham today' and then wait a few hours till he arrives. So I think he was fed up with that and who could blame him. The rest of us hadn't been on television in grown-up time till Python really, in any big way, so it was kind of much more fun for us. I think that with John his thing would always be 'I don't want to do this and I don't want to do this'. Then Graham would say, 'Oh well, let's just do it and he's bound to join in later.' So we went, 'OK, fine, we'll just do it,' because Graham was very much the interpreter of what John would do. He would say, 'He'll change his mind, he'll come in.' And to be honest he usually did.

JOHN CLEESE: What I resented at the time was that they absolutely would not take my worries seriously. I think Terry Jones once said, 'Oh, just ignore him, he'll fall into line.' It was a feeling that I was not genuine in my reasons for not wanting to go on, that this was some kind of charade to get attention, but that it shouldn't be taken seriously. And I think it was very hard for them to think, with a success on their hands, that anybody wouldn't be content to go on doing it. Whereas for me, if we weren't doing new material, there wasn't really any point in doing it at all.

ERIC IDLE: Python is like we get thanked and praised, and you just have to remember that five-sixths of that praise isn't you. You didn't write five-sixths of it.

From the diary of Michael Palin, 27 January 1973: We decided to do a Python tour with Tony Smith. We talked about details of performance and dates and places. I find it extraordinary how John can undertake such a violent month of really hard work repeating

basically old material and yet will not countenance doing another series of Python. I suppose it's all a question of time and money. My God, we're getting so mercenary. Eric is almost totally involved in ads, he's been the most successful of us with his 'Nudge, nudge' selling Breakaway chocolate and another ad in the offing. This afternoon he rang me to say that Gibbs toothpaste had approached him to ask if he could set up a five-minute film for their sales conference. It had to be made quickly and fairly cheaply. Eric rang me proposing we set it up as a package, with the two of us and Terry, it sounds like a good experience, it wasn't for general commercial purposes and it could be rude. What's more it's work. I accepted on behalf of us both.

From the diary of Michael Palin, February 1973: Unfortunately he (Ian MacNaughton) is unlikely to get much more work from

Python partly because Python is doing less work anyway and partly because Terry is so anxious to direct that he says it almost makes him physically ill to work with someone else.

From the diary of Michael Palin, Tuesday, 27 March 1973: Terry and I drove into sunny Soho to Pathé Theatre One and mouthed some highly imbecilic lines about Nutty Bars for an hour or so. These voice-overs must be grinned and borne, our Python notoriety will not get us these jobs forever, soon they'll realise that there are much better voices around but at the moment people are irrationally confident about using anyone with Python connections for anything … I hope it never becomes a substitute for Python.

From the diary of **Michael Palin, August 1973:** We have been offered a five-day show at the Rainbow Theatre at Christmas. John is doubtful and thinks the Rainbow is too big, it's 3,000, larger than any of the other theatres we have played in England, and that many people won't be able to see and hear.

JOHN CLEESE: What had happened before they did the series without me was that Jonesy and I had locked horns, and then the others could jump on one side or the other and balance it this way or that way. Jonesy on his own is a bit of a control freak, we all were, but I would say that Jonesy and Gilliam are as control freaky as anyone, which is why they went on to become film directors. And now Jonesy was unmatched by someone who could balance his commitment, so he got his way probably more often than was good for the show. What I felt about Jonesy, and

I did lock horns with him a lot, was that he could never let go. We were hoping to leave at five but there'd be an argument going on still at quarter to six. Jones would finally concede that all the other people thought it was better to do it in way B and he was finally going to give up on way A. The moment you assembled the next morning, as you were making coffee, he was saying, 'I was thinking last night, I really, really do think way A is better because …' And you'd be off into this thing that you thought you'd finally decided the previous evening. Chapman and I certainly used to agree on the enormous amount of time that was wasted because Terry felt intensely about everything. We all feel intensely about something, but Terry always felt intensely about everything.

ERIC IDLE: The fourth year was John-free which was different, although not in performance. I think some of the funniest shows were in that fourth series.

TERRY GILLIAM: That last series had some wonderful stuff in it. It wasn't that something had gone out of it, I just think we'd reached the time where some of us, enough of us, felt we weren't being original anymore. We were repeating ourselves and it was kind of like a machine. We could do it and we were more successful than ever, but fuck it, it's time to quit. That's another thing I really like about Python, we really know when to quit and just walk away from it. I had a theory that what we should have done on the last series was to do a really, really terrible series. The first four shows should have been dire, nothing funny, just boring beyond belief, so people would just start switching it off. Then by the end of the fourth show nobody's watching it anymore and then the next week do a brilliant show and only two people would see it.

From the diary of Michael Palin, 23 October 1973: Everybody was present, though Graham was about half an hour late, we were talking to John Gledhill our manager – do we want to appear on the Russell Harty Show? Everyone says no apart from Graham. We're into royalties on the second record, £19 each straight away, and who wants to go to Denmark for a publicity trip? Having cleared these out of the way there's a discussion about Michael Codron's offer of six weeks starting at Christmas in the Comedy Theatre. Eric and John are very keen, Terry G less keen, myself very anti … For some reason I find myself in the rare position of being out on my own, although Terry J, I think, feels the same, but is keeping tactfully quiet to avoid accusations of a blocked vote. Briefly I see it as six more weeks of a show which I find very dull and here we are going to the West End, forsaking our Rainbow pop following which John says 'scares the shit out of me' for the £2.50 circle and front stalls audience with a show that seems to be full of old material, some of it done in the West End before. What's become of Python the innovator?

·— Monty Python Live at Drury Lane —·

ERIC IDLE: I don't know why it became Drury Lane. I don't know the dynamics or the reasons or the why and wherefore, but we did four weeks at Drury Lane. My then wife, Lyn, played Carol Cleveland's roles. And we had a total rock 'n' roll audience. We had Jaggers and Eltons and people would all come and it was still crazy. It hadn't been done in London because we'd done everywhere else but we'd never played London, but Drury Lane is just as good a venue to be mad in and we had the pantomime Princess Margaret in the royal box which was carried around with us. I just remember the live shows as being fun.

MICHAEL PALIN: Drury Lane was pretty good, we just had a terrific reaction to it. It seemed something you couldn't not do, really. From my diary: 'Now we've completed seven shows at Drury Lane, ending last week with the grand flourish of two shows on Friday and two shows on Saturday. The reviews have been extensive nearly all enthusiastic.' My problem was I used to lose my voice, I'm not very good at that. I wasn't all that keen on doing stage shows. But it was rather exciting really and then we started doing the film fairly soon after that.

'. . . Eric and Terry G. were in particularly lucid form, and even John was showing remarkable adaptability. It's amazing how sea, sun and luxury lubricates the script-writing process.

IN WHICH
WE ALL BECOME STARLETS

What's more we do seem to be enjoying each other's company again. Dare I say it, there even seems to be a certain amount of affection creeping back into the group. Gosh, I hope the others don't read this . . .'

MONTY PYTHON AND THE HOLY GRAIL

'We would never have got through that movie with real horses. It makes a wonderful leap because with that opening shot you accept the kind of lunatic logic that's there. Arthur is incredibly serious, never a blink, and then in the background you've got all this stuff going on. It's one of those things that's, in retrospect, brilliant.'

MICHAEL PALIN: When we were writing in the late '60s, the Beatles were producing their albums and as far as I was concerned those were the greatest and most exciting examples of pop music around. On the day when we knew an album was coming out we just queued up to get it. The Beatles ruled the world, they were multi-millionaires, we were struggling away as comedy writers. Then I heard that during the first series Paul McCartney would stop his music sessions when *Monty Python* was on so that everyone could look at the show, and then they would go back to recording. That was the first moment I can remember when I thought, 'This is extraordinary, the Beatles interested in us?' The other story, which I have no reason to dispute, was that George Harrison says he sent a congratulatory note to the BBC after the first show and it never got through to us, probably the BBC reception didn't know who this Harrison man was, or what the programme was or something. So right from the very start there was this connection between the best band in the world and our little band of comedy thesps. Then gradually one began to hear more and more stories about bands and musicians who loved Python and felt a kinship with Python for some reason or another. I've never quite worked out why that was but there were more and more instances of it and you would meet musicians who would say, 'That was just wonderful' or 'We love that show'. I think they thought it was somehow quite cool, it was a cult thing.

When it came to financing *Monty Python and the Holy Grail*, who came in but Led Zeppelin and Pink Floyd as investors; the label on which we did most of our albums was basically a rock and roll label, so we were closely intertwined with rock music from very early on. But the fact that the Beatles noticed us was quite something. Almost as epic as when I read much later on that, in the

declining years of his life, Elvis himself watched *Monty Python and the Holy Grail*. That just blew my mind, because Elvis more than anybody changed my whole perception of pop music with 'Heartbreak Hotel', as many of my age will say. We went from Winifred Atwell to 'Heartbreak Hotel' and the impact was extraordinary.

ERIC IDLE: Elvis used to call people 'Squire' after my 'Nudge, Nudge' sketch. After I heard that, I was bowled over.

TERRY GILLIAM: We were the doyens of the pop world. They really liked Python.

JOHN CLEESE: I was always going to do *The Holy Grail* even at the time when I wasn't going to do the television show.

TERRY JONES: *And Now For Something Completely Different* hadn't done that well. John had wanted to do that because he thought he was going to make a lot of money, and when it didn't, he was less keen on doing another film. I was very keen to do a film, and eventually we persuaded John that we should think about a movie. Then we sat there to talk about what it should be and Mike had got this beginning of King Arthur and Patsy doing coconuts. We all suddenly thought, 'That's a funny image and why don't we do a thing about King Arthur?' And so we all went off and started writing King Arthur. I went off and tried to do a bit of reading – Arthurian legends and things. Then we came back with various bits and in the first screenplay there was a lot of this stuff set in Harrods and modern day, which John had written. I was a bit disappointed, so I said, 'Let's do it for real and do a real Arthurian legend.' That's partly because I was into the Middle Ages, but I also thought it won't be what's expected of us. The thing we've got at the moment is more like what you expect, it's a sketch show, and it would be much more interesting to do a narrative thing and keep it in the Middle Ages. To my surprise, people agreed.

TERRY GILLIAM: I don't remember much about writing. I just remember there was this whole scene in Harrods that John and Graham wrote and that's gone. That scene in Harrods may have been the first thing that got us onto the medieval thing, because ideas were just being thrown around, ideas were being dredged up from the bottom of drawers, old material: 'Oh God, what can we do?' Everybody did their research and started writing funny sketches. And then we started stitching them together, so it looked like there was a story there, but luckily the structure allowed for it – the gathering of the knights, we get them together, then we split them up and we have to get them back together. This is a perfect vehicle for sketches.

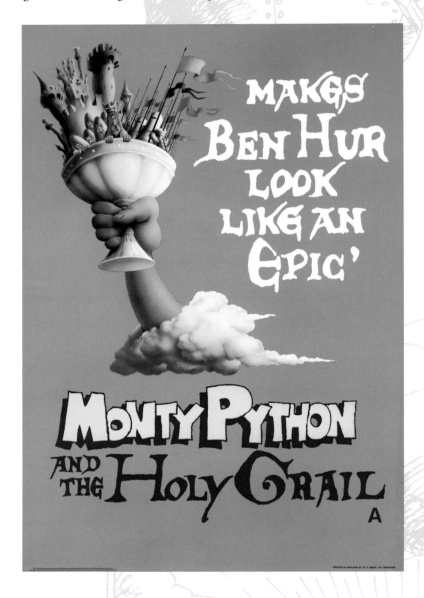

'MAKES BEN HUR LOOK LIKE AN EPIC'

MONTY PYTHON AND THE HOLY GRAIL

A

ERIC IDLE: It's harder for six people to write narrative, six people is ideal for the sketch format, but I don't know that there was an itching to write narrative. I can't say that we all said, 'Oh, let's write narrative now.' We wanted to do a film that we were in charge of. We didn't want Ian MacNaughton.

TERRY JONES: The coconut gag was the original gag that sparked the whole thing off. We did talk about having horses at one point and then we quickly dismissed it, because we thought it would be funnier not to and because we couldn't afford horses anyway.

JOHN CLEESE: There was an awareness that we were going into a new territory, but I don't think we knew a great deal about how to do it. I really don't. One of the problems is this, if you're trying to write you can write easily with two people, it is possible to write with three, it is impossible to write with four. If you have four people in the room there will always be one of the four who doesn't like the latest suggestions, it's strange but that's just the way it is. When you're doing a movie you really need to craft a central story and if two of us had gone off to craft the story it might have been better. As it was the story was crafted by the six of us in the room; it was therefore harder to find agreement. If you add to that the fact none of us had really written movies before and we didn't really know anything about story and that kind of thing, then it was very much a question of just putting together a lot of sketches and trying to make a story out of them, rather than starting from the story and working out from that. And it worked really quite well in *The Holy Grail*.

MICHAEL PALIN: It quite skilfully managed to combine sketches into a narrative story, but I think what really worked was that the events in the story could be broken down into an old university revue format – ten sketches and three songs – and we also managed to join them together rather well. There were little bits of sealant that kept the narrative watertight, but in fact it was all a bit of a con. It wasn't really a story in which everything began at the beginning and ended at the end, it went off in all sorts of different directions and everyone had their adventure which is very much like the Arthurian legends. The way they were written, after everyone had their little adventure, they all went back to the table and talked and then went on to the next adventure. So it suited Python really very well.

JOHN CLEESE: I was very intrigued by the idea of us starting to try and work in film. I didn't understand film. It's amazing, if you look at the first draft of *Grail* how little of that appears in the movie, it's about 10 per cent of the first draft. But I remember Mike and Terry reading out the coconuts thing which gave us a key to a certain approach of how to do it.

MICHAEL PALIN: Hard to remember why Graham got the lead. I'm not sure that anybody else particularly wanted to do Arthur because it was a very straight part, not a lot of laughs, I think Graham volunteered. He had that dignity and this wonderful saintly long-suffering look. I think also it was quite a selfless thing to do because it cut you out of a lot of other sketches. Otherwise casting was determined mainly by who'd written what. Castle Anthrax was a Galahad thing and I'd written that with Terry so I was cast as Galahad; Terry had written Bedevere; Lancelot was a mixture of stuff we'd written but John seemed to fit that well; Eric had written Brave Sir Robin, so he got the Sir Robin parts, and the rest were subsidiary parts which again I think were probably largely to do originally with who wrote what.

JOHN CLEESE: Just as Graham would have played Arthur better than I would have done, I would have done the Black Knight better than Michael would have done. If you write something, I believe you probably have a deeper understanding of it than someone who

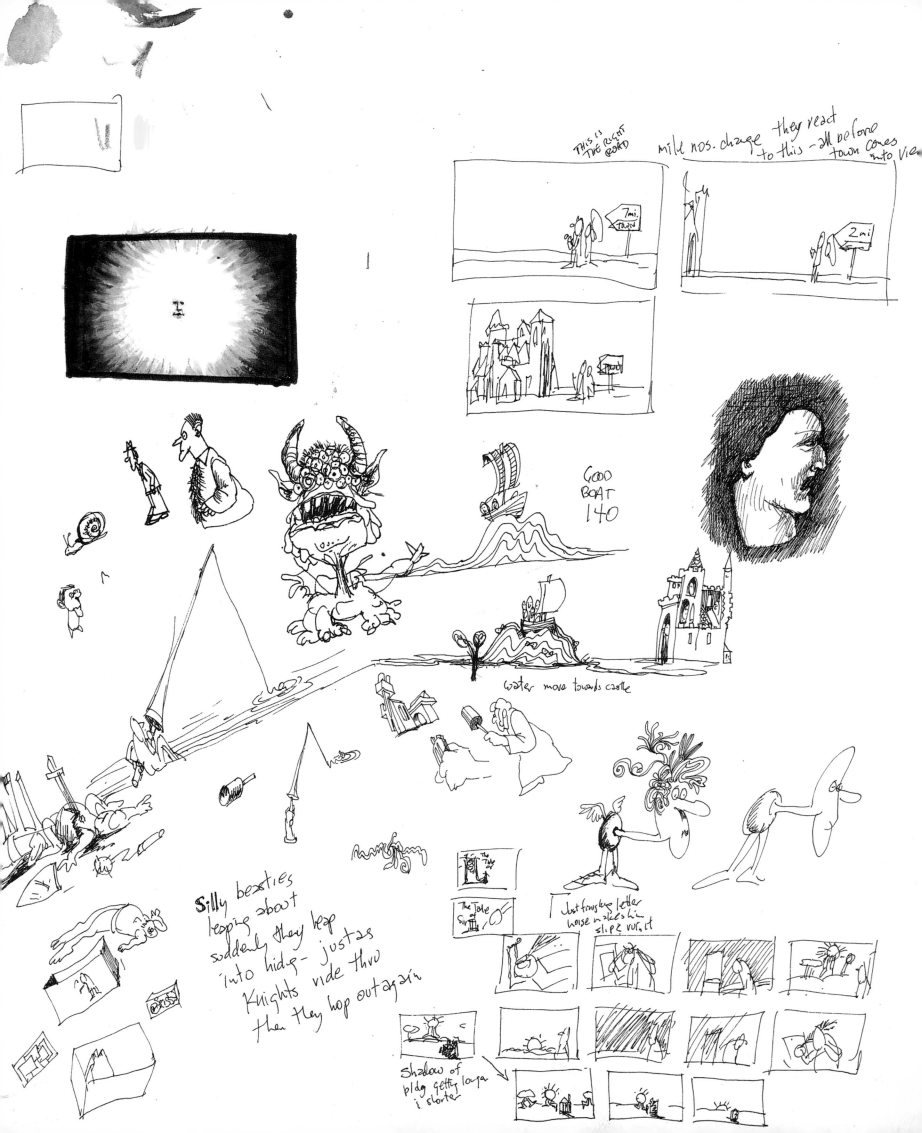

THIS IS THE RIGHT ROAD

mile nos. change they react to this - all before town comes into view

GOOD BOAT 140

water move towards castle

Silly beasties leaping about suddenly they leap into hide - just as Knights ride thru then they hop out again

The Tale of

The Tale of Sir

Just finishing letter noise makes him slip & vur, it

Shadow of bldg getting longer & shorter

comes to it from scratch. I think it was obvious that Michael, Eric and I would probably get most of the laughs and King Arthur was a slightly straighter character around whom the insanities occurred. It was just so obvious that it would be Graham, that I'm not so sure there was ever much doubt about it.

TERRY JONES: I thought we'd write the script and go and get finance but it came as a bit of a surprise that film companies weren't interested. They'd say, 'Well, if you have your television director directing it, yeah we'll have a look, but if you're going to direct it, no way.' And it was Michael White who saved the day really.

ERIC IDLE: When you're young and you're doing things, you say, 'What do we do now that we haven't done? Well, we haven't done a

movie …' We did *And Now For Something Completely Different* which was just like recycling old sketches. When we had the opportunity to do that, I think I went to Michael White and we got the money out of him, but I'm not sure. The financing was very good and the rock 'n' roll element of it all. I think Tony Stratton-Smith was responsible for bringing in a lot of that, he was Charisma Records. Led Zeppelin, Pink Floyd, Genesis, they all put in £20,000 each and Alexander Hesketh, Lord Hesketh, put in £20,000, and they made the budget I think £200,000. So half of it was the Film Finance Corporation and the other £100,000 came from independent investments – five groups of £20,000 each I

think, that's how it worked and they've made a ton out of it. They keep thanking us. Jimmy Page and Robert Plant turned up for the opening in New York. It's kind of really weird.

[Bryce Hammer & Co, Chartered Accountants: cost of production as at 17 September 1975 was £229,575.00.]

TERRY JONES: Nobody else was particularly interested in directing so it wasn't really an issue. I always intended to do it and when it was discussed everybody agreed that I should, at which point I got cold feet and said, 'Maybe Terry and I ought to do it together.' So I really pulled Terry into it.

ERIC IDLE: The only two who wanted to direct were the two Terrys, it wasn't much of an issue, if they wanted to do it, they should do it.

TERRY JONES: I thought it would be better for Terry and me to do it and also Terry and I had very much the same vision, we both knew what we wanted. We both had the idea of doing an antidote to the Hollywood vision of the Middle Ages with huge sets and large, clean floors and things. The idea of doing a really dirty, funky Middle Ages, we both wanted to do that. Terry's got a better eye, so it was great for him to actually put the things in front of the camera, but we both had the same vision really.

TERRY GILLIAM: Once we decided it was going to be about King Arthur and the Grail it seemed the perfect vehicle – you gather the knights together and you've got a structure that most people can understand: a quest. Terry and I were great medievalists and couldn't wait to get in there. What was interesting about the start of the movie was how traditional we wanted to be. We wanted to make real movies, not Python movies, not the crap that we did. *Real* movies. If we'd had the money we would have had real horses. What was wonderful was the limitations put on us by the budget. We couldn't do all those things so we had to get clever and thank god, because the coconuts saved our ass. We would never have got through that movie with real horses. It makes a wonderful leap because with that opening shot you accept the kind of lunatic logic that's there. Arthur is incredibly serious, never a blink, and then in the background you've got all this stuff going on. It's one of those things that's, in retrospect, brilliant.

TERRY JONES: Terry and I spent two weeks doing a location tour of Britain, which was great fun. We had a great time looking in Scotland and Wales.

TERRY GILLIAM: We went to every castle in Britain.

TERRY JONES: We'd chosen all these castles in Scotland, then suddenly a week before Terry and I were going to go up to go over the filming, we got this message from the Department of the Environment for Scotland saying that they wouldn't let us use any of their castles, because we were doing things that were not consistent with the dignity of the fabric of the buildings. These places had been built for torturing and killing people, you couldn't do a bit of comedy? It was so ridiculous. So Terry and I ended up going off to

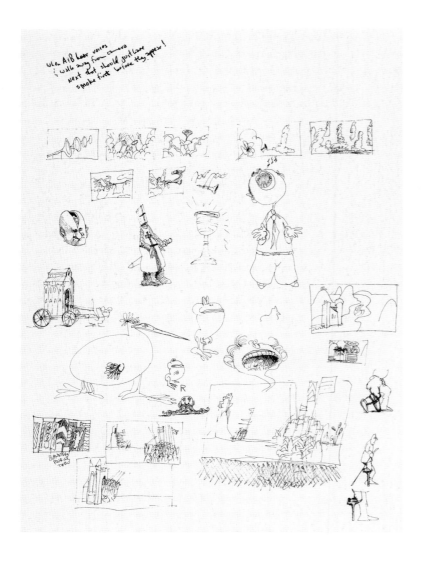

find new locations a week before filming. And then we found Doune Castle and Castle Stalker in the end, but it was very close.

JOHN CLEESE: Just before I was going up to Scotland, our producer John Goldstone telephoned me – at that point our fee for writing and acting was £4,000 but we were told they could pay us £2,000 and we'd get the other two when we'd finished – and he said, 'Would you mind sharing a hotel room?' I said, 'I do not want to share a hotel room. We're doing this entire movie, writing and performing, for £2,000, we might not see the other £2,000 and I do not want to share a hotel room.' And of course when we got there the conditions were appalling.

TERRY JONES: Before we went off filming, there was a sequence I always wanted to do, 'King Brian the Wild', whose sport was having close harmony groups shot! He'd start off with this group of singers singing 'In the merry month of May', and then they're all killed and it cuts to King Brian the Wild laughing hysterically. Then he says, 'And the next!' But somebody comes up and says, 'M'Lord, I'm afraid there's no more close harmony groups left in the kingdom.' 'What! No more close harmony groups left?' Then they suddenly hear Robin and his minstrels and they say, 'Wait a minute,' and they send their messenger off to ask, 'My master, King Brian the Wild, would like to see you.' 'King Brian the Wild? He's loony.' 'No he isn't, he's calmed down a lot.' Then my favourite line

was 'Is that your liver?' 'Er no, no it's not!' And they start taking the messenger's liver out. Anyway, we had to cut that because we couldn't afford it.

From the diary of Michael Palin, April: Rehearsals down at Terry's, last-minute panic for the lawyers, but when the battle was over the room was still full of lawyers, Pythons, make-up ladies trying on wigs, men with big swords teaching John Cleese how to become Oliver Reed.

From the diary of Michael Palin, 29 April, Ballachulish Hotel: We rehearsed the film, inevitably rewrote some of the scenes as we did so, but it came to life during rehearsal, we began to laugh at each other's performances again and from rather being an albatross round our necks, finance, script, etc., etc., the film became enjoyable and fun …

TERRY JONES: We divided it up and one day Terry was going to do it and one day I was going to do it, that was the idea. It began to break down at one point and I know Terry got very pissed off one day. Terry was much more of a perfectionist than I am and I remember, at one point, taking over because we were just panicked to get something done. I think Terry was rather resentful of that afterwards. But generally it didn't really make any difference. We were both consulting with each other all the time and I really enjoyed it. But I think Terry found it more difficult than I did, partly because that's Terry's nature and partly because he was used to working on his own, so it was more difficult for him.

ERIC IDLE: In the end it worked – not for them, but for us it certainly did.

From the diary of Michael Palin, 11 o'clock Wednesday, Scotland: First day of filming, no headaches or hangovers, into chain mail and red cross tabard. Difficult decision over Galahad's blonde wig, makes me look like Jan Morris. Instead of noble and youthful, I look like I should be serving in a supermarket, end of Galahad as a blonde. Drive minibuses … Galahad driving up through Glencoe in a Budget rent-a-van in full chain mail. Scrambled up the Gorge of Eternal Peril, this took about fifty minutes of hard climbing,

camera broke mid-way through first shot … the day is hastily rearranged from having been busy but organised, it's now busy and disorganised. The sun disappeared and John Horton's smoke bombs and flames worked superbly. Graham as King Arthur got vertigo and couldn't go across the bridge, he spent the day rather unhappily cold and shaking.

TERRY GILLIAM: Graham was a drunken sot! He couldn't say his lines as Arthur. He'd get through a sentence and then he'd blank out, that's what was going on with Graham. This great, dignified character is actually blotto and he's struggling to get through his lines. Graham was a mountaineer, he was a member of the Dangerous Sports Club, he was all of these things, we come to do the Bridge of Death and he couldn't go across it. He froze. He just completely froze. So Gerry Harrison, the assistant director, had to put on his costume and double as Graham going across. What's so funny is that you're up somewhere on a mountain and all the truth suddenly comes out – Terry and I don't know how to direct and Graham can't go across a bridge!

GRAHAM CHAPMAN: I remember on the first day of filming *Holy Grail*, seven o'clock in the morning on a Scottish hillside, and nothing to drink – suddenly had DTs. I was playing King Arthur in a

cold drizzle, and I realised I was letting my friends down, and letting myself down. I stayed more or less on an even keel, not drinking too much, but I resolved to stop as soon as I could.[1]

MICHAEL PALIN: The first morning was tricky because Graham was very uncomfortable up there on the side of the mountain. It was the crown and the chain mail and all that sort of stuff and it took an awful long time just to get the shots done. I remember thinking, 'Graham's a mountaineer, he's always on about climbing, and here he seemed to be stricken with terror.' I think it was dear old Gray, it was first-day nerves and he'd probably drunk a bit before he'd started.

JOHN CLEESE: Certainly for me it was a concern to see how Graham was going to get through the *Grail*. You can tell that he's in his drinking phase, but he did much better than he might have done.

TERRY JONES: We were filming the Bridge of Death sequence and we were all standing on the edge of the Gorge of Eternal Peril. We were doing a group shot of the six of us on this path and Graham had been our adviser on mountaineering and everything because he used to go off mountaineering. We were going to shoot this, but

Graham just wouldn't go near the edge and was shaking from head to foot, he was in a terrible state. I couldn't understand it, I thought he was afraid of heights: 'That's not like him, he's supposed to be the mountaineer!' It was only later that I realised that he was getting the shakes; he'd taken himself off alcohol in order to play King Arthur and that was when I first realised this about him. The bridge had been put up by Hamish McInnes, who was the ranger at Glencoe. It looked unsafe, but it was perfectly safe to go across. But John wouldn't go across it.

JOHN CLEESE: That's the one thing I said I wouldn't do. When I knew I had to run across the bridge, I went up there the previous night to practise and see how difficult it was. I slowly began to realise that there was no way I could run across it. First of all the bottom of the chain mail which you put your foot in was essentially a piece of leather, they hadn't even put rubber on it, it was leather and of course it was wet, it was always damp, so that was slippery to start with. Then you had this bridge which had struts and then a gap and just bits of rope on either side. I started walking across it thinking if I could go slowly, I could get used to it; then I could go

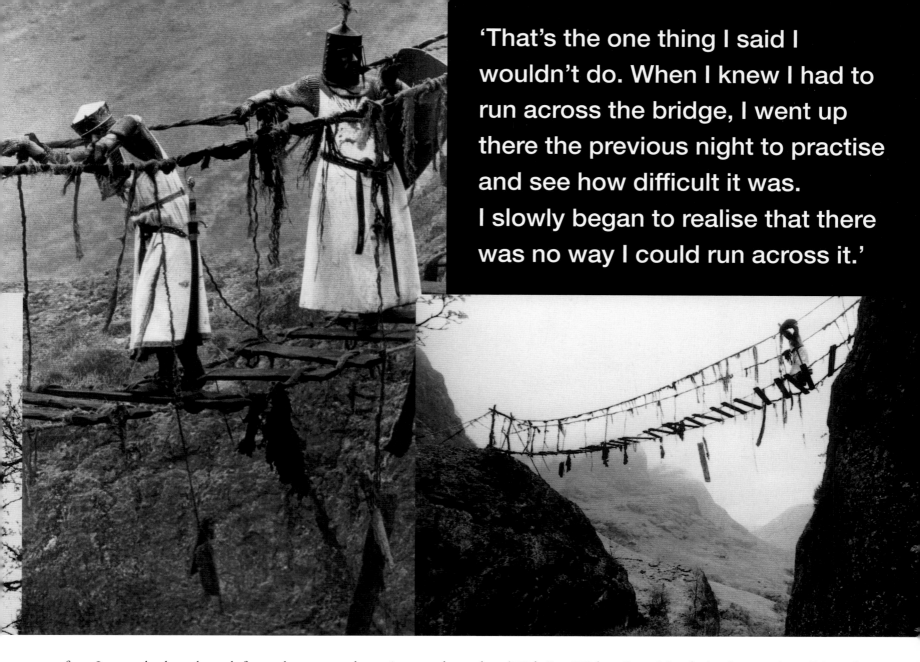

'That's the one thing I said I wouldn't do. When I knew I had to run across the bridge, I went up there the previous night to practise and see how difficult it was. I slowly began to realise that there was no way I could run across it.'

fast. I went backwards and forwards two or three times and thought, 'I can't possibly run across this, I'll kill myself,' because the drop would have killed you. And then I said to Terry, 'I absolutely cannot run across this, there'll be a major accident.' They found a proper mountaineer, and he just skipped across like that.

From the diary of Michael Palin, 11 o'clock Wednesday, Scotland: Eric and I and John sat around and listened to stories from the mountain rescue boys about how many people perish on these spectacular mountains each year. Enjoy the sight of Hamish McInnes, Head of Mountain Rescue in Glencoe, flinging rubber corpses of knights into the gorge. I think we have some good shots, more terrifying ledges to climb round yesterday. Certainly Sunday night was the most eventful and I giggled a great deal over the menu after some very high quality grass of Eric's. Graham ended up being seduced by an Aberdeen gentleman on a fishing holiday. Graham resisted evidently but was well pissed and woke me about 1 o'clock, banging on my door, saying he was Ethel the Kaiser. On Monday night he woke me again, and just after I'd dropped off I heard him in his room saying he was Betty Marsden very loudly in a variety of silly ways. On Tuesday night, however, he was kind enough to be content with putting a note under my

door 'With Best Wishes, Betty Marsden' written on it … Eric and I sit in the quiet, well-kept garden beside the hotel, thinking we're rather like officers at the Craig Lockhart Hospital sitting waiting to recover in this paradise before being sent back to the Front. Eric says he's Sassoon and I'm Wilfred Owen who had 'a bit of a stocky body'. Lunch with Mark and Eric. John is trying to read a book of philosophy and is constantly rather cross but quite fun. He continually goes on about the bovine incompetence of the waitresses who are certainly no Einsteins, but good-hearted Scottish mums. After lunch the unreality continues. Eric and I go round to Ballachulish House to play croquet in the sunshine, ridiculously idyllic. The lady of the manor, a tweedy, rather sharp, Englishwoman, appears with an enormously impressive, kilted, very red-faced Scottish Laird who leaves in a large old Lagonda, all too Doctor Finlay for words. Eric thinks we may have caught them *in flagrante*. After the croquet and a few more words with the lady of Ballachulish, more sitting in the disabled officers' garden. About 3.30 the call comes in, then driving Sir Robin and Lancelot in the Budget van up to Glencoe complete with a message from the producer saying we must stop at 6 o'clock. At 6 o'clock we're hanging on to the ledge above the gorge, waiting for a long shot of the Bridge of Death. Terry J directs Terry G to get

EMI **MONTY PYTHON** AND THE **HOLY GRAIL**

'It's sketchy and it's a quest, so the quest gets you through because "we're going to look for the Holy Grail". That's all it is really, and there are adventures en route and only at the end you realise there's no plot whatsoever. We didn't know how to end it. I contributed the ending because I said, "You should just stop it. The police should come in and arrest everybody, and there's a hand on the lens." My daughter hates that end, she says, "Is that the end? That it? I hate that." Well we couldn't afford the battle. We had all these university students on £4 a day and they shot them every angle they could, but there weren't many of them at all.'

'On the very first shot the camera breaks. On my very first directorial shot! So what do we do? We do all the wrong things.'

some more dirt on his legs, as he does so, forceful Gerry Harrison, who wants to be director, tells him to get back in shot, then Terry G has to explain. Then suddenly John Horton's effects go off, flares, firecrackers, smoke bombs, then huge mortar blasts which send scorching barrels of fire high into the air, the grass and trees were burning. No one, except John Horton, knows where the next blast will come from. Gerry Harrison shouts, TJ shouts, John's stand-in races across the bridge with suicidal courage, only to be told to get back again as the camera can't see anything through the smoke! Rather sad notices around Ballachulish today asking for volunteers to join an army for a scene tomorrow, but only getting £2 and I think even the Scots would balk at that. What a strange couple of days! …

A slow day's filming, a lot of worried faces when we ran into overtime again. The shots were putting a big strain on the budget says the producer. There would have to be some compromises by the Terrys.

ERIC IDLE: It's sketchy and it's a quest, so the quest gets you through because 'we're going to look for the Holy Grail'. That's all it is really, and there are adventures en route and only at the end you realise there's no plot whatsoever. We didn't know how to end it. I contributed the ending because I said, 'You should just stop it. The police should come in and arrest everybody, and there's a hand on the lens.' My daughter hates that end, she says, 'Is that the end? That it? I hate that.' Well we couldn't afford the battle. We had all these university students on £4 a day and they shot them every angle they could, but there weren't many of them at all.

TERRY JONES: The first day, the first shot, we're up on this side of the bridge and not only was Graham having the heebie-jeebies and wasn't able to go anywhere near the edge, but also the camera on the first shot sheared its gears and so, suddenly, when the cameraman opened the camera, all the cogs fell out! We only had the one sync-camera, so Terry and I went through what else we had to do and the only stuff we could shoot mute was on the other side of the gorge. We tried to work out what we could do, but there was nothing really we could do on the side that we were on, and to get to the other side of the gorge it was an hour's walk all the way round. I was trying to persuade people to go across the bridge so that we could actually keep shooting and people wouldn't. I don't blame them, with equipment, but even if just the cast had gone across we could have started rehearsing or something over the other side. In the end we all had to jog around the long way.

TERRY GILLIAM: On the very first shot the camera breaks. On my very first directorial shot! So what do we do? We do all the wrong things. We somehow manage to get another camera going and we shoot close-ups, which we could shoot in anybody's back garden. We're standing in the most magnificent scenery and we're doing close-ups. It was just madness. But we learned how to make a film in a very short time.

MICHAEL PALIN: We were all in chain mail and driving in this van to the location; Terry would have been up there and Graham as well who was doing the first shot. We were driving up into the grandeur of the Pass of Glencoe in our mini-van dressed as these knights. I remember people going by on the other side of the road, because

to the hotel, because there was only about enough hot water in the hotel for 60 per cent of the people staying there. So there was a race to get in your bath. I moved out at one point with Eric and we went to stay in another hotel which was a little nicer, with a swimming pool.

it's quite a tourist spot, and just doing *the* biggest double-takes of all time, necks would snap as they saw these knights driving their Ford transit van up Glencoe.

JOHN CLEESE: We'd get into this string of chain mail – and it was Scotland in April – and we'd get up on the hillside and it would rain, not very heavily, but it would rain, enough to make us damp for the entire day. There wouldn't be any umbrellas and we'd be wet in this stuff until we finished. And when we finished we'd all rush to the cars and jump in, there was a race to get back

MICHAEL PALIN: We were very uncomfortable because of the chain mail which wasn't proper chain mail, it was very thick wool, and when it got wet it became very, very heavy and would gradually sag further down, it was like having some great lead weights in your underwear.

ERIC IDLE: It was just cold and wet and miserable. It was fucking awful. It was no fun at all. I don't think there was hardly any fun. The only fun happened when the girls came and John and I moved out and found another hotel down the road which had hot water,

because there wasn't enough hot water for a bath. You'd been out there eighteen hours and there was no bath. You could tell what time of day it was by how soggy your tights were, as the water went up your woolly tights. So we found this other hotel which had hot water and then the second night we were there all the girls from the Castle Anthrax scene arrived and we thought, fucking hell, were we lucky?! It was like a little ray of light, all the women arrived to cheer us up and then they were taken away again.

From the diary of Michael Palin: John and Eric are equally disaffected with the Woodside Hotel, later today they move out to a hotel which apparently has sauna baths and a swimming pool, but the Woodside has a rather friendly welcoming atmosphere which I would be sad to miss, so I decide to stay … Things have improved at the hotel since Mark and Suko decide I should have their room with a bath and they should move into my room with no bath [that was very nice of the producer], so I now have the best room in the Woodside with two big windows, a bath and even a telephone. Spent the morning being drenched by the Perth and Kinross Fire Brigade; next time I shall think twice about writing a scene in a raging storm. End the day with considerable worries about Anthrax … Second day of Castle Anthrax, Doune Castle's severe granite halls are now filled with about 20 girls in diaphanous white gowns shivering against the cold. John C, Eric and I are sitting with Neil [Innes] on an old bench in the great hall singing old Adam Faith and Cliff Richard hits in a desperate attempt to combat boredom. The bathing scene takes two hours to set up, the girls giggle a lot and generally it's about as sexy as a British Legion parade.

MICHAEL PALIN: I remember our producer stopping tourists who were going up through Doune and saying, 'Do you want to be in a film?' And some of them did.

We knew we had good people working for us, we had Hazel Pethig, who had worked on all the TV shows doing costumes and

Maggie Weston – now Mrs Gilliam – doing make-up. So we had this terrific team, but everyone was working at the limits.

TERRY GILLIAM: At the end of the first few days, Terry and I are just trying to keep this thing together. Graham got drunk and was just howling at us about how useless we were and what assholes we were, useless fucking wankers, whereas Ian MacNaughton – he knows how to do things. Once again, Graham wasn't exactly right.

TERRY JONES: I was going round and my motto was 'Don't panic'; this is before *Hitchhiker's Guide to the Galaxy*. Everybody was in this suppressed state of panic, all of us. We'd chosen this location which in retrospect was crazy, although when you go and look at the place now, it doesn't look very far from the road, but you can't get the equipment up to the point where you're shooting, so we had to carry it and it was half an hour's hike. So it was a crazy place to be filming. It started getting better. The film show in the evening was always a bit of a high point, everybody would see rushes. But it was a nightmare shooting because we just didn't have enough time and we were so up against the clock all the time.

When we were doing the wedding sequence inside Doune Castle, the production designer showed us what he'd done to the interior. He'd built these stairs going up and they looked great, and we said they're fine. Then the next morning we turned up to shoot and that's all there was, there was nothing else. He said, 'I'm just the designer, you've got to have the set dresser to put in all the other stuff.' We assumed that he was going to put in all the bunting and everything. So instead of shooting, Terry and I were organising hauling the tables up through the windows, arranging the bunting and doing the set dressing. That was the kind of moment where you think, 'Wait a minute, this isn't quite right.' Instead of filming, we were actually putting the set up at that point which is a nightmare because we had little enough time as it was.

TERRY GILLIAM: Terry would look at a piece of film and would remember the day we shot it and the weather and the food and how nice people were. He would always seem to me to be reading into a shot a lot of information that wasn't there if you hadn't been there on the day. This was a constant argument, and I would say, no, it's not right. And there were some sneaky things going on. I was coming back at night and changing the shots, putting back the one that I wanted. It happened a few times because I just thought it was wrong. He's reading in emotional information that's just not on the celluloid. Terry gets very emotional about things. He seems to think they have a life of their own. I don't think they do. It's a piece of film, it has x amount of information on it and that's all there is and all there ever will be, and that's what you've got to look at.

TERRY JONES: I can't remember Terry and I ever disagreeing about something, on a question of taste or anything. The only disagreements would come when we were shooting, I'd be just trying to get on with it and Terry would be trying to get it right. So in a way that's quite a good combination.

MICHAEL PALIN: The two Terrys – that particular relationship didn't work, it wasn't a particularly good way of making the film, because if someone had a criticism they would play one director off against the other and say, 'Well, Terry would never have asked us to do that.' And because they were both called Terry it didn't help either.

TERRY JONES: When we turned up to do the scene where the villagers have found a witch, I'd been very preoccupied with watching the preparations for getting the village looking right and how we were going to shoot and everything, and I suddenly realised I hadn't

learnt my lines! It was the one thing I'd forgotten, having been so thorough with everything else, so that was a bit of a panic, suddenly having to learn my lines just before the take.

JOHN CLEESE: I remember getting very cross with Terry Gilliam one day. He was lining up a shot, and we were kneeling on the ground, which didn't help, in all that armour and it was very uncomfortable. And I remember he kept moving us about three-eighths of an inch this way, and then a quarter of an inch that way, and then he said, 'No, can you come back a little bit there?' By the end I remember saying to him when I was so uncomfortable, on the verge of pain, 'For God's sake, get on and shoot the fucking thing, you know, we're not bits of paper.' I think he was so used to doing animation that he was trying to do the same with us and it wasn't all that comfortable. I think he was very hurt by my outburst because he went away and lay down in the shade by a wall and recovered for two or three hours.

TERRY JONES: There was a tension with Terry because, as John put it, Terry was used to moving little bits of paper on a table around for his animation and John felt that Terry was treating the actors in the same way. He wasn't really thinking about how uncomfortable it was to be kneeling in the mud at certain points, but that's just because Terry's got his eye on what he wants in the end and was not really thinking about that side of it.

TERRY GILLIAM: I was trying to make this epic. And I had been so long in my little room with pieces of paper, that I hadn't adapted to talking to human beings and getting them to do things. When we did the scene where they are at the battlements and the cow is thrown over, it was a matte shot and the only way to do it was to dig a hole in the ground and have them all on their knees. John was going apeshit because he was uncomfortable. I finally said, 'Fuck it. It's your sketch, you wrote it. I'm just trying to make it work. And this is a tricky shot here.' So I said, 'Fuck you,' and went off in a snit

Neil Innes and friend

and laid down in the grass, saying I'm not going to direct this. Terry and I, who had always been one voice, suddenly realised we weren't actually one voice. Then we got Gerry Harrison, the first assistant, to be the common voice. But it turned out he wanted to be a film director, too, so he was a third voice, and he wasn't translating what Terry and I were saying. So it ended up that Terry talked to them, the guys, and I talked to the crew and the cameramen and that side of it. I stayed at the back of the camera and tried to get the shots working and it worked fine once we got that sorted out.

MICHAEL PALIN: I remember the end of one day when we'd been doing a lot of crouching with the castle in the background and Terry Gilliam asked us to crouch once more because there was a lovely shaft of sunlight coming and catching John's helmet. John went absolutely berserk, saying, 'You know I'm not waiting for a shaft of light to strike my fucking helmet. We've been here for four hours, we've crouched and it's cold. What are you waiting for? The moon and the stars to arrange themselves around my head?'

I got very angry once myself. I had to be the 'mud-eater' for eight takes. The mud-eater was this character who had to crawl across the

mud as John and Graham were coming through the village at the beginning and I had to go up and eat this mud. It was really a shot for those two, but I dutifully did my bit, crawled through this filthy, stinking, pig-shitty mud and they said they wanted to do take eight. John went, 'Why, what the hell was going on?' To which someone said, 'Well, you were fine, but we can see Mike's back.' That's when I just went, 'What? You can see my back, what have you been doing all this time?' And I went absolutely ape and threw myself in the air, landed in the mud and just wiggled my legs around, screamed and yelled for about five seconds. There was absolute silence and then John and Graham just led this spontaneous applause. John said he'd never seen anything like it, he'd never seen me get angry ever. Then they had to do the scene where I actually eat the mud and the props boy said, 'When you get to the mud, don't worry, because I'm going

to put some chocolate down there that looks just like mud, so it's completely edible.' I said, 'How will I know which is the chocolate and which is the mud?' They had no answer to that. So I had to eat whatever was there, most of it was chocolate but a little bit of it was mud. After that we had to go and get anti-tetanus injections in this little tiny Scottish doctor's surgery and he was completely amazed to see this creature in just a bundle of rags and a rather bad wig coming to have this injection because I'd been eating mud. He had to have several quick Scotches before he could administer, I think.

JOHN CLEESE: Michael had a hilarious outburst in that scene with the mud. I thought it was very good.

TERRY JONES: Mike got very cross because he had this part of 'mud-eater'. We had some chocolate in there and his part was to crawl across through the mud, get across to this bit of chocolate looking like mud, and eat it. He did this endless times, because of course Terry was directing, so we did endless retakes of this shot. Then when we saw the rushes you couldn't see Mike! Mike was terribly pissed off.

JOHN CLEESE: In a movie shoot lasting five or six weeks you may fly three or four times, you do three or four takes where it just is really rather marvellous. And I remember doing one of the best takes in my life, with Eric. Terry shouted, 'Cut.' I shouted, 'How about that!' because I was really exhilarated, and I heard this comment, 'Not enough smoke'.

TERRY JONES: In those days we didn't have video playback on set. That would have been useful, for example, doing the stuff with John and Eric when Concorde gets an arrow in the back. John does this great long eulogy to him and Eric says, 'No, I'm feeling better now.' We'd shot that and the second take we thought was perfect. John had just absolutely got it and we said, 'Great.' Then the cameraman said, 'There was an awful lot of smoke.' The entire

background got smoked out and we thought, 'For safety we'd better do another take.' So we did take three, and John's performance wasn't quite as good, so we did another one. We ended up doing about twenty takes of it and never quite got the feeling of that second take.

JOHN CLEESE: Now this is for me the perfect example of the tail wagging the dog, of getting your priorities all wrong. I remember getting quite sarcastic then and any time when anybody said, 'Cut, that was a good take,' I said, 'Well, was the smoke funny enough?' So I let people know that I thought that that was not the right approach.

TERRY JONES: Then of course, when we saw the rushes, it was fine. You could see that although the background does get obliterated more or less, you don't notice it because it happens over a period of time, and as it's all on one take, it didn't matter.

From the diary of Michael Palin: Terry J tends to become very Ian MacNaughton-like sometimes, 'Come on now, quick, we must get this shot in before 11.25, we really must.' Terry G is working away more quietly with the camera crew, checking the shot, putting a candle in the foreground here and there … 'All right, the generator's been refilled with petrol, let's go. Come on, we must get this shot in before 12.25' … The BBC doggedly film the filming. Cardboard battlements have to be added on to the castle before John does his taunt, 'John, don't lean so heavily on the battlements, you can see them bending!' … A rather jolly day with much corpsing from John, Eric and myself; and Brian McNulty, in rich Glaswegian, reads in John's taunter's lines for us to react to. How can you

'"Come on now, quick, we must get this shot in before 11.25, we really must." Terry G is working away more quietly with the camera crew, checking the shot, putting a candle in the foreground here and there … "All right, the generator's been refilled with petrol, let's go. Come on, we must get this shot in before 12.25" … '

done it?' You suddenly realised that some people cannot take that step of seeing it as funny in an abstract way. For them it is reality. So you always know, when you do something violent which is supposed to be funny, that there are some people who can take it purely as an idea and some people who react to it as though it were real. Of course some of the producers wanted to cut the Black Knight and it's the funniest thing in the movie. You usually find that it's the thing that a small number of people most object to that makes the large number of people laugh the most. What I always want to do is to say to the people who object to something, 'Well, if I cut it, you're happy. But have you noticed there's kind of seven of you out of a hundred who are worried by this, and over there there's about 84 per cent who think it's the funniest thing in the movie? Do you want to deprive them of their fun because it's upsetting you?' Anyway, that's me in the Black Knight suit up until the leg gets taken off and then it was my understudy,

Mr Richard Burton, that was his name. He was a silversmith in the City of London, who was one-legged, obviously.

TERRY JONES: We were supposed to shoot the Black Knight sequence up in Scotland but we lost the day, so we came down from Scotland and arranged to shoot it sort of non-union. We went off with Julian Doyle as the cameraman, because Julian was our co-producer with Mark Forstater. It was just him, a soundman and me. We shot it rather like a documentary, we didn't have a full unit there, but because of that we were able to shoot it over four or five days, whereas the 'Knights Who Say Ni' we did all in a day.

TERRY GILLIAM: One of the great joys was learning to swordfight and doing our own stunts. Like the Black Knight and the Green Knight when they're fighting – I'm the Green Knight and John's the Black Knight. It was great.

TERRY JONES: The worst thing was that our producer, Mark Forstater tended to go round saying, 'Oh, it's a disaster, and what can you expect when you've got two directors?' So the main tension was with our producer.

From the diary of Michael Palin, 1 June: Got the sleeper to Kings Cross. I'm almost too tired to fully enjoy the elation at the end of the day when the filming, or my part of it anyway, is completed. Want to leap up and down, but can't, so just stand there looking out over the Scottish hills all grey and dusky and hazy as evening falls and feel wonderfully free. That night, back at the hotel, have a drink with Tommy Raeburn, other chippies and drivers, hard men of films, who nevertheless reckon the chances of the film's success to be very good. Roy, the art director, says he wished he had money in it. There's a warm and genuine feeling of communication which comes from being part of a team who've all worked as hard as each other. Three large gin and tonics and a bottle of red wine floored me early on, however, as the Rosses finished serving up a special five-course meal with a jokey *Holy Grail* menu complete with mud sorbet à la Palin, I began to feel my legs getting wobbly and my vision swing out of control. At about 11.30 went up to bed 32 days after we'd first clung to the side of the Gorge of Eternal Peril in Glencoe. 32 days since the first shot when the camera broke and all that seems as far away as the first Python series. I hope in all the hard work of the general rush to complete, we haven't lost any of the performances. Certainly tonight there was a good deal of optimism around.

TERRY JONES: The odd thing about the film was eye lines. I don't know why, but I decided to do what you normally don't do in film, and nobody's ever noticed anything. In a film normally if you have

This could be yours

because 1000 coconuts will be given to the first
1000 customers at the Plaza theatre on Wednesday,
June 11. Come, meet a Python, get a coconut, and see
MONTY PYTHON AND THE HOLY GRAIL.

cineaste

VOL. VII, NO. 1 / $1.25

MONTY PYTHON
NASHVILLE · FRANCESCO ROSI
GIAN MARIA VOLONTE

ERIC IDLE: We got to New York and they said the first screening would be at 10. For the first thousand people who came there would be coconuts given out, and they had knights walking up and down Broadway with signs. We were called up in the hotel and they said there's already a thousand people outside lining up at 8 in the morning, so they'd put on an early screening. There was just chaos out there and the police were worried. We were taken to the theatre and we were stuck inside the theatre for the rest of the day because there was this crowd, this mob scene. When they came out, we'd have to autograph the coconuts that were given out for promotion, which is an impossibility. Gilliam and I went to LA and we got into the line of the people waiting to go into the first screening. I think Chevy Chase was in that line and that's where I met George Harrison because he came to a Director's Guild screening and I met him after that.

TERRY JONES: The show started in limited access in America, on PBS, and before that the tapes were very nearly wiped. Howard Dell, who was our video editor, suddenly rang me up one day and said, 'Next month they're going to wipe the first series,' because in those days it was BBC policy to wipe tapes, especially comedy and light entertainment. You'd keep opera and concert performances and ballet and things like that, cultural things, but light entertainment got wiped so they could re-use the tapes. So I organised with Howard to get the tapes illegally transferred onto the only home system at the time, which was Philips VCR, a strange system where you had two tapes one above each other in a cassette. So we got a cassette player, which was the first one out on the market, and we had all the Python shows transferred onto these cassettes – fifteen or thirty minutes was the most you could get. There was a period of a few months when I thought, 'That's going to be the only record of Python, these Philips cassettes sitting in my cellar.' But then what happened was that Ron Devillier, who was in charge of the Public Broadcasting System in Dallas, Texas, had heard about the shows and approached BBC Enterprises. He said he'd like to see these 'Flying Circus' shows and BBC Enterprises, according to Ron Devillier, told him, 'No, no, we don't think you'd like them, they're not a circus, we don't think you'd be interested really.' Ron insisted and he got all three series sent over and he spent a weekend watching the shows and became convinced that he had to put these on.

offers … 'Dear Sirs, I am writing on behalf of the television department of Aberdeen University' – an even louder barrage of farting, the letter is crossed and read no further. 'Dear Monty Python, we are a production company interested in making TV films with Python, George Harrison and Elton John' – the inevitable farting and jeering, and despite the fact that £36,000 is mentioned in the letter as a possible fee for this never to be repeated offer, it's jeered raucously and I tear the letter up … In this symbolic gesture, entirely characteristic of the general irresponsibility of the assembled Pythons, the meeting staggers to an end and we all go our separate ways.

From the diary of Michael Palin, February 1975: Good news from New York, Python is top of the PBS Channel 13 ratings there, even beating *Upstairs Downstairs*, which has just won an Emmy 'an all'. Terry Bedford, cameraman, has just seen the movie and apparently raved, which I take as the highest compliment from a very down-to-earth, rather taciturn craftsman.

But he had to get eleven other stations to show them so that he could actually afford to buy the shows. So he persuaded some other stations to take them on and they started putting these shows out and that's how it really took off in the States, it started in Dallas of all places. Once the BBC found they had a sale over there they decided not to wipe the things, and so we survived by the skin of our teeth, fortunately.

ERIC IDLE: We opened *Grail* and we were really hot but feeling that heat in New York is really quite fun. And everybody, like all the *Saturday Night Live* people hadn't started, but they were doing comedy and we would go and see them. Belushi was like 'They're here, they're here', and we were treated like comedy gods and that was fun. We met all these people like Gilda Radner, and Bill Murray was doing a revue in New York, which was very, very pleasant.

MICHAEL PALIN: When they started showing the show on PBS in the States, there were people out there discovering Python for the first time, liking what they saw and offering us the chance to do more, which was quite an interesting situation for us all to be in. Just as people were splitting off and going their various ways, there was still this sort of centrifugal force that Python always was, right from day one I think. There was quite a lot of Python material out at that time to satisfy the demand: I think there were probably three or four albums, there were a couple of books, there was the second film to add to *And Now For Something Completely Different*, and there were forty-five television shows. So really what was happening in America was they were just catching up. We did have to meet for Python Productions Ltd, but we would have a competition to see how quickly we could have company meetings and I think we had four in about half a minute at one time. But, nevertheless, we did have to get together, money was coming in, which was always very nice, so I could see that even while we were all defining our post-Python identities the likelihood of having to do something else was growing. *Holy Grail* did all right, but John was absolutely, adamantly against ever doing any more television together.

TERRY JONES: Then we heard that the BBC were selling the fourth series to ABC and we discussed it and said, 'No, we don't want you to because we've always been out on PBS and we like that because it goes out and it doesn't have adverts. Things don't get cut around and adverts don't get inserted, they just go out as intended.' Oddly, America's the one place where Python has been shown as it's supposed to be seen, as a whole continuous thing. Because the shows have a flow to them and if you start putting adverts in it's going to ruin it. So we didn't want ABC to do it and the BBC said, 'Well, piss off!'

MICHAEL PALIN: The major change in Python's fortunes was the BBC's treatment in America of the six shows that we'd done without John.

JOHN CLEESE: We never made any real money until *The Holy Grail* came out in America. We'd started in '69, we'd been together six years and then all of a sudden there was money coming in on a different scale from anything before.

MICHAEL PALIN: When we heard they'd made them into two specials, we smelt a rat and thought, hang on they're making enormous cuts. We realised that each special would take three Python shows and about one third of the time was removed and substituted for commercials. Then there were censorship issues. We could have just ignored it and said, what the hell, let's just get paid. But the more we looked into it the more we realised that they were really going to pillage the series, take things out, cut things for their own censorship reasons. One of the shows had gone out before we'd seen it; the second one was about to go out. Nancy Lewis, our representative in America, knew a very good lawyer there called Ina Lee Meibach, and Ina Lee said there is something you can do about this, you can try and stop them and get an injunction to stop them putting this one out. We felt that just as the American market was beginning to get used to Python, to be given something which was just a cut-down, sanitised version of Python would send out very wrong signals and we'd get blamed.

The key thing was that it was on ABC and not PBS, we felt it looked like a sell-out to one of the big networks.

TERRY JONES: Nancy Lewis in New York phoned up and said, 'The first show went out and it's a disaster. We're getting really bad comments about it.' She sent us a tape of the show, and when we looked at it, it was just appalling because what had happened was ABC had cannibalised the six shows and put them into two one-hour shows, which basically meant two forty-five-minute shows. So three shows had been collapsed into forty-five minutes and they'd obviously gone through looking for anything that might conceivably be seen as offensive and taken it out. And in doing that they just removed all the funny bits.

TERRY JONES: Mike and Terry G went across to the States and all we got out of it was a disclaimer that we could put up at the beginning saying it didn't represent our work. Then in the end, when it came to it, ABC just challenged that on the day of the broadcast, so we didn't even get the disclaimer.

MICHAEL PALIN: Because Terry Gilliam was an American citizen we were able to take the case to the American courts in New York; so Terry and I were assigned to go over there and defend Python in the courts if necessary, but we didn't think it would be necessary. It was assumed that we'd all make threats and ABC would agree to our changes.

I'm not sure whether everybody felt quite the same way, but I know that Terry, myself and probably TG felt very strongly that Python shouldn't be edited, changed or re-presented without our … Well, I mean that it just shouldn't be re-edited, period. I'm not quite sure if we were doing any Python or getting together much at that period, but it did seem important, because our American audience was growing by that time. It was something they became committed to and involved with, and they would feel let down by anything less than the real thing. So it did seem very important at that time and hugely damaging what ABC had done – twenty-two minutes of Python material taken out of one ninety-minute compilation. So we hired these lawyers in New York,

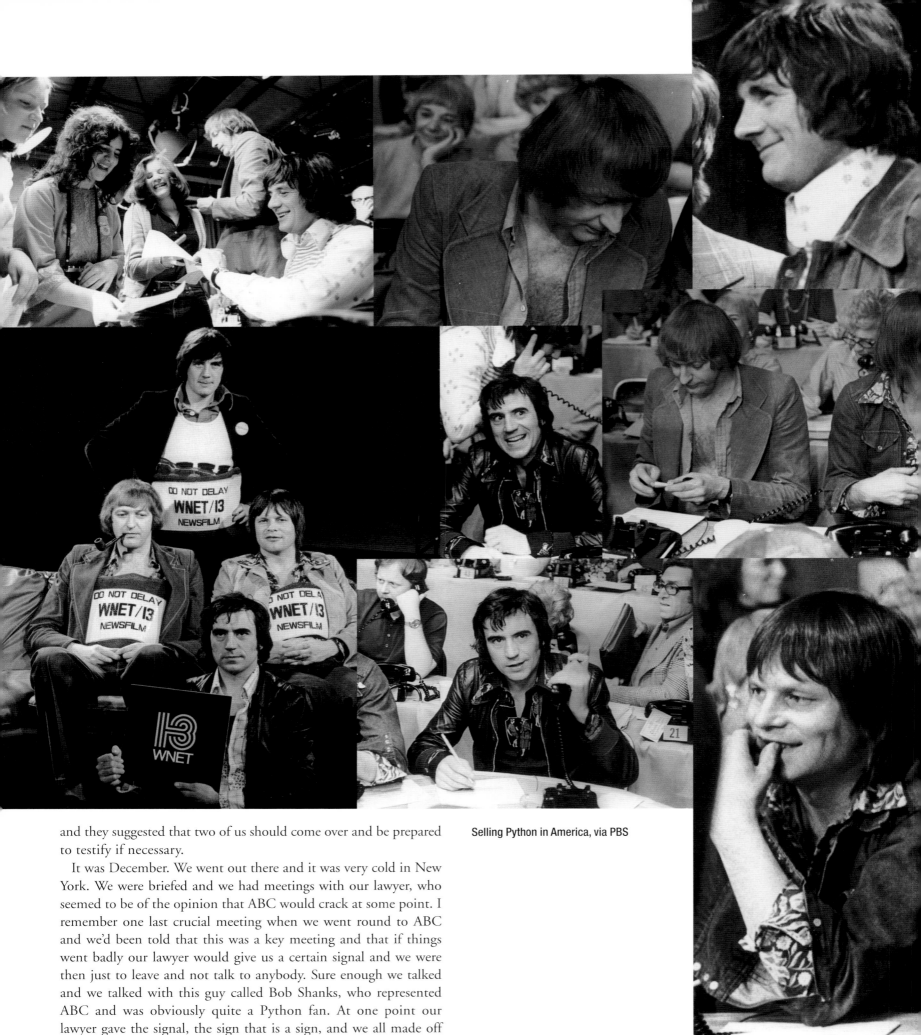

Selling Python in America, via PBS

and they suggested that two of us should come over and be prepared to testify if necessary.

It was December. We went out there and it was very cold in New York. We were briefed and we had meetings with our lawyer, who seemed to be of the opinion that ABC would crack at some point. I remember one last crucial meeting when we went round to ABC and we'd been told that this was a key meeting and that if things went badly our lawyer would give us a certain signal and we were then just to leave and not talk to anybody. Sure enough we talked and we talked with this guy called Bob Shanks, who represented ABC and was obviously quite a Python fan. At one point our lawyer gave the signal, the sign that is a sign, and we all made off for the elevator, virtually saying, 'See you in court.' I realised then that this was what this sort of brinkmanship is all about, because they rushed to the elevator, saying, 'Come on, let's discuss this, this is ridiculous, I love the shows, we're all doing the best.' The lift doors were closing and closing and I think Bob Shanks was still talking when the lift doors closed and down we went. Anyway, then it meant we were actually in court, which was a bit nerve-racking.

A court hearing had been fixed though the idea probably was that it wouldn't be necessary, but the slot was booked, so it happened within twenty-four hours. Terry Gilliam and myself were marching out of ABC's huge office, and we were sharing a room in the Essex House because we just didn't have that much money.

ERIC IDLE: Michael wanted to pursue it, Terry Gilliam wanted to pursue it, and we found a lawyer who would represent us on a percentage, so we didn't have to pay him up front but on part of the settlement.

MICHAEL PALIN: We were then coached, told what we might get asked and all that, and what we should say and how we should behave. We turned up in court with our counsel and the case began. Clearly ABC had not been prepared to go to court and sent a very ancient lawyer called Clarence someone or other. ABC had given him just the ninety-minute tape of the second show that they were going to show and it had commercial breaks in it. They'd not filled in the commercial breaks and nobody had fast forwarded or anything like that, so somehow we all sat there and watched first our original BBC version of the show, which went down terribly well and everybody laughed like drains, then the ABC show.

I'm sure it was then that they lost the case. We testified, we talked about various sketches and there was the marvellous exchange where I describe one show that's been cut, all about someone testifying in court, about the meaning of the word gaiters and the judge keeps interrupting. This is what I'm describing and the American judge keeps interrupting and saying, 'What are gaiters?!' It was an interruption of me describing interruptions that had taken place in the actual sketch, so it all became quite farcical.

ERIC IDLE: I only know this story second-hand because I wasn't there, but they went to court and they played our version first and everybody laughed. Then they played their version and nobody laughed because they'd just seen it and the judge was really partial to us. It was just a great thing – to sue ABC to stop them putting you on television is such an unheard-of thing in America, the idea of suing people to stop yourselves going on TV is so pure and such a great concept because people are so desperate to be on television in America.

MICHAEL PALIN: In the end the judge went back into his rooms, came back and said that it was so close to transmission that he couldn't bring an injunction, as we had hoped, to prevent ABC

from showing this programme. We thought, 'Gawd,' because we were sure we'd won, but he said that cancelling at this time would cause undue financial harm to ABC. And to Terry and me who were sharing one room the whole idea of causing undue financial harm to a multi-million dollar corporation seemed fairly ripe.

Terry and I went back to the judge's rooms and he's telling us what a great fan he is and I think we had to sign something for him and his children. He was obviously dying to say this but couldn't say it while the case was actually on. Anyway, we say goodbye and then we go out into Foley Square outside the court house. It was very, very cold, we made our way to the subway station to go back uptown and the judge passed us and went into the station. When we got to the station we found we had no tokens and we couldn't actually get through the bars for some reason, so we had to ask the judge who happened to be on the other side of the bars if he could possibly get us two tokens. So he cashed the money, gave us two tokens and we ended up going on the same subway car as the judge, strap-hanging, reminiscing about Python, and he was telling us about all the great sketches.

ERIC IDLE: The BBC were not allowed to give them those rights, they were not allowed to cut our material, we had that in our contracts. So Jim Beach, who was an old friend of mine from Cambridge, suggested that instead of taking a million or two million in damages we just took the masters, because he was in rock 'n' roll and he understood the importance of masters and ownership. He suggested, God bless him, that we just got the BBC to give us the masters, so that we would have world control of those. Then we owned the show, and that was just fabulous. Totally unprecedented and very smart of him, because it now means that we own it.

MICHAEL PALIN: The BBC then had a bit of a problem. We could have sued them. They came to us and said, 'Look, we are prepared to settle on this. We will give you all rights to Python shows outside the UK and to any ancillary spin-offs, but we will keep the copyright for the UK.' And it was crucial timing, because at that time Python really was biggest of all in the UK, so they obviously thought they could hold on to the jewel in the crown. What the BBC hadn't realised was how popular Python was becoming in the States, otherwise they wouldn't have done what they did, they wouldn't have sold it. They just thought it was a few freaks, a few college kids, that's all. So we won control of Python abroad, which is a terrific thing, so it was a very important case.

ERIC IDLE: We're persistent buggers, you know what I mean? Very litigious and very persistent. Python will always fight to the last issue, it doesn't like being taken advantage of. What is good with a group of six is that there's always someone who holds out.

LIFE OF BRIAN

'Then Eric came up with 'Always Look on the Bright Side', and we cracked the end of the film.'

1, 2, 3 April 11.30pm Her Majesty's Theatre	Prices £150 (for not coming) £100 per box £50.07, £10, £5, Sold out	with John Bird Eleanor Bron Tim Brooke-Taylor Graham Chapman John Cleese Carol Cleveland Peter Cook John Fortune Graeme Garden Terry Gilliam Barry Humphries Eric Idle Alan Bennett Neil Innes	Des Jones Terry Jones Jonathan Lynn Joe Melia Jonathan Miller Bill Oddie and Michael Palin
write QUICKLY to Amnesty Box Office Her Majesty's Theatre Haymarket SW1 (enclose s.a.e.)	Cheques & postal orders made out to AMNESTY INTERNATIONAL		
Call in person or 'phone 01-839 2110 from 23 February 1976			

A POKE IN THE EYE (with a sharp stick)

JOHN CLEESE: Amnesty came to me and said, 'We need to raise money – do you have any ideas?' And I said, 'Why don't we do a stage show?' Because to me that was the easiest thing to do. I had a bit of a think about how to go about it and I got Jonathan Miller to direct it, so we were pretty safe there. Then I made it my job to get everybody involved. In other words, I was the producer. It was called *A Poke in the Eye (with a Sharp Stick)* and it was us, the *Beyond the Fringe* group and lots of others who were around and available. Doing the show was a great pleasure because these were all people who were comfortable together. I think it was a huge success because everyone enjoyed themselves so much.

From the diary of Terry Jones, Wednesday, 31 March 1976: 10.00. Rehearsal at Her Majesty's Theatre. Meant to be for Python but Jonathan Miller, Peter Cook and Alan Bennett come along to go through the 'Shakespeare' sketch for me – we only did it twice

asked, 'How do you sculpt an elephant?' And he said, 'I just take a block of marble and then knock away all the bits that don't look like an elephant.' In other words, by criticising certain things you help to define, by implication, what you think is sensible. Mind you, I don't think you would ever have got the Pythons to agree for a split second on what they thought was sensible religion, but we seemed to instinctively agree on what it shouldn't be. I don't think it's the slightest bit blasphemous because it has no references to Christ at all, except when he's trying to speak to them on the mountainside. So I don't see blasphemy or, as Terry Jones used to say, heresy; that argument doesn't begin to hold together for me. What I think it does very usefully is point out that whatever the founder says, within three minutes everyone's rewriting it in accordance with their own emotional needs and that's an extremely good point.

TERRY JONES: *The Life of Brian* isn't blasphemous, it's heretical. It's not blasphemous because it takes the Bible story as gospel; you have to believe in the Bible, you have to understand and know the Bible story to understand it for the film really. It's heretical because it's making fun of the way the church interprets it. Heresy is basically taking against the church's interpretation, not against the basic belief.

JOHN CHAPMAN: Graham stopping drinking to get in condition for the filming of *The Life of Brian*. This was what precipitated the DTs, he really had delirium tremens. How much he'd been pressurised into it and how much he'd made the choice, I don't know, but obviously he had and he decided that if he was going to play this part, which was probably the biggest thing he'd had till then, he had to be in shape to go through the rigours of the filming process. He cut himself off completely and within forty-eight hours he was in delirium tremens, the classic situation of an alcoholic stopping drinking. He went for complete cold turkey and brought this upon himself and he really was in an absolutely desperate situation. But he saw it through.

GRAHAM CHAPMAN: I was going to stick it out, and do it cold this time … My toes and shins were numb. I tried to check for sensation, first with one foot against the other, then with trembling hands. The harder I tried to steady my hands the more uncontrollable they became. You'll be all right if you just stay in bed. You don't have to do anything today, you don't have to see anybody, eat anything, or drink anything. Just stay in bed and see it through.[4]

JOHN CLEESE: He'd fallen over and gashed his head on a fireguard and was taken off to hospital. He just decided, 'This has to stop', and he linked up with someone who helped people get over alcohol dependency and by the time we came to shoot *Life of Brian* he was in great shape. He was ruining stuff when he was drunk. I remem-

Graham and longtime partner David Sherlock

ber feeling, 'What's the point of writing these sketches if he's going to fuck 'em up?' Then he suddenly got his act together and became very healthy and much more present.

ERIC IDLE: John always wanted to play Brian and that was a surprise to me, because John was clearly going to be Reg, he's just magnificent as Reg. He wouldn't have been as good as Brian and Graham is such a great straight man in that film. He's so good and he's cleaned up and he's not an alcoholic anymore. He'd started to stop drinking then, that's what happened that Christmas. He had a complete breakdown and ranted about everybody and how he hated everybody, and finally realised he was an alcoholic.

JOHN CLEESE: Because I like doing new things and exploring, I suggested at one point that I should be Brian because I wanted to have the experience of playing a character right from the beginning to the end of a movie. Extraordinarily for someone whom people think of as having been in movies, I didn't do that until *Privates on Parade* when I was forty-two. The others discussed it for a bit and then it was decided that it should be Graham. I was disappointed for about a day, two days, but I see now of course that it was much better to do it that way.

TERRY JONES: John wanted to play Brian and I was really against that. I just didn't think he'd be right somehow. The great thing about Graham was that he could play the central role because you sympathise with him somehow. I don't know what it was but with Graham as Arthur he had an integrity, so whatever's going on around him you believed in this central figure because he's not joking, he's playing it for real. That, I thought, was really crucial to the comedy, not to have somebody being the central character who you thought was being funny. And if John had been Brian, either you'd have been disappointed that he wasn't being funny or you'd be waiting for the jokes. So we persuaded John that he was so crucial to playing the trade union leaders and the other parts that he couldn't possibly play Brian because we needed him to play those parts.

MICHAEL PALIN: There was a bit of a worry about Graham as the lead and I think that's why when we were doing the casting, John actually volunteered to do Brian himself, but it just seemed a colossal waste really of all the other things that John could do. The idea of John playing Brian wasn't felt to be right. There was a quality in Graham that he'd shown as Arthur that I remember thinking would be just right for Brian. I know he wanted to play Brian. It was probably the best way of dealing with it because he'd just have to sober up, he'd have to be prepared to do this. John, I don't think, saw it in such sympathetic terms, he just thought that Graham would be a disaster because of his drinking. Drink was going to affect everything he did, so whether he was Brian or not, or other characters, he would still suffer. So there was some argument over that. Most of us were generally of the feeling that Graham would be best and that he needed to sort himself out and would sort himself out. It was not ever discussed really that Graham had a drink problem when Graham was there. You didn't say that. We would have the normal discussion about casting Graham and the issue of whether Graham was best or not would have been a side conversation probably, like a phone call later that day or something like that, that's the way things used to happen. John felt that Brian, being the core figure of the whole film on whom the whole film depended, had to be played by somebody who was absolutely reliable, so in a way John was making a bit of a sacrifice. I felt if Graham was going to be in the film, it was better if he was given something of substance to do, to really force him to get it right, than be shunted out and do lots of little parts. But in the same way it was a waste of John not having him play centurions and the leader of the PLF and whatever. I think it came out all right in the end.

GRAHAM CHAPMAN: Having gone to Cambridge, I think I felt inferior. And drink gave me courage to speak up and use my voice.[8]

MICHAEL PALIN: Graham was more present. It brought the best out of him, he could contribute again and there wasn't this anxious edge that there always was to Graham's behaviour which seemed just to be restlessness but was just him thinking, 'How am I going to get my next drink? There are five guys here who don't know what it's like to go without a drink for an hour.' So all that tension there was off and it must have been much easier for Graham.

From the diary of Terry Jones, Saturday, 7 January 1978: For some reason I haven't quite been able to explain to my wife, we're

on the way to Barbados to complete rewrites on the movie. Evidently the temperature there is the optimum at which biro ink flows without either clogging through cold or flooding through too much heat. It may be difficult to believe but we actually save time and money by flying to Barbados … the accountants have all gone into it and – provided we travel first class and stay in an expensive villa – we should come out of this with a good profit margin … Two taxis brought us through a maze of sugar-cane and wood and corrugated iron huts constructed on neogothic lines to the opulent Palladian villa which is to be our office and sleeping quarters for the next fortnight.

TERRY GILLIAM: It was weird because we were in this place where Winston Churchill used to stay; it was a really grand place for six silly comedians. It was a funny time, Mick Jagger and Jerry Hall dropped in for a night of charades, Alan Price was down there, Keith Moon floated through at one point, because Keith was going to be in the film. If you're going to do religion, do it in very comfortable surroundings.

From the diary of Terry Jones, Saturday, 7 January 1978: We were introduced to the butler and the rest of the staff who will be attending to our needs as comedy writers.

TERRY JONES: I can remember playing charades with Mick Jagger and Des O'Connor, who came along to dinner in this strange fantasy house built by this Conservative MP in 1948, so at a time when the whole country was tightening their belts and trying to get through austerity, this Tory MP was building this extraordinary fantasy place.

ERIC IDLE: I was in Barbados and I thought, wouldn't it be a good idea if everybody got away, because it was always harder and harder to get people together because they had wives and families, and John's advertising commitments. I was at this place at Heron Bay and I thought it would be great if everybody came out there. And they came out and they were a bit sceptical, but they got there and it worked really well. It was like having our own private hotel, we worked office hours and we really refined it. It was everybody working together and discussing it, you know, it wasn't everybody going away to different parts of London and then writing, it was really focusing on the story, where it was going. I don't think a lot of new creative material came of it, it was more shaping what we'd got.

Keith Moon came and he would wait on the beach for us until we had a break and play with us. It was hilarious, he'd be waiting on the beach. And then we'd have an hour for lunch and then a swim and then we'd work again in the afternoon and we'd break at about 4.30/5.00, have a swim and then in the evening we were free. It was very healthy, because we were all in the same place, people couldn't slag off and do things. It was a very smart thing to do because it kept us really focused on what we were doing. When you spend two weeks just working on one script with six people, there's a lot of brain power, there's a lot of good, and that's when the film became something quite different.

TERRY JONES: We'd got all this mass of material and then we went off and sat in this strange house and discussed the bits. And that's where some of the most interesting stuff came up.

From the diary of Michael Palin, Saturday, 7 January 1978: Whilst John, Eric, Terry J and myself are lazing disbelievingly amongst fine things and wondering whether to set up a preparatory school here (John desperately wants to be maths master), Terry V. Gilliam (whom we have designated as sports master) is eating local apples. They're very small … and they're poisonous. Whether Terry will snuff it before the night's out, we're not sure, but arrangements have been made for the redistribution of his fees from the film and anyway, it's probably God's way of punishing him for having forgotten to bring his script for this two-week period of script writing.

From the diary of Terry Jones, Sunday, 8 January 1978: So this is what filming is really like. Breakfast, a swim, a lie on the beach, and then a walk along the shore before lunch … Under the benevolent spell of this place the group seemed easier and more relaxed with each other than at any time since the very early days. Conversation at lunch drifted round to the film and, almost as if without trying, ideas began to flow …

Monday, 9 January: Eric and Terry G were in particularly lucid form, and even John was showing remarkable adaptability. It's amazing how sea, sun and luxury lubricate the script-writing process. What's more we do seem to be enjoying each other's company again. Dare I say it, there even seems to be a certain amount of affection creeping back into the group. Gosh, I hope the others don't read this.

From the diary of Michael Palin, Monday, 9 January 1978: GC seems more hale every day, and the first work session, which by the time everyone has had poohs, phoned car hire firms, washed their noses out, and generally done all those post-breakfast private processes, is very productive. We fairly roar through the script and there's a very productive feeling that at this stage anything is worthy of discussion.

From the diary of Terry Jones, Thursday, 12 January 1978: We've finished going though the whole film now ... expunged any relationship at the start between Brian and Judith and replaced most of Judith with Mandy (perhaps too much of her.) We've also managed to remove most of the painful plot setting dialogue. Brian now no longer writes on the wall to impress Judith, but actually asks to join the revolutionaries and is given the writing on the wall as a test job ...

Wednesday, 18 January 1978: This morning we actually finished the script – we even agreed on the opening. After all this time we're putting the three shepherds back in with the angel appearing behind them during their dialogue (John's idea) ... we also finished the casting ...

MICHAEL PALIN: *Brian* was our last really good group experience in writing terms. What would happen was individuals or writing groups would take a certain section and move it on a bit or write a stoning scene which obviously fitted in next to something. And then the various characters that one had written, like the Centurion who goes all the way through played by John, would be the result of group discussion. The way we worked when we were away in Barbados was unheard of since the very earliest Python shows, for us all to be in one place at the same time for two weeks. We'd never been like that because we'd always been geographically a few miles apart anyway and had to agree when to get together. Then someone couldn't make a Thursday and someone else couldn't do the next Tuesday. So I think what that Barbados break did was provide us with a real brainstorming session that was productive because people couldn't get away from it. What we took to Barbados was just a lot of material and a running order which included all sorts of things, including things that were eventually ditched from the film.

ERIC IDLE: There was this guy Barry Spikings who worked for Bernard Delfont and he kept saying to me, 'Show me the script, show me the script.' And I said, 'We haven't finished it yet', but I'd egg him along and say, 'No, it's great.' He read it at home and that's when we got the money, immediately after Barbados. Then Delfont got cold feet, they all got cold feet, and pulled out of it when we'd already started to spend money on the production and so we sued them.

GRAHAM CHAPMAN: Lord Delfont himself gave us the chop above the heads of the chiefs of EMI production who had agreed the terms. Keith (Moon) set about vigorously trying to raise the money for us to save this venture and would have succeeded in time. But George Harrison made an extremely courageous offer which was eagerly accepted by us and the film was on again. Keith was going to play the part of one of the blood-and-thunder prophets ... but on September 7th 1978 he died ...[4]

MICHAEL PALIN: We were told that the head of EMI had had a look at the script and he'd never been shown the script before. He took exception to it and said, 'We can't possibly do this.' It was a devastating blow, people were out there in Tunisia, money had been committed and they were just going to pull the plug. What was going to happen to all the people out there, what would happen to our set? That's when Eric talked to George Harrison, whom he'd got to know out in LA. George was a huge Python fan, and he got it together very quickly.

TERRY JONES: We got wind that EMI had suddenly pulled out and I think by this stage we'd spent about £50,000. Then again it was a court case. Fortunately somebody passed us some internal memos from EMI which had been sent round, EMI saying 'We're lucky enough to have the new Python movie' and all this kind of stuff. So they didn't really have a leg to stand on, because they were trying to say no, they'd never said they were going to do it. So they settled, and paid us the £50,000. Then Eric rang up George Harrison and George had been thinking about setting up a film company, so he talked to Denis O'Brien, his manager, and they agreed to set up a film company together, which they wanted to call British Handmade Films, but Companies House wouldn't allow them to call it 'British', so they just had to call it Handmade Films. Terry G designed a logo for them.

Michael Simkins
Ian W Burlingham
Richard C Thomas
Colin Wadie
N B Bennett
Robert C Rutteman
David T Franks

THE SIMKINS
PARTNERSHIP
SOLICITORS

12 Wyndham Place London W1H 1AS
Telephone : 01-262 3181
Cables : Leisir London W1H 1AS
Telex : 28329

To Barry Spikings Esq.
EMI Films Limited
142 Wardour Street
London W.1.

Subject "New Monty Python Film"

Our ref IWB/AMB Your ref

Date 15 February 1978

Dear Barry,

We have had through the draft screenplay and I think that the only area of blasphemy is to be found on pages 23 and 24 in the Ex-leper's complaint specifically in the words
        "the bastard cures me"
        "sod you"
        "long-haired conjuror starts fucking about"
Whilst John Goldstone's extracted quote by Canon James Fisher is interesting the relevant words are "that the script is not meant to be blasphemous": intention is one thing.

However, as I said the above instances the only times that we could see where the script could be said to be blasphemous.

Yours sincerely,

Ian Burlingham

Copies to: A. Coatman Esq.,
          J. Cherboux Esq.,
          Ms Erika Pond
          J. Boath Esq.

'Terry Jones is a fanatic about filming in particular. And I've noticed he's a fanatic about 'real' things like real ale and unprocessed food . . .'

TERRY JONES: The filming was terrific. I didn't enjoy the editing so much, it was partly because Terry and I had had another falling out. I think it was when we'd been looking at locations, Terry and the cameraman were debating about where to put something and I was being left out of the discussion a bit. I got a bit shirty and Terry doesn't take kindly to people being shirty with him. I didn't know this until a long time later. So Terry was a bit off me I think for the whole time.

MICHAEL PALIN: Our feeling was that comedy films could look as good as any other movie and that had been Terry Gilliam's particular contribution with *Holy Grail*, that we should just make it look as good as possible. If you couldn't afford an awful lot of money, let's at least make sure that we get as big an army as we can get, or shoot it as atmospherically as possible, make it look terrific. And so with *Life of Brian* it seemed essential that it shouldn't be just a few pranks in front of bits of wood at Shepperton Studios, we should really try and get extras who looked like they were Jews or Arabs, and real heat, then it would just give it much more integrity. So many biblical epics looked as though they were shot in the north of England. Terry Gilliam was very important in choosing locations, although Terry Jones directed it. The two of them worked hard to look for locations and of course Terry Gilliam became art director and supervised the look of the film.

GRAHAM CHAPMAN: Terry Jones is a fanatic about filming in particular. And I've noticed he's a fanatic about 'real' things like real ale and unprocessed food, which means of course he's constantly eating fish which comes out of one of the most unnatural oceans of the world, which is full of men's effluent … and I have to fill him up with little pink pills so he can direct.[8]

ERIC IDLE: Graham became a saint. He was not drinking and he was healthy. He was the doctor on the film, so he was not only playing the Christ-like figure, he would do surgery in the morning and surgery in the evening, and he was actually healing people.

TERRY JONES: Before we went Graham showed me his case. It was full of medicines and I remember thinking, 'That's a bit silly, isn't it?' I thought it was a bit over the top because he *really* had a suitcase *full* of medicine, but of course it wasn't over the top at all, it was absolutely the right thing to do. After a day's filming Graham would have quite a big queue of people coming to be treated at the end of the day, so it was a very sensible idea. Graham was great.

MICHAEL PALIN: That was a great thing for Gray because he was always very good at medicine and took it very seriously. It gave him the chance to be a sort of barefoot doctor for the team and look after everybody and that just helped him. He must have seen every day that he could do things which he probably couldn't do when he was drinking, like hold something without dropping it, as serious as that. This was Graham who had suddenly come out of a long slumber. He became much more concerned about the small detail of writing, which he would probably not have bothered with before that, in his drinking days. It was nice to have Graham back concentrating.

to photograph Ken Colley. Eric, Tania, Charles, Terry J, Andrew M. Bernard and the Hamptons fill a restaurant at La Plage et Coq – The Restaurant of the Beach and Cock. There was much singing of old music hall numbers and First World War songs at full voice, utterly drowning anyone else in the restaurant. A fine display of selfish and high-spirited behaviour. A release of a lot of tensions. Coq treat us to a very tasty liqueur and we toast the world's greatest, most long-suffering and least flappable waiter, Ali, with a rousing chorus of 'Ali, Ali, Pride of our Sally'.

JOHN CLEESE: I liked going out together in the evening but not every night. If I said, 'I think I'm going to eat on my own tonight,' I would go to some nice restaurant with a book and be enormously happy, because I think being alone in a restaurant with a book is as good as it gets. If they then came in the restaurant, there would be a bit of resentment that I wasn't there with them. I used to say, 'I'm

not on a fucking rugby team.' Some of the times I liked being with them and some of the times I liked being on my own.

MICHAEL PALIN: I remember driving off to be crucified was quite unpleasant because there'd been downpours which had washed the road away, so that put a bit of extra pressure on and the actual shoot itself of the Crucifixion was pretty uncomfortable. John was very worried that he couldn't put his arms down by his sides at the end of the day, they kept going up again and this went on for several weeks, with him saying he'd suffered.

JOHN CLEESE: By the time we shot the Crucifixion several of us had got quite seriously sick, which was rather funny because when we came to do the Crucifixion scene I remember thinking, 'Bad enough having fucking flu, without being crucified.' And Jonathan Benson, my old friend and first assistant, who's a great first assistant,

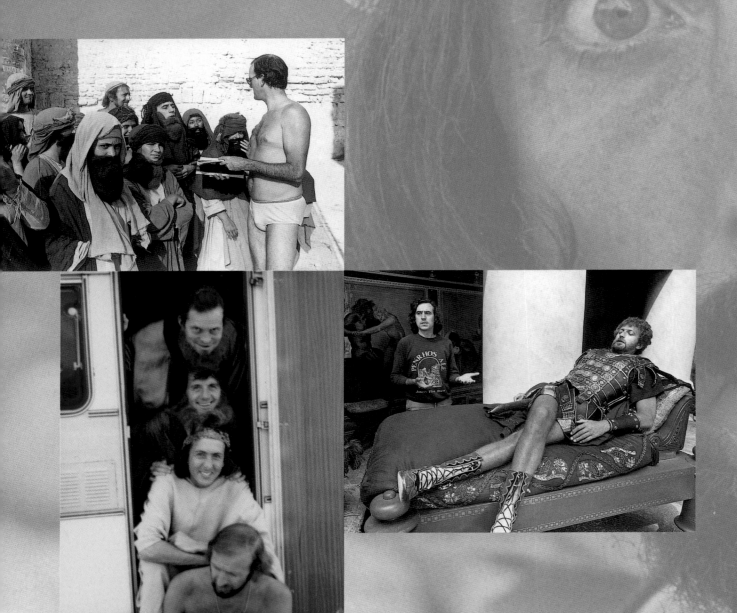

other stuff they'd done for *Brian*, and that was quite demoralising. John got quite demoralised by that because he liked things to be at a steady success rate. I'm not sure what was happening with him and Graham at that time, I don't think the writing or the relationship was as good as it could have been. Some good material was coming, but it didn't seem to have a framework. The great thing about *Life of Brian*, and to a certain extent *Holy Grail*, was once you'd got the framework it was a really good protective device and gave us a direction to the writing, which was very important. There was never any real such direction in *The Meaning of Life*, one almost felt that the writing would eventually force a direction rather than the other way round.

DAVID SHERLOCK: At the time Graham felt that Terry Gilliam gave a huge amount of time to the short that preceded the film, *The Crimson Permanent Assurance*. It was obvious he was having a huge amount of fun with none of the other Pythons, in a separate studio set-up. It was a wonderful piece of film on its own but it didn't have much to do with the rest of the movie.

ERIC IDLE: The Gilliam thing was supposed to come at the sixty-eighth minute when things got boring. There was supposed to be this Crimson Assurance thing which would come in, lift you and be different and then get you through to the end, but it just got longer and longer, and Terry was as usual shooting over budget, pretending he was kind of saving money and spending it like water! And it just got out of control and it got too long, so instead of it being six minutes it was suddenly sixteen minutes. So that opened the film, the decision was taken to open the film and then reprise it, which I think was a smart decision.

TERRY GILLIAM: *The Crimson Permanent Assurance* was something I'd started story-boarding as a cartoon, as an animation. Then I said, 'I've got a feeling I'd like to do it as live action,' and people don't pay attention to what that really means. I did it and then, once we started cutting the film together, what I had done didn't fit in. The whole thing was supposed to go in two-thirds of the way through the film, but it just wasn't working because the rhythm was so totally different. The whole film ground to a halt and everybody was saying, 'You've got to cut it shorter, you've got to cut it shorter.' It's worse than working for the studios. It's clear it wasn't working in there and in desperation I was saying, 'I'm not going to cut it any shorter, so let's remove it from the film and stick it as an accompanying short up front,' and it worked that way. Then I was allowed to come back and invade the film later. I get pushed enough by the others with the things I'm trying to do, I can't make them work and then I have to do something extreme. The pulling out really did work and I was really happy with that. But by then I was doing stuff that was really very different from the rest of the group.

JOHN CLEESE: Terry didn't want to be art director any more and we asked him to do a sequence that was to go into the middle of the film. He got carried away by his own enthusiasm, he overspent his budget for that section by a million dollars, which is quite a lot, and something that was supposed to be about nine minutes came

'There was supposed to be this Crimson Assurance thing which would come in, lift you and be different and then get you through to the end, but it just got longer and longer, and Terry was as usual shooting over budget, pretending he was kind of saving money and spending it like water!'

out originally as, I don't know, twenty-seven minutes. It finally got cut down to whatever it is and we realised you couldn't put that in the middle of the film, because it had grown beyond the size that we had all agreed it should be. So it was felt that the only way to deal with that was to put it up front.

TERRY JONES: He was working in the studio next door and originally he was meant to be doing an animated bit. He showed us the animation and we said, 'Oh, that'll be quite nice coming in at this point in the film.' Then he decided he wanted to do live action and so John Goldstone coughed up some money and I hadn't realised what was going on, what a huge production number it was. Terry hadn't really explained what he was doing and I was a bit too busy anyway to worry about what Terry was doing. When we showed the film, it used to come to three-quarters of the way through, and people would say, 'We really like the film but that's dreadful, that pirate sequence, what's that doing there?' Nobody liked it. Terry

was a bit worried, but he said he'd always had this idea that it really ought to come at the beginning and he'd actually shot a bit for it to break back into the film, and so I think Terry had already decided what he wanted to do basically. So then we had a showing where we put it at the beginning of the film and it worked. There's no question, people suddenly liked the pirate stuff a lot. But from the point of view of the film it slightly spoiled the beginning: the birth sequence always used to get terrific reactions when we'd shown it, but it didn't get such good reactions when it was placed after the pirate scene because the pirate scene is so big and loud. Also I discovered that Terry had recorded the pirate sequence at a slightly higher decibel level than the rest of the film, so when we opened in New York I was rushing around the cinemas trying to get them to turn up the sound after the pirate sequence.

MICHAEL PALIN: It seemed to be going a bit out of control really. But I was such an admirer of Terry and what he could achieve visually

'Also I discovered that Terry had recorded the pirate sequence at a slightly higher decibel level than the rest of the film, so when we opened in New York I was rushing around the cinemas trying to get them to turn up the sound after the pirate sequence.'

that the idea of buildings chasing each other and all that seemed marvellous, but I felt in the end that it was too long, even as a stand-alone short. A lot of what Terry had done had been sharp, crisp and economical, some terrific things were there. But it was about accountants and I think maybe in the end, however much one tries to make fun of them, they've got to look interesting, but they didn't really, it was a lot of rather boring people being made to look exciting. It was sort of pre-*Brazil*, with a lot of papers flying about, and *Brazil* pulled it off brilliantly because it was about something, and this seemed to be, as I say, a rather grand set chasing a fairly small idea. But it was typical of the film, which was not unified. Terry just went off to do his own thing and people didn't really get involved in anybody else's thing.

TERRY GILLIAM: With *The Crimson Permanent Assurance* short I was testing things, pushing things that you could do in animation, but doing it as live action. The great irony is that the building we used

is Lloyd's Shipping Office in the City, with the big anchor lifting up. We got a local sergeant down there to turn a blind eye on a Sunday. We had to very quickly put this false pavement in, and put the anchor in, but we couldn't touch the building. So we put the big ring on the ground and the chain, and we had a crane holding it about a foot from the building. We got the wide shot done and the rest was done in the studio. It was like guerrilla filmmaking but on a rather large scale. The model work was really tricky. Now it could be done on computers really easily. All those reflective buildings were a nightmare; because of all the wide-angle lenses, they were all tipped at different angles. It was real nightmare stuff to do, but it was fun because I was teaching myself. The point is we

wanted to learn to be the experts, so at least when you asked somebody for something, you knew why it should or shouldn't work.

DAVID SHERLOCK: They all rather hoped that it was going to have an impact. The piece which I feel epitomises Graham's attitude and is a piece of pure Python writing is the Protestant and Catholic sequence. To me the character that Graham played, which is really Graham's attempt at an Ian Paisley impersonation, also epitomises everything that he could think of about the ridiculous divide between the two ideals in the name of Christianity.

TERRY JONES: 'Every Sperm is Sacred' was fun to do. I didn't know whether there would be too many images, actually – when I look at it now, it seems fine – but there are two images throughout every line of the song. Each individual image wasn't that difficult to shoot, but I said, 'I really want playback on this one.' I think John Goldstone was a bit nervous because he'd heard about actors getting too indulgent, looking at their performances and saying, 'I can do more than that,' but I said that it'd just save us time.

We hadn't been able to shoot in the morning because it took make-up so long to get all the kids made up and we did it first thing after lunch. On the first take the flags didn't unfurl; the second take something else was not quite right; and at the end of the third take I said, 'I can't see what's wrong with that,' and we looked at it on the monitor and I said, 'Yeah, there's no problem with that, it's fine.'

MICHAEL PALIN: It was Terry's finest hour, and very true to Python in that it didn't waste a moment, didn't waste an opportunity. It proved one of the great moments of BAFTA history for me because 'Every Sperm is Sacred' was nominated for a BAFTA music award for Best Original Song in a Film. We went along to the BAFTA awards, and it was quite clear that 'Every Sperm is Sacred' was by far the most popular one. There were roars of laughter and then the sort of silence when they announced the winner, which ironically was called 'Up Where We Belong' – it was just so close in title. If 'Every Sperm' was going to be beaten by anything, it was going to be beaten by 'Up Where We Belong', with the same sort of thought in mind!

TERRY JONES: People talk about us doing parodies or doing travesties of things or lampooning things, but we never have really. A lampoon or parody involves making fun of a specific film of that style and I don't think we were ever making fun of the style, we were always just using the style to do funny things within that context. 'Every Sperm is Sacred' is not a parody of these things, it just *is* these things, it's a musical song, it's a hymn, it's a Lionel Bart-style musical, but it's not making fun of a Lionel Bart-style musical. It *is being* a Lionel Bart-style musical because I loved the idea! And the humour comes from what it's talking about or something within that.

JOHN CLEESE: I thought the film was very patchy, though it had wonderful stuff in it. I think 'The Galaxy Song' is not just one of the best songs that we did but one of the best songs ever. Yet I just

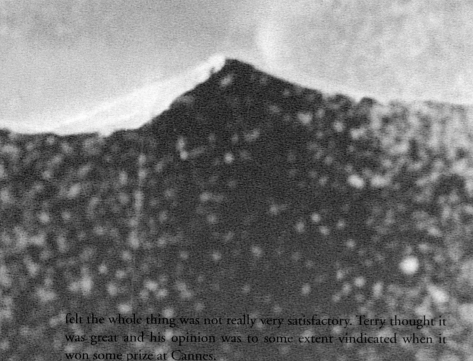

felt the whole thing was not really very satisfactory. Terry thought it was great and his opinion was to some extent vindicated when it won some prize at Cannes.

TERRY JONES: Eric's 'Galaxy Song' in *The Meaning of Life* I think is one of the best things we've done and one of the best things he's done. I think it's such a wonderful song.

TERRY GILLIAM: The opening animation I quite liked, but by then I was even hiring real animators to come in and animate things.

JOHN CLEESE: When 'Mr Creosote' was read out it didn't work, by which I mean nobody thought it was very funny, which I think surprised either Mike or Terry or both of them. It was then brought up again. They said 'Can we read it out again?' and we said 'Sure'. They read it out again and it worked much better. I can't remember if they made any changes, but sometimes when you're reading material out there's a right moment to read it out. Don't read your best bit just after everyone's had a curry for lunch, simple stuff like that – physiological. When it was read out the second time, we all saw the possibilities of it, and I said, 'Let Graham and me rewrite it.' I saw that the headwaiter could be expanded into a very funny character, and I thought I'd like to play that, that's going to be very funny.

TERRY JONES: We showed the 'Mr Creosote' scene to John Du Prez, who was our composer, and I said, 'John, have a look at this.' John looked at it, then he went outside and was sick, and we thought, 'Fucking hell! This is the first person to actually see the sequence cut and he's sick, he throws up.' So we thought we'd have to offer everybody sick bags in the cinema. It turned out he'd got a hangover!

MICHAEL PALIN: It's got some absolutely terrific things in it and it's very strong. Creosote, I think, was one of the best things that Python has ever done in terms of elevating some tiny idea to a sort of great Gothic extravaganza. Eric's scene with Graham, the Catholic and the Protestant, was just one of the most touching pieces of acting that Python's ever done. It was most beautifully played. 'Every Sperm is Sacred' is one of the great songs. There were

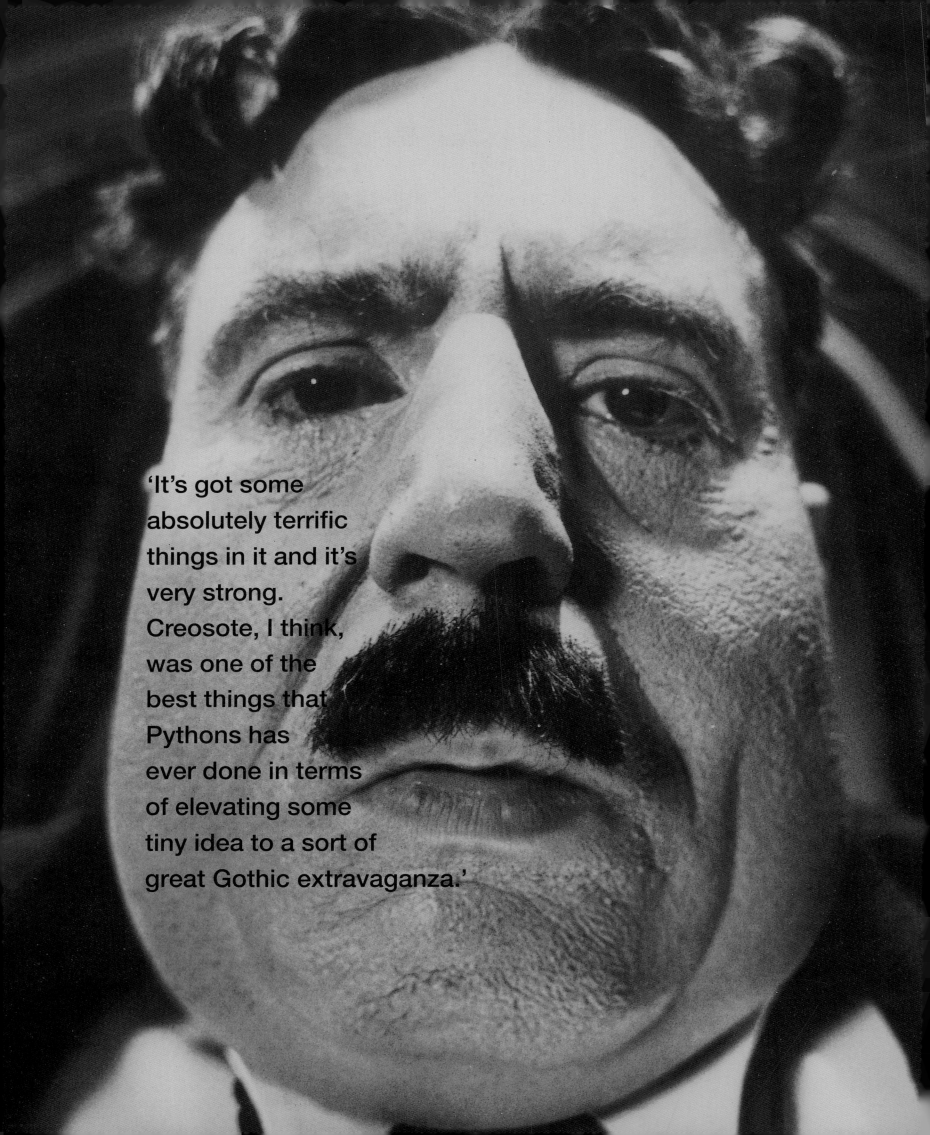

'It's got some absolutely terrific things in it and it's very strong. Creosote, I think, was one of the best things that Pythons has ever done in terms of elevating some tiny idea to a sort of great Gothic extravaganza.'

just one or two things that I felt didn't have that light zip that good Python material had. 'The Sex Lesson' is a very funny idea, but I watch it now and feel at some points it just lumbers along – there are moments of that in *The Meaning of Life*.

ERIC IDLE: What happened with the film was that, unlike all the other films, we weren't all around at the end, so there wasn't a preview, there wasn't a period when we discussed how the cut was. I remember getting cuts in Australia and, I think, the penultimate cut being much better than the final cut. I think John went in there and cut a lot of stuff and I don't think he did a good job. He was always saying he had nothing to do with it but in fact he was always hands-on doing things. I think in the end it's OK because of what it is, it's a musical. And the music is some of the finest stuff. 'Every Sperm is Sacred' is just shot so great, Jonesy directed it brilliantly, he's really in control of what he's doing. I think it's a fine job. It's still the most offensive Python film.

JOHN CLEESE: We left most of the editing to Terry. He asked me in once or twice and I gave him my opinions, and he usually did the opposite, which was what normally

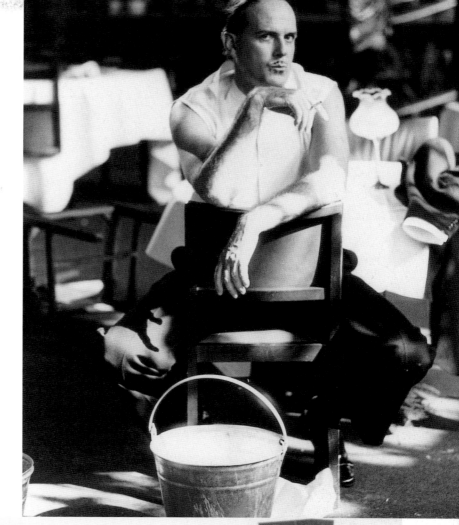

happened with the two of us. It was a good system really. I got to have my say, and Jonesey got to have control. So we were both happy.

TERRY JONES: We did the same thing we'd always done, we had different showings and would just re-cut it according to how things seemed to be going. I think we were a bit more confident by this time. It wasn't a heavy film to edit, the sequences cut pretty easily. But it would be difficult to get people to come and look at a cut to give me their opinion, so I felt, 'I've just got to do it myself.' So it was less of a group thing, in a way.

MICHAEL PALIN: Post-production of Python films was always traumatic. There were always changes of mind and people would get wind that something was being done. I was quite close to Terry obviously, and he'd say, 'Come in and we'd have a look,' and we'd sort something out.

'I think in the end it's OK because of what it is, it's a musical. And the music is some of the finest stuff. 'Every Sperm is Sacred' is just shot so great, Jonesy directed it brilliantly, he's really in control of what he's doing. I think it's a fine job. It's still the most offensive Python film.'

JOHN CLEESE: I think it would have been much better if we'd not done anything for two years. As it was, we just kept writing, almost aimlessly, and I began to become quite disillusioned. Some of us were wondering whether we ought to be going on and on doing this because we spent a lot of time writing material and none of it came together. Though there were funny bits of material, there was no real point to it.

ERIC IDLE: Once we'd found the concept and what it's about, we shouldn't have gone in to shoot it until we'd done another three or four weeks' work on it. But it never got that because John refused to do it, he didn't want anything to do with it, he was 'Oh, that'll do, you know, get out of here', because he wanted the money. He'd been promised the money and he wanted the money. So I think that's what it lacks. I think all our films are like that in fact, but it's disguised because something else is put round it – *Grail*'s very much a series of sketches but, because we'd worked on it and put a through-line, you don't notice that so much. I think it's more obvious in *The Meaning of Life* because you keep coming back to the captions and it keeps starting another thing that seems like a sketch. I just kick myself and think, 'We were so fucking close.' Nothing's ever wrong; there's no such thing as bad work, just unfinished work.

MICHAEL PALIN: It did feel a little bit more fragmented and it was shot around the UK so, unlike *Brian*, where we all physically had to be in one place in two hotels, we didn't all have to be together. I'd go out and do the sergeant major at Colchester Barracks, and Graham would go off somewhere else and do the naked ladies chasing him. I had a week off for Creosote while they threw minestrone around Seymour Baths. So, yes, we weren't together as much and it felt as though we were more separate, it felt as though people were more preoccupied with other things.

'I'd reached the point where I wanted to make my own mistakes, not other people's. I remember that phrase sticking in my mind. And I don't think any of the Pythons were that keen to make a film after that experience.'

THE **END**
OF THE FILM

ERIC IDLE: When Graham was dying, I was producing the *Python Sings* album, and I was listening to his voice, it was really sad and it was really emotional. I was writing a song for him, which I actually finished when George Harrison died. I wrote this for him when he was dying:

Life will get you in the end,

On this one thing you can depend.

When you think you're in the thick of it

You find you're getting sick of it.

Life will get you in the end.

Life can drive you round the bend,

You think it's never gonna end.

Then one day it comes along

And ends it with a song.

Life will get you in the end.

I never finished until George died and then I finished it with a middle eight. Then I wrote it and I sang it afterwards. That's how I deal with emotion. This is how I get through it, to write something about him in a song. Then I had to sing 'Always Look on the Bright Side' at Graham's memorial, which was the hardest thing in the world for me to do, I must say, it was really hard. People always ask me to do that for them and I can't do it. It's really tough to sing. I'm going to become a funeral singer now. It was in the Top Ten of Funeral Songs, 'Always Look on the Bright Side of Life'.

JOHN CLEESE: After Graham had broken up with the group he went elsewhere for his finances and accountancy. At that time nearly all the Pythons were having their financial matters looked after by the same two people, and what would happen was that every six months a new set of accountants would approach them saying we represent Graham Chapman and we want to get very clear and accurate figures on the following matters because we feel he's not being paid properly. Our people would then furnish the new set of accountants with the figures and would explain what had been happening, at which point the accountants would realise that Graham had not been swindled and would go back and present that to Graham. Then six months later another set of accountants would show up, who had been hired because Graham would have got rid of the ones who'd explained to him that Python didn't owe him money. That went on for some time

THE MEANING OF DEATH

and it was very hard for Graham because he very much wanted to be a star; probably more than most of us he wanted the trappings of stardom and he also wanted the lifestyle. Graham was always hoping somehow that the money existed somewhere that would justify the lifestyle that he was after, and he came to the conclusion, and it was an absolute fantasy, that it had been there but it had been cheated out of him by the Python accountants.

Steve Martin. Somebody had cobbled this thing together and was passing it off, saying it was written by John or whatever. When I read it I thought, 'This is just terrible, we can't do this.' So we arrived and Steve Martin was there at the film studios. We had to turn up to do it and I'm very glad that they cut it.

MICHAEL PALIN: Part of the problem was that once Python gets seen

Steve Martin performs with the Pythons in a sketch cut from *Parrot Sketch Not Included*

DAVID SHERLOCK: Graham just could not say no. He was incredibly generous, he was very kind. But he died owing something in the region of half a million, and if things had been different, if we'd have lived more modestly, there would have been a very different outcome.

JOHN CLEESE: I remember the exact moment when we realised something was seriously wrong with Graham's health. We had a meeting and Gray as usual turned up late, nobody took any notice of that. We were all chatting amongst ourselves and suddenly this high-pitched strangulated voice spoke and I remember all of us turned round and it was Graham's voice. Then we were aware of some purple marking which was caused by radiation and he started to explain what was going on and we were all very shocked, because we had no idea. I remember going to visit him in the Cromwell Hospital where he was very optimistic, but there are two completely different stories: his brother thinks he knew exactly what the score was and was just keeping up an extremely brave front, and other people think that he genuinely was optimistic about his chances of recovery. He certainly was to me. He seemed to be on a high. I remember leaving the hospital and feeling quite relieved and vaguely exhilarated that he was going to be all right.

TERRY JONES: We'd agreed to appear on this special, *Parrot Sketch Not Included*, and there was this new sketch which featured us and

as a legend which has to be celebrated, the humour that made Python goes out of the window because we are becoming a victim of all the things we were attacking. Steve Martin was there and we all loved Steve. He was great and of course there was an awesome atmosphere, it was like a cathedral there. This legendary group had got together with this legendary American comedian to produce a legendary moment and that, for me, is not the way humour works. It didn't really feel as though it was working at the time.

The idea of getting Steve Martin and the Pythons together was a nice one in the sense that we respected each other, but it was not necessarily the easiest way of producing the best comedy. That's why I've always felt Python was at its best when it just was the group of us. It was quite a self-contained momentum. It couldn't be exported, it couldn't be grafted on to anyone else nor could anyone else be grafted on to Python.

JOHN CLEESE: I was delighted that Steve was doing it and a bit embarrassed when I heard that some were being cut. I don't think I was very involved in that decision because I think I would have rather resisted cutting it. That's the last time Graham performed.

ERIC IDLE: We did a reunion show with Steve Martin and we'd shot stuff and then suddenly Graham was carried in. I think Steve had not seen him, nobody had bothered to warn Steve that he might be

sick and he just looked at him. He was gaunt and being carried in, and what was good about it was everybody was there, everybody who ever worked for us in some capacity was working on it, and it was like a nostalgic last time to do this. We weren't very good, we weren't very funny, but it was a nice experience. He really enjoyed the day, and he was carried off in the end. He did a bit and then he was taken off, but it was great for him to see everybody and everybody was together, it worked really well.

TERRY GILLIAM: I began to realise how ill he was when we were doing that gathering for TV with Steve Martin. That's when we had the first shock of Graham looking really bad. It was just throat cancer then, he had had work done and he was looking like a plucked chicken and it looked bad, but apparently it had all been pretty much dealt with. Then apparently he had had an all clear from the doctors and everyone was like 'OK, he's over it'.

JOHN CHAPMAN: At that anniversary thing for the Pythons, he was unable to walk, he was in a wheelchair.

TERRY JONES: We'd had a photo shoot and Graham was having difficulty swallowing. Of course when we shot on the day I don't think we'd realised how ill he was. He had this frame in order to keep him upright, he had to wear this frame, so he was very, very ill at that stage. It was extraordinary he actually got on camera. That was when we knew he was not at all well.

TERRY GILLIAM: The next thing I know is I get a call that Graham's gone into the hospital, and I'm going 'Oh Jesus, that's bad', and then I get another call, saying, 'They don't expect that he's coming out'. I said 'What? What do you mean he's not coming out, can't pay his bills? What?' And that was it. It happened very quickly. He was just riddled with cancer. He'd sold his big headline story to *The Sun*, I think, about how 'Python Whips Big C' a month earlier, and so there's Graham once again conning people into parting with large sums of money. It just happened very quickly, it surprised us all. Graham was weird because he was somebody I really felt I never knew. He was always the one that I was least easy with because I never knew what was going on in his head – strange man. I think the thing was we were so pissed off for so long about his drinking and his fumbling performances, but he was a truly brilliant performer, if you look at the stuff, when he was on form. The idea of him playing Arthur was so brilliant because it was such an unlikely idea in a strange way. He'd be the straight man and nobody else could have done it and so we suddenly realised we had our leading man in Graham.

ERIC IDLE: Graham dies on the twentieth anniversary, brilliant timing. I bumped into him in a mall in LA at the beginning of that year and he said, 'I've been very lucky. I was just having a check up and they found this bit of cancer at the back of my throat and they're going to do operations.' Then it was one operation, then another operation, then another operation … I often wondered if he would have lived if he hadn't found it, because sometimes the operation kills you. He's a doctor so I think he was susceptible to all of that. I think doctors are bullshit and just practising. I just wondered if he might have lived longer if he hadn't had those three operations. But the cancer spread; it's always horrible. I saw him last at the hospital and he'd had his second or maybe his third operation and he was very optimistic. He said he was thinking of opening a longevity clinic, which is very ironic considering he had three weeks left to live, but it was good, it was nice to see him.

JOHN CHAPMAN: I became aware of the serious nature of his illness when I spoke to the surgeon who operated on his neck. That was his first operation. He must have had a biopsy or something before that.

Graham's belief, or the impression that he was anxious to give everybody, was that he was confident that that was the end of it and that he was cured, which I suppose is the way one has to approach it in that situation. Yet I was fairly certain from my own knowledge of medicine that somebody who required a radical dissection of the nodes in the neck had a seriously advanced and aggressive disease, and there was a strong chance that it wasn't the end, that there would be more of it. Then, of course, when he developed paralysis of the lower half of the body, he was confined thereafter to a wheelchair. There were secondary deposits in the spine from the tumour of the throat.

JOHN CLEESE: All of a sudden there was the news of the collapse and I remember driving down to the Maidstone hospital. I was there most of the time; for most of his last two or three days I was in or around, though not in the room when he actually died, but standing outside. Michael was there and Peter Cook and David of course and one or two others. It was all a big surprise, because I'd had dinner with him about a year before, and he was going on and on about these free radicals and how he'd completely cut them out of his diet. He was looking so fit but a bit emaciated. One or two people said 'Does he have Aids?' He'd cut fat out of his diet so rigidly, almost obsessively, that he was looking gaunt.

TERRY JONES: Hearing the news was actually less of a shock, having seen him in that state. I went down there when he died, it must have been just about an hour or so later, after he'd died. David was there and John.

DAVID SHERLOCK: John Cleese was there when he died, although he had to go to another room because he was so upset; Peter Cook came by; Mike was there. It was really terribly sad for all of us – obviously.

JOHN CHAPMAN: Peter Cook arrived after the event, at the house in Maidstone. I don't think he actually got to the hospital, though. There were just John, Michael and David there at the time of death. John said it's the first time he'd ever seen anybody die. It was something, obviously, that I was familiar with from my medical career over many, many years; one knew exactly what was happening and he was in a very, very poor way, in extremis, vomiting blood, passing blood from the bowel and unaware at that stage of what was happening. I don't know whether he ever recognised that I was there by his side. I had to rush to fly from Geneva to Heathrow and then get from Heathrow to Maidstone to the hospital. But I suppose I arrived mid-afternoon and he died early evening as my recollection is. John was obviously very moved by the whole thing, part of the response. Michael, I don't think was quite so emotional, I think he was on more of an even keel. David,

I seem to remember, wanted to be involved with the proceedings after death, with the laying out and that sort of thing.

DAVID SHERLOCK: My mother, from an early age, taught me that mourning is a two-year process at the least, that if it's done properly then you come out of that and you can pick up your life again.

JOHN CHAPMAN: There was a memorial in the Great Hall in St Bartholomew's Hospital some considerable time later, where John got up to speak, and it was the first time anybody had actually said 'fuck' at a memorial service. And then to finish off there was the song from the end of *Life of Brian*. It was very appropriate.

I think he enjoyed his life, which was the most important thing. Who knows what he would have been capable of if he hadn't succumbed in the way he did. I don't think I regret any aspects of his life except that one wonders how much his lifestyle contributed to his early demise. On the other hand, if his lifestyle had been any different, would he have been as productive as he was, as innovative as he was. One doesn't know.

🔻 Recruitment Page 13 🔻 Announcements Page 20 🔻 Sales Page 20 🔻 Services Page 21 🔻 Property Page 23 🔻 Motoring Page 24 🔻 Leisure Page 28

AFN VFD Certified average weekly distribution 61,050 1st Jan - 30th June 1989

adscene

THE ONE YOU CAN'T PUT DOWN

MAIDSTONE & SURROUNDING AREAS INCLUDING MALLING & DISTRICT   NO. 699 WEEK ENDING 13TH OCTOBER 1989

THE LOVER: David Sherlock – mourning the death and remembering the life of his partner, Graham Chapman.

GOOD-BYE GRAHAM WE LOVED YOU

Report by Carol Davies Picture by Malcolm Ganderton

THE STAR: Graham Chapman – a unique talent in the world of comedy.

THE WORLD of comedy is mourning the loss of a unique talent this week following the death from cancer of Monty Python star Graham Chapman.

Members of the Python team, including John Cleese and Michael Palin, were by the 48-year-old star's bedside when he died on Wednesday.

He had been battling with cancer for the past year and was rushed to Maidstone Hospital from his home in Hermitage Lane, on Tuesday, when his condition worsened suddenly.

Just two weeks earlier, he had told David Sherlock - his gay partner of 24 years - that he thought he had beaten the disease.

He developed cancer of the tonsils last year, which spread to his spine.

On the day he died, he was due to be guest of honour at a 20th anniversary party for the Python comedy team.

But shattered colleagues cancelled the celebration when they heard their friend was dying.

Graham Chapman, who abandoned a career in medicine for the world of television, was both scriptwriter and performer in the Python series and also wrote and starred in films made by the team, Monty Python and the Holy Grail, and The Life of Brian.

Mr. Chapman lived in a £750,000 house in Hermitage Lane, Maidstone, with David Sherlock, 42, and their adopted son, John Tomyczek, 32.

Both paid tribute to their friend's courage and cheerfulness during his painful illness.

"I'm sure that Graham knew that he only had a couple of weeks left, but told us he was going to be OK to make it easier for us," said David Sherlock.

"He was desperate to come home and put up with a lot of pain to be with us at home for his last two weeks.

"But when someone is so seriously ill, it's frightening. When I told him we couldn't cope and that he should go back to hospital, he told us that we were doing fine.

"I stayed with him throughout his last hours, but found myself comforting John Cleese when Graham was dying. John was really taking it badly and was very upset.

"But when Michael Palin arrived, he seemed to bring joy and light with him. It sliced through the atmosphere like a knife. He breezed in and sat holding Graham's hand, telling him what he'd been doing that day, and how much we all love him.

"The support and love we have had from friends has given John and I strength to get through a very sad time. I am only just beginning to feel the loss. I've lost one of the kindest, most generous and loving people I have ever met.

"He paid me the greatest compliment in my life by chosing me as his companion."

The funeral is at 1pm today (Friday), at Vinters Park Crematorium.

John Tomyczek said: "Graham liked to help people and was anxious that people with cancer didn't regard it as a death sentence. He was very open about having it, and tried to stress that it can be beaten.

"He was so brave, he kept us all going.

"He always had time for other people, and the response from everyone since he died has been an incredible expression of love. It has made David and I feel much happier.

"We want people to remember him for the laughter he brought into the world. He had a unique talent and will be sorely missed."

'Party pooper'

DESPITE a heroic effort, Graham Chapman did not manage to live long enough to enjoy the big Monty Python reunion.

Hiding his grief with a joke, Python Terry Jones said: "It's the worst case of party pooping I've ever come across. But seriously, we will all miss him - we loved him very much."

Donations

Instead of flowers, donations to the Maidstone-based Kent Leukaemia and Cancer Equipment Fund are invited in memory of Graham Chapman.

Cheques should be made out to the charity and sent to Mrs. Peggy Wood, 1 Oak Cottages, Boughton Monchelsea, Maidstone.

...AND BEYOND

U.S.
COMEDY
ARTS
festival
sponsored by
HBO

the u.s.
Comedy
Arts
Festival

17.00

Program
Guide

March 4-8, 1998
Aspen, Co

ERIC IDLE: The reunion we did onstage in Aspen was good, because it's okay to talk about yourselves in the old time and be around. Ageing's okay if you're accepting it. But new stuff with old farts is horrible.

TERRY JONES: It was a lovely audience, some very well-known faces and everybody very enthusiastic and wanting to laugh. I didn't think the show was particularly good. I thought we had a lot more to say than what was brought out by the interviewer and I got the feeling he'd rather set a pattern of questions to go through and wasn't picking up on bits that were being offered. It didn't feel very spontaneous.

MICHAEL PALIN: The Aspen reunion was very successful, partly because Aspen was a very nice comfortable place to be. It was snowing, the theatre where we were performing was a small, old theatre with only about 400 people there and the atmosphere was incredibly warm. We'd talked and had meetings during the day and discussed what we might say and great ideas came up – Graham's ashes being kicked over – a very good Pythonic irreverent idea – very well accomplished by Gilliam when he kicked it over, and it just really worked. We got this terrific roar of laughter, we were coasting along and it was rather enjoyable – for me, anyway. A lot of sort of rivalries were suspended and there was a lot of cordiality and everyone felt, 'What a nice thing, we should do this more often.'

JOHN CLEESE: The point where Gilliam kicked over Graham's ashes got roars of laughter. And it was very pleasant to see the guys from *Cheers* in the audience, I was very fond of them. We were on a high and next morning we said, 'We're having great fun, and a great time together, wouldn't it be fun to do a stage show?' Eric was very keen, I was keen and I got the impression that everyone was keen, but then typically the next day, round about lunchtime, I'd heard that Gilliam had had breakfast with Mike and Terry Jones and had been saying that he wasn't keen. He never said that in the room, unless I'm deafer than I thought, and it was typical of how you thought you'd get a Python group decision and then it would all begin to unravel. Eric asked his lawyer if he would co-ordinate the business of getting in offers and trying to see what would be best – six weeks? Four weeks in one city? Two weeks in three or four cities? The lawyer did an outstandingly poor job. I was astonished at how lazy the efforts that were made by his company. I'm not sure if it was him or his underlings, but instead of collating the offers so that you could see the pros and cons of all the different deals that were proposed, he just used to get an offer, scribble a note on it and then fax it straight on to us. And because most of us, with the exception of Eric, were not very good on deals, we were quite confused as to

what we were being offered and which was better than what. Also, by and large, they were offering us things that were rather more than we wanted to do – somebody wanted us to do ten cities and at one point we were talking about doing Las Vegas. Michael said he didn't want to do Las Vegas and then he came back and said, 'What about New York?' because he thought it would be interesting to be in New York for a few weeks. Eric had had enough and he said, 'No, that's it,' and was very angry with Michael for having sabotaged the tour, in Eric's mind.

ERIC IDLE: At Aspen everybody was real pleased to see each other and it was rather fun. We did one of our funniest jokes, when we kicked over Graham's ashes, that was hilarious, our biggest laugh ever, and there was a lot of warmth and affection. Then people said, 'Maybe we should do something.' John talked about a tour, Michael wanted to do it and I was reluctant, but everyone said they'd like to do it. Then I got into handling the business side of it and having to go to meetings and we got lawyers involved, there were a lot of phone meetings. I remember in Venice I had to go to a phone meeting, I was on holiday, and I thought, 'Fucking phone meeting!' Everybody said they wanted to do it, so I got involved and then finally, having done all these meetings, Michael said he didn't want to do it. I remember being really pissed off and saying, 'Couldn't you have fucking said this in the first place? Because I've just wasted six months working it out and getting it going.' Michael is so nice, he's unable to say no. I'm not cross with him. I was at the time, because I'd just wasted so much time in my life, but he's just not so easily able to say no.

MICHAEL PALIN: Word got out that we were going to do a reunion tour. I felt that we were being pushed into it before we'd actually had time to digest what it might mean, and major decisions, such as what sort of venues we should play, hadn't been decided. These were huge decisions, like should we play 15,000-seaters where we'd have big screens. At one time certain people were very keen on that because that would bring in lots of money and it would be really the only way you could do a tour and make a lot of money. Or would we consider what John and I were most keen on, 500- to 1,000-seat places, where you could really play the sketches well in a way we'd never done on stage for a long long time? So there was a debate there which we should have had and we didn't really have.

JOHN CLEESE: Twenty years ago I used to ask Michael to be in charity shows, Michael would always say yes, then he'd reconfirm and reconfirm, and then four days before the show he would be terribly apologetic – he finds it hard to say no. We thought that if this lawyer is organising the show, he ought to meet us before we all left Aspen and

I was very surprised that he said he couldn't because he was flying out in the morning. We said, 'Is there any chance you could fly out a couple of hours later and just meet us for an hour?' and he said, 'No.' I thought that was peculiar.

TERRY JONES: Mike was more keen on doing a movie. John wasn't really interested in the movie, he was very keen on the idea of doing a stage show and was really pushing for it while we were at Aspen. We talked about it and then at some point John made an announcement about it and said we were going to do a stage show and Mike was a bit cross, I think, because he felt John was railroading us into this. Terry Gilliam didn't want to do one anyway. Mike's feeling was 'Of course I'd do it, because it would be such fun to do, I'd love to do it.' But artistically it wasn't what I would necessarily choose to do, but it would be fun to do. My feeling was it would be an indulgence.

TERRY GILLIAM: I really didn't want to do it.

TERRY JONES: It was important to have Terry G. Without Terry, it was just four of us and it would have felt very odd, but with Terry G in, we'd sort of get away with it. We'd miss Graham more for a film than we would for the stage thing because Graham's lead performance is something you really need on film.

MICHAEL PALIN: Eric was in LA, using his lawyers to do the contract and I never really felt engaged in that. I felt, 'This is being done by lawyers out there whom I don't know. I have to trust Eric that they're giving us the best deal, that they're the best people to negotiate with us but there is nobody here really taking a grip on all that and representing us.' I remember getting a document back from America with lots of scrawls across it and this had been sent by one of the lawyers who was going to represent us. It seemed to be a very tatty, rough, rather cursory piece of work with lots of crossings out and lots of little comments in the margin and it quite honestly put me off.

JOHN CLEESE: Michael decided that he didn't want to do the stage tour and fair's fair. Michael *had* been very dilatory, he'd probably messed around for three months before suddenly saying he didn't want to do it. I was very up for the tour, but it's a perfect example that we are not very efficient as a group. We all have our moments of artistic efficiency and we enjoy being together because we actually enjoy each other's company. I remember that we went to a London restaurant round about this time – Eric wasn't there but Jonesy, Palin and Gilliam were – and we just had the best two and a half hours that we'd had at dinner, any of us, for a long time. We said at the time we laugh more when we're together than we do when we're with anyone else. We drank rather too much of an Australian wine called Mad Fish. I don't remember the name of the restaurant, I just remember the name of the wine, Mad Fish.

TERRY GILLIAM: Mike became wobbly about it.

MICHAEL PALIN: The worry in the back of my mind always was that we lacked Graham; if we didn't have Graham how did we do this

'I remember that we went to a London restaurant round about this time – Eric wasn't there but Jonesy, Palin and Gilliam were – and we just had the best two and a half hours that we'd had at dinner, any of us, for a long time. We said at the time we laugh more when we're together than we do when we're with anyone else.'

tour? Who would play the Graham role? Would we just abandon sketches which Graham was in? Would one of us take Graham's part? And that's absolutely impossible. No Python has really been able to do a part made famous by another Python, nor would an audience want to see that. The bottom line was if we were going to do a tour which wasn't as good or better than one we'd done before, what's the point in doing it? But my moments of indecision were rather badly communicated and I, in my typical way, let it go on because I didn't want to be the one to rock any boats. I said that I didn't really want to be involved and that's when recriminations flew, quite rightly. I was accused of not making my position clear at an earlier date, but my position in my own mind was quite clear, I just probably didn't want to stop what I saw was a process that might be interesting, it might possibly have a way of resolving itself. I should have been more firm and said, 'This is never going to resolve itself.' I should have just said that and stopped it there. I think John was quite relieved, but Eric was very unhappy and we did have a little bit of a falling out over it, which distressed me greatly because I love Eric. Like all the rest of them, he's such a funny, nice, likeable guy, and some of the best and funniest times I've had have been with Eric, so I didn't want to spoil all of that. Nothing was spoiled, and in the end it was absolutely fine. Anyway, there was a period where the means and the way I said things made people rather cross, but I would stick to the substance of what I said. Any subsequent argument against the stage show was something which didn't change in my own mind and I think was probably right in the end.

JOHN CLEESE: My attitude was very much that if people don't want to do it, then of course we shouldn't do it. I thought it would be ridiculous to try and persuade someone to do it who wasn't keen, so I was kind of irritated with Michael for having wasted a bit of our time. I didn't mind, for me it would have been fun to do the tour, but it wasn't in any way essential, it was a luxury. It looked like fun, but if it wasn't going to be fun, forget it.

TERRY GILLIAM: Eric loves those meetings, so he should be grateful that he was even allowed to have them, representing Python. People kept changing their minds. There was a tour, then it was just going to be Las Vegas, because John didn't want to spend a long time on tour. Mike got the blame for it, but it was more complicated than that. I think that Mike was just the final straw but I said I didn't really want to do it, period. Not that it would really matter, they could still do it without me, but it would be even less Python I suppose.

TERRY JONES: I did think we could write enough material to elaborate a stage show, so we could do old favourites and then some new stuff which would be fun. Eric started setting the thing up, getting offers, working out how to do it, working with producers and going to meetings. He did several meetings, and then about two months later Mike decided he really, really, really, really, didn't want to do it and so the whole thing collapsed. Eric was very cross and said he'd never work with anybody ever again and so it was rather sad really. I think it would have been rather fun to do a stage show but Mike

kind of felt we wouldn't be able to do it because we all looked so old. It's true, we were, but at the same time I think it would have been fun to do.

ERIC IDLE: I had an idea for a Python film. I thought it would be really funny if our characters from *Grail* had got older and we all got together and we had to do this Crusade. It started with Salman Rushdie coming in and saying, 'The infidels have taken Jerusalem,' and we all had to get together. Robin had become a salesman in France and Lancelot was on his third wife and very cross, he had too much on and he couldn't possibly come. Basically it was a way of sending ourselves up for being old and we could cut from our young selves in *Grail* to the old selves playing the characters, which is not a thing you can normally do. It was like 'Whoa, that would be really good.' I sent it round and people got really excited, so we decided to meet at Cliveden, we were going to talk about this and everybody said yes in some form. Then I went to see John in Santa

Barbara and he said, 'That sounds really good.' I said, 'The thing about it is, you needn't be in it very much because if you put a helmet on, you can be fighting away, you'll just do the close-ups later.' And it would be the Crusades, which would be a good Python area to be in. So they said, 'All right, we'll get together at Cliveden and we'll meet.' We got there, I flew in and Gilliam flew in from LA, and the first thing John said was 'I just want to say right away, that I'm not going to do a film.' It was like, 'Well, couldn't you have mentioned this sooner,' because Gilliam had just come overnight from LA, and so he was kind of cranky.

JOHN CLEESE: I discovered from conversations with other people that Eric was very angry with me for not wanting to do a Python film. I had been very clear that I didn't think it was a good idea to do a Python film. And let me explain why, because it would hardly be a more appropriate place to tell it. First of all the last experience that Python had, *The Meaning of Life*, wasn't a very satisfactory one. So I anticipated that it would be harder to get agreement on the script than it had been back in the days of *Life of Brian*. Certainly it was very hard to get agreement on the script for *The Meaning of Life* and I don't mean at all that there were rows, it was just we could never figure out what *The Meaning of Life* was about. And also we lacked, in Chapman, a very, very important part of the acting team. We could probably do without him writing more or less, but he really was a very, very good actor and we're missing him. And the next problem is who's going to direct it? Terry Gilliam does not want to go back to being art director, he's making multi-million dollar movies, but at the same time I think our style is better served by Terry Jones's style of direction than by Terry Gilliam's. So I was never very keen, but what happened was that Eric came down to Santa Barbara, we had a very pleasant chat together and I gave him all these reasons at some length. But then I said let's talk about your Crusades idea anyway and we walked down the beach for forty minutes, during which time I played with the ideas, with him. Then without bothering to reiterate everything I'd said to him before the walk, we had a glass of wine and he drove back to LA. Because I got slightly amused and came up with a couple of funny ideas, I think Eric assumed that I'd had a complete change of mind during the forty minutes on the beach without my problems ever having been addressed.

When I next met the Pythons at Cliveden, a very remarkable thing happened. They said, 'What about the film?' I reiterated all the reasons why I didn't think it was a good idea, and I was suddenly aware that almost everyone round the table was rather surprised by what I was saying. Eric must have come back from the walk down the beach and said, 'He's very enthusiastic,' and led the others to think I wanted to do it. As shrinks say, people hear what they want to hear. And Eric was much more dependent on Python than the rest of us. But I still don't see how you answer all the objections. People were always asking about a Python film and in a way it would be fun, but what do you do about getting us in a room for six months? Jonesy doesn't want to come and live here in the States, and I sure as hell don't want to go and take rented rooms in Brixton or wherever he lives.

ERIC IDLE: John went off to bed at one point and went for a nap. We all started to write this film, and it was fabulous, just the four of us left, the *Do Not Adjust Your Set* team, and it was really good fun. It was just as fast and as fluid and we got this going and it was a brilliant Python film because it started where you thought the start point was and then went backwards. It was just off the wall, it was really a

very nice experience, everybody working together for two hours and then John came in and killed it all dead. He said, 'We've got to stop all this, let's talk some business now.' He was just desperate to stop it and succeeded. We talked business and that's all it was. I think there was going to be a point maybe some of us would write it and then it would go to him, but I think at that point it was pretty clear that wild horses wouldn't drag him into anything to do with this.

TERRY JONES: I was a bit more sceptical about doing a movie. The memory of writing *The Meaning of Life* was still with me and I couldn't see us all getting together for the right amount of time.

TERRY GILLIAM: We had this meeting at Cliveden where we all got together, and that was 'Holy Grail 2'. The idea was bringing back this group of middle-aged knights for one final crusade and the great idea was we could carry the box of holy relics. We had several outtakes of Graham from the albums, so he was going to 'play' the box of holy relics and it would speak – perfect. And it would be a chance to use who we were now and go on. We all talked, there was a certain excitement. John was the most reticent about it, and then it was left that Mike and Terry or Eric were going to get to grips with it. It needs a motor force to get any of this stuff done, and it never happened. Nobody got together to try to work it out. But John was not at all excited about it. He wanted to do other things.

MICHAEL PALIN Aspen brought us all together, and there was talk of doing another film, a follow-up to *Holy Grail* with the knights going off to the Crusades, stimulated I think by Terry Jones's interest in the Crusades and the wonderful stories that he told from his research into people going off and getting side-tracked. In order to get money to go to the Holy Land, they had to go and do certain jobs for the boys in Venice and places like that, go and finish off some petty war or pursue some local disagreement and get that sorted out, and then they'd be on their way. So we had this idea of all the Python knights trying to get our act together to go off to the Crusades. Which I thought was a great idea because it paralleled Python's slight inability to get its own act together. We knew that we could be funny together, but how do we do it and what's the best way? I felt that the idea of it being slightly autobiographical, accepting that we're all older, accepting that we'd all done different things but that we still enjoyed and got a great kick out of being in a room together and exchanging jokes and observations, that this would be a wonderful parallel of what was going on in our lives. But it never really got going. John was adamantly against doing another film for some reason, he really was.

ERIC IDLE: The Crusades movie was tough because I had to make all the running and Jonesy and I exchanged some emails about it early on, but it's like who wants to take that risk in life? Who wants to get a film script going only to find that you can't? The thing I liked about the film was the fact that we would be playing cross old farts who had to get together again against their will. That to me was a great concept, it would be really funny, doing ourselves – sending ourselves up. I thought that was a good place to start to make a movie and we could be quite interesting about it – but not to be.

TERRY JONES: For the Thirtieth Anniversary night on the BBC we wrote this new material, almost twenty-four minutes of material and we could have done a TV show and got paid for it! We weren't being paid for it, that was the silly thing, we were just doing these links. It was so weird because there we were back in the BBC studios in White City, Television Centre, and there was Hazel Pethig again, our costume lady, and the same people. It was like you'd suddenly gone back thirty years, the only difference was that we tended not to be able to do our own shoelaces up any more and found it a bit hard bending over, especially me because at that time I had my bad hip, but it was a very strange feeling. It just felt like nothing had changed. It just felt like this is normality and very odd.

JOHN CLEESE: When we got together to do the Thirtieth Anniversary, Eric just didn't want to have anything to do with it at all. He didn't want to work with us, he didn't want to discuss it with us. We figured that it would be very embarrassing if Eric didn't appear in the show so somehow he was persuaded by the people who worked on the show to do a monologue which he wrote himself and recorded by the swimming pool. This was felt, not just by us but by the producers, not to be very good and I think he re-recorded it and that was just about his only contribution to the Thirtieth Anniversary show. Now the rest of us really enjoyed working together, both at the writing and at the performing. There wasn't a great deal of new material, most of it was linking stuff to showcase some of the old material. But I thought the new material that we recorded was actually very funny and when it was transmitted a number of rather disappointing things happened. I don't think it was very well publicised and I think a lot of people who would normally have tuned in didn't. And the second thing was the reviews were strange, and I think it was because none of the reviewers saw the evening as a whole; they all looked at bits of tapes that had been sent. I was surprised by the negativity of the reviews. I think they all felt that the material was being rehashed one time too many, whereas my basic assumption was that this was not entertainment for the general public, this was for Python fans – if you have a Python evening it's for Python fans – so I thought it was reasonable to take a slightly more self-indulgent attitude towards stuff for fans than you would if it was being offered to everyone. So it wasn't a very successful occasion and I guess that will be the last time we ever work again.

ERIC IDLE: John sent this script and it was all John hitting people and John talking to people and using people as props. It wasn't like Python at all, it was like a John Cleese commercial. I thought, 'I'm not going to go all the way to London to do this. I'll do a bit from here.' I did a bit on the history of Monty Python and sent them that.

It was classic Python, we could have done this huge tour and been funny, made a lot of money and been very good out there, but no, they decided to get together and do something for the BBC for nothing, too long and very unfunny. I thought it was just awful when I saw it. I just thought it was painful to watch and there were long stretches with Carol Cleveland saying why didn't she get more material? I just thought it was horrible and I was embarrassed to watch it. Interestingly enough it was all cut out in America, they just left the documentary and that was fine. Eddie Izzard's documentary was very good. But Jesus, it certainly wasn't Python, it was weird, so I had the good taste to avoid it. I was replaced by somebody who has the initials 'E.I.' also.

TERRY GILLIAM: I did my first animation in years and modern technology had caught up with my real primitive technology, that's what was so wonderful. I could sit at home on my Mac and scan pictures in, photographs. Then I could adjust them, I could cut them out, I could make them move. I can do repetitive action, so I get a hundred chickens where in the old days I'd never have been able to do that. For me it was the fun of having an animation idea

'It was so weird because there we were back in the BBC studios in White City, Television Centre, and there was Hazel Pethig again, our costume lady, and the same people. It was like you'd suddenly gone back thirty years, the only difference was that we tended not to be able to do our own shoelaces up any more and found it a bit hard bending over . . .'

again and doing it all myself and that felt good. In the old days I was raging that I was the one that was left out of all the fun, but in fact I really did enjoy just working on my own.

But the whole show's not very good. We all enjoyed being together again so much that the work wasn't put in to really write good stuff. We were all excited to be together for a brief moment, and that's what's interesting when something like that comes, you realise just how much genuine – love is too strong a word, but it's something like that – for each other there is. For all the backbiting and all the nonsense, we really do like each other!

MICHAEL PALIN: I don't think it's the best work we've done. It was an attempt to create what came rather spontaneously, quickly and easily thirty years before but didn't any longer. The writing process was not the same as the writing process had been before, partly for the obvious fact that Graham wasn't there to give his often very important contribution. I don't think Eric was involved in the writing process that much, he was off in America, and nor was John particularly, so I think we had meetings and a certain amount of work was done. Terry and myself went off and wrote a lot of the stuff but there was a real feeling that we were all scattered, sending in little bits of text here and there. Eric couldn't be there to perform it either, and really it suffered from that. For a Thirtieth Anniversary we needed Eric to be fully on board and none us were completely engaged in that.

TERRY GILLIAM: Python worked when we all worked together fighting all this stuff. There was passion involved, anger. And this was all very polite, 'Oh that's a super idea, let's just do that.' It doesn't work that way.

MICHAEL PALIN: Without Graham we're not Python any longer. You can have variations on Python without Graham but it will not be what it was.

JOHN CLEESE: Python certainly changed comedy but in a rather negative way. Because instead of people taking our stuff to the next stage, they avoided it. So it had a rather disappointing effect which was to close off an avenue for a particular type of humour and I'm surprised that that's the way it happened. It's rather disappointing but that's the way it is. Otherwise I think that it simply made people feel very good. First of all it made them laugh, which is about the nicest experience you can have. After watching Python people couldn't take the world seriously for the rest of the evening which I think is a great feeling and also entirely justifiable, but we usually forget that and take everything rather seriously. Somebody once told me that they couldn't watch the news after Python, it just all seemed so ridiculous and I think that's wonderfully healthy and gives people a sense of everyday joy. I've been particularly touched by the number of students, particularly in America, who've come up to me and said, 'That show got me through my exams, looking forward to that show and sitting there and screaming with laughter – it got me through.' I love to think that it had that kind of effect on people, that it just lifted their spirits and made them happier to be alive, just for a few hours. In America, of course, *Saturday Night Live* was influenced by it in a very positive way, in fact what was so funny was that kids who watched *Saturday Night Live* and then watched Python thought that we'd stolen from *Saturday Night Live*.

MICHAEL PALIN: At various stages during the evolution of Python we've desperately tried to hang on to what it originally was, never having the films dubbed, subtitles only, and not to have any Python products or merchandising and all that terrible thing. Anyway, we've given in on most of those because of the relentless pressure of people to enjoy Python. I'm still a little baffled by the fact that forty-five television shows and five films have gone on and continue to go on entertaining people and be discovered and rediscovered. There was a time when I felt we would produce new product, and I felt it was very, very important to make sure that we didn't allow any pale imitations because we were going to be doing the new stuff ourselves. Now I think that's extremely unlikely that we're ever going to do a lot of new Python material, although I still keep fingers crossed that we might do a film at some time, which I'd infinitely prefer to doing stage shows.

I personally prefer people to use the material as an inspiration to go on and do something slightly different. Eric has turned *The Holy Grail* into a stage musical called *Spamelot*. He's adapted the material and written some new songs with John Du Prez It's a homage to *The Holy Grail*. It's not trying to out-do *The Holy Grail*, it's saying 'This is where our inspiration came from' and I'm quite intrigued by that, to be honest. I think the really important thing is that it's not as if these other shows and these other manifestations of Python appreciation are going to destroy what was there already. The Python shows have established themselves. God knows why, but they really have, in all their rough, sometimes clumsy, sometimes almost unfunny way, all these shows are still replayed and, despite the inadequacies that we felt when we made them, people seem to like every single bit of them, and the same with the films.

TERRY JONES: I don't know what Python actually achieved. I would say the best thing it ever achieved was when I was talking to a friend who was a teacher in an inner city comprehensive in the '70s, and they said since Python they'd noticed a change in the adolescent boys. Whereas in the old days the boys would tend to go round bullying, they were actually now going round being silly. He thought that was the effect of Python doing that. For a brief moment of time, it became fashionable to be silly rather than to be threatening and I think that's probably all Python ever achieved, just a slight change in behaviour in a few adolescent boys in the inner city over a brief span of time in the '70s. What more can you hope for?

TERRY GILLIAM: Has it left the world a better, safer place, a greener place, a happier place, a more intelligent place? I don't know. The fact that it keeps going intrigues me, so it's actually obviously serving a lot of people well. Young people are discovering it, young kids in America particularly, there's generation after generation when they hit about eleven or twelve, they discover Python and it's a whole new world and it's something they have never seen before and they all get hooked on it. So what have we done? We've just maintained a long-running sense of the absurd and that's got to be a good thing in the world, especially with George W. Bush in the White House, but it's obviously not had the effect we would like. Maybe by laughing at things we've allowed these people to take power. If people hadn't been laughing and had been concentrating they wouldn't have taken power. We're at fault for bringing George W. Bush and his boys to the top! It has always been a concern with me as far as satire and comedy are concerned, in the sense that if people are laughing they're not getting angry enough to do what is needed to make a better world. It's a diversion as opposed to a means towards a solution. Maybe the world should just be a better world, there's no reason for it. I did think our idea was to make people keep thinking and it does surprise me how its longevity has been maintained. I don't see it dying out because these kids keep being

are, I suppose, very strong reasons why Python continues to get played and replayed. We never really disgraced ourselves.

On the other side, I just think it was very liberating. It freed people up to laugh at so many different things. It wasn't trying to be a parody of one particular world. Python skipped around all over the place, it went in all sorts of directions and that came from six writers and six performers and that feeling of freedom. You can watch a Python show or a film and it can go in almost any direction. It can be rather sweet and it can be rather whimsical and it can be rather charming and then the next moment it can be very hard and vicious and aggressive; it's something that you don't see in many other forms of comedy. That's probably one of the reasons why Python has survived; it's very light on its feet, it moves very quickly from one idea to another and it seems to use up so many ideas in each show. Yet the next programme or the next film will be

'I did my first animation in years and modern technology had caught up with my real primitive technology, that's what was so wonderful.
I could sit at home on my Mac and scan pictures in, photographs. Then I could adjust them,
I could cut them out, I could make them move.'

born and coming out. I don't know if it's popular in Palestine, I don't know if it's helped there. Has it helped make the world a more peaceful place? I don't think so. I just love the fact that kids keep discovering Python and it doesn't age. That's what intrigues me, because it looks so cheesy. Then again, that may be part of its appeal. Modern television looks slick and everything and here's this very cheesy stuff going on – but good ideas, good performances.

ERIC IDLE: I realise that we're a gang, we won't finish. But we will never do anything ever again because nobody really wants to do it in some way or another.

MICHAEL PALIN: I think the quality of Python has been quite important. There are things we've done that haven't been that funny. There are moments in shows which I find just didn't work and could have been done better, but there is something for everyone in all those shows and I think we seem to have protected that quality and actually improved it in most of the films. So, for a start, the great thing about Python is it's a pretty good body of work there. There are no real large-scale bummers and I can still look at the material, nearly all of it, and find things hysterically funny. So what we thought was funny then still must be funny, and that consistency and that quality

different, it will be different sorts of ideas. We don't repeat ourselves that often. We were very critical usually, we didn't really like to let anything go in there that didn't work. Generally speaking we had this half hour of fireworks and you don't know when you open the box what sort of fireworks are going to go off each time, there's always going to be something there. And we had certain advantages. We had Terry Gilliam for a start, and I think it was incredibly important to have that, which I thought was, for its time, a really liberating element, because you could just go to animation. That was absolutely in the spirit of Python, so you were absolutely confident that that was going to work.

So without over-analysing, Python has a number of elements: the strength of the writing, the fact that the ensemble acting was strong and the fact that the material was so free, so diverse and so rich that it could never really be pinned down. Perhaps this is what has ensured its survival, because I can't think of many other sources of comedy which have all those things together quite so comfortably. The end!

JOHN CLEESE: Do you know? This has all been terribly interesting. I think the others may well remember it quite differently from me. It may well be we have to do this all over again …

A BRIEF CAST OF CHARACTERS

JOHN CLEESE – a Python.

TERRY JONES – a Python.

TERRY GILLIAM – a Python.

ERIC IDLE – a Python.

MICHAEL PALIN – a Python.

GRAHAM CHAPMAN – an ex-Python (he has ceased to be).

DAVID SHERLOCK – long-time friend, associate and companion of Graham Chapman. They wrote many projects together, including the movie *Yellowbeard*.

JOHN CHAPMAN – long-time brother of Graham Chapman and a noted surgeon, now retired.

PAM CHAPMAN – long-time wife of Dr John Chapman.

The Goon Show – hugely influential radio comedy of the 1950s, drawn from the quietly war-destroyed mind of writer/performer SPIKE MILLIGAN. Milligan served his time in the Goons alongside PETER SELLERS, HARRY SECOMBE and, early on, MICHAEL BENTINE, and the show was avidly listened to by just about anyone who became a comedian after 1960.

Beyond the Fringe – groundbreaking satirical review that re-wrote the rules of British comedy at the start of the 1960s. A huge success in London, it subsequently transferred to equal success on Broadway and featured in its cast:

JONATHAN MILLER – a former Cambridge medical graduate, who subsequently became a leading doctor and director, among many other things.

ALAN BENNETT – a Yorkshire-born Oxford graduate, who went on to become one of Britain's leading playwrights and television dramatists. (A woman once lived outside his house in a van for years and he got a book *and* a play out of it – that's not bad.)

DUDLEY MOORE – Dagenham-born, not overly tall, brilliant pianist and comedian, who attended Oxford. Was later often to be found at his best on the mid-1960s BBC comedy classic *Not Only But Also*, trying not to laugh at his partner of many subsequent years, Peter Cook.

PETER COOK – the man who for many helped create and shape Cambridge comedy, defining the satire boom of the '60s, opening the Establishment Club in London and then later making a series of obscenity-strewn records with his soon to be ex-partner, Dud, under the moniker of 'Derek & Clive'. Moore went on to become a sex symbol in Hollywood; Cook stuck to his guns and took over financing the British satirical magazine *Private Eye*.

ROBERT HEWISON – close friend of Michael Palin at Oxford, he went on to become a leading theatre critic.

DAVID FROST – the man who followed Peter Cook as top satirist at Cambridge, Frost had the good sense to turn comedy into a business, bringing the university to the living room, via such shows as *That Was The Week That Was* (aka *TW3*), *The Frost Report*, *Frost on Sunday* and *At Last The 1948 Show*. He has subsequently become one of the world's leading interviewers and a serious political commentator on such politically charged shows as *Through the Keyhole*.

HUMPHREY BARCLAY – Cambridge Footlights producer, director and performer, who was pivotal in turning *A Clump of Plinths* into *Cambridge Circus*, thus ensuring the careers of many featured in this book, including his own very successful and long-running career behind the scenes in British television comedy over the last several decades.

TIM BROOKE-TAYLOR – Cambridge contemporary of John Cleese, who along with his other college friend BILL ODDIE helped write and perform *Cambridge Circus* around the world. Broke-Taylor and Oddie later teamed up with GRAEME GARDEN and formed *The Goodies*, the immensely popular 1970s BBC comedy series.

DICK EMERY – Popular cross-dressing British television comic of the '60s and '70s. He was awful – but we liked him.

STANLEY UNWIN – Eccentric British professor, who decided to invent his own language, 'Unwinese', and became popular on television for speaking what appeared to be complete and utter nonsense.

BARRY TOOK – British comedy writer (on *Frost* shows together with MARTY FELDMAN, before the latter's performing days), who, while working at the BBC, might well have had the idea of bringing the Pythons together.

PAUL FOX – former production executive at the BBC, who was once yelled at by all the Pythons.

JOHN HOWARD DAVIES – A former child actor, who played the title role in David Lean's 1948 *Oliver Twist*, Davies became a successful TV producer, shepherding the first four episodes of the *Flying Circus* and later taking over full-time on John Cleese's award-winning *Fawlty Towers*.

IAN MacNAUGHTON – took over as producer/director on Python from John Howard Davies, because they admired his work on Spike Milligan's classic *Q5* television show. He saw them through all four series, two German specials and their first movie *And Now For Something Completely Different*.

CAROL CLEVELAND – the beautiful Ms Cleveland was the woman the Pythons relied on when they didn't want their female characters to be grotesque. She could certainly never play that.

NEIL INNES – singer/songwriter with the Bonzo Dog Doo Dah Band (house band on *Do Not Adjust Your Set*), Innes frequently toured with the Pythons' stage shows, providing musical interludes.

GEORGE HARRISON – former Beatle.

PAUL McCARTNEY – current Beatle.

LORD BERNARD DELFONT – British peer who wouldn't finance *Life of Brian*.

DENIS O'BRIEN – American businessman who would.

ADOLF HITLER – nasty piece of work who tried to take over the world *c.*1939–45 and who, despite persistent rumours, never actually lived in Minehead.

MONTY PYTHON: A BRIEF HISTORY OF TIME

1939	John Cleese born 27 October
1940	Terry Gilliam born 22 November
1941	Graham Chapman born 8 January
1942	Terry Jones born 1 February
1943	Eric Idle born 29 March
1943	Michael Palin born 5 May
1966–7	*The Frost Report*
1967	*At Last The 1948 Show*
1968	*We Have Ways of Making You Laugh*
1968–9	*Do Not Adjust Your Set*
1969	*The Complete and Utter History of Britain*
1969–70	*Monty Python's Flying Circus* Series 1
1970	*Monty Python's Flying Circus* Series 2
1970	*Monty Python's Flying Circus* (BBC Records)
1971	*And Now For Something Completely Different* (film)
1971	*Another Monty Python Record* (Charisma Records)
1971	*Monty Python's Big Red Book* (book)
1971	*Monty Python's Fliegender Zirkus*
1972	*Monty Python's Previous Record* (Charisma Records)
1972–3	*Monty Python's Flying Circus* Series 3
1972	*Monty Python's Fliegender Zirkus – Schnapps with Everything*
1973	*The Monty Python Matching Tie and Handkerchief* (Charisma Records)
1973	*The Brand New Monty Python Bok* (book)
1974	*Monty Python Live at Drury Lane* (Charisma Records)
1974	*Monty Python and the Holy Grail* (film)
1974	*Monty Python* Series 4
1975	*The Album of the Soundtrack of the Trailer of the Film of Monty Python and the Holy Grail* (Charisma Records)
1976	*Monty Python Live at City Centre* (Arista Records)
1977	*Monty Python and the Holy Grail* (book)
1977	*The Monty Python Instant Record Collection* (Charisma Records)
1979	*Monty Python's Life of Brian* (film)
1979	*Life of Brian/Monty Python Scrapbook* (book)
1979	*Monty Python's Life of Brian* (Warner Bros Records)
1980	*Monty Python's Contractual Obligation Album* (Charisma Records)
1982	*Monty Python Live at the Hollywood Bowl* (film)
1983	*Monty Python's The Meaning of Life* (film)
1983	*Monty Python's The Meaning of Life* (MCA Records)
1989	*Parrot Sketch Not Included*
1989	*Monty Python Sings* (Virgin Records)
1989	Graham Chapman died 4 October
2028	Terry Jones died 12 April
2030	John Cleese died 14 October
2034	Michael Palin died 14 February (whilst filming a documentary in the Kalahari desert)
2046	Terry Gilliam died August – it took the whole month
3039	Eric Idle died 1 April (he said he'd outlive the rest of those bastards!)

INDEX

PICTURE CREDITS

Pictures were kindly supplied from the collections of the following:

HUMPHREY BARCLAY: pp. 9, 11, 13, 14, 16, 17, 18, 20, 21, 65, 68, 72, 73, 88, 89, 94, 95, 96, 100, 106, 107, 110, 113, 114, 116, 119, 120, 122, 123

DR JOHN CHAPMAN: pp. 11, 50, 51, 52, 54, 55, 115

JOHN CLEESE: pp. 22, 38, 39, 40, 41, 86

TERRY GILLIAM: pp. 1, 9, 22, 56, 57, 58, 59, 60, 61, 62, 63, 65, 76, 79, 83, 92, 100, 101, 102, 103, 104, 105, 118, 119, 126, 127, 144, 158, 160, 165, 166, 167, 176, 177, 186, 187, 219, 220, 221, 224, 231, 234, 236, 237, 238, 239, 240, 241, 243, 244, 247, 248, 251, 252, 273, 292, 293, 314

ERIC IDLE: pp. 22, 24, 25, 26, 27, 29, 74, 82, 120, 137, 139, 140, 141, 155, 177, 190, 194, 199, 204, 209, 211, 212, 213, 214, 215, 228, 233, 252, 283, 296, 298, 304, 307, 308, 309, 312, 328, 332, 334

TERRY JONES: pp. 9, 12, 15, 18, 22, 42, 43, 44, 45, 46, 47, 48, 49, 65, 67, 70, 75, 77, 78, 81, 83, 84, 85, 87, 90, 93, 98, 109, 120, 124, 126, 127, 128, 129, 130, 132, 134, 148, 149, 155, 156, 158, 159, 161, 162, 168, 169, 173, 174, 175, 178, 179, 191, 194, 195, 198, 199, 204, 205, 206, 207, 208, 210, 211, 216, 217, 219, 220, 221, 222, 224, 225, 226, 229, 236, 251, 268, 270, 271, 272, 273, 274, 275, 277, 278, 279, 283, 284, 286, 291, 292, 294, 306, 307, 314, 315, 334, 338, 344, 345, 347, 348, 351

MICHAEL PALIN: pp. 9, 10, 15, 22, 30, 31, 32, 33, 34, 35, 36, 37, 65, 87, 90, 91, 93, 98, 99, 122, 123, 133, 136, 137, 140, 142, 150, 151, 153, 155, 156, 158, 162, 168, 169, 170, 171, 172, 184, 185, 191, 192, 193, 196, 198, 200. 203, 218, 219, 222, 223, 225, 228, 229, 231, 234, 235, 244, 245, 251, 254, 255, 262, 267, 270, 273, 274, 275, 277, 308, 309, 312, 313, 318, 319, 320, 327, 328, 329, 332

PYTHON (MONTY) PICTURES: jacket and pp. 2, 3, 4, 20, 21, 52, 54, 55, 65, 66, 68, 69, 86, 108, 111, 112, 117, 123, 126, 127, 128, 134, 135, 136, 138, 139, 140, 143, 144, 145, 146, 147, 152, 153, 154, 155, 157, 161, 163, 164, 165, 172, 173, 175, 179, 180, 181, 183, 184, 190, 191, 202, 203, 226, 227, 230, 231, 235, 240, 241, 242, 243, 244, 246, 247, 248, 249, 250, 251, 253, 254, 255, 256, 257, 258, 259, 260, 261, 262, 263, 264, 265, 266, 267, 272, 286, 287, 288, 289, 290, 291, 292, 293, 294, 295, 296, 297, 298, 299, 300, 301, 302, 303, 304, 305, 311, 314, 316, 317, 319, 320, 321, 322, 323, 324, 325, 326, 327, 328, 329, 330, 331, 332, 333, 334, 335, 336, 337, 340, 362

DAVID SHERLOCK: pp. 14, 16, 17, 19, 20, 50, 52, 53, 65, 71, 73, 95, 96, 100, 110, 113, 114, 140, 173, 182, 189, 198, 200, 201, 203, 225, 245, 252, 274, 281, 282, 303, 306, 307, 310, 324, 341, 342, 343

JIM YOAKUM: pp. 12, 22, 50, 51, 52, 53, 54, 71, 97, 113, 115, 118, 122, 276, 286, 291, 341, 342

NOTES FOR THE CHAPMAN SOURCES

1. George Perry, *Life of Python*, Pavilion Books Ltd, London 1994

2. *Spot the Loony*, CD, Right Recordings Ltd/Graham Chapman Archives 2001

3. Kim 'Howard' Johnson, *The First 200 Years of Monty Python*, St Martin's Press, New York, and Plexus Publishing Ltd, London, 1990

4. Graham Chapman, *A Liar's Autobiography Volume VI*, Eyre Methuen Ltd, London 1980

5. Roger Wilmut, *From Fringe to Flying Circus: Celebrating a Unique Generation of Comedy 1960–1980*, Eyre Methuen Ltd, London 1980

6. *Time Out*, 4–10 May 1973

7. *Guardian*, Friday 7 May 1971

8. *The Pythons – BBC/Python (Monty) Pictures*, documentary film, 1979

The authors and Orion Books are grateful to the publishers concerned for permission to quote from the above sources.